Praises for The Life-Saving Divorce

"This practical and straightforward book combines a traditional high regard for scripture with the latest results of academic research by Christian scholars and applies it to pastoral realities. The problem of abuse within marriage is shamefully common but rarely mentioned, especially in churches. The approach of this book is both empathic and well researched, employing the latest stats alongside clear advice. A must for anyone involved in pastoral work and a lifeline for those suffering within marriages."

—REVEREND DR. DAVID INSTONE-BREWER, WWW.DIVORCEREMARRIAGE.COM

"Gretchen is giving freedom for captives. She helped me think deeply about deeply held wrong ideas related to divorce!"

—PASTOR NEIL SCHORI, PASTOR AT THE EDGE CHURCH,
KEY WITNESS IN THE DREW PETERSON MURDER CASE

"I describe Gretchen as generous, wise, courageous. She has helped me as a pastor have both a theology and a practice that reflect the heart of God toward people who divorce and people who consider divorce."

—PASTOR COLE BROWN

"It's so much easier for a pastor to prioritize the institution of marriage over the people within that institution. Yet any marriage defined by power and control has already been broken at the foundational level. This book exposes the tactics of those who leverage marriage to serve themselves and shifts blame away from victims who tirelessly work to salvage beauty from betrayal. Gretchen shines as a ray of hope into a dark place, offering us a better way."

—PASTOR JEREMIAH RICE, CERTIFIED CO-FACILITATOR OF DOMESTIC
ABUSE INTERVENTION GROUPS USING THE DULUTH MODEL

"Mark my words—*The Life-Saving Divorce* is going to be a *huge* catalyst for change in the Christian community. Gretchen not only has years of experience working with Christian divorcees, but she has done hardcore research and produced an incredibly powerful, compassionate, and insightful solution for the destructive issues found in many Christian marriages. If you have ever wondered if God is okay with you and your divorce, you need to read this book."

—NATALIE HOFFMAN, AUTHOR OF IS IT ME? MAKING SENSE OF YOUR CONFUSING MARRIAGE

"I'm so thankful for Gretchen and this book… Gretchen uses her God-given gifts and her years spent leading divorce recovery groups to help regular people like me, who are *still* in a fog of disbelief (after 24+ months of leaving), come to grips with why divorce is okay with God in certain situations. She's helping fight the imaginary taboo that regularly accompanies Christians who divorce. This book will help you. And please buy it for a friend who may feel trapped because of her devotion to our Lord—and her vows. It could save her life."

—SHERYL WEAVER

"Sympathetic, liberating, rational. She helped me not feel the pressure of having to sustain a marriage on my own and [helped me understand] that divorce is a valid option instead of continually being made to feel less than or staying with someone who doesn't want to stay with you."

—JEFFREY LEWIS

"I have been in ministry for roughly 20 years as a pastor, church planter, missionary, and mentor of church leaders. After reading this book I am both exceedingly grateful that it now exists and heartbroken that I did not have this resource the first 20 years of my ministry… The book is an excellent resource for church leaders, people struggling in their marriages, divorced Christians and church members in general as Gretchen covers everything relevant to the topic... This will be *the* book I recommend to those considering divorce or already divorced and *the* book I will purchase for church leaders in hopes that they read it and better shepherd their people as God desires. I know it has already empowered me to do just that."

—RACHEL RAMER

"Her voice is crucial, liberating, hopeful. She helped me see my life and marriage through God's gracious eyes."

—RICHELLE WISEMAN

"When I think of Gretchen, I think of the words: Needed, truth-telling, and hope. She filled in the data and research behind the things I knew by experience, both personally and from others I know. There is so much bad Christian advice that doesn't acknowledge destructive marriage and abuse; this truth is so needed in the world."

—JODI POMPA

"This book should be read by pastors and family ministry leaders in every church. Those reaching out to us for help deserve our empathy and support. This book is a perfect example of why it's important for pastors (and others) to listen and learn from survivors."

—DIANA HOEKSTRA

"Gretchen is supportive, unapologetic, and confirming. She helped me understand I am not alone in my divorce walk, [and] that the Christian community need not vilify already damaged spouses who have to seek divorce."

—HOLLI LEWIS

"Many in the church are unaware that the Bible's divorce laws were originally given as a protection for women. They are, as Jesus puts it, a concession God makes to preserve life in a world full of hard and fallen hearts. In this important book, Gretchen Baskerville calls attention to the best biblical scholarship on the topic and combines it with wise counsel from the trenches of ministry."

—REV. DR. TIM MOREY

"She gives hope, mercy, and strength. She helps lessen the shame carried by divorced woman of deep faith."

—MARILYN SMITH, MSW, LCSW

"If you are in an abusive relationship, if you have a loved one who is in one, or if you are struggling to discern the Biblical truths of divorce: read this book. It is wise. It is safe. It is gentle. It is not demeaning towards anyone. It is not condemning, and it is not high-handed... You will feel loved and cherished. In the beginning, Gretchen tells you to imagine her wrapping her arms around you, telling you it's going to be okay. That feeling stays with you throughout the entire book. You will be okay. Your babies will be okay. You're going to make it. You are not alone. You are enough.

For interwoven in every sentence, in every word—and I cannot stress this enough—is the fact that Gretchen is not the only one holding you. She simply adds her human arms to the arms of the One who holds the universe, yet has written your name on the palm of His hand. You are not forgotten. You can do this. You can make it. Hold on. Get that life-saving divorce."

—JOELLE

"Transformational, honest, refreshing. I realized God didn't want me to give my life for my marriage. I am worth so much more than that."

—E. FARLEY

"Gretchen helped me process my parents' divorce in such a way that I don't have to feel guilty about it at church and now know how to defend why it was a good thing for our family."

—SARAH BARNARD

"Gretchen has provided a resource that is both deep, thorough, steeped in sound Biblical exegesis and grounded in solid abuse and trauma awareness. Every church leader and pastor should not only have this on their shelf but refer to it often and provide it to those who are struggling with their marriage."

—BRENDA CAMPBELL WAKEFIELD

"Gretchen is perceptive, honest, and compassionate. She is someone who understands the importance of focusing on women's wellbeing..."

—SHIRLEY FESSEL, MA, MEd

"Gretchen gives hope, grace, and solidarity. She has opened my mind to think about how the church is pastorally responsible from the pulpit as much as one-on-one, and how rigid dogma isn't the best tool for keeping people from harm."

—CHARLOTTE NAYLOR DAVIS

"Her words are vital, practical, and relatable. Gretchen helped me stop shaming myself for leaving my abusive marriage."

—KATHERINE LEONARD

As a small token of my thanks for buying this book, I'd like to offer a free bonus gift exclusive to my readers.

This life-saving PDF is called "7 Effective Ways to Deal with Criticism When You Divorce."

No one likes to be criticized, but it's a fact of life! When you finally face the reality that your marriage may be over, one of your biggest worries is: "How will people respond?"

Having facts will give you confidence and peace in the midst of this storm. Your friends may be well-meaning, but often they are ill-informed about divorce and the effect of divorce on children.

The 7 tips in this fact sheet will bring you strength and courage. It explains—

- How many divorces are for very serious reasons, not frivolous ones
- Why it's better in some cases for kids if you leave rather than staying
- Why kids of divorce are not likely to have drug/alcohol problems
- Why your divorce probably won't cause your children to divorce.
- And more…

You can download your free gift here:
www.LifeSavingDivorce.com/FREE

The LIFE-SAVING DIVORCE

Hope for People Leaving Destructive Relationships

GRETCHEN BASKERVILLE

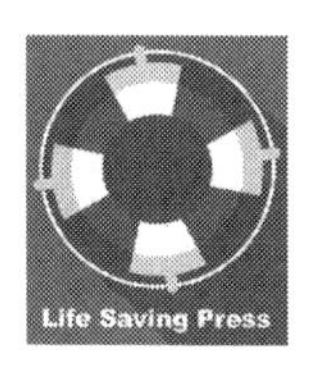

© 2020 Life Saving Press LLC

All rights reserved. No part of this publication may be reproduced, distributed, or transmitted in any form or by any means, including photocopying, recording, or other electronic or mechanical methods, without the prior written permission of the publisher, except in the case of brief quotations embodied in critical reviews and certain other noncommercial uses permitted by copyright law.

All names and identifying features of interviewees in this book have been changed to protect their privacy.

Printed in the United States of America. Second printing, July 2021.

ISBN 978-1-7343747-2-8

Life Saving Press LLC
21143 Hawthorne Blvd., #441
Torrance, CA 90503

Most Scripture verses, unless otherwise noted, are taken from THE HOLY BIBLE, NEW INTERNATIONAL VERSION®, NIV® Copyright © 1973, 1978, 1984, 2011 by Biblica, Inc.® Used by permission. All rights reserved worldwide.

Other translations used include:

The Christian Standard Bible. Copyright © 2017 by Holman Bible Publishers. Used by permission. Christian Standard Bible®, and CSB® are federally registered trademarks of Holman Bible Publishers, all rights reserved.

Holman Christian Standard Bible®. Copyright © 1999, 2000, 2002, 2003, 2009 by Holman Bible Publishers. Used with permission by Holman Bible Publishers, Nashville, Tennessee. All rights reserved.

The NEW AMERICAN STANDARD BIBLE®, Copyright © 1960, 1962, 1963, 1968, 1971, 1972, 1973, 1975, 1977, 1995 by The Lockman Foundation. Used by permission.

The New King James Version®. Copyright © 1982 by Thomas Nelson. Used by permission. All rights reserved.

The ESV® Bible (The Holy Bible, English Standard Version®). ESV® Text Edition: 2016. Copyright © 2001 by Crossway, a publishing ministry of Good News Publishers. The ESV® text has been reproduced in cooperation with and by permission of Good News Publishers. Unauthorized reproduction of this publication is prohibited. All rights reserved.

The *Holy Bible*, New Living Translation, copyright © 1996, 2004, 2015 by Tyndale House Foundation. Used by permission of Tyndale House Publishers, Inc., Carol Stream, Illinois 60188. All rights reserved.

The Holy Bible: International Standard Version. Release 2.0, Build 2015.02.09. Copyright © 1995-2014 by ISV Foundation. ALL RIGHTS RESERVED INTERNATIONALLY. Used by permission of Davidson Press, LLC.

NET Bible®, copyright ©1996-2017 All rights reserved. Build 30170414 by Biblical Studies Press, LLC.

GOD'S WORD®, © 1995 God's Word to the Nations. Used by permission of God's Word Mission Society.

The Holy Bible, Berean Study Bible, BSB. Copyright ©2016, 2018 by Bible Hub. Used by Permission. All Rights Reserved Worldwide.

Thank you to the many brave people who
anonymously shared their stories
about their Life-Saving Divorce
after abuse, infidelity, and betrayal.
Your courage and strength are inspiring.
I'm glad you've found safety and peace.

[The Lord] will say to the prisoners,
"Come out in freedom,"
and to those in darkness, "Come into the light."
They will be my sheep, grazing in green pastures
and on hills that were previously bare.
—Isaiah 49:9 (NLT)

[The Lord] will restore to you the years that
the locust hath eaten...
—Joel 2:25 (KJV)

QUICK GUIDE

The Life-Saving Divorce Book

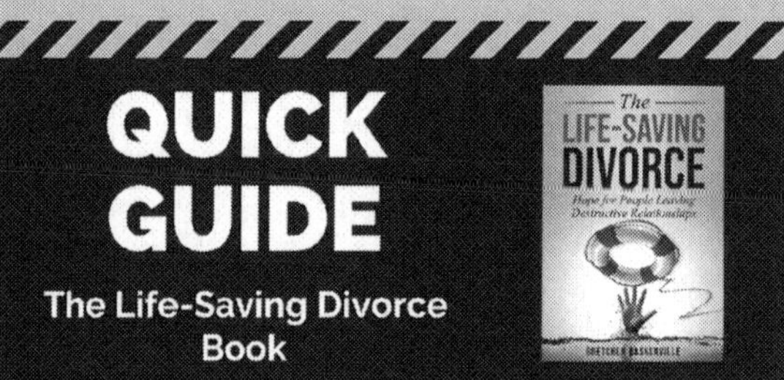

The
LIFE-SAVING
DIVORCE
Hope for People Leaving Destructive Relationships

Read the Introduction and Chapter 1 first, then jump to other topics.

If you have kids under 16

Chapter 7 - Gives you hope about kids' outcomes after life-saving divorces.
Chapter 2 - Ideas of how to talk to your kids so they can avoid a bad marriage to begin with

If your pastor says you didn't try hard enough or it "takes two to tango"

Chapter 3 - Helps you destroy the 27 myths about divorce that don't apply to Christians who really love God and seek to please him.

If your church doesn't condone divorce for abuse.

Chapter 6 - Helps you see that God wants to protect the faithful spouse. The Bible does allow for divorce for sexual immorality, violence, emotional/verbal abuse, substance abuse, etc.

If you wonder if you're being abused, or if this is a normal marriage

Chapter 4 - Gives you examples of physical, emotional, sexual, and financial abuse and neglect. Explains gaslighting and Abuse Cycle & Duluth Wheel

If your friends avoid you

Chapter 8 - Helps you find safe friends and a safe church. Even well-meaning friends may distance themselves during this time. They don't know what to say.

If you wonder if it's time to leave

Chapter 5 - Gives you the 10 most common turning points: the final straw that makes people finally walk away.

If you ask, "Will I ever be happy or ever find love again?"

Chapter 10 - Gives you hope for the future, because those who stayed in long-term toxic marriages are likely to be happier if they leave, regardless of whether they remarry or not.

CONTENTS

Acknowledgements xiv

Introduction xvi

CHAPTER 1: WHAT IS A LIFE-SAVING DIVORCE? 1

Nearly half of divorces are life-saving divorces: those marriages with serious problems (adultery, physical abuse, emotional abuse, drug/alcohol addictions, or sexual immorality). As a divorce recovery leader, for the past 20 years I've listened to heart-breaking stories of good spouses who tried to hold their marriage together at all costs.

CHAPTER 2: UNDERSTANDING DIVORCE AND DANGEROUS MARRIAGES 11

How did I get into this? How many dangerous marriages are there? Are abuse, infidelity, and addictions common? And how do I keep my children from getting into bad marriages? What role do age and education play? How do social and religious pressures (such as legalism) affect marriage quality? Why is the divorce rate declining? How does no-fault divorce affect the rates of suicide and domestic violence?

CHAPTER 3: MYTHS OF DIVORCE—DID I TRY HARD ENOUGH? 57

Most good spouses tried very hard to make their marriage work. They gave it their all. Here's how to respond to 27 common myths: false messages such as, "it takes two to tango," "marriage problems are always 50/50," or "it's best to stay for the kids." This chapter also addresses religious messages such as, "obviously you don't care about the sanctity of marriage," "you don't take the Word of God seriously," or "you must forgive and forget."

CHAPTER 4: AM I BEING ABUSED? 125

This chapter helps you figure out: "Is it abuse, or is this a difficult marriage with normal ups and downs?" Some people are confused; they feel scared even though they've never been physically struck. Here are 100 examples of physical, emotional, sexual, spiritual, and financial abuse, including explanations of terms like "gaslighting," "the abuse cycle," and featuring the Duluth Wheel of Power and Control diagram.

CHAPTER 5: TO STAY, OR TO GO? 173

How do you know if it's time to go? Learn about 10 common tipping points, those "Aha" moments when people sense it is time to leave. Only you know what you can take, and only you know when "enough is enough." Learn the steps for protecting yourself using "safe words," plus 50 tips to prepare yourself financially, physically, and legally to get away and get to safety.

CHAPTER 6: WHAT DOES THE BIBLE SAY? 210

God cares about and protects vulnerable spouses. The Bible says there are several acceptable reasons for divorce: infidelity, physical abuse, emotional abuse, sexual immorality, neglect, and abandonment. This chapter includes key Bible verses as we look at the teachings of Jesus, the apostle Paul, and Moses, as well as the Jewish customs and culture in biblical times.

CHAPTER 7: RAISING KIDS AFTER DIVORCE 242

About 8 in 10 children of divorced parents have no serious longterm social, emotional, or psychological problems. More than 9 in 10 have no drug or alcohol problems. Is divorce hard on them? Yes, of course. But if you are in a high-distress marriage, even if there's no screaming, fist-pounding, or overt conflict, it is likely better for your children that you divorce rather than stay in a tension-filled home where you're all walking on eggshells.

This chapter also discusses kids in high-conflict, vengeful divorces. About 1 in 10 divorces is not typical; it involves a hostile ex-spouse who attacks with vitriol, threats, name-calling, multiple court appearances, stalking, false accusations with no evidence, parental alienation, or years of child custody battles. Learn how to parent your children in these situations, and how to document your ex's behavior so you can protect yourself better.

CHAPTER 8: SAFE CHURCHES AND FRIENDS 295

Nearly 1 in 3 churchgoing Christians who divorce switch to another church during the process. They love God, but they worry about judgment and gossip. Safe friends and a safe religious fellowship can be an encouragement. When you go through a divorce, some good friends may walk away, or they want to cast judgment on you. It's good to find supportive people who've walked in your shoes. This chapter helps you identify pastors and friends who are safe.

CHAPTER 9: MALE VICTIMS OF ABUSE AND BETRAYAL 329

For every seven women who are abused, there is at least one man. In this chapter, we look at the stories of two men's life-saving divorces from wives who were abusive or adulterous. They explain what kept them in these long marriages and how they finally realized it was over. Men often feel shame about being abuse victims; they deserve to be heard, cared for, and understood.

CHAPTER 10: MOVING ON: FINDING HAPPINESS AGAIN 358

Although those first two or three years are stressful, you can survive! Shock, anger, fear, worry, and loneliness are part of the process. Recovering from trauma takes time. Know how to rebuild your self-respect and find your separate identity. Find your voice and become better at protecting yourself and your kids. Discover why those who get life-saving divorces are likely to be happier than if they had stayed—whether they remarry or decide to stay single.

Further Reading 412
About the Author 419
Index 420
Helpful Links 424

ACKNOWLEDGEMENTS

I wish to acknowledge those who urged me to write this book long ago, including those who've attended my divorce recovery groups and single mothers' groups since 1998. Thank you to my husband, my adult children, my pastor, and my best friend who co-founded the original group with me.

Thank you to my interviewees—all of you, devout Christians—whose heartbreaking stories made your courage and faith in God that much more inspiring to me. I am so glad that, through this book, many others will now have the chance to be inspired by your strength, and I praise God that you have found safety and peace for yourselves and your children.

I want to give a shout out to the pastors who wanted me to know that they stand beside victims of abuse and are in favor of life-saving divorces. I especially want to thank Dr. David Instone-Brewer (Cambridge) for reviewing the wording in my chapter on the Bible and Divorce. (Any errors are mine, not his.)

Thank you to the researchers, the quiet academics, and the professors at universities who keep sounding the alarm year after year that some homes are just too destructive to be safe, and that spouses and children would often be better to leave.

Thank you to the men and women in the Executive Roundtable who lit a fire under me and got me to finish the book.

To my many followers on social media (you know who you are), to those who sent me private messages, gave me book recommendations, and told your stories on Twitter, thank you! I learned a lot from you.

To those who did sensitivity readings for the manuscript, but wanted to stay anonymous, you deserve a lot of credit for finding my errors and recommending better wording. I appreciate your advice. Thank you to Brenda, Kelly, Tiffany, Sandy, and Mike for tipping me off to issues I hadn't fully considered. And finally, I want to acknowledge my excellent editor, Kay Ben-Avraham, whose strong guidance helped make the book much better than I ever envisioned.

INTRODUCTION

What's a Nice Christian Girl Like You Doing Promoting Divorce?

Good question! I am a Christian, and I am pro-marriage. I believe in the sanctity of marriage: God meant marriage to be loving, undefiled, and lifelong. I'm not interested in opening the floodgates and encouraging people to bail out of marriage.

I attend church, I tithe, I volunteer, I serve, and I pray. I came to Christ when I was 5 years old. I love the Lord. My parents have had a loving Christian marriage for sixty years and counting! As a young person from a genuinely good Christian family, who attended a Christian college, one of my biggest goals was to be an affectionate wife and loving mother. And I set out to do everything right.

But things didn't turn out the way I'd planned.

In fact, they turned out *dangerous.* The loving marriage my faith had promised me if I followed all the rules crumbled before my eyes, and I soon found myself terrified and in totally unknown territory, with kids depending on me, judgmental messages about divorcees pounding in my head, and an increasing sense that I *had* to get out of there.

In those dark years, by his Spirit, God showed me his provision for me and my children. He helped me get a "Life-Saving Divorce," and he helped me rebuild my life afterward.

In time, God had healed and strengthened me so much that I could turn around and help others who were in my same situation, leading divorce recovery groups and walking beside abused women and men as they grew in the strength of the Lord to recognize the abuse, get to safety, and form a new life for themselves.

I started working on this book twenty years ago, then put it down. Then three years ago when I remarried, my husband said, "You've got a lot to say on this topic, and you need to interview more people."

So for the next three years, I interviewed women and men from all parts of the country and all walks of life. I have hours of recordings, and hundreds—perhaps thousands—of pages of transcripts. Their stories are included in this book (with names and identifying features changed to protect their privacy) in the italicized excerpts you see appearing in various chapters.

I didn't know anything about the people I interviewed before the interview. I didn't know if they were divorced or separated. I didn't know the reason their marriage ended. I didn't know how long they'd been married or when they got divorced. I wondered if I would get some "I felt unfulfilled in my marriage" stories, but I didn't get even one.

What I got were some stories that were so heinous, I couldn't sleep at night.

I heard about abuse and betrayal I never dreamed possible.

Despite having been a divorce recovery leader since 1998, I was so shocked by some stories, I asked for evidence (and it was provided). I also heard stories of people who cannot divorce due to physical problems and financial constraints: people who must live in a terrible situation 24 hours a day, 7 days a week, sometimes barricading themselves in their bedroom. I've asked how I can help and have done what I can. I felt honored that each of these precious people shared their stories with me.

But for those who got a life-saving divorce, everyone I interviewed is grateful to the Lord that they got out.

They may not be as financially stable as before; they may be going to therapy and needing a lot of support; they may have a child who was broken by the abuse in the home; but they say their lives are better now. They may still have court battles over custody and support with their ex-spouse, but they are glad they got to safety.

This book isn't meant to tear down marriage. (I love being married.) This book is about "Life-Saving Divorces," that category of divorces that are for very serious reasons. These divorces are designed by God to help innocent spouses and children escape from someone who threatens their lives or emotional and physical health.

We all know that some marriages are the opposite of God's design. Some are mean, selfish, adulterous, or one-sided to the extreme… and they are often kept secret from other people at church. You probably have known of at least one marriage so terrible, you were sad but relieved when it ended. Maybe you had mixed feelings.

The Bible talks about people who are too destructive to be allowed to stay in our churches; how much more is this true in a marriage? God knew people would be terrible to their spouses, and he condemned it. God told the Israelites: "…Let no one deal treacherously against the wife of your youth."

This book is about treacherous marriages, including high-distress marriages with undercover problems where there is no violence, screaming, or visible conflict. I want to help people reach out to the Lord for help and guidance. In my divorce recovery groups, I saw some couples reconcile, but I also observed many, many cases where sinful and marriage-endangering behavior continued. God allows divorce in cases such as this. I am here to tell you:

You can love God and get a divorce.

Many interviews were conducted for this book. All names and other identifying information have been changed to protect anonymity. Their stories and quotes are set in italic type.

WHAT IS A LIFE-SAVING DIVORCE?

For more than two decades, I've been working with Christians going through divorce. Tears stream down their faces as they talk about how hard they tried to make their marriage work, how much they prayed, how many times they went to counseling.

These people are not quitters.

They are committed Christians who believe in the sanctity of marriage. They take the Bible seriously, and they take marriage seriously. They looked forward to marriage all their lives, coming to the altar with an eagerness to love, give, and commit.

They were realistic about the ups and downs of marriage. They knew there would be challenges.

They knew marriage takes hard work and compromise. And when they married, they gave it their all. They forgave over and over and went the "extra mile" repeatedly, trying to be more forgiving, more agreeable, more loving.

This book is based on more than twenty years of experience leading divorce recovery and single mother's groups, and on interviews with Christian men and women, those who took the Bible seriously and sought to follow the Lord in everything they did. They looked forward to a lifelong marriage, but they ended up unknowingly marrying someone whose vows were words only.

Over the years, I've heard many stories of marriages filled with betrayal, cruelty, infidelity, sexual immorality, violence, and chronic emotional abuse. I've cried and prayed with people as they've agonized about what to do. These believers begged God to heal their marriages, but the betrayals were so intense that their God-given instincts kicked in, and they finally walked away.

As the former slave Frederick Douglass said—

> "I prayed for twenty years but received no answer
> until I prayed with my legs."[1]

Listen to the Stories of Christians—In Their Own Words

He was a competitive bodybuilder,
and everything revolved around him: food, competition, training.
I wanted to support him because he didn't have family who cared.
He didn't work, so I supported the family.
The moment I told him I was pregnant, everything changed.
He started bringing women around to the apartment
when I wasn't home.
He smacked me in the face and pushed me into the wall.
This went on for 25 years—cheating and abuse—probably 20 affairs,
eight women I knew by name.

One day I found one of his notebooks. I read his description of me.
He'd had his eye on me while I was still married.
He described me as the "perfect victim":
financially stable, active at church, and trusting.
I realized he was going to kill me. I contacted his ex-wife and we compared stories.
She was just as terrified of him as I was.

I realized he was drinking all day.
He just keeps it going. And most people didn't know.
We had a conversation: "Do you want booze or me?"

---

1 Frederick Douglass as quoted by Rufus K. Noyes, *Views of Religion* (Boston, MA: L. K. Washburn, 1906), 65.

He said, "I'll have you."
But he didn't stop. He hid bottles in the garage fridge and sat out at the pool.
It was all deception. He had no intention of quitting. He just wanted me to believe it. He didn't have a job. Had no interest in getting a job. He wasn't doing anything.

I've always been a naïve person. That was a major factor in why I ignored
so many signals that my wife was a narcissist.
I remember when we were still engaged thinking,
"Get out now. This may be your only chance." I stayed 29 years.

Now, my daughter is 41 years old... Not surprisingly, she has been in abusive relationships, including one where she was hit in the back of the head. We've had many conversations about what to expect when you have a relationship with an angry man, but the main theme of our talks is the same: If you are hit once, you will be hit again.

I was pregnant at the time, and my husband backhanded me across the mouth.
We were on our way to his parents' home. My mouth was swollen, and I was all bloody.
My mother-in-law asked what happened to my mouth, and I lied.

The emotional abuse and brainwashing finally reached the point where I was so depressed, I lay there on the couch,
and I thought about pain pills as my only way out.
I was being so destroyed; all I knew is that I must get away from him.
And I wasn't strong enough to get away.
I wish I had heard messages from the church
saying you can be healthy as a divorced person.

This Book Is a Big Hug

If these stories resonate with you, I want you to know: I see your pain. I am walking over to you and putting my arms around you. I know you gave your marriage everything you had. I know the suffering you have experienced. I know the nights of crying in despair.

God knows and cares, too.

He will walk with you. Your life isn't over. God promises to bind up your wounds and heal your broken heart. Then he gives you a new life of hope and courage.

To the women and men who feel trapped in dangerous marriages and don't know there's a way out—

To those who have gotten life-saving divorces and now face blame or loss of social standing from their churches—

To the desperate, the fearful, the hurting—

To the ones who feel so horribly alone—

This book is for you.

My Story

My name is Gretchen Baskerville. I've been a Christian divorce recovery leader since 1998, leading groups in several churches in the Los Angeles area. I am a Christian and very pro-marriage. (My parents have had a loving Christian marriage for sixty years and counting!) As a young person from a genuinely Christian home, all I ever wanted was to be an affectionate wife and loving mother. And I set out to do everything right.

But like so many other Christians, I met and married someone from my church singles group and assumed he was a good choice. My parents approved of our dating, but things were not as they seemed. My new boyfriend told me that he used to have a sexual addiction, but it was long in the past, he said. I suggested we see a pastoral counselor. The pastor listened to the story and spent several months counseling us. He was convinced my love would heal my fiancé's wounds from childhood. He was confident everything would be fine after the marriage.

I was looking forward to a great marriage. I believed my pastor was right. That must be how things worked. I was a radiant virgin bride in a beautiful white dress, and I loved my new husband and was so attracted to him. I was looking forward to a passionate sex life. We had a wedding at the church my family had attended for years. Everyone came.

But the sexual addiction was not "long ago." It was now.

After our wedding, he started acting out again. We tried everything: Christian counseling, Sexaholics Anonymous... and finally he claimed he'd found a therapist who really understood him. I grew to have concerns about this particular therapist—concerns which later proved justified when the therapist acted out with a client, got sued, lost his license, and fled the state—but I was pregnant at the time, and desperate, and I didn't feel I had a choice.

To be a good wife, I thought I had to forgive and try harder to make our marriage work.

Instead of getting better, our marriage went downhill. I told myself it was okay, that "happiness in marriage is over-rated." We did more Christian counseling. I prayed and fasted. We went to church marriage retreats.

And finally, in our tenth year, I discovered his sexual addiction was worse than ever before. I was in shock. That was the turning point. It was clear the marriage had to end.

I went through a devastating, but ultimately life-saving, divorce. I wasn't prepared. I didn't anticipate it. Some people say that divorce is worse than the death of a spouse. All I know is that it was the most painful event I'd ever experienced. Although my parents—and my ex-husband's parents—were in favor of the divorce, I concealed the truth from all but my closest friends.

I thought that I was disqualified from God's best in life.

I was in despair. My dreams of being a loving wife with a happy family evaporated; in fact, I was confident I would never be happy again. I thought that there would be no meaningful contribution I could make to this world, and that I was destined to walk around with a black cloud over my head.

Life was over. I was done for. I had missed Plan A, Plan B, and who-knows-how-many-other plans for my life.

These fears defined me, and I alternated between being numb and crying in despair. Many of those dark days, I was barely able to care for my little children. I couldn't look into their eyes, because I couldn't bear the pain. I knew I had nothing to offer them. I was convinced they would turn out to be juvenile delinquents, emotionally troubled, and hopelessly dysfunctional.

The Lord is close to the brokenhearted
and saves those who are crushed in spirit.
— Psalm 34:18 (NIV)

During those months after the divorce, I prayed and read my Bible, and slowly a glimmer of hope appeared. I started realizing that I had let these fears dominate my life rather than letting God's words of hope and courage determine what I believed about myself. The Bible said I was precious to the Lord and that he would put my feet on a firm path.

I found many stories in the Bible that told of people who had been through tragedy but had still gone on to greatness. I read a lot of autobiographies of courageous people, and I realized that everyone has failure and disappointment in life. Yet there was hope: In the stories of people I admired, I began to see a theme emerge, of good things coming out of pain and tragedy.

Jesus promised that he would give me strength in my weakness—

My grace is sufficient for you, for my strength is
made perfect in weakness.
—2 Corinthians 12:9 (NIV)

I started leaning on the Lord, trusting him to keep that promise. The more I held to God's promises, the more strength and courage I found. Slowly the Lord pulled me out of the terror and up onto solid ground.

I obeyed his commands—to keep trusting God, to keep doing good for others, to keep taking care of myself, and to be generous even when I felt hopeless.

I didn't know how I would support myself financially, because I earned only $500 per month at the time. In Southern California, that wouldn't even cover my house and utilities, not to mention food and clothing and gas.

But my father said I needed to trust God and pay one bill at a time—don't worry too far out into the future.

When we project our fears out into the future,
we always forget to project God's mercy and power
into the future at the same time.

God was faithful. By the end of the first year, I had made it through successfully—paying all of my bills, borrowing from family, and providing the basics for my kids. By the end of my third year, I was able to find a glimmer of financial stability and began to see the light at the end of the tunnel. The smile came back to my face... I had found hope and peace.

What Is a Life-Saving Divorce?

Many people in the church think all divorces are the same: sinful. Selfish. Something that only flighty, frivolous, immature people do—people who don't respect the sanctity of marriage, who don't take the word of God seriously, who get bored, or who don't have the strength of character to go the distance in marriage.

But the truth is, none of these things describe a life-saving divorce.

When we talk about a life-saving divorce, we are talking about *leaving a marriage that is so destructive, the family can no longer function*. The situation is so intolerable that the innocent spouse and children must get away. They fear losing their good name, and they don't want to lose the marriage they thought they had and desperately wish were still possible, but they cannot tolerate the destruction and betrayal any longer.

I don't mean to suggest that a person always goes into marriage with the intention to be a destructive spouse. Some individuals hoped and prayed that marriage would fix them. They knew they were messed up from childhood. They too had been told that marriage would somehow cure their problems. When it became clear this was not the case, many drifted into addictions and self-focused behavior. But that doesn't mean the other spouse must stay with them and get dragged down themselves.

Destructive behavior, whether deliberate or not, is a valid reason to leave. And you don't have to hate a person to divorce them. You don't have to paint them as all bad. People are complex. Some are good in certain areas but unable to be safe marriage partners.

Almost Half of All Divorces Are Life-Saving

A life-saving divorce refers to the 40% of divorces in America that occur for very serious reasons. For example—

- infidelity
- abandonment/neglect of duty
- physical or sexual abuse
- chronic emotional and verbal abuse
- financial abuse
- serious drug or alcohol addictions
- sexual immorality and deviations, such as child molesting or child porn

A life-saving divorce is a way for a wife or husband to leave a destructive marriage when their spouse has repeatedly betrayed them by breaking their vows to love, honor, and cherish.

Those who treat their spouse like the enemy or like a slave to their whims, rather than like a partner through life's ups and downs, are not safe to remain married to.

A life-saving divorce happens when every stone has been turned and every effort has been expended. The tipping point is when some incident, great or small, makes you realize there is no rational reason to believe your spouse will ever change.

I do believe in miracles, and I have seen some unfaithful spouses come to their senses and make the effort to completely change their lives, but—

God does not promise to heal every marriage.
God does not magically fix every marriage.
Your righteous prayers do not guarantee that God will change your spouse.
You can love Jesus **and** *get out.*

What Will This Book Do for You?

The Life-Saving Divorce will help you get to safety and come to peace emotionally and spiritually. You (and your children) will find hope and happiness again. I would even suggest that your faith will increase as you see God's love and faithfulness to those who have been heart-broken by betrayal and abuse.

I will repay you for the years the locusts have eaten…
—Joel 2:25 (NIV)

I am writing this book as a layperson, not a professional. I'm not a lawyer, a licensed clinical counselor, a pastor, or a social worker. What I am is a woman who has known betrayal first-hand, gotten a life-saving divorce, raised children, and worked for more than two decades in the Church either leading divorce recovery groups, single mother's groups, women's Bible studies covering abuse topics, or meeting with and praying for people sent to me by churches in my area.

I should note also that in this book, the term *divorce* is broadly used to cover divorce, separations, and breakups of long relationships, not only official, legal divorces.

This is a topic near and dear to my heart, and it's one I know a lot about—but it's important for me to say that the thoughts and advice contained in this chapter, as well as in the rest of the book, should not be taken as legal, medical, or psychological counsel. For those things, you should consult a professional.

God Allows Divorce

In these pages, I will show you that God allows divorce in destructive circumstances. You will read Bible verses that teach that divorce was invented by God to protect innocent spouses and children trapped in highly destructive marriages. (You will also be reading the verses on divorce that most Christians have missed!)

In the case of a marriage where one spouse is treacherous, God does allow the other spouse to get out, maintain their honor and standing as a good Christian, and to have the option to remarry if they wish.

God is not mocked. When a self-centered spouse makes a sham of the covenant of marriage, turning it into one-way street rather than a loving, faithful, and supportive partnership, God provides a way out for those who wish to go.

Hope for Your Children, Hope for You

This book will support and comfort you as you walk the path to safety. It will show you research that says kids, on average, turn out fine after divorce; and it will offer ways to take good care of your kids during and after the divorce, helping them to get through the rough parts and come out the other side healthy and flourishing.

It will teach you to identify myths that say if you only tried harder, prayed and fasted more, and lived more righteously, God would have automatically fixed your marriage. It will help you recognize signs of abuse, and it will help you plan how to get to safety.

It will also teach you how to find God and a good future in the midst of the pain. And it will give you guidance on how to respond to those who don't think you tried hard enough, and how to choose safe friends and a safe church, to find the support you need to get out of a dangerous marriage and rebuild your life.

The good news is, there is life after divorce.

And that's the other part of this book: how to move on. How God loves and cares for you, never leaves or forsakes you. There is peace and a future for you and your children.

God has a plan for your life, even if you go through divorce.

"For I know the plans I have for you," declares the LORD, "plans to prosper you and not to harm you, plans to give you hope and a future."
—Jeremiah 29:11 (NIV)

UNDERSTANDING DIVORCE AND DANGEROUS MARRIAGES

About ten years after my divorce, I found a box in the garage. It had keepsakes from our wedding twenty years before, and one of the items was a fill-in-the-blank workbook we used during our premarital counseling at church. I opened it.

I was curious to see how we had answered the questions and to find out what I had missed. How had I failed to see the danger? Surely there must be something that would explain how I could have married my ex-husband. After all, on the first page of this bestselling workbook it said, it was designed "to help you decrease the risk element in marriage."

What I saw surprised me: We had answered truthfully, but the topic of dangerous behaviors never came up.

The workbook had a lot of good advice and Bible passages about God's purpose in marriage, but the examples of marriage difficulties were minor, such as communication problems that almost any kind-hearted couple could solve by listening better, understanding each other's views and expectations, and compromising a bit.

In the workbook, the word *infidelity* appeared only once, and the author said that such behavior was inconceivable in Christian marriage.

The word *domination* and the phrase *unfair use of anger during conflict* came up, but no warning bell was sounded, no advice was given. This wasn't identified as a serious problem.

An example of being overly *controlling with money* and *questioning all the receipts* was mentioned, but the comment was mild: "This is not how to start a marriage."

Why didn't the author say more? Intimidation, domination, and control are serious red flags for domestic violence, but the book did not raise a warning. Shouldn't a premarital book do this?

The words *adultery, lying, cheating, betrayal, gambling, pornography,* and *addiction* didn't appear in the premarital workbook at all. Nor did words such as *abuse, slap, hit, push,* or *fight*.

The only mention of substance abuse was an example of an alcoholic who one day stopped cold turkey and had a complete life change at the request of his spouse, along with the comment that that this change might happen in your marriage! The opposite and far more likely scenario—where a spouse gets arrested for drunk driving, functions poorly, has mood swings, may be violent, loses jobs, or spends the vital family resources on drinking—was never addressed.

The workbook never brought up risky behaviors: Abuse, adultery, prostitution, chronic lying, drug addiction, gambling, battering, child sexual abuse, or other behaviors that would destroy the trust in a marriage and jeopardize its future. There was no instruction to break your engagement or even to get counseling. It was as if these marriage-endangering problems didn't exist in anyone you might meet at church. And when "undesirable behaviors" did crop up, the readers were told they could "learn to adjust."

At one point the workbook said, "The best way to help another to change is to make changes in your own life," but it never gave any suggestions of how you might do that. It never mentioned that one option might be to stop "adjusting" and "compromising," and to draw a line in the sand. It didn't say anything about requiring better behavior and possibly cancelling the wedding.

Serious problems do exist.

I had married a man in my church's singles group who wasn't trustworthy: someone with a sexual addiction.

Finally, I realized:

This workbook assumed every Christian was
a person of good will who had their spouse's best interests at heart.

I was shocked and closed the workbook.[2] It was full of premarital topics, but it did not address the red flags, outline the risk and likelihood of dangerous marriages, or recommend ending an engagement in such cases. How was this possible, when the Bible warned us about the existence of predators in our churches and told us not to associate with such people (1 Corinthians 5:11)?

That's when I started looking for anything that could help me understand. I had a lot of questions.

- How many dangerous marriages are there?
- Are abuse and infidelity common in marriages?
- How common is abandonment and neglect in a marriage due to alcoholism or drug addictions?
- Are there seriously troubled people in our churches, or did I manage to marry the one-in-a-million guy (and *not* in a good way)? Sure, the Bible told us there were wolves in our midst who took advantage of others, but how many?

I turned to research to find out. Many believers faithfully view the Bible as God's Word, and as an infallible guide to God's truth and wisdom for our lives.

We can look to the Bible for this wisdom as we ask questions and search for answers.

In my case, these answers to the questions I had about divorce and dangerous marriages were to be found in modern-day research. I soon came to more deeply appreciate the Bible's wisdom in warning us against untrustworthy people, and in showing us how to protest abuse (see Chapter 6 for more on Scripture's teachings about life-saving divorce).

I came to appreciate it so much because the answers to my questions were horrifying. There are a *lot* of dangerous marriages out there. More than 40% of divorces are for very serious problems, and we were pretending as if they didn't exist. We just automatically looked down on divorcees as quitters.

As Christians, this is so important for us to understand. When we

---

2 I bought the latest edition of H. Norm Wright's book ***Before You Say "I Do,"*** just to see what the author had changed, but didn't find much. Every word and illustration I mention in this chapter exists (or does not exist) in today's Kindle version of the book.

continue teaching and spreading a false message—that everyone who divorces is lazy, selfish, and sinning—we inadvertently put pressure on many devout believers to stay trapped in marriages that are draining the life out of them and traumatizing their children.

Instead, we need to see what's *really* going on in many of these marriages and families.

In the Church, we have a high view of marriage and family—as we should! But sometimes our desire to hold marriage and family up ends up damaging people. When we believe dangerous marriages are extremely rare, or are easy to fix, we apply pressure to couples to stay together.

Yet as we look at the statistics, we see that our teachings about marriage and family are contributing to making marriages more unstable and perilous for people (especially women and children, as we'll see in Chapter 7), and that life-saving divorce not only happens much more often than we think, but that it is necessary and godly: an escape route designed by God to free people from bondage.

In the final section of this chapter, we will discuss ways that we as the Church can help make dangerous marriages less likely to happen. Many of our churches' teachings do not prepare people (especially women) to spot "red flag" warnings that mark probable abusers (the "wolves" that the Bible warns us against), and our concerns about pre-marital sex pressure people to marry quickly and/or young, which tends to make dangerous marriages more likely.

Learning more about divorce research helps show us what things we as the Church can be doing that would make people far less likely to enter unsafe marriages in the first place, and that would make them more equipped to identify and escape unsafe marriages once they're in one.

How Many People Get Divorced, Really, and How Many Are Life-Saving Divorces?

Myths about divorce are hard to shake. Most of us believe them because we've heard them all our lives, and the people around us in our churches (including, often, our pastors!) believe them, too. So we don't question them. We hold onto them, and we pass them along.

But believing them has dangerous real-world consequences, especially for people trapped in marriages that threaten their wellbeing and safety.

As God's people, we are called to devote ourselves to the truth, and to setting the captives free. One of the ways we can do this is by learning the truth about life-saving divorces, and helping tear down the beliefs that keep victims in the power of their abusers. Research can help with this!

In this chapter, we will look closely at the question, *Why do people divorce?* This question is important because many Christian communities, leaders, and churchgoers don't know the true answers and instead believe lies—lies that help prop up abuse and misery. And we truly want our marriages to be loving and stable. We want children to see good examples of their parents in a caring partnership.

But before we start to examine that question, I want to say a few words about Christians and divorce.

Divorce is a hard subject and can be hard to understand in a "big picture" sense, no matter who you are. But for us as Christians, there are some additional roadblocks to understanding.

Not only do we as Christians have a powerful drive to get married and stay married at all costs—our church communities tend to hold the institution of marriage and the family in a position of highest importance—we also get upset and defensive when we're faced with the reality that we're only doing a slightly better job of staying married than the secular world is.

This strong inward motivation to value marriage and family over the individual believer, together with our upset and defensive feelings when we're presented with facts that contradict what we want to believe about ourselves as the Church, combine to keep us from seeing what's really going on—in our churches as well as in our own personal lives.

Though we probably wouldn't put it this way to ourselves, the truth is that we really want to believe that we're superior. We love to picture us, the Church, as a community of people who have the truth the world needs, who have the answers, and who are living life God's way, full of the fruits of right living.

We like to put forward a good image with our lives, often because we love Jesus so much that we want to have our lives look like a picture-perfect advertisement for Christianity, to make non-Christians want to learn more about our God.

Admitting brokenness and allowing our pain, confusion, and suffering to be seen are hard for us to do.

Sometimes we even feel as though we are letting God down by not performing perfect peace and joy all the time. We feel much more comfortable if we can believe that we Christians are doing better with our lives than non-believers are. And when the facts show otherwise, we get very, very uncomfortable, scared, defensive—even angry!

This is a strange reaction on our part, if you think about it. For people who have devoted our lives to Jesus, it should come as no surprise to us to face the fact that we are sinners in need of a Savior, *just like everyone else*.

God is not shocked to discover that we are needy, broken, confused, and hurting.

That's why he came to save us.

That's why he promises us his presence and his love.

He knows we need him. He knows we don't have all the answers. And do you know what? Non-Christians know it, too! They are far more likely to be drawn to the Church when they see *honesty* than when they see people putting on a show of perfection.

We don't have to feel attacked or threatened when we learn that Christians divorce almost as much as non-Christians. We don't have to go into denial and ignore the truth that attending church, loving God with our whole hearts, praying, and reading Scripture don't guarantee us a long and happy marriage. We don't have to plaster on a forced smile for the outside world while we feel like we're dying inside.

The Bible has prepared us for things like this.

It teaches us that the Body of Christ is made of fallen people who aren't perfect, and we don't have all the answers. We're *forgiven*, and we're walking with Jesus on the long road to maturity.

The Gospel is not strengthened by our defensiveness and our desperation to prove that we're better than everyone else. It's strengthened when we admit, in humility, that we need God's help just as much as the rest of the world, because we are as broken and in process as they are.

So as you read the research in this chapter, see if you can keep these things in mind. If you can keep your defensiveness at bay, you will be able to see more of the truth that God wants to show you. Some of the myths you have perhaps believed, and that may be still keeping you captive, can be defeated and replaced with God's truth—even through reading about the work of researchers who have been studying divorce!

Why Did I Get Divorced?

As I mentioned at the beginning of this chapter, when I was going through my own life-saving divorce, I needed answers to some big, fundamental questions. I wanted to make sense of my own divorce: why it happened, and what the likelihood was of encountering the same problems when I remarried. I wanted to do it right. I didn't want to suffer that way again, and I wanted my children to see a good husband-and-wife relationship. Like any good parent, I wanted to give my children the best chance of having good marriages, too. I didn't want them to go through the kind of pain I went through.

When I began researching divorce, I was asking the question: why did this divorce happen to me? Is the quality of my spiritual life the only factor in finding a good mate and having a happy marriage? Are there any other factors—inside or outside of my control—that contributed to this divorce, or is it all my lack of faith and effort?

Surely my belief that "any Christian who is godly enough can have a great marriage" couldn't be wrong, could it? Everyone I knew and trusted held to this belief.

The guarantees had seemed so rock-solid, so certain.

I quickly realized that there were a lot of factors, outside the spiritual realm, that did make a difference in the quality of my marriage, and that led to the necessity for a life-saving divorce.

There were factors outside of my control that made my marriage dangerous.

I was also blown away when I learned the sheer number of Christians who are divorced. I learned that essentially 1 in 3 marriages involving churchgoers—and 1 in 4 of conservative Christians—end in divorce.

Immediately I wondered, why hadn't I heard more about this? Why didn't I see other divorcees in my church? In the 2000-person megachurch that I attended for forty years (and that's just the adults, not the kids), why couldn't I point out more than ten people who were divorced like me? Surely the researchers must be wrong! If they were right, there should have been at least 500 of us (not 670, because some individuals divorce multiple times). Where were they?

This opened my eyes to the social pressure and stigma against divorce that exists in the church, and the degree to which that stigma forces people into hiding.

Before I divorced, I knew two people in my church singles groups who had previously divorced, and they kept it hidden, a never-discussed secret. It was taboo, completely hush-hush. They pretended their second marriage was their first.

Why?

Because church people would treat them like second-class citizens if they were honest about their divorces, and the price was just too high.

If you, like me, have been burdened with the belief that you're the only one who failed at this marriage thing—keep reading. You'll discover that you're in good company. There are lots of devout, faithful Christians who have needed to get life-saving divorces.

It's not just you.

"No-fault" Divorce: Destroying Family Values, or Saving Lives?

The first state in the U.S. to adopt "no-fault" divorce was California in 1969, signed into law by then-governor Ronald Reagan and put into effect in 1970. A few other states already had similar laws, but California's bold move by the movie-star-turned-politician grabbed the headlines.

There is no federal divorce law in the U.S., and each state has vastly different laws. In general, no-fault divorce is the opposite of "fault" divorce. In other words, in a no-fault divorce, you don't place blame on one spouse for ending the marriage. The reason can be "irreconcilable differences," "incompatibility," or something similar. It also allows one spouse to file for divorce without the other's consent; it can be a unilateral move.

"No-fault" divorce has often upset religious people and others who are traditional and conservative. Many Christians see no-fault divorce as running counter to the Bible's teachings. They feel it promotes moral decay, destroys family values, and disrespects the sanctity of marriage.

For many Christians, no-fault divorce just seemed like as "easy out" for those who didn't take seriously the effort and commitment that marriage requires, even making a mockery of marriage vows. "No-fault" seemed to give a free pass to those who wanted to abandon their faithful spouse and kids and go live the party life.

For Christians, no-fault divorce is a mixed bag. In this next section, we will examine the pros and cons. Once we're through, you can make your own decision.

Pros: Reasons It Is Good

1. *Lowering the suicide, domestic violence, and murder rates.* In states that adopted no-fault divorce, researchers discovered that over the course of time, the suicide rate for wives dropped by 8-16%. The domestic violence rate by and against both men and women dropped 30%, and the homicide rate for women murdered by intimates dropped by 10%.[3]

No-fault divorce reduced the suicide rate, domestic violence rate, and murder rate.

These are very significant decreases, and they point to the fact that no-fault divorce meant that people who needed to leave their marriages were finally able to escape and find safety.

In many cases, because of no-fault divorce, people were able to get out of a dangerous marriage before it could turn violent, or they left a dangerous marriage faster than they would have been able to otherwise. In some cases, people filing for no-fault divorce did so in order to leave a dangerous marriage, even when they didn't have enough evidence of danger to convince a judge.

All of these things resulted in fewer cases of domestic violence, fewer deaths at the hands of abusive spouses, and fewer cases of death by suicide.

In this book, you will read many stories of men and women who are so abused and in despair that they turn to suicidal thoughts. When divorce is almost impossible to achieve, cannot be initiated unless the abusive spouse

---

3 Betsey Stevenson and Justin Wolfers, "Bargaining In the Shadow of the Law: Divorce Laws and Family Distress," *The Quarterly Journal of Economics* 121, no. 1 (Feb. 2006): 267, 268, 286.

agrees to it (which they rarely will), or comes with so much stigma and loss of social standing (even resulting in being shunned or ostracized from the only community you have ever known) that the victim cannot envision any good future for themselves either inside or out of their abusive marriage, sometimes suicide seems like their only way out.

No-fault divorce gives distressed and miserable people a way to end their marriage rather than their life.

2. *Giving the victims of abuse and betrayal the ability to get out without their spouse's consent.* The truth is that a lot of marriages are not ended by the unfaithful spouse, but by the long-suffering spouse who cannot take it anymore.

Many divorces are initiated by abuse victims who have endured cheating, domestic violence, chronic emotional abuse, depression, and suicidal thoughts—people who had to get out. The abuser would never agree to a divorce. They would do everything to stonewall and block it and fight it in court.

Often those who neglect, abuse, or betray their marriage want to have their cake and eat it, too, enjoying the benefit of having a responsible spouse who takes care of the household and kids while they do their own thing. No-fault divorce allows the spouse to leave unilaterally, without any consent from the betrayer, abuser, or addict.

3. *Getting safe, even if you're not wealthy.* In the past, before no-fault divorce, the legal process took a long time, had a lot of barriers in some states, and was expensive. People who weren't wealthy often stayed in miserable, violent marriages because they had no realistic choice, or they walked out the door and disappeared.

Wealthy people from states that had very strict laws could travel to a liberal divorce state, establish residency, and file for divorce. Or if a wealthy person's state allowed divorce for infidelity only, and their spouse had abandoned or abused them, they could fabricate evidence and lie in court. (For example, in New York in the 1800s, people faked evidence of adultery because that was the only legal reason for divorce in the state.)[4]

---

4 Nelson Blake, ***Road to Reno*** (New York: Macmillan, 1962), 119.

But poorer people were stuck. They simply could not afford a divorce that required them to move to another state or pay for court fees, expensive attorneys, private investigators, and long arguments in court. Unilateral no-fault divorce tilted the scale so that people who needed a life-saving divorce, especially low- and middle-income people, could escape bad marriages, too.[5]

4. *Reducing public humiliation.* Contrary to popular belief, many people in life-saving divorces don't want to air their dirty laundry for all to see. They would prefer to end their marriage as privately as possible. They don't want to talk publicly about the misdeeds of their spouse (especially if they depend on that person's job for child support), discuss the disrespectful treatment they received, or tell about their own torment in a room of strangers. They don't want to expose themselves to ridicule or bring humiliation to themselves or their children.

No one wants to be the subject of gossip or feel judged by others. No-fault divorce allows them to get out without pointing fingers, and without enduring public judgment and further emotional turmoil.[6]

5. *Keeping the courts from being bogged down.* Many Christians especially want to clear their name and make sure the world knows they were not at fault for this divorce. But this adds significant legal costs and requires more resources in the court system, a system that already has hundreds of thousands of people utilizing it every year.

For those who object to big government, this is a genuine issue. In fact, about 1 in 3 states no longer allow people to file a fault divorce (one that casts the blame on the other party).[7]

This is why you cannot tell if a person had a life-saving divorce just on the basis of their having obtained a no-fault divorce. (Note: No-fault divorces are not *always* faster than fault divorces. Some states will waive

---

5 Philip Cohen, "Hell in a Handbasket, or the Democratization of Divorce?" ***Family Inequality*** (11/27/2003), accessed 10/1/19, https://familyinequality.wordpress.com/2013/11/27/handbasket-democratization/. Although I've read a lot about the plight of poor spouses who could not afford a divorce, and even seen it in my own family tree, this article clarified it as an issue of fairness.
6 By the way, The United States is one of the few countries that has no-fault divorce. As of 2019, people are still trying to introduce and pass a bill that will give people in the United Kingdom the right to no-fault divorce.
7 Beverly Bird, "Which States Are No-Fault States," ***Legalzoom.com,*** accessed 10/16/19, https://info.legalzoom.com/states-nofault-divorce-states-20400.html.

their waiting period for those who file a fault divorce, so if you have evidence, it's important to discuss these options with your attorney.)

6. *It hasn't increased the divorce rate over the long run.* After the jump in the divorce rate from 1970 to 1984, it has dropped over the past 50 years almost back to the 1970 level. As of 2010, all states now have no-fault divorce, *yet the divorce rate continues to drop*. It declined 21% between 2008 and 2017, and it appears to be dropping further.[8]

No-fault divorce has saved lives, without significantly increasing divorce rate long-term.

Some people try to explain it away, saying the marriage rate has dropped too, so of course we have fewer divorces. They will say that more people are cohabiting—which is also true.

But the divorce rate in this illustration, and in the graph pictured below, is a percentage of all *married people, plus recently divorced people*, not a percentage of the whole U.S. population, so it is a valid comparison.

It means that, even if more people were married back then, more were divorcing back then, too.

Chart: Divorce Rate from 1970 to 2019[9]

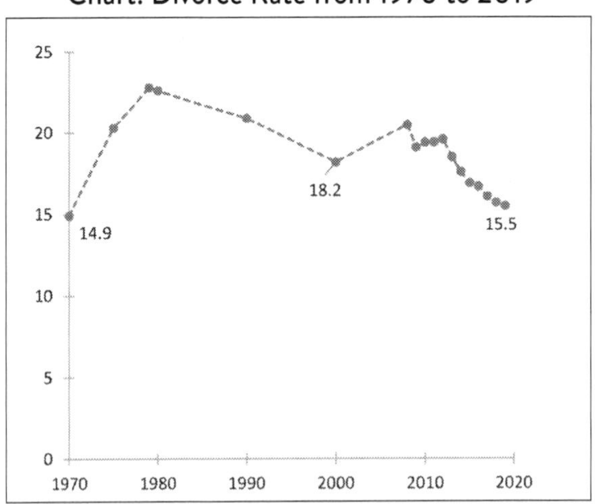

8 Philip Cohen, ***The Coming Divorce Decline*** (College Park: University of Maryland, 2018), 2.

9 Reynolds, L. (2020). Divorce rate in the U.S.: Geographic variation, 2019. *Family Profiles*, FP-20-25. Bowling Green, OH: National Center for Family & Marriage Research. https://doi.org/10.25035/ncfmr/fp-20-25.Method of calculation:The divorce rate = [(number of women divorced in the past 12 months) / (number of women divorced in the past 12 months + number of currently married women)] x 1000.

Cons: Reasons It Is Bad

1. *It allows an executive to run off with his secretary.* No-fault divorce allows one person to walk away from the marriage for any reason. That doesn't sit well with those of us who care about fairness, family values, and the sacredness of marriage. As Chapter 6 will show, religious leaders tried to trap Jesus by asking him about no-fault divorce for frivolous reasons (such a wife burning a meal). Jesus said those reasons were not sufficient for divorce.

2. *Divorce is tough—sometimes even devastating—to the financially dependent spouse and children who get discarded.* The first year, these "rejected" spouses go through a lot of anger and turmoil. They struggle with the avalanche of transitions. Now they have to deal with the shock, accept reality, get a better job (or any job), support traumatized children, find childcare, and locate a new place to live.

But just like the spouses who file for divorce, the "left" spouses usually feel better within two or three years. And their children usually turn out fine, on average.

One of the leading researchers on divorce, Dr. Mavis Hetherington, wrote,

> "In the early period, the "left" spouses were the most unhappy and resentful, but by the end of the second year, there were few differences between those left and the "leavers."
>
> "[In] the second year there was an upsurge in emotional wellbeing as people began to adapt to their new life situation."[10]

Divorce Is Declining

Contrary to what you may have heard from news media, family organizations, and conservative think tanks, the divorce rate is about as low as it was 50 years ago. And it appears to be continuing downward.

The good news is that fewer young people are divorcing. They are pulling the divorce rate down. The baby boomers, as a group, still have

---

10 E. Mavis Hetherington and John Kelly, ***For Better or For Worse*** (New York: WW Norton & Company, 2002), 50-51.

a high divorce rate, but that will be less of a factor as that generation passes. Millennials have comparatively lower divorce rates. And that trend will likely continue.

On average, millennials (unlike their parents) are waiting until they are older and have more life experience (and sometimes more education) before tying the knot. They are being more selective when considering mates. Because of this type of caution and careful consideration on their part, researchers expect the divorce rate to continue to decline.[11]

Why People Are Divorcing

As was mentioned in Chapter 1, about half of divorces in the U.S. are life-saving divorces. Those are the divorces that happen for very serious reasons, such as infidelity, physical abuse, chronic emotional abuse, abandonment, drug or alcohol abuse, and sexual immorality.

Christians often challenge me: "Can you prove that about 50% of divorces are really for serious reasons?" They've always heard that 95% of divorces are for falling out of love, even though there is no evidence for that claim.

And that's the problem: If we don't see it in our own church, we don't believe it. If we haven't experienced it in our extended family or close friendships, we are skeptical.

Common sense is valuable, but we also need to admit that we hang out with the same people much of the time. We are only seeing a tiny little piece of the big picture. That's why we need surveys done by universities and organizations that talk to hundreds—even thousands—of people across the country, surveys that simply want to document what is happening. They don't have a vested interest in one particular result over another.

In contrast, we want to be skeptical about organizations that have something to prove. For example, if a drug company presents the test results of the safety of a drug they sell, we would be smart to ask for an outside organization to verify them. Of course that manufacturer will say the drug is safe—they'll make money if people think it's safe and buy it!

Because of things like this, history has shown us that it is best to

---

11 Cohen, *The Coming*.

have research done by *neutral researchers*, who have no reason to favor a certain outcome. Also, we want large surveys or national surveys using scientific methods that can be reviewed by critics to make sure the results are accurate.

When you see such a survey, with a lot of participants
from all regions, ages, and walks of life,
you have a better chance of finding out what's really going nationwide,
even if you're not seeing it in your area.

I will give evidence through four surveys that life-saving divorces are more frequent than commonly thought.

Several studies on "reasons for divorce" have been done, surveying people from all parts of the country and all walks of life. When you look at the results, you will see that *more* than 40% of divorces are for life-saving reasons.

Let's start with the research about the reasons people divorce. If, as we've said, it's not true that 95% of divorces are for "falling out of love," what does the research show? What is causing most divorces?

Survey 1 included 1,147 people who divorced after age 40. Researchers asked each participant *the most significant reason* for their divorce.

They gave the participants twenty different choices of answers, from mild ones (like "my spouse is not so attractive anymore") to extreme ones (like "my spouse cheated," or "my spouse was abusing me").

Half of the participants reported that their reason was an extreme one—that means that 50% of these folks needed a life-saving divorce.

The Twenty Different Answers Offered in the 2004 Survey

Cheating	Verbal, physical, or emotional abuse	Control freak	Stepchildren got in the way
Sexual incompatibility or poor sexual performance	Inability to have children	Didn't want to have children	Always away at work or business
Not carrying weight in marriage (sharing chores, etc.)	Physical appearance declining	Different values, lifestyles	Money problems
Religious differences became intolerable	Cultural differences became intolerable	Alcohol or drug abuse	Abandonment
Homosexuality	Fell in love with someone else	Major age difference	No obvious problems, simply fell out of love

Survey 1: "What was the most significant reason for your last divorce?"

Sample of Most Serious Reasons Reported[12]

16% – Adultery, cheating, infidelity
16% – Emotional, physical, verbal abuse
12% – Alcohol or drug addiction
3% – Not carrying weight in marriage (neglect of duty/refusal to provide)
3% – Abandonment

50% of divorces

(There may be other serious reasons among the other answers given, but these are the most obvious.)

12 Xenia P. Montenegro, "The Divorce Experience: A Study of Divorce at Midlife and Beyond," ***AARP the Magazine*** (May 2004), accessed 1/10/20, https://assets.aarp.org/rgcenter/general/divorce.pdf.

What about people who divorced before they were forty?

Survey 2 interviewed 208 people who had divorced between the ages of 20 and 55. Instead of being given options to choose, they were asked an open-ended question: "What do you think caused the divorce?" The wide variety of their responses were categorized into eighteen reasons.

This survey also shows that a high percentage of divorces—in fact, 42%—are for very serious reasons.

18 Types of Answers in the 2003 Study[13]

Infidelity	Incompatible	Drinking or drug abuse	Grew apart
Personality Problems	Lack of Communication	Physical or mental abuse	Loss of Love
Not Meeting Family Obligations	Employment Problems	Don't know	Unhappy in Marriage
Financial problems	Physical or mental illness	Personal Growth	Interference from Family
Immature	Other		

Survey 2: "What Do You Think Caused the Divorce?"

Sample of the Most Serious Reasons Reported (% Cases)
22% – Infidelity
11% – Drinking/drug use
6% – Physical or mental abuse
3% – Not meeting family obligations

42% of divorces are for serious reasons

(58% are for other reasons.)
(There may be other serious reasons among the other answers given, but these are the most obvious.)

13 Paul R. Amato and Denise Previti, "People's Reasons for Divorcing," *Journal of Family Issues* 24, no. 5 (July 2003): 602-626.

Granted, on the face of it, we might not necessarily know what some of the potentially "milder" phrases mean. Does "employment problems" mean the spouse couldn't keep a job, or does it mean the spouse had a bad relationship with his boss? Does "religious differences" mean they disagreed on churches to attend, or does it mean one spouse is donating all the rent money to TV preachers? Does "personality problems" mean being married to someone who interrogates you about every dime you spend, or being married to someone who doesn't enjoy family activities? Does "financial problems" mean being married to a person who spends the family income on gambling, or someone who earns minimum wage and needs dental work? Hidden within some of these seemingly milder reasons may very well be other examples of life-saving divorces.

But for our purposes, we only need to notice that there are many more life-saving divorces than we have been led to believe.

In fact, ***Survey 3*** shows even higher numbers of life-saving divorces. In a large, 2,323-person study in Oklahoma, respondents were given a list of reasons and asked to indicate which reasons were major contributors to their last divorce. 58% indicated infidelity, and 30% indicated domestic violence (there was no option for substance abuse).[14]

In ***Survey 4***, a smaller survey of divorced people going through premarital education classes, where participants could select more than one factor, they selected infidelity (59.6%), substance abuse (34.6%), and domestic violence (23.5%) as "major contributors for divorce."[15]

For a long time, we in the church have tended to think about divorce, and about people who have gotten divorced, as though only five percent of those divorces happened for good reason. As you can see from these studies, that's not true.

If we focus only on the *obvious* reasons from the lists above, we can estimate at least 42% of divorces, and probably about half of divorces, are for very serious problems, the kind of problems that make the

---

14 C. Johnson, S. Stanley, and N. Glenn, et al., "Marriage in Oklahoma: 2001 Oklahoma Baseline Statewide Survey," (2002): 15.

15 Shelby B. Scott, Galena K. Rhoades, and Scott M. Stanley, et al., "Reasons for Divorce and Recollections of Premarital Intervention: Implications for Improving Relationship Education," ***Couple and Family Psychology: Research and Practice*** 2, no. 2. (2003): 131-145. There were 54 participants in this PREP premarital education course.

marriage miserable: unfaithfulness, physical or mental abuse, drug or alcohol abuse, refusing to support the family, or simply walking out the door.

When the desperate spouse says, "I can't take any more suffering and betrayal," we call it a "life-saving" divorce. And only that spouse knows how much they can take. What may be acceptable to someone else, may be excruciatingly painful to you.

Those who believe 95% of divorces are due to frivolous reasons are simply wrong.

What Are the Risk Factors for Ending Up in a Dangerous Marriage?

If our goal is to have good marriages and healthy children, we want to educate our community. We want to identify risk factors, red flags, and dangerous behaviors before or during the engagement, to make sure the couple is aware, so they can decide whether or not to proceed.

Having said this, knowing red flags isn't enough, because so many flags are only evident in hindsight. For example, a man who pins his girlfriend to the ground and tickles her until she is breathless and gasping for air may seem affectionate—until after the wedding, when he restrains her physically or blocks her path or uses his height to intimidate her.

That's why we can do more than just help people learn to spot warning signs (a "preventative" strategy). We can arm them with tools that will help them at any stage, not just before the marriage.

We can teach people that they may not see any signs at all—that many people don't. And we can reassure them: even if you did see troubling behavior but married anyway, how could anyone predict it would get so bad? There are abusers clever enough not to show their hand until you are vulnerable. It's not your fault—and you can still get out.

All that matters is getting to safety, whenever that happens.

Good Marriage Versus Dangerous Marriage

How do we define a good marriage, so that people know whether they are in one or not?

One Christian therapist said: "A marriage must be safe and loving (or at least respectful), where both people are grateful for the other's capabilities. Otherwise it is not *marriage*. It could be kidnapping or incarceration or servitude, but it isn't a marriage."[16]

That's where discussing life-saving divorce in advance comes in. As a mother, I've taught my adult children to watch for manipulation, control, and isolation techniques used by abusers. My kids know that a marriage to a person who can't or won't stay faithful is not worth their time, energy, or loyalty.

They understand that both spouses must sacrifice to make the marriage safe, loving, and respectful. If only one is doing it, it needs to be addressed. If it continues to be a destructive one-sided marriage, it may be time to get out.

So how do we reduce the risk of getting into a bad marriage in the first place?

This next section will discuss a few of the biggest risk factors, so we can get closer to answering that question—risk factors like:

- marrying young, fast, or early
- having less education
- being financially dependent
- having low income
- using biblical patriarchy to keep wives powerless
- holding to an overly legalistic view of sexual purity
- formula thinking, or "prosperity gospel"
- church peer pressure

Why Does Marrying Young Make Getting Stuck in a Dangerous Marriage More Likely?

The United States Census surveys have found that people who marry younger are at a higher likelihood for divorce later in life.[17]

There are many reasons for this, but most of them have to do with

---

16 Michael Alvarez, personal conversation.

17 M. D. Bramlett and W. D. Mosher, "Cohabitation, Marriage, Divorce, and Remarriage in the United States," *Vital and Health Statistics* 23, no. 22 (July 2002). Table 21: Women (all races) ages 15-44. Probability of divorce after 10 years of marriage. Note: This report is a free download online and measures many more factors, and breaks down by race.

the amount of experience these people have in living an independent, adult life, and in the amount of thought that was put into the choice they made to marry that specific person, rather than someone else (or rather than not getting married until later, or at all).

More importantly, people who marry quickly in this way are at a much higher risk for marrying someone who will later prove to be dangerous, making a life-saving divorce necessary.

Young people are still maturing, emotionally as well as physically. Often, people who marry as teenagers are not yet finished with significant personal growth, and they aren't ready to make a life-long commitment.

Think of the foundation of a house: All the supporting structures need to be in place, and the cement thoroughly mixed, poured, and set, before the walls, roof, plumbing, and electrical systems can be installed securely. That foundation has got to be solid to bear the weight of a home.

Similarly, in our youth, our "cement" may not yet be set; we haven't ever lived on our own before, or we don't yet have experience earning a paycheck or managing our own finances, or we don't have a clear sense of what our personal goals are in life. Perhaps we haven't yet carried significant responsibilities like paying rent, holding down a job, developing good professional skills and relationships, planning and making our own meals, and taking charge of our medical needs and bills.

For young women especially, having little practical expertise in the professional and financial areas of life can leave them too vulnerable to their husband's wage-earning status—they may not know how to make their way in life without a husband, which means that they feel like they have no choice but to stay with a man who is abusing or terrorizing them, simply because he's making the money.

This pressure to stay can be even stronger when a woman has children and is unable to picture how she might support her children if she were on her own.

Young people who marry early, especially in Christian circles, are more likely to be marrying one of the first people they've dated, or one of the first people who has shown any interest in them. They're more likely to be motivated to get married, not because they want to marry *this specific person* and have good reason to believe that person will be a steady, caring, and devoted life partner, but because:

- Authority figures, or the community, are pressuring them to "settle down."
- They want to obey God and save sex for marriage, and they really want to have sex—or they already had sex with this person and think they have to get married to them now, to make up for it.
- They are pregnant and are getting pressured.
- Marriage is expected of them; it's assumed that it's just "what you do."
- They have been taught that marriage is proof of their entrance into adulthood.
- They have been taught that it is holiest to only have one person that you have ever loved.
- They believe that marriage is the best step into maturity in God.

This is why it's so heartbreakingly common for earnest, committed believers to make the mistake of marrying someone who later proves to be a dangerous person to be married to. And the same pressures that push Christians into unwise marriages are still there later, pressuring them to *stay* in marriages that have turned harmful, abusive, scary, and damaging to the children.

In fairness, some early marriages are not the young person's idea. Some girls are pressured, coerced, and bullied into marrying by their own families.

It's difficult to believe that the United States allows child marriage, but if a parent or a judge consents, child marriage is legal in 46 states in America.

Between 2000 and 2010, an estimated 250,000 child brides (under age 17, and some as young as 12) got married. Although some of those older ones were likely consensual, many were not. Many are girls who are raped by adult men or family members and are forced to marry their rapist in order to save face for the family or avoid criminal charges for the perpetrator.[18]

---

18 Nicolas Kristof, "11 Years Old, a Mom, and Pushed to Marry Her Rapist in Florida," ***The New York Times*** (5/26/2017), accessed 05/30/2017, https://www.nytimes.com/2017/05/26/opinion/sunday/it-was-forced-on-me-child-marriage-in-the-us.html. The reason 250,000 is a nationwide estimate is that only 38 states provided data on child mariages (167,000 for those 38 states). One of the leading advocates for changing child marriage laws is Sherry Johnson, a Christian who was raped at age 9, gave birth at age 10, and forced to marry her rapist at age 11. She wasn't able to escape this violent, neglect-filled marriage until age 17, when she had six children.

"Bullied by their parents into marriage, [Fraidy Reiss, founder of Unchained at Last] says, girls may feel powerless to object— and fearful of telling a judge that they don't want to wed. If they try to flee an abusive marriage, they are turned away from shelters and may be treated as simple runaways."[19]

These marriages that began with rape are likely to continue with violence and coercion. They have the highest divorce rate of any age group, and rightfully so.[20] Many of these girls are handcuffed to men who control all the money and power, because even though the girls are wives and mothers, they are still minors. Some cannot divorce until they are older.

These are truly life-saving divorces.

Why Does Having Less Education Make a Dangerous Marriage More Likely?

The United States Census surveys[21] have found that having less education increases the likelihood of divorce in first marriages, and as we've seen, a large portion of those divorces are for life-saving reasons.

EDUCATION – Women with a high school degree or further education tend to divorce less.

Less than high school: 42% likelihood of divorce
High school diploma: 36%
More than high school: 29%

Marrying early, being young, and having less education go together.

We've already seen that being older, having life experience (such as paying bills), carrying the responsibility of having a job, following the instructions of your boss, and learning to plan your calendar are good preparation for marriage. You've developed the skills in advance; you've seen a bit of life; and you are truly ready to make a well-considered decision about marriage.

---

19 Ibid.
20 Vivian E. Hamilton, "The Age of Marital Capacity: Reconsidering Civil Recognition of Adolescent Marriage," ***Faculty Publications*** 1430 (2012), accessed 12/28/2019, https://scholarship.law.wm.edu/facpubs/1430.
21 Bramlett, "Cohabitation," Table 21.

Similarly, when a person—especially a woman—doesn't get an education and may not have her own job or income, it leaves her vulnerable if her spouse treats her badly.

I interviewed several divorcees who had been caught in this situation. Even those who had parents nearby were not always able to depend on them for help. Some felt they had no choice but to stay with an abusive or unfaithful person. They had to beg for spending money. They got the message that they were less important in the relationship—more of an employee or a servant than a partner. Their wishes and preferences just didn't count as much as his did.

This stripped away these women's self-respect. Their relationships spiraled downward. This is more common than you might think, as the high divorce rate shows.

Many women in my divorce recovery groups decided to go back and finish their education. For some, it opened doors to much higher-paying jobs. One woman went from a childcare job to a supervisory job in a childcare center in a public school district, more than doubling her income. When she started dating again, she felt more confidence and ended up marrying a man who respected her, treated her well, and had similar life achievements.

And there's another dynamic: Having attained an educational goal gives many people a sense of dignity.

One 55-year-old Christian man shared that he had been selfish and immature as a young newlywed, and that his wife felt confident about saying no to his bad behavior and setting boundaries because she too had an education and a job.

She stood firm, not allowing herself to be trampled on, which taught him a good lesson, and was a major factor in keeping their marriage loving for the past 30 years.

Why Does Low Income Make a Dangerous Marriage More Likely?

The United States Census surveys have found that low household income increases the likelihood of divorce in first marriages:

FAMILY INCOME – Lower incomes increase the likelihood of divorce.[22]

---

22 Bramlett, "Cohabitation," Table 21.

Less than $25K: 53% likelihood of divorce
$25K-$49K: 31%
$50K or more: 23%

A friend of mine is a licensed therapist in Chicago who has worked with a wide variety of clients in his career, from the richest to the least wealthy. Now he is working mainly with low-income families.

He said, "Having no money makes everything in life harder."

He points out that most of his clients are hard-working, decent people, but they are under the tremendous stress of long hours, poor working conditions, and the constant fear of not being able to put food on the table. They often find themselves in despair.

They have not failed morally. They aren't lazy.

They are overwhelmed.

When things go wrong, they have little or no financial reserves to smooth over the problems. Sometimes to pay for a car repair or a medical bill, they go into debt they may never be able to pay off. It may become more than they can handle. When their child loses their only coat, it is one more blow.

The parents cannot afford counseling for themselves or their children; they cannot take a day off; the stress of day-to-day life leaves them with few options. Their bodies break down with the strain, but they cannot afford to rest or get good medical care.

In some cases, since they cannot afford counseling or pay for medicine, the inexpensive alternative is alcohol.

In addition, prescription medications for long-term pain (which were thought to be non-addictive) turned normal people into victims of the opioid crisis, leading to overdoses, depression, or suicide.

If there is no family or community assistance in these cases, these marriages may go downhill and become unsafe.

I don't want to put any blame or shame on people in this position. They are in a tough spot. They have been doing their best for a long time, trying to stand up in the face of waves that never stop coming. They need more support than they get. It is too much.

Let's talk about another form of "low income" that comes from financial abuse. In several of my interviews, husbands (or, more rarely, the wives) would make good money, pay for housing, utilities, and food, then spend the rest on themselves: for prostitutes, sports tickets for their friends, international travel (with friends, not the spouse), expensive recreational vehicles, and nice clothes, while their spouse and children were literally in rags scraping to get by, unable to afford therapy, enjoy recreational activities, or join a school sports team.

When there is this level of disrespect and selfishness, you can see this isn't a safe and loving marriage.

Why Can Biblical Patriarchy Make a Dangerous Marriage More Likely?

When I started interviewing divorced Christians several years ago, I was surprised by the number of women (and one man, whose story is in Chapter 9), who told me their marriage was destroyed by biblical patriarchy.

They explained that they might have had a better marriage, or might not have chosen this particular spouse, had they not been following the messages of biblical patriarchy.

Now, I want to be clear: Many people model their marriages along traditional gender lines, and there's no problem with that. (My marriage looks pretty traditional: I do all the cooking, my husband handles most tasks that require physical strength.) Believers see models of manhood and womanhood in Scripture that they want to adhere to in their life together. In many marriages this works beautifully, and the couple is very happy together. They are excellent parents who are deeply committed to their children.

What we're talking about here is when those teachings are used to abuse—when something beautiful is made into a weapon.

Different Christians read Ephesians 5 in different ways. Some—like me—emphasize verse 21, where all believers (not just wives) are encouraged to submit to one another in love. Other people focus on verses 22-24, where emphasis is put on a wife submitting to her husband. But however we interpret these verses, the one thing both sides can agree on is this: husbands must not treat their wives in a domineering, uncaring fashion. That Bible passage commands husbands six times to treat their wives with love, so there's no excuse!

Biblical patriarchy is a hierarchical, authoritarian view of men and women. Those who promote this view say they wish to show the "glad harmony portrayed in Scripture between the loving, humble leadership of redeemed husbands and the intelligent, willing support of that leadership by redeemed wives," according to the Danvers Statement.[23]

According to this view, the man is the leader and benevolent ruler of the home; the wife is the submissive helper who sets aside her interests and preferences to serve her husband.

The effect of this arrangement is *to grant the power to the husband, and to entrust the wife and children's wellbeing in his hands.*

Again, there are plenty of couples whose marriages run along traditional gender lines and work very well and lovingly. The messages about men and women themselves aren't a problem when they are being lived out in a good and loving way, and when abuse is clearly condemned.[24] It works just fine when the man uses his power for good and the wife is not being mistreated.

But when these messages reduce the woman's voice, discourage her from vetoing an unwise decision, pointing out sin, setting a boundary to protect herself, or having any preferences at all, they've created a system ripe for abuse.

In a fallen world, it's dangerous and naive to assume everyone will use this one-sided power for good. Some do, but not all. It's like the bestselling premarital workbook I described at the beginning of this chapter:

The writers of this statement assume every "redeemed" person has good will and has their spouse's best interests at heart.[25]

I interviewed one Christian woman who lives in a very religious county in the U.S. She was homeschooled by her stay-at-home mother. Her community was influenced by Bill Gothard's biblical patriarchy teachings, as well as other teachers who said that women couldn't have

---

23 "The Danver's Statement," ***CBMW.org*** (Wheaton: Council on Biblical Manhood and Womanhood, 1988), accessed 1/10/20, https://cbmw.org/about/danvers-statement/.
24 For example, the Council on Biblical Manhood and Womanhood has a clear statement condemning abuse that can be found here: https://cbmw.org/about/statement-on-abuse/
25 In chapter 2, we examine some of the dangerous messages that biblical patriarchy promotes.

driver's licenses, couldn't read books their father hadn't screened and approved, and taught that daughters were the personal possession of their fathers and had no say in whom they would marry.

The young woman and her husband followed the courtship model promoted by homeschool leader Josh Harris in his book *I Kissed Dating Goodbye,*[26] getting to know each other in her parents' living room under the watchful eye of her relatives.

Everyone followed the proper steps—but that didn't ensure a good marriage.

The woman's husband has physically and emotionally abused her. He has frequently demeaned her in public (but never in front of a pastor), raped her, and is addicted to porn. Over the past 15 years, six professional counselors have met with them and have expressed their concern about her husband's behavior toward her and her children. Friends have witnessed his vicious behavior and submitted written statements to the judge to defend her in court. Her pastors know what is going on. But she says—

Our pastors have clearly told me they would not support a divorce. And certainly not divorce and remarriage. That's a common view in my culture and community, in fact my whole county. Being a divorcee is something people look down on.

Here's a young, intelligent, well-spoken woman who might have had a good marriage and raised children in a home with peace and safety—but that's not what happened. Instead, her children have had the trauma of witnessing their father abuse their mother. He's also psychologically abused them by threatening to kill their pets.

Those incidents alone are two of the seven categories of childhood trauma that correlate with health problems later in adulthood that we discuss in Chapter 7 on children and divorce.

She has made a clear-eyed decision not to divorce but to stay legally separated, because she gets more emotional support from her tight-knit church community if she appears to be open to reconciliation. She knows she could divorce and leave the community and church, but she has chronic health problems and feels this is the best option for now.

Many families and churches caught up in the biblical patriarchy movement have done an injustice to young women by leaving them

---

26 Josh Harris has publicly apologized for the damage his book has done.

defenseless, without any way of providing for themselves if something goes wrong. Powerful teachers, such as the now-disgraced biblical patriarchy and Quiverfull leader Doug Phillips,[27] and alleged sexual abuser Bill Gothard,[28] marketed their curriculum to homeschooling families for years, actively discouraging both young men and women from getting higher education. They and their ministries profited financially from these teachings.

These teachers of biblical patriarchy were so destructive that Michael Farris, one of the founders of the ultra-conservative Home School Legal Defense Association (HSLDA), said this in 2014:[29]

"The philosophies of Gothard and Phillips damage people in multiple ways."

"Innocent people follow teachers in good faith thinking they are following God. And when the directives turn out to be **only man's ideas,** the followers often find that someone in their **family has been damaged in the process**…"

---

27 In 2013, Phillips resigned from his ministry Vision Forum after confessing to cheating on his wife. He was also excommunicated from his church, Boerne Christian Assembly, in 2014.

28 Sarah Pulliam Bailey, "New Charges Allege Religious Leader, Who Has Ties to the Duggars, Sexually Abused Women," ***Washington Post*** (1/06/16), accessed 08/13/19, https://www.washingtonpost.com/news/acts-of-faith/wp/2016/01/06/new-charges-allege-religious-leader-who-has-ties-to-the-duggars-sexually-abused-women/?tid=sm_tw. More than 30 women have said they were molested by Bill Gothard, according to this ***Washington Post*** story. Survivors of Gothard's teachings and his organization have been sharing their stories and healing from the damage they suffered. These stories have been made available at the website www.recoveringgrace.org. A lawsuit filed by numerous women alleging sexual abuse and harassment by Bill Gothard was withdrawn due to the statute of limitations; however, the women said they "were not recanting our experiences or dismissing the incalculable damage that we believe Gothard has done by his actions…" https://spiritualsoundingboard.com/2018/02/26/breaking-lawsuit-against-bill-gothard-and-the-institute-in-basic-life-principles-dismissed/ (accessed 8/13/19). See also: https://www.christianitytoday.com/news/2016/january/more-women-sue-bill-gothard-iblp-alleging-sexual-abuse.html (accessed 8/13/19).

29 Two quotes found here: Julie Ann Smith, "From Silence to Exposure: Why did Homeschool Leader Michael Farris Speak Out Now?" ***Spiritual Sounding Board*** (8/30/2014), accessed 08/13/09, **https://spiritualsoundingboard.com/2014/08/30/from-silence-to-exposure-why-did-homeschool-leader-michael-farris-speak-out-now/**. See also this article in the ***Christian Post*** where Farris wrote: "The philosophies of Gothard and Phillips damage people in multiple ways[.]" Napp Nazworth, "Homeschool Advocate Michael Farris Responds to Sex Scandals of Homeschool Leaders Bill Gothard, Doug Phillips," ***Christian Post*** (8/29/2014), accessed 8/13/19, https://www.christianpost.com/news/homeschool-advocate-michael-farris-responds-to-sex-scandals-of-homeschool-leaders-bill-gothard-doug-phillips-125549/.

"I've come in contact with many **young people who were raised in patriarchal or legalistic homes**. Almost none of them are following these philosophies today. **Some have rejected Christianity altogether.**"

An entire generation has been infected with damaging teachings that told women they were powerless to choose when and whom they married; that their desire to make their own choices was a sign of rebellion; and that they should willingly submit to this system, belonging to their fathers and then to their husbands.

Phillips and Gothard's followers saw them as speaking with God's authority. But as Farris says, their teachings were "only man's ideas."

Granted, not everyone will benefit from a college education or trade school. Not all can afford it, and perhaps they would not find subjects they would enjoy. But it is irresponsible for faith communities to give a message such as this, denying the benefits of having a college education and actively discouraging it.

And of course, it is not just a matter of education—we are talking about an entire system that leaves women (and young men) dependent on authoritarian spiritual leaders, by deliberately restricting them from having skills and experience they need to make it outside their own culture.

Why Can Legalistic Views about Sex Sometimes Make a Dangerous Marriage More Likely?

Just as we discussed with biblical patriarchy, I want to emphasize that there's nothing wrong with believing sex belongs in marriage. That isn't where the trouble comes in, when we look at this aspect of Christian teaching about sexuality (sometimes called "purity culture"). As one Christian blogger put it:

"By 'purity movement' I don't mean a home that believes that sex before marriage should be avoided. That's just a basic Christian tenet. But the purity culture has extra-biblical rules attached to it: dating is wrong; one should always court; parents must chaperone; parents should set kids' boundaries; kissing before marriage is wrong; clothing should be stringently monitored and modesty

enforced; girls who aren't pure are 'chipped teacups' or 'stained napkins' (those are analogies that are often used in rallies)."
—Sheila Gregoire[30]

Some legalistic versions of purity culture take biblical patriarchy and extend the father's control to his children and to *their* marriages. Despite what leaders may say, their messages often suggests that a daughter's worth is based on her virginity, that she belongs to her father, and that he has the right to determine whom she marries. (Tellingly, this pressure to be a virgin is applied much more heavily to daughters than to sons.)

In certain Christian churches and groups, this overly legalistic treatment of sexuality leaves believers thinking that if they feel they are sexually attracted to someone, they should marry that person, to avoid "burning with lust." In these circles, premarital sex is condemned so much, it is seen as being the unpardonable sin. So there is a lot of pressure to have hasty marriages.

These twistings of a normally biblical teaching put supreme emphasis on a woman's virginal status, and often people who grew up with such teachings were taught that dating was sinful or was "practice for divorce." These folks were pressured to marry the first person they dated, and to marry young, as a way of being purer in the sight of God—something that only faith in Christ, not "right sexuality," does for us.

Unfortunately, as was discussed above, these practices make it far more likely that a young person might marry unwisely, before they are ready, or without recognizing the true character of the person they have married.

Here's the story of a woman of faith who cared about the church's teachings on premarital sex. Her virginity and sexual morality were very important to her. She was active in her church and always wanted to be right with the Lord. And she had been taught that if you honor God in your sex life, he will bless you with a good husband.

By teaching her to focus on formulas, her church rendered her defenseless. By telling her that marriage would be great as long as she

30 Sheila Wray Gregoire, "10 Things that Scare Me About 'Purity' Culture," ***To Love, Honor, And Vacuum*** (1/19/16), accessed 12/28/19, https://tolovehonorandvacuum.com/2016/01/purity-culture-10-things-that-scare-me/.

was a virgin on the wedding night, they failed to equip her for reality. So she got some Pollyanna-ish messages: "Marry someone who says he's a Christian; it will all work out." Or "marry someone recommended by a Christian friend; it will all work out." Or "marry fast so you don't burn with lust; it will all work out."

None of those simplistic messages led to the expected result: a good Christian marriage.

> *My father was a military man—a loving guy—a man who turned over his entire pay to my alcoholic mother. He taught me how to do everything. He was the real nurturing figure.*
>
> *But when I left home, I walked into the world unprepared...*
>
> *I married very young. I wanted to have sex and didn't want to burn with lust.*
>
> *I was a virgin, and we married fast... He was bipolar, and he simply disappeared one year later.*
>
> *Before my husband left, he had introduced me to his best friend. He said if anything ever happened to him, I should marry this friend. So of course, I looked to this friend for trustworthy advice. I was naïve. I had been taught that wives obey their husbands, and so after my husband disappeared, I found myself lonely and later sexually attracted to this friend. I wanted to be a good, respectable Christian wife and mother. Once again, I felt it was important to marry rather than to burn with lust. So we married during our lunch break just after we started dating.*
>
> *That husband was a serial cheater. He told me I had to accept that he had girlfriends on the side. And over time, the girlfriends got younger and younger. I divorced him.*
>
> *Then I started dating a guy who said he was a big-time Christian. We went out on one date, and the next day he came back with his truck filled with all his possessions. He said my pastor had given him permission to marry me. It never occurred to me that he might be lying. He acted as though God had chosen me for his wife. I allowed myself to be swayed by his Christianity, never stopping to ask if he was God's choice for me. My assumption was that if* he *said I was God's choice for him, that was all that mattered.*
>
> *He decided we should buy a house, but my wishes didn't matter to him. He picked a house and demanded that I cash out my 401(k)*

retirement plan as a down payment. He contributed nothing to the purchase of the house. Although I sensed this was a bad start, I wanted to be a good, submissive wife. Being a married woman was important in the church I attended.

Over time it became clear that my husband was not the Christian leader he claimed to be. He drank to excess, and he wasn't viewed at church as a man with leadership potential. In fact, he was mad I had been given a lot of responsibilities in the church. My husband would be angry and jealous.

By this time, I was pregnant and feeling sick constantly. I knew something was wrong, and I wanted him to take me to the hospital. But he refused. [That was the way our marriage was.]

I hung in there nine years. I didn't want another divorce. I worked, paid the bills, and raised his son and daughter as well as our little one. I put his children through private school and earned all the money.

[Lying and financial fraud were also part of his scheme.] I discovered my husband had opened accounts in my name online using my social security number and driver's license. He slept with a bank teller to get an ATM card for my savings account and drained it. He forged my signature on my checks, and he embezzled from his former business partner.

One of his tricks was to tell me a friend needed money for rent, but that I couldn't know who, because the friend would be embarrassed. He wanted cash for the friend. I gave him cash multiple times. Speaking with that friend later, I learned the friend had been approached by my husband requesting cash for my imaginary "financial problems."

My husband admitted he was staying with me just so he could save up money to get a bigger house. I felt beaten down, used, and destroyed. His two children were devastated. I couldn't take any more and left.

Finally I went to my best friend and told her I'd like to find a good husband. She introduced me to her churchgoing, evangelical brother, but failed to mention he was a violent man, a felon, and con artist. I didn't ask a lot of questions up front because I thought he was a good Christian. He spoke in church, but I had no idea he was dealing drugs. He became Husband #4.

One day I found one of his notebooks. I read his description of me. He'd had his eye on me while I was still married. He described me as the "perfect victim": financially stable, active at church, and trusting. I realized he was going to kill me. I contacted his ex-wife and we compared stories. She was just as terrified of him as I was. I got a restraining order, divorced him, and moved.

My pastor told me that one of the biblical grounds for divorce is abandonment, and he said it included abandonment of marriage vows. When a husband is abusive, he has abandoned his vows and is acting as an unbeliever. He said if the unbeliever wants to leave, let him leave.

After 4 divorces and you're nearly 40 years old, your self-esteem is in the toilet and you've got nothing to offer. For the never-married women who say, "Any marriage is better than none..." No, a bad marriage will wipe out your self-esteem. Don't change to make someone happy. Trust your own judgment; don't assume a Christian will be a good man.

I've known other women who've had four marriages, but it wasn't until I interviewed this woman that I understood the role Christian legalism plays in the lives of people with multiple marriages. I'm sorry to say, I used to judge such people.

But now I realize she was just trying to obey God by avoiding sex outside of marriage. She wanted to please God. She didn't marry because she was promiscuous. In fact, it was just the opposite; she married to avoid sin. And that meant marrying men she thought were good Christians without taking the time to ask a lot of questions first.

How has she turned the ashes into beauty?

In my profession, I now work on a lot of disabled/elder abuse/ exploitation cases on a civil level. We go after exploiters for financial abuse and breach of fiduciary duties. I gather and analyze all the financial stuff, then build the story. We file a civil suit in either state or federal court, and we turn over that information to the local police/sheriff's department, and we work with them to build a criminal case to take to the district attorney. I could not do this if I were not passionate about not seeing people get abused. We win the civil cases every time. Every time. This is how God used my experience to help others.

How Does "Formula Thinking" or the "Prosperity Gospel" Make Dangerous Marriages More Likely?

This woman has used her pain to help others. She's an intelligent person. She's good at her job. She's been a devout Christian since age 9. She has always loved being at church and has done a lot of volunteering, including leading women's Bible studies. How did she end up marrying so many dangerous men?

1. She truly wanted to please God and be a perfect Christian. She didn't want to be a failure in God's eyes or to embarrass her family. She didn't want to live in sin.
2. She was taught formulas that blinded her to danger. The message was something like this: If you don't have premarital sex, God will give you a good spouse, great sex, and a long, happy marriage. If you do have premarital sex, your life will be wrecked. (Multiple men and women have told me they believed that having premarital sex would cause them to burn in hell; and that incurable sexually transmitted diseases or marital abuse might be the natural consequence of their sin.)

What this woman experienced is a perfect example of being a victim of the false "prosperity gospel" message:

The message says that if we are good people, God will bless us abundantly. If we aren't being blessed, that's because we aren't righteous enough, we're hiding a secret sin, or there's some sin we are unaware of (but it is there, deep inside).

Most people think of the prosperity gospel as the message that if you are good enough and donate enough money to the church, God will give you health and plenty of money.

But there's another version of this message that occurs in many churches when it comes to the topic of dating and marriage. It goes like this: If you follow the proper steps, you will be guaranteed success. If you don't, you'll have a horrible marriage, and it will all be your fault. You reaped what you sowed, and now you're stuck.

So when an perfectionistic Christian who wants to please God and make her family proud, marries to avoid sinning and ends up in a miserable marriage, that person somehow imagines it must be their fault. They didn't want to fail God.

They did what they thought was right. But it still went wrong.

There's no way to win. In their minds, divorce is just one more thing that will displease God. This leaves them stuck and confused. They heap on themselves a pile of guilt-inducing thoughts and stay in a dangerous marriage.

"Formula thinking" teachers will always figure out a way to make it your fault if their advice doesn't work. And frankly, people who care deeply about God and tend to be self-critical find ways to blame themselves for a spouse's bad behavior. Instead, let's put the blame where it belongs: on the person who chooses to abuse or betray!

Even well-intentioned teachers and pastors can reduce marriage advice to an overly simple formula. If the youth group leader teaches that you must fit a certain mold and have a certain personality type, how will you find someone who loves you for *you*—with your particular God-given gifts, talents, and personality?

The truth is that the only guarantee we have in life is the guarantee of God's love and presence with us.

Marriage is a risk. God gave you brains, a voice, and feet to walk away if your marriage is toxic. Chapter 6 covers the Bible verses that show you can divorce for physical abuse, chronic emotional abuse, and neglect due to situations such as serious addictions. You have power, whether you know it or not:

- You have control over how much time, energy, money, and loyalty you give to someone or something.
- You have discernment about what is right and wrong.
- You can sense when your spouse is treating you like the enemy and looking for ways to exploit you.
- You can sense when your spouse is ruining the kids and pitting them against you.

The Apostle Paul warned believers about Christians within the church who choose to go the wrong way:

These people are hypocrites and liars,
and their consciences are dead.
—1 Timothy 4:2 (NLT)

Is your spouse's conscience dead? Do they no longer care if they hurt you? When you tell them they've hurt you, do they show concern, remorse, and make changes so that they don't do the same thing again? Or do they just ignore or blame you, excusing themselves, saying it's your fault they behave badly?

If you love the Lord, the Scriptures entitle you to follow your own conscience—even if that means choosing something others in your church or family might disagree with. Of course, relying on wise counsel when making serious decisions is biblical, but the Bible also advises believers to use their own judgment and wisdom. The Apostle Paul says you, as a believer, can make decisions based on your own conscience and your love for God:

One person considers one day more sacred than another;
another considers every day alike.
Each of them should be fully convinced in their own mind.
Whoever regards one day as special does so to the Lord.
Whoever eats meat does so to the Lord, for they give thanks to God;
and whoever abstains does so to the Lord and gives thanks to God.
—Romans 14:5-7 (NIV)

No mere human can claim to be God's spokesman. Only Jesus can claim that.

Pastors, family members, and friends are just flawed human beings like everyone else. They are not the Holy Spirit. Although wise and loving counselors are helpful, no one gets to decide what is wise and discerning for your life.

In the early church in Rome, Christians didn't always agree on what was a sin and what was not. Some thought one day was more holy than the others. Others thought eating meat sacrificed to idols was a sin.

Paul told them that as long as they were trying to honor the Lord, they were free to decide.

For people (like me) who want to follow clear rules, this is scary and radical. But the truth is that if you love the Lord, you have freedom of conscience.

The early church father Augustine summarized the same idea—

"Love God and do whatever you please:
for the soul trained in love to God
will do nothing to offend the One who is Beloved."[31]

Why Does Church Peer Pressure Make a Dangerous Marriage More Likely?

Skeptics read the story in the last section and say: "Wasn't she trained to identify the traits of godly and ungodly men?" Or, "Where was her father? He should have stopped this."

They don't understand the power that pastors and youth leaders have, or the power that Christian friends, radio programs, websites, and Christian books have, with their expectations and assumptions, and their emphasis on marriage and submission (where submission is defined as obedience) at all costs.

In an extreme example of this teaching, the wife is taught to stay silent, even when she sees her husband about to make a serious mistake or do something sinful, illegal, unreasonable, or dangerous. Speaking up or giving advice is condemned as "trying to usurp leadership" or "emasculating" her husband, rather than a sensible and godly thing to do (Proverbs 13:18).

Some of church teachings imply or actually teach children, adolescents, and young adults that they will go to hell if they sin by having sex and not marrying that person, or by divorcing.

One Twitter user described what she called the "catch-22 [of the] evangelical laws of marriage," saying that although she did not love the man she married, she was "ushered into marriage for the sake of sexual purity," and later, when the marriage proved dangerous, she "couldn't leave if I wanted everlasting life, [but] couldn't stay if I wanted to keep my life."

Despite our best efforts, we may be actually encouraging dangerous, reckless marriages. We are giving messages that wound good people. The formulas don't always work, and now the truth is coming out, and the church is paying the price.

---

31 Paraphrased from A. S. Ingram.

According to LifeWay, nearly 1 in 3 divorcees who had been frequent church attenders just before their divorce decided to switch churches. In their new church they are just as involved as ever. That tells us they love the Lord and are committed to the church, but perhaps they just don't want the criticism or judgementalism from their former church.

Another 1 in 5 divorcees left the church entirely.[32] Many of the people I interviewed felt so abandoned by their church leaders, they had to take time off from church attendance. They couldn't sit there and listen to another sermon that bashed all divorcees as quitters.

How Do We Do Better?

So how can we do a better job?

It's simple (though not easy): Our priority should be on teaching and mentoring people to have good character. Our focus should be on an individual's integrity and trustworthiness, not on their marital status. We need more reliable, kind, and safe individuals in the world, good citizens who will carry out their duties faithfully and honestly in every area of life, as unto the Lord. Marriage is not what makes people good. It should not be the goal. "Character counts," as one bumper sticker said. Marital status is secondary.

We will have more healthy, safe, and loving families if we have responsible, fair-minded, and good-hearted people. In fact, I would suggest that if the quality of the individuals is high, then our marriage quality will be high, and our families and churches will thrive more. Those who love to exploit others and feel entitled to take advantage of people beneath them should not be encouraged to marry; nor should they have power over anyone, either in business or in private life.

In the past, Christians gauged the health of our marriages by looking at divorce rates. We saw it as a way of proving that faith in Christ made us better people, better spouses, and better families.

One Christian researcher[33] pointed out that Christians who attended

---

32 Lisa Cannon Green, "Threat of Divorce Hard to Spot Among Churchgoing Couples," ***LifeWay Research*** (10/29/15), accessed 12/13/19, https://lifewayresearch.com/2015/10/29/threat-of-divorce-hard-to-spot-among-churchgoing-couples/.

33 Brad Wright, as quoted in this article: R. E. Wright and Christina Zozula, "Bad News about the Good News: The Construction of the Christian-Failure Narrative," ***Journal of Religion and Society*** 14 (2012): 9, Table 1.

church frequently had a lower divorce rate than Christians who didn't. Christian leaders cheered! Surely, we thought, this was evidence that our churches were changing lives, and that those who attended frequently were becoming better people.

But what if that wasn't the whole story? What if it was only partially true?

What if *some* of the lower divorce rate *really* meant abuse victims felt peer pressure to stay in destructive marriages?

What if the "divorcees are quitters" message from sermons, Bible study groups, and small group leaders compelled people to stay in terrible marriages out of fear that they might be criticized, rejected, or even put under church discipline?

What about churches that excommunicate, demote, or fire divorcees in leadership: pastors, youth leaders, Bible study leaders, elders, deaconesses, or those on the worship team?

For pastor's wives, divorce means losing your reputation and your livelihood:

My daughter begged me to divorce. I had health issues, anxiety, complex post-traumatic stress disorder from the abuse. I felt torn. You don't get divorced in Evangelicalism, not when you're a leader. Being married to a pastor puts a layer of bondage on it. It is another level of expectations laid on you. Our divorce was the first one in the family.

This woman finally got free, but she cannot speak on the record about her story. She fears retaliation from her ex-husband, who is still a major figure in Christian leadership.

What Can Be Done to Make Dangerous Marriages Less Likely?

After all this, you may be asking: what can I do to make it less likely in my own life that I would end up in a dangerous marriage, or that I would lose years of my life suffering in a dangerous marriage? What can I do to make these things less likely in my children's lives?

How about in the Church? What can pastors, spiritual leaders, and churchgoers do to help make dangerous marriages less frequent and end faster? What can we as the Church do to help make marriages safer for everyone?

The answer is: A lot!

Resist the pressure and take your time. If you are single, you can begin resisting the pressure to marry fast and/or young. It is wise to take your time in choosing a life partner, because it usually takes time to spot warning signs.

Establish yourself in the world. Especially for young women, you can invest in your education and career, developing your own skills and independence in the world. Having years of experience living an adult life on your own will give you a strong sense of self-confidence, a sturdy grasp of your worth in God's eyes, and a deep-down knowledge that you can make your way in the world when you need to.

This knowledge gives you confidence. You know how to earn a paycheck and afford rent and groceries. You can handle the basics of adult life, even when you're a household of one.

For women who marry too early, or whose families or religious communities discouraged (or forbade) them from attending college or working outside the home, they enter marriage at an extreme disadvantage. They are at the mercy of their husband for their livelihood—literally for the roof over their heads and the food on their table.

Without the experience of providing for and supporting themselves, these women can be terrified to leave even a highly abusive husband, because they do not know how to make it on their own. This fear is even more profound when they are worried about how they will feed and house their children if they leave the marriage.

Ask yourself: Why marriage? Why this marriage? For all single people, whether male or female, use this time of singleness to ask yourself *why* you want to marry. As I got back into dating after my long years of singleness, my Christian counselor asked me three questions:

- Do you want a man?
- Why do you want one?
- Do you have room in your life for one?

At the time, I was taken aback; after all, I'm a good Christian woman who likes marriage and family. Wasn't it just a given that I would want to remarry?

But I went home and spent several days thinking about those questions in depth. I was a very happy single woman, so was marriage truly what I wanted? What needs did I have that a new husband could meet? Was I too busy with work, ministry, or travel to invest the necessary time that a good marriage requires?

These questions were valuable for me. I recommend them for you. (And yes, I did remarry soon after that. But the questions gave me clarity. Asking them meant I chose marriage with eyes wide open.)

Are you considering marriage because everyone's doing it, because your parents or church expect it, because you want to be allowed to have sex, or because our society uses your marital status to prove that you've grown up and are a successful person?

Is it because married people are more highly regarded in the church than single people? Is it because you think the best (or even only!) way for God to bless you and mature you is by getting married?

All of these are unwise reasons to marry. They are not about the person you're marrying, who that person really is, and what you can realistically expect your life with that person to be like. And they're not about what will actually be good for you.

Instead, these reasons are based on poor theology (a good theological understanding is that God values single people, and God blesses and matures us in life regardless of whether we are married or not). And they are about image (wanting to look good to others) and performance or pressure (giving in to what everyone else expects of you).

But guess what?

Those people you're trying to please, or to impress,
are not the ones who will be in the marriage with you.

They won't be the ones most affected by how your spouse behaves. Their bank accounts aren't the ones that will be jointly shared with that person. They won't be the ones raising your children with you (or watching first-hand as those children suffer at the hands of your abusive spouse).

And they won't be the ones on the front lines, living with anxiety, if the marriage turns dangerous. They have no skin in the game.

Because of this, they *do not get to have a say* in whether or not you get married, and to whom. That is your choice, and yours alone, and you are allowed to hold off on making it until you're certain that the person you're choosing to marry will be a trustworthy, reliable, and safe spouse.

Reject the formulas. Has your church taught you that there is a guaranteed way to have a happy marriage—that if you do it right, go to church, pick someone who loves God and the Bible, ask for your father's permission, and save sex for marriage, God will reward you with marital bliss and an amazing sex life?

There's nothing wrong with doing these things, but when they are taught as a formula, beliefs like these set Christians up for heartbreak and disappointment when they encounter the reality: that marriage is a risk, and no matter how devout you are, no matter how well you follow the "rules," some of you will still find yourselves trapped in a dangerous marriage.

Instead, we can learn to be suspicious of false promises of guaranteed happiness (even from people who say those promises are coming from God!), and to keep our feet on the ground and our expectations realistic. We can remind one another that the rain falls on the righteous and the unrighteous (see Matthew 5:45), and that people, not God, are the ones making these false guarantees.

This makes it easier for us to notice potential problems in a relationship or a person, rather than indulging in magical thinking ("Oh, it'll go away once we're married," "Getting married will change him/her," or "God can do anything, I'm sure he'll fix this somehow once I walk down the aisle").

Start noticing the reality. For those of you who are in dangerous marriages, all is not lost.

Though it is harder to get *out* of a bad situation than to simply not get *in* it in the first place, none of us are immune from making mistakes, or from giving in to cultural and familial pressure, or from not having been taught how to spot warning signs.

It is not your fault that you are where you are,
and you are not helplessly stuck there,
nor are you a lost cause.

As Scripture says, "Today is the day of salvation" (2 Corinthians 6:2, ESV). You can begin to wake up to your situation right now, and to start reaching for new support, new learning, and new resources to bring about a change in your circumstances.

God cares about you and will walk with you every step of the way.

You can start reading books (like this one!) about how to recognize abuse and get free of an abuser; you can start the process of finding a safe church and maybe a support group who can accompany you through your learning process and possibly through a life-saving divorce; you can start investing in your education or skills, finding a therapist for yourself, pursuing a career or taking on a job so you can have your own income, and more.

I've seen chronically depressed women affected in amazing ways by going into the workforce for the first time—even in low-paying jobs—simply because of the self-confidence that comes from earning a paycheck of their very own.

Learn about healthy communication skills. Whether single, married, or divorced, we can all learn communication practices that can help keep us safe. Learning how to have constructive (not destructive) conflict, to identify and be honest about our needs and feelings, to recognize the signs of a person who can't or won't care for those needs and treat us with respect and care—and learning how to walk away from those people without guilt—are all invaluable areas of personal growth that we can work on, no matter our life circumstance.

Help reinforce healthy, life-saving concepts in church. In our churches, we can remind one another that we don't have to marry the first person we date. We can also remind one another that people who have premarital sex with someone don't have to marry that person to "make up for" the mistake—Jesus is the one who forgives and cleanses us of our sin. Getting a marriage certificate doesn't do for us what only Jesus can do.

We can learn about life-saving divorces and stop shaming people who have divorced, so that believers who are stuck in dangerous marriages don't need to be so afraid of being judged and badly treated in the church if they get a life-saving divorce. Rather than being viewed as losers, they need to be seen as people who faced tremendous obstacles and had the determination to do what was best for themselves and their kids. It took courage!

Together, we as the body of Christ can begin to take away the stigma around divorce that has kept so many people suffering in silence in horrible marriages for far longer than they needed to be.

Resist pressure from other believers. Uncles, aunts, parents, grandparents, pastors, and fellow church members can drop not-so-subtle hints about how "picky" we are about marriage partners, or lecture us on what they think we "should" do, as much as they want—but they're not the ones who will be making the vows.

It's better to lose some face in the eyes of other believers than to become trapped in a life of misery—one that we may spend years or decades barely enduring, only to end up needing a life-saving divorce, and encountering that loss of status or approval anyway!

Instead, let's give ourselves the permission to exercise our God-given wisdom, take our time, get to know ourselves well, develop our confidence and skills, and consider marriage for the right reasons and with realistic expectations. The nagging relatives and pushy fellow believers will just need to wait.

Talk to your children. In age-appropriate ways, you can tell your children about your experiences with marriage, teaching them about how to recognize a disrespectful or potentially abusive person, and making sure that they understand that marriage and singleness are both valid options in life.

You can help educate them about good conflict resolution strategies, and about the wisdom in waiting to marry and marrying for the right reasons. And you can teach them about how life-saving divorce is God's escape plan for people who are stuck in a dangerous marriage.

Let them know that you will love and support them no matter what choices they make in their lives. You're not going to pressure them into marriage, and you're not going to shame or shun them if they get a divorce.

Model to them that it is good and godly for them to value their own safety and wellbeing, and that it is good to ask for what you need and insist on respectful treatment in your intimate relationships.

Permission—And a Hug

If your spouse has a pattern of breaking their marriage vows to love, cherish, nurture, and be faithful to you—and if you feel you have tried hard, forgiven over and over, and gone the extra mile—I believe you are free to go, *if you so choose.*

If your marriage involves so much destruction that you are in despair, depression, or in danger of suicide, I believe you are free to go, *if you so choose.*

You can love Jesus and walk away from your destructive marriage.

Bible Passages to Consider

You are free to end your association with a sexually immoral, drunk, emotionally or financially abusive person.

But actually, I wrote you not to associate with anyone who claims to be a brother or sister and is sexually immoral or greedy, an idolater or verbally abusive, a drunkard or a swindler. Do not even eat with such a person.
—1 Corinthians 5:11 (CSB, emphasis mine)

You are free to throw off a yoke of slavery.

It is for freedom that Christ has set us free. Stand firm, then, and do not let yourselves be burdened again by a yoke of slavery.
—Galatians 5:1 (NIV)

You are free to walk away from selfish, mean, out-of-control, abusive people.

But mark this: There will be terrible times in the last days. People will be lovers of themselves, lovers of money, boastful, proud, abusive, disobedient to their parents, ungrateful, unholy, without love, unforgiving, slanderous, without self-control, brutal, not lovers of the good, treacherous, rash, conceited, lovers of pleasure rather than lovers of God— having a form of godliness but denying its power. Have nothing to do with such people.
—2 Timothy 3:1-5 (NIV, emphasis mine)

God doesn't like violent people.

The Lord examines the righteous,
but the wicked, those who love violence,
he hates with a passion.
—Psalm 11:5 (NIV, emphasis mine)

MYTHS OF DIVORCE—DID I TRY HARD ENOUGH?

In my divorce recovery groups, I've learned this—

Very good spouses are very hard on themselves.

It's common to listen to people who've been beaten, intimidated, or cheated on for ten, twenty, thirty years or more. Some fled to battered women's shelters ten times before they finally divorced. Some lived with family or friends for a while, then gave in to promises of repentance and a fresh start and decided to try again. And again.

Some tried living on their own but felt they had nowhere else to go and returned to the chaos.

Some face homelessness as their only alternative and decided a roof over their children's heads was worth the trauma of living with the other parent.

It breaks my heart to listen to their stories of how hard they tried, how much they denied the seriousness of the problem, how many pastors and counselors they saw, the books they read, and why they stayed. They hoped beyond hope—yet their dreams were crushed.

Many women endured abuse until their adolescent son or daughter said, "You've got to divorce him, Mom."

Many men decided to "stay for the kids."

People tell me all the time, "I wish I had gotten away sooner, but I just couldn't." Or "I knew my marriage was over, but I just didn't have the strength." I resonate with that feeling; that was where I lived for a long time, myself. It's far more common than we imagine. But what keeps us in dangerous marriages too long?

Sometimes, it is our own self-doubt and criticism: *Am I trying hard enough?*

How many times have you asked yourself one of these questions?

Is there something more I can do?

- Have I forgiven my spouse enough?
- Have I prayed enough?
- Have I set a good enough example?
- Am I sexually available enough for my spouse?

As I interview people, I've found that good, responsible spouses have made *every* effort to fix the marriage. They've read marriage books. They turned themselves inside out to be a good wife or husband. They've prayed, tried to be nicer and more agreeable, and forgiven over and over.

Many people like this think there is a purpose for God having them in a troubled marriage. They think it is to knock off their rough edges or to learn to suffer as Christ did. And indeed, God knows how to bring good for us out of even the worst situations, but that is quite different from saying, "I *have* to stay in a horrible situation so that God can bring something good out of it."

Consider the story of Amanda, who sacrificed everything—even her mental health—to hold the marriage together for twenty years.

Amanda's Story

Amanda was brought up in a devout missionary family and grew up overseas. She and her husband met on the mission field and decided to become missionaries, too. Once they moved overseas her husband was chronically emotionally abusive, and it got worse and worse over time. She excused it as cultural stress.

She thought if they found the right counselor, he would finally wake up and realize what he was doing and would change. They had gone to Christian counselors over and over. They'd talked to the missionary-sending agency. The organization was concerned for them. But a pattern emerged: They would meet with counselors, and every time the counselor would turn the attention on her husband, he would get angry and refuse to go back to therapy.

I read part of The Excellent Wife, a book that told me to submit more and be more loving, and my husband would become a better husband. My husband noticed and even said I had changed. But he wasn't willing to change himself. Our life on the mission field became more dangerous...

I knew that he was paranoid. The mission agency was concerned and sent us to counselors. My husband told me I deserved to die. He threatened to punch me in the stomach when I was pregnant. He needed psychiatric help. A neuropsychologist at the Veteran Administration interviewed him and saw the mental illness, but my husband refused to follow the recommendations for dealing with his condition.

I was still putting a lot of the blame on myself, trying to be a better wife. And so as I started sharing with a woman I met at a ladies retreat, she kind of started saying, "You know, that's not okay that he's doing this."

I knew I had to get away. I filed for separation and eventually for divorce. But it was still crushing. I kept asking myself, "Why didn't he love and value me?"

Finally, Amanda was worn out. After watching decades of abuse, the woman's siblings (all of whom had good Christian marriages) said, "Enough is enough. Get out." But she felt desperate and trapped:

I didn't tell anyone because I didn't think anyone would believe me. I was ashamed. I didn't want to shame my husband. I was afraid of the fall-out from him.

Yet I was being destroyed. All I knew was that I must get away from him. I wasn't strong enough to get away. My siblings have good marriages. They hired a babysitter and sat down with me. They said, "This is not you. All you want to do is sleep. We think you need to get out of your marriage. How would you feel if we made your husband move out of the apartment?"

I was so relieved. I just couldn't do this anymore.

Today the children and I have our own home just a block from my parents. We are not a broken home; we are a peaceful home! I am a lot happier. I have started laughing again. I have this great belly laugh. I can be silly and goofy with my kids. My parents said I had stopped doing that for a long time. They said, "We were so worried about you, because you were not the person that we knew." The Lord has carried me through so much and brought so much joy into my life and so much peace. I've found a lot of healing.

Today she is happy, and her depression has lifted, because of her life-saving divorce. And her children are doing well.

If you are reading this book—if you've put up with chronic abuse, put-downs, betrayals, indifference, or cheating—if you have given it your best—my answer is: *Yes, you tried hard enough!* Yet many Christians are told by their pastor, Bible study leader, or fellow churchgoers, that they must go back and try harder.

27 MYTHS ABOUT YOU AND DIVORCE

In this chapter, we discuss 27 assumptions people often make about divorce and divorcees. I've called these assumptions "myths" because they are false ideas and beliefs, and they appear both in churches and in secular society.

These myths keep us from getting out earlier, and they cause us to second-guess (and third-guess, and fourth-guess) our decision to leave. We hear them and convince ourselves to stay and try harder. Many spouses hear these voices in their head tearing at them. It's important to identify these myths and, like the superheroes in movies, put on your emotionally protective armor and fight them off with the Truth.

Myth One: You Just Fell Out of Love

This myth says that most marriages fall apart because two people just fall out of love. This is an exaggeration. In reality, about half of divorces happen for life-saving reasons:

- chronic emotional or mental abuse
- physical or sexual abuse
- addictions
- sexual immorality or infidelity
- betrayal
- criminal activity

- incest
- financial abuse
- spiritual abuse
- neglect or abandonment

Though some people divorce due to falling out of love, growing apart, or having different values, many others give very serious reasons for divorce.

Myth Two: You Just Don't Take God-Ordained Marriage Seriously

This myth says all divorce happens because people just aren't committed these days. They don't take their marriage vows seriously. They don't have the grit to keep their promises made before God. They don't care about their kids. They are quitters. They want the quick way out. They've been affected by Hollywood's moral decay.

But this myth is not true of people who need life-saving divorces. Most of the people I see were very committed to their marriage vows, took their responsibilities seriously, and believed in the sanctity of marriage. They invested in the marriage. They valued family. But their spouse chose to be abusive or to cheat—and in doing so broke the covenant. An abuser or cheater forfeits the right to remain married.

Think about it this way. If a person hadn't been committed to their marriage, hadn't wanted it to be lifelong, and hadn't been optimistic about change, they would have exited at the first sign of abuse. Abused spouses, de facto, are the ones who took their vows seriously and thought they could fix the marriage. They tried over and over.

If you are a person who took your vows seriously, say to yourself:

I kept my vows before God—to love, nurture, and cherish—
but my spouse did not.
Some divorces may be due to selfishness. Mine wasn't.
I can take the Bible, God, my faith,
*and the institution of marriage seriously—**and** still choose to get divorced.*

Myth Three: You Just Didn't Try Hard Enough

This myth assumes you haven't put in much effort. You gave up too easily. People who hold to this belief strongly say all terrible marriages can be fixed if one spouse tries harder—or prays harder—and all divorces happen because people quit too soon when they should have kept trying.

The truth is: People in the most destructive marriages often try harder than anyone else.

Researchers have found something surprising about marriages that have highly destructive factors (abuse, drug or alcohol addiction, or infidelity): The innocent spouses in these highly destructive marriages often *increase* their efforts to save the marriage. That is, in the face of these very serious problems, the committed spouses continue to work to save the marriage—and are *more likely* to believe that divorce can be prevented if both of them "try harder."

This paradox amazed the researchers.[34] In other words, the more severe it was and the more hopeless it looked, the harder people tried. They weren't looking for the easy way out.

Even in the most horrible marriages, often the spouse who is being abused or mistreated hangs in there for a long time. Early in the relationship, some knew their spouse had problems and persevered anyway, setting aside their own happiness, health, and peace to keep the relationship going.

They never dreamed that small red flag would grow and become terrifying. Their desire to be married and stay married was extremely high. They kept trying until the day they finally said, "Enough is enough."

The first time you walked back into an abusive home and faced an abusive spouse was the day you proved to the world that you were dedicated, going beyond the call of duty, to hold your marriage together.

Sylvia's Story

Sylvia's husband confessed to her that he was molesting children. He checked into a 28-day treatment program, but within three months after his release, he told her he was struggling. Sylvia forgave him and kept hoping for the best. She held it together several more years, assuming he

34 Alan J. Hawkins, Brian J. Willoughby, and William J. Doherty, "Reasons for Divorce and Openness to Marital Reconciliation," ***Journal of Divorce & Remarriage*** 53, no. 6 (2012): 453-463.

was doing better—until he molested the babysitter right in front of their daughter. Even then, she struggled to give herself permission to leave.

> *I felt uncomfortable about divorce. I knew any rational person would divorce an admitted child molester. Part of me knew I had tried everything. The other part of me wasn't sure.*
>
> *I talked to a counselor. He said I had left no stone unturned, and I was free to go.*
>
> *I finally decided that the only way I could handle the guilt and the conflicting feelings was to divorce now and stay unmarried for five years, just to see if he would change; and if he changed, we could remarry.*
>
> *So I proceeded with the divorce, and for the next five years I turned down all but one date.*
>
> *Five years later, my ex-husband had improved maybe 10%, but nothing close to what I needed to feel confident that he was safe and we could have a healthy marriage. I was glad I walked away. I don't recommend others hang on for years after a divorce, but I look back now and see that as something I needed to do for my own conscience.*
>
> *I have no regrets about the divorce. I am happy and stress-free now. Eight years later, my ex-husband admitted to law enforcement to having more than fifty victims. I am so glad I asked him to leave.*

Myth Four: You Didn't Attend Church Enough

This myth suggests you would have saved your marriage if you had attended church more or been more devout.

The truth is that people who go to church still get divorced, and the percentage of divorces among people who go to church—even those who go to church multiple times a week—are only a bit lower than the percentage of divorces among people who don't. (You can read more about these facts in Chapter 2.)

Churchgoing doesn't make dangerous marriages safe,
and it doesn't make dangerous spouses magically change.

A related myth is "I can convince my pastor/church to approve of my divorce, since they know I am a godly person." In churches that don't allow divorce for any reason, that effort is unlikely to succeed. You can talk to the pastor over and over, but at some point the old adage "You can't fight city hall" is true. Many people find it best to make their own decision and switch to another church. (See Chapter 8 on finding safe churches.)

"The idea that pastors get to decide whether a woman is 'abused enough' to get a divorce is ludicrous."
—Julie Anne Smith

Myth Five: Christians Are Required to Forgive and Forget and Reconcile Over and Over... Forever.

This myth says you must forgive—and trust—after every abuse and betrayal. If you give up too soon, says this myth, you will surely miss a miracle.

Some believe that verbal repentance and tears show true remorse and change, and therefore you must reconcile. If your spouse cries, confesses, claims to be "the worst sinner I know," and otherwise puts on an emotional spectacle of remorse, this myth says that a good Christian spouse *has* to take them back and stay married to them, remaining tied to them emotionally, physically, financially, and sexually.

We've all been told stories of a woman in a terrible marriage who stayed and suffered and prayed for years, and miraculously today she and her husband are tremendously happy. These exceptions are held up as common. They are not. Serial adulterers, pedophiles, and abusers have poor success rates and are often treatment failures.

If someone demands that you put up with a pattern of abuse, neglect, or sexual immorality, they are out of bounds. You and you alone know what you're going through and how much you can endure.

Reject any and all versions of this myth:

- "You are sinning because you refuse to give your spouse another chance."
- "You must forgive and trust your spouse again. You must go the extra mile forever, because Jesus said, 'love your enemies'."
- "You are unforgiving if you divorce."
- "You cannot demand good behavior. That is not being submissive."
- "Once you've forgiven, you cannot hold it against them. They have to do something worse."

Look for the Pattern: Pattern of Abuse, or Pattern of Repentance and Change?

The Bible says there will be people who are in the church—even church leaders—who do wrong and just won't change.

> ***But actually, I wrote you not to associate with anyone who claims to be a brother or sister and is sexually immoral or greedy, an idolater or verbally abusive, a drunkard or a swindler. Do not even eat with such a person.***
>
> ***—1 Corinthians 5:11 (CSB)***

We are to stop associating with them. But sometimes your friends or pastor will insist that you ignore your God-given instincts and give it another chance. This is not biblical. Jesus calls his followers to forgive, but he doesn't call them to trust again or to reconcile unilaterally.

The Bible instructs us to look for "fruits of repentance"—evidence of sustained change over time, not just sporadic fits of remorse with more abuse in between. (To learn more about this, and about the Abuse Cycle, see Chapter 4). Paul says we are to live in peace with everyone, "as far as it depends on you" (Romans 12:18, NIV). He's saying the other person may never become a good, trustworthy person. In the end, some people feel entitled to continue in their destructive ways. This makes it impossible to live in peace with them. To live in peace, you need to get away.

Being a Christian doesn't mean that you need to entrust your safety and peace of mind to a person who has a pattern of hurting you. In fact, Scripture tells us to get away from angry, divisive, or destructive people.

> ***Do not make friends with a hot-tempered person;***
> ***do not associate with one easily angered...***
> ***—Proverbs 22:24 (NIV)***

The Apostle Paul warns his fellow Christians about those who pick fights and cause hurt and division. Paul says, "Warn a divisive person once, and then warn them a second time. After that, have nothing to do with them" (Titus 3:9-10, NIV). Living in peace is important to God.

One wife shares her experiences with her husband's display of repentance that had no fruit, no pattern of change, to support it. His actions didn't match his words.

[My mom is] my best friend, couldn't have asked for a better mother to be born to. I was raised by a loving single mother who had divorced my father because he was violently abusive and threatened to kill her. The police had told her to leave. And then when I was about nine, she met my stepdad, who she ended up marrying when I was twelve. And he is 100% my dad. You would not be able to tell that biologically we're not related. We get along super well, and they have a tremendous marriage. [They are] an example that I look up to… a supportive husband, a supportive wife, just like harmony.

And I think when I was twelve, my thoughts about marriage were probably kind of like a Disney princess story. Like, you fell in love with a guy and he loves you back, and it's all going to be wonderful. Very naïve.

[My family had just moved to Canada from Europe, and] Canadian men were kind of exotic to begin with, like the rough cowboy type. I actually met [the man I later married] through work. I was doing commercial real estate leasing.

Her friends were divided on him. She had a good education, but she liked that he was a driven entrepreneur and business owner.

I'd never had a serious relationship before—and I earnestly prayed to God… And then I felt this overwhelming sense to google this guy. I ended up on a photo page from one of his friends, and he had posted pictures of my husband's baptism. It was like I was hit by lightning. I thought, oh my goodness, I like this guy, and he's a Christian. This is meant to be. I told myself that was God telling me that this was supposed to be my husband. And I completely ignored all the red flags after that.

I lived outside of downtown, so more in the suburbs. And he absolutely hated the suburbs and barely ever wanted to come to my place. I always had to travel. No matter what time of day, if I wanted to see him, I had to come to him.

There was one occasion where he finally came over to my place just to have dinner, and the next day I was going to participate in a 5-kilometer run; I'd never done that before. And if you know me, I hate working out, and I hate running.

> *So it was a big deal for me, because I had trained and was really excited to do this. And he left without saying anything about it, so I said, "Hey, my run is tomorrow. Don't you want to wish me good luck?"*
>
> *He just turned around and kind of scoffed at me. "What? For a 5K? That's easy." And then he just walked away. Instead of encouraging me or even showing up at the race... No, [he didn't do anything] like that. That was the first moment where I thought, "Hm. That's a little odd."*

But she justified it by thinking, "Oh, he's a pro athlete, and he works out so much, he's so fit; I'm probably just exaggerating. This isn't a big deal."

> *He has a pretty large group of guy friends, and they've grown up together and went to church as children and teenagers. They seemed like solid guys, and I was very impressed with the level of friendship that they had. I got along with [all of them]. And my ex-husband always seemed super-generous with everybody. [He was] always pulling out the wads of cash that he made with his businesses, and he just came across as a very genuine and friendly guy.*
>
> *Having said that, though, even when we started dating, he was always quite cold to my parents, never engaging in real conversation with them, always talking about money and [about how] his main focus in life is to get out of the rat race. His conversations with my parents were always about money and success, never about emotional things or about our faith.*
>
> *He fooled me and our friends. Nobody but my parents figured him out. His last girlfriend had stood him up at the altar... twice. He took no responsibility for it. I think the fact that he never took personal responsibility for any of that, was a red flag. It was always all her parents' fault.*
>
> *That's the red flag that I completely ignored. He claimed it was because her parents hated him because he wasn't educated and he was just a snowboarder. Looking back, I think that she had come to her senses early enough and dodged a bullet twice. But I felt really sorry for him, and I think that's one of the reasons why, when I, too, before the wedding [asked myself], "Is this really what I want?"*

I [immediately] told myself, "No, I can't do that to him because somebody else already stood him up twice. I can't do that."

And there were other indications:

[For example, despite being an outdoorsman and an extreme athlete,] he refused to drive over to my place or to come pick me up, not even during winter snowstorms.

I wish I could say that I pushed back in those years, but I can't recall a single moment when I did. Before I met him, I was very independent. I had my masters' degree; I bought my own condo; my career was going really well. I was in a really good place in my life. You know how they always talk about your love tank, and your self-esteem tank and everything? I felt like all my tanks were pretty much overflowing. And I think that's why I was able to take so many of these blows.

I was so focused on giving to him that I don't think I even realized in a lot of cases that what he was doing was not right. I just tried to talk it away. Like, "Oh, he's very busy, so I should [be the one to] drive downtown," not realizing I work 8:00-5:00 every day and have a demanding career. But I figured, he's a business owner, and I should feel sorry for him; it's my responsibility to accommodate his schedule. So in retrospect, I think I was kind of a pushover.

He basically told my parents, "I'm going to propose to her, and once we're married, I want you guys to [get out of our lives] financially and not interfere with anything." To which my mom said, "If you hurt her, I will kill you." My parents were very hesitant about him and tried to warn me, but I just didn't listen. And I think a big reason for that was because I was convinced that God wanted us together. He pretended to be quite spiritual. He was always reading Christian men's books and talking about them.

I told myself we were going to be opposed so much by evil and Satan because we were this amazing, godly couple doing wonderful things for God's kingdom. I didn't know if he was just blowing hot air or not. I don't think he was truly ever repentant, but if he was, he definitely didn't put his life in God's hands or take any kind of spiritual responsibility. But in that year, especially after we got engaged, I was just so blinded by everything he said that I stopped noticing everything he did or didn't do.

Our wedding rehearsal was a turning point. Friend after friend made heartfelt, touching speeches about us as couple. His friends, my friends... It was magical and beautiful, until it was his turn. He stood up, thanked everyone for coming, thanked his parents for staying married, and sat down. That was it. It was like a slap in the face. Nothing about being excited to get married or about me as his wife. Nothing about us joining together the next day.

Starting then, I slowly got the message: I didn't matter. At the wedding, we acted like event planners, not a loving team. There was no connection. On our honeymoon, he got a rental car that was breaking down, and for the first time in my life I felt a panic that I'd never felt before. I knew deep down that he wouldn't look after me or care for my safety whatsoever. This was my first taste, my first realization, that this person is not interested in my best interests at all. In fact, he told me directly: "Nothing, not even you, is going to stand between me and my success."

He would pick fights in restaurants and at holiday events and blame me. He would say it was all my fault. I had ruined the night or the weekend. I would beg him to make up and talk things out, and he would flat-out refuse and go to sleep. He wouldn't even want to talk to me. The message was, "You're so disgusting, and it's all your fault." He wanted me to apologize, so I did. I would immediately—even if I thought I was right—I would apologize. But then he would still say, "No, I'm too mad, I can't even look at you or touch you." And then he would just roll over and go to sleep, and I would cry the whole night. [He was always giving me] the silent treatment, the cold shoulder.

I actually quit my corporate career and joined his company to work for him. Big mistake. He would yell at me and make me work till 11:00 pm if there was a deadline, and he would not care whether I had eaten or if I was exhausted. I actually moved in with him because he hated the suburbs so much, even though my condo was brand new and he lived in this simple, decrepit house. He had fixed it up a little bit before I moved in, but he was always very, very cheap with money. I felt like as soon as I said, "I do," all the money always went back to his businesses. And he actually started two new businesses during the course of our marriage. He reinvested all that money back, never invested in us or our house.

We had a furnace that was so old and broken that during the winter, I would come home from work had to keep my parka on so I could stoke an actual fire in the fireplace to warm up the house. And I had to sit there in my parka for a half an hour until it was warm enough to take it off. Every single time I wanted to buy something to make it a bit nicer, he would argue with me over it. It was never allowed.

His lack of concern for her and his fixation on his business continued. He would scream at customer service reps on the phone, but when they would go to a restaurant, he would make an elaborate over-the-top scene, demanding that she thank and say goodbye to the waiter. Then they would go out to the car, and he would scream at her. Her wellbeing didn't matter. Though there was plenty of money to invest in the businesses, she was driving an old car long distance in the below-freezing Canadian snowstorms.

He always ruined my birthday and either gave me no gift or a crappy gift. Where I am from, birthdays are a big deal. One birthday, when there was no gift at all, he just delivered a speech to me over dinner. I was so disappointed, I said something. He just ripped into me for the entire night. How ungrateful and selfish I was! How materialistic!

Before I got married, I was a pretty chill person, But I turned into anxiety-ridden person. I developed a form of OCD where I would constantly check everything. Years later, I'm still trying to understand how this could have happened. I'm starting to get a bit more clarity on narcissistic abuse and how it changes your brain. From time to time, I would get sick, and he would make me go sleep out on the couch. If we fought, I had to go sleep on the couch. He never once slept there.

I would see other couples at the supermarket having a good time together shopping, and I would just say to myself, "I guess that's not for me. Maybe I don't deserve it, or maybe it's not in the cards for me." You start making all these agreements with yourself where you tell yourself this story: "This will not be my life. This will not be my marriage." [Common kindness is such a normal thing], and I think you lose track of what's normal and what isn't.

I think back on his overall obsession with money and success. The businesses were always number one; making money was always number one. Like I said, he would keep the money tabbed very, very tight. We were not allowed much. But he would take exorbitant trips, like with this Entrepreneurs' Organization. There was always a forum retreat, as it was called. And he went to several different international locations. Then he joined a Christian entrepreneurs' organization, and they would go on weekends away. So he was always quite well off in the vacation department, but I was not allowed to come, because it was just for him and his fellow members.

She had enough and separated from him for a year, but she came back and tried again after reading Eggerichs's *Love and Respect* book.

[I told myself] I'm just going to go harder and pray to God that he gives me the wisdom to deal with this. [I decided] I should cut my husband some slack because he's working so hard. But then, if you hear the same thing year-in, year-out and you're treated like garbage on a day-to-day basis, that just gets really old really quick. You actually lose respect for someone.

We separated again for a year, and when I finally felt things were good enough, I moved back in with him. We actually moved into a rental property together for five days. As soon as my parents drove away after dropping me and my stuff off, I had this overwhelming urge to lock myself in the bedroom with my cat and not come out. He immediately became haughty and arrogant again.

I was really done. I was ready to file for divorce. I contacted a lawyer. [When he realized this, suddenly] he claimed he had this big repentance and come-to-Christ moment, and he wrote me a letter where he listed every single thing and every comment he had ever made to me. Which, looking back, is kind of creepy. Who would even remember everything? I didn't even remember everything that was in that letter.

[He] really made it seem like he had true repentance. I felt like it

was the Holy Ghost convincing him of every single thing he had done. And he joined a church.

And then, all of a sudden, he came up with the story that he was an addict. He was addicted to work, and that was the root cause of all of our problems. He claimed he was going to support meetings for addiction, and I figured it was going to be like AA. But a month later, I found out it was just him and a few entrepreneur buddies meeting once a week, lamenting about their sorrows. So it wasn't even properly facilitated or anything. [I wish that] was the last deceptive thing he did to me.

I truly believe his whole repentance schtick was just a fraud, and now I'd been duped once again. I don't know if you've ever heard of the term "love bombing," but he did that the first year after I left. [He] would leave notes under my office door when he would travel out. And I would find little cards and treats on my car: things he'd never done before. And every time—as soon as I kind of gave in a little bit—it would all disappear again. It was just a game to him.

This was the first time I feel like the mask dropped since the separation, and I could just see that he was ticked off. I think he saw it as winning and losing. I think to the outside world and his family, and everybody that's holier-than-thou in his life, it's deemed a failure that he is now going to divorce. I think he was just mad that he couldn't keep up with the façade and get me back.

I don't think it's ever been about me with him. I think he just wanted—and he said this, too—he wanted a European wife. I was just like a trophy wife to him. But he never looked beyond skin deep. I think it never really occurred to him that I have deep feelings and needs and ambitions and hopes; it was just about him, how he could be as successful as possible, and how other people could see him being successful in marriage and business and everything else. But looking back, I don't think he ever truly cared about who I am as a person.

Looking for the Pattern: A Pastor's Advice

An earnest Christian wife went to her pastor. She had already filed for divorce, and her husband had moved out, but six months later she was feeling alone and overwhelmed by the task of raising her children by herself. She was having second thoughts, and a lot of conflicting emotions. She wondered if she should reconcile and invite her husband to come back.

She told me, "I want to share this letter publicly with other Christians who are considering divorce. I wrote to my pastor because I was tormented with uncertainty about my divorce. My pastor knew I had clear biblical grounds for divorce, but years of dysfunction had clouded my judgment. I had forgiven my husband's sexual immorality over and over, and I wondered: should I try again? My pastor sent me this wonderful email. It helped me make the decision. I hope it helps others, too."

Pastor: I believe you are scripturally free to make any decision you wish. If for any reason, you wanted to reconcile and make another go at it, that's a choice that is available to you. Even when there has been a scriptural breaking of the marriage, there can be forgiveness and reconciliation.

The key question, however, is "What has happened other than the passage of time?" Anybody can be forgiven for a failure or indiscretion. What you need to conclude, however, is whether the "condition" in his life is different in any way.

Wife's reply: No, my husband's apologies sound like they were written by someone else. He is still irresponsible and selfish. He cannot even please his boss and keep a job.

Pastor: It is understandable that he would want to reconcile. He doesn't have to apologize for that. He's done wrong. He knows it. He wants his wife and family back. I don't fault him for that. His words have to be heard through the filter of what you know him to be, however, and whether in your judgment there is any hope for change in the condition that has contributed to his way of viewing life, himself, you, and his conduct.

Wife's reply: No—he hasn't even changed during this six-month separation.

Pastor: Do you want a happy marriage? Are you a tolerant and forgiving person? Are you willing to go the extra mile?

Wife's reply: Yes, to all of those things.

Pastor: How many extra miles do you have to go, however, before concluding that, sadly, this person whom you have loved and with whom you have tried to forge life simply doesn't have what it takes to make a faithful commitment to you and earn your trust?

Wife's reply: No more miles.

Pastor: As I said, the key question is, "What has changed other than the passage of time?" Also, remember that it is not you who have chosen to end the marriage. He has. His conduct has broken the marriage bond. All you are doing is acknowledging it and bringing the civil records up to date about the true condition of the marriage.

I vote for remaining free.

She says, "I was grateful for this very special letter, and I wanted to share it with you. My pastor's words gave me the strength of conviction to stay strong and continue with the divorce. I'm glad I did."

Myth Six: You Must Be Exaggerating! Everyone Would Know If Your Spouse Was THAT Bad.

This myth says that abusers, narcissists, and sex offenders are easy to spot. You can tell just by hanging out with them. If it's not obvious to everyone, you must be wrong.

- "I don't think he's an abuser. You're being overly dramatic."
- "I've never seen him be mean to anyone. I think you're lying."

Abusive people do not show their abusive side in front of bosses, friends, or people they want to impress. They rarely beat or torment their spouse or children in front of two witnesses, a video camera, or an audio recorder. They are clever. Abusers don't want to be caught, and often the victims say nothing in hopes that the person will change, or out of fear no one will believe them.

Some abusers—especially in religious circles—are friendly and charming in front of others, but turn into the opposite behind closed doors. One woman described her husband as Dr. Jekyll-and-Mr. Hyde: He was a man who would go out of his way to help people stranded along the road by fixing their flat tires, but he would viciously attack her when he got home, satisfying his violent temper without compassion or remorse. "I knew no one would believe me if I told them he was abusive," she said. It took her years to get out.

In a recent interview with a woman with chronic health issues, she mentioned how deferential her husband appeared at church; but in the presence of her hobby group, he was blatantly selfish, demeaning, and mean-spirited.

In her own words —

Around people he didn't want to impress, he acted differently. He would stand there and watch me struggle with something. My friends thought it was appalling. He would act resentful about helping. One time at a birthday party, witnesses heard him say,
"If you don't get into the car,
I'm going to leave without you." He meant it.
Many witnesses agreed to tell the court what they had observed over the years.

Even experts cannot recognize abusers immediately—not from the outside, and not if the abuser wants to impress them.

I once asked a pastor if he could identify an abuser. This pastor had been raised in an abusive home and specialized in the area in grad school. He said, "In a social or work setting, I can't identify abusers, even if I see them every day. If they want to befriend me because I'm a pastor, they won't reveal their abusive, controlling side to me."

In other words, if a trained professional cannot detect an abuser, how can others?

As we see in the news every day, sexually abusive doctors, bosses, and even pastors can hide for years. Abusers, narcissists, and sociopaths are excellent con artists and fantastic at concealing double lives. Many spouses don't discover they've married an abuser until the honeymoon or in the first year, or when they are vulnerable (such as when they get pregnant or seriously ill).

Often the badly behaved spouse won't admit the full details of felonies, abusive behavior, addictions, or affairs. And ironically, the innocent spouse will hide facts, too, but for other motives.

In the words of Sylvia, the ex-wife of the child molester—

My husband was a child molester, but I didn't want people at church to know.
I told them we were divorcing "for biblical grounds."
When they asked for details, I said, "No, I want to keep it private."

Falling on Your Sword

In divorce recovery support groups, many women will conceal their husband's criminal activity, such as sex offenses, physical abuse, child porn, drug addiction, DUIs, and/or other behavior for years. If asked, they will mention other, less serious problems. I call this "falling on your sword," meaning the innocent spouse minimizes the other spouse's bad behavior and covers up the reason for the divorce.

"Falling on your sword" often happens when one person wants to get out of the marriage and—at the same time—wants to hide their spouse's illegal or immoral behavior. They do it to:

- protect the other spouse's reputation (because their own reputation is tied to it in some ways, and/or because they think exposing their spouse makes it their fault when the spouse suffers consequences for the wrongdoing)
- protect their own reputation (it's embarrassing to admit you missed red flags and married someone horrible)
- protect the children's reputation (to protect their privacy and keep people from asking them about the situation or judging them)
- keep a roof over their head (if they need child support or spousal support and cannot survive on their own, the last thing they will do is say anything that will jeopardize their spouse's income or job)

These are normal, understandable reasons, but they keep the abused spouse (and the children) in danger for too long. If you are being abused, you can contact the National Domestic Violence Hotline at 1 (800) 799-7233 or TTY 1 (800) 787-3224, or go to http://www.thehotline.org/

If your abuser is monitoring your internet or phone usage, ask a friend to lend you their phone or computer. Public libraries have internet access; so do some retailers, such as the UPS store. Also, see Chapter 4 on abuse, and find in Chapter 5 a checklist to plan your escape and collect the documents you need for your attorney. Some attorneys may advise staying in your house and getting a restraining order to keep your spouse away.

Myth Seven: "It Takes Two to Tango" and "All Marriage Problems are 50/50"

This myth says you cannot claim to be innocent. You must bear significant blame in this marital breakdown.

Some variations on this myth include:

- "You're just two sinners sinning."
- "You must have done something to deserve it."
- "Marital problems are always 50/50."
- "You both share responsibility."
- "You can't claim to be the innocent spouse. Everyone's at fault."

This myth heaps false guilt on you, by making everything 50% your fault. It's called *mutualizing*. Abusive and unfaithful spouses, and even some counselors, are experts at this; they mutualize the sin and blame it on you.

- "If you hadn't _________, I wouldn't have __________."
- "I cheated because you ______________."
- "You deliberately pushed my buttons."
- "If you do that again, I'm going to blow up, and who knows what I might do when I get angry."
- "Even if I did those things, you claim to be a Christian, and you should forgive me and get together again."
- "So, what's your part in this?"

The truth is: It only takes ONE destructive spouse
to make a marriage dangerous.
There is nothing the victim can do to ensure
the other spouse does not sin.

A wise Christian counselor met with a man and his unfaithful wife (she had cheated on him many times). Watch how the counselor handled it: She didn't allow the wife to make her husband equally guilty. In the husband's words—

My adulterous former wife said she was repentant and said she wanted to do counseling to put our marriage back together again. We found a Christian counselor and set a meeting. …Right away, my ex started in on how she did things because of me. Each time the therapist stopped her and said, "Don't you think you had other choices?"[35]

---

35 Comment on a public website, dated 5/28/18, accessed 12/13/19, http://www.divorceminister.com/how-to-prepare-for-christian-couples-counseling-post-infidelity-discovery/#comment-6612. Used with permission.

Unfortunately, not all counselors and friends are this savvy. In some cases, well-meaning but overly idealistic friends may not even listen to your claim of innocence, especially if they have heard and bought into your spouse's explanations, denials, and lies. They can't bring themselves to face the truth. They cannot accept that someone they like—someone like your spouse—can be that way. They interrupt, dismiss serious problems, and try to pin the blame on you. They cannot enter the pain because they dislike uncomfortable things that might require them to act, so they avoid it.

Dr. Judith Herman, researcher on trauma and recovery, calls these people "bystanders," and says:

> "...the bystander usually succumbs to the temptation
> to look the other way.
> This is true even when the victim is an idealized
> and valued member of society [or the church]."[36]

Even if you grew up in the church and your family is held in high esteem, this attitude silences you and allows the cheater or child molester to spin stories in their favor. The innocent spouse must be allowed to share their story and be given an opportunity to relate the facts without being accused of being bitter or unforgiving.

After all, God is angry about infidelity (Hebrews 13:4). Shouldn't everyone be?

If you don't find anyone who will listen at your church, look for others who have walked your path.

We all need time to evaluate our part in how a marriage fell apart, but that is between you and God after you get to safety and have time to think. If other people stop you as you tell your account, shift the blame to you, or demand you answer their questions, they are probably not the right friends for this season in your life. Find someone wise and safe.

Myth Eight: It Is Your Fault Because You Aren't Perfect, Either

This myth says both people are guilty of anger in the marriage, so both

---

36 Judith Lewis Herman, ***Trauma and Recovery*** (New York: Basic Books, 1992), 8.

are wrong. Some people use the Bible verse Matthew 7:3 to silence the invested spouse, asking—

> ***Why do you look at the speck of sawdust in your brother's eye and pay no attention to the plank in your own eye? (NIV)***

People who misuse this Bible verse say you are not allowed to call out the sins of your spouse because you sin, too. This is called "sin-leveling."

Definition of Sin-Leveling

Sin-leveling is a way of silencing victims and keeping them from asking for fairness and justice. This view says all sin is an affront to God, and therefore your sin is equal in God's eyes to your spouse's sin. Sin-leveling says no human being deserves anything good from God because we are all worthless sinners in his sight. Therefore, you shouldn't ask for justice, because real justice in God's sight is to hand you over to death for your sins.

For example, in this false theology: The wife explodes at her husband for having an affair. She is told rage and anger are sins. So, no matter what he did, the wife has no right to show anger. She cannot claim to be a victim.

Here's how one church appears to have used the sin-leveling tactic to keep alleged child sexual abuse victims silent. The mindset was described like this—

> "One of the clearest signs of 'rebellion' is when a person sees himself as an injured party, because no injury that can be perpetrated against the person could ever surpass the horror that the person's own sin is in the eyes of God."[37]

This mindset suggested they were rebellious when they talked about their horrific experiences. This twisting of theology silences and minimizes victims' stories and justifies the pastors' decisions to do nothing. Thus, pastors encourage perpetrators and enable them to continue.

---

37 Website host, Kris, "A Theory of Why Sovereign Grace Churches Seemed to Side With Perpetrators," *www.sgmsurvivors.com* (3/22/18), accessed 8/18/19, http://www.sgmsurvivors.com/2018/03/22/a-theory-of-why-sovereign-grace-churches-seemed-to-side-with-perpetrators/.

The result is victims who are discounted and abusers who are protected.

Sin-Leveling Phrases Often Quoted:

- "When you point your finger, there are three more pointing back at you."
- "Judge not, lest you be judged. You must confess your own horrible sins first."
- "All sin is the same in God's eyes (and therefore your sin of anger is no different to God than your spouse's sin of infidelity)."
- "You must claim to be the worst sinner you've ever known." (Once an abuser or pedophile does this, they are viewed as the "more righteous person.")[38]
- "Standing up for yourself is spiritual pride. You are guilty of unforgiveness and bitterness, and so you are worse than the abuser."
- "He who is guilty of one point is guilty of the entire Law." (This is twisted to mean that taking a pen from work is the same as your spouse's sin of beating you).
- "You have no rights. All your good deeds are like filthy rags. You have no righteousness and no right to demand good treatment."

Although these phrases may sound pious, sin-leveling is dangerous to victims. We all know that molesting a child and abusing a spouse are bad. We know that murder is worse than cutting off someone on the highway. Staying silent when someone deliberately injures another or breaks the marriage vows is wrong.

It is important to speak up when someone is injuring or betraying another.

If people do not care about victims—if they turn the tables and make the victim into the bad guy—how can anyone have confidence that they will do what is right? It undermines the delicate trust that makes rule-of-law societies run smoothly.

I often find women who feel terribly guilty that they yelled at their husband, or defended themselves physically, or left him an angry note.

---

38 Kris, "A Theory."

In their minds, this just as bad as a husband's long-time pattern of put-downs, threats, slaps, and selfishness. So even the victim falls prey to the false teachings of bad theology like this.

Sin-leveling is also nonsense. It doesn't work in real life.

Imagine a police officer who would not arrest a burglar caught red-handed because the officer, too, had sinned.

The police officer identifies criminal behavior in real life and arrests a suspect based on the officer's judgment on whether that suspect was involved in a crime. That is the practical reality of sin.

And sin-leveling is not biblical. Jesus taught his disciples to identify con artists. These are people who appear to be on your side and gain your confidence, but they deceive instead.

Jesus wanted his disciples to look at the ungodly results of behavior and call it bad fruit. That is what Jesus calls his disciples to do today. If a person lies, call it a lie. If a person uses a pattern of anger and violence to get their way, call it abuse. If a person cheats, call it infidelity.

Look at the pattern of behavior—not the person's image or popularity, not their fine-sounding words, but their actual actions. Is there a pattern of bad fruit?

Watch out for false prophets. They come to you in sheep's clothing,
but inwardly they are ferocious wolves. By their fruit you will recognize them.
Do people pick grapes from thorn bushes, or figs from thistles?
Likewise, every good tree bears good fruit, but a bad tree bears bad fruit.
A good tree cannot bear bad fruit, and a bad tree cannot bear good fruit.
Every tree that does not bear good fruit is cut down and thrown into the fire.
Thus, by their fruit you will recognize them.
—Matthew 7:15-20 (NIV)

Jesus encourages us to identify bad behavior, not to ignore it because we are sinners, too.

Sins of Thought vs. Sins of Action

Jesus said if you lust, you are guilty of adultery. And he talked about hatred and murder in a similar way. That's the Christian theology of sin. Both sins fall short of God's righteousness.

But practically, in real life, we know the consequences are different for hatred and murder.

Conscientious people are tough on themselves. They often make sin-leveling accusations to themselves in their own minds, telling themselves they cannot speak out or take a stand unless they are perfect. In fact, self-critical statements and self-doubt are often signs that you care deeply about right and wrong.

In contrast, abusers usually aren't willing to express any misgivings about their own actions. They often want to make it seem that they are immune from any guilt, failings, or problems. As one forensic psychologist said, they wish to "present themselves as free of psychological difficulties."

Myth Nine: You Can't Demand to Be Treated Right, Because Christians Have No Rights

Similar to the teaching of sin-leveling is the concept that we as Christians have no rights. This false belief says: Due to our sin, we deserve only judgment and death from God.

Then this teaching is stretched to further include the idea that we also deserve nothing good from anyone else in the world. It strongly implies that Christians aren't allowed to speak up when they are being injured. We should be grateful we're alive.

This teaching is nonsense.

When an abusive spouse denies your biblical right to faithfulness, respect, and care, this is a sign that something is not right. Beware of those who ignore your claims and silence you by invoking a "no talk" rule or a "no gossip" rule and try to keep you from telling the authorities, friends, and clergy.

When you have no voice and no power to shine the spotlight on injury, you are being silenced.

The Bible *encourages* injured people to speak up. In Scripture, God constantly calls on judges and kings to protect the rights of the vulnerable. People who are being treated unfairly, taken advantage of, and cheated, are invited to call on their leaders. Jewish courts heard cases and handed down justice during biblical times.

Open your mouth for the mute,
for the rights of all who are destitute.
Open your mouth, judge righteously,
defend the rights of the poor and needy.
—Proverbs 31:8-9 (ESV)

Give justice to the weak...
maintain the right of the afflicted and the destitute.
—Psalm 82:3 (ESV)

Myth Ten: It Is Your Fault Your Spouse Cheated or Watched Porn Because You Didn't Give Them Enough Sex

This myth says that men who are getting enough sex at home do not have affairs or molest children. Therefore, the wife is to blame if her husband acts out. (It is much rarer—because many church communities falsely believe that men are sexual creatures and women are not—for this myth to be leveled against men whose wives cheat, too. Men usually get accused of not being loving and helpful enough around the home.)

The truth is that you cannot cure someone else's sex addiction or deviant sexual behavior by having more sex with them.

Respected infidelity researcher Dr. Shirley Glass, in her book *Not Just Friends,* writes:

"Most people mistakenly think it is possible to prevent affairs
by being loving and dedicated to one's partner.
I call this the 'Prevention Myth,'
because there is no evidence to support it.
My experience as a marital therapist and infidelity researcher
has shown me that simply being a loving partner

does not necessarily insure your marriage against affairs."[39]

As the old saying goes (and the Bible agrees)—

*There aren't any acceptable reasons for cheating, **just excuses**.*

Of course, there are some people who will blame you for your spouse's cheating. Yet those same people—if Christian—don't say, "Your spouse has a right to have sex with others if you sin." If your spouse cheats because they constantly need to see themselves in the eyes of a new adoring love, they need to go to counseling and figure out what's going on.

A single incident may be repaired, but it takes hard work, and the unfaithful spouse must be committed to transparency and investing in the relationship. You can't make it happen by yourself.

If a spouse cheats, the innocent spouse can forgive; but building a trusting marriage cannot happen until the adultery stops. Anyone can forgive a single incident (in fact, many people do), but serial adulterers don't usually stop. They cheat, then come home to a loving spouse who pays the bills, keeps the household running, puts food on the table, and makes sure the kids are cared for. Many serial adulterers don't leave or file for divorce. Why should they? They've got the best of both worlds.

Child Molesters and Child Porn

Many Christians want to believe that God will magically cure every child molester who acts repentant. But that is delusional thinking. To date, academic literature indicates that pedophilia doesn't go away. The only published study that says it might was debunked.

James Cantor, a clinical psychologist at the University of Toronto who specializes in the treatment of pedophiles, says some pedophiles might think they've been cured when they haven't.[40] Pedophilia is considered "a lifelong condition."[41]

---

39 Shirley P. Glass, ***Not "Just Friends,"*** (New York: Free Press, 2003), 2. This book is also excellent on how to rebuild a marriage after an affair.

40 Justin Lehmiller, "Pedophiles Can't Be 'Cured' and It's Dangerous to Suggest They Can," ***Vice*** (1/25/19,) accessed 8/20/19, https://www.vice.com/en_us/article/mbzj5q/pedophiles-cant-be-cured-and-its-dangerous-to-suggest-they-can.

41 A. Mokros and E. Habermeyer, "Regression to the Mean Mimicking Changes in Sexual Arousal

We are talking about a long-term pattern of attraction to kids, or as researchers define it: "a persistent sexual interest in prepubescent children."[42] There are also people who have a pattern of illegal sexual activity targeting early adolescents (10-14) or late adolescents (15-19). And of course, there are people who are opportunistic and will violate any vulnerable person in their path, including children. (They may not be classed as pedophiles, but they are clearly dangerous.)

I've interviewed many Christian women who were married to men who have a pattern of committing sexual offenses (either child porn or molesting minors). In most cases, husbands were active churchgoers and lay leaders—and sex offenders.

These men often confessed to something minimal, like "attraction to children." They cried tears of repentance but continued in their sin. Some religious leaders are ill-informed and believe that attraction to children can be fixed by a sexually eager spouse. Nothing could be further from the truth. Pedophiles may have sex with adults, but their interest is in children.

To quote one child molester who also had frequent sex with his wife, "The addicted part of me sees kids as good for one thing: sexual pleasure."[43]

These Christian wives did not realize that pedophilia never goes away. They worried about their children and other children who might be affected. They hoped and prayed and forgave. They knew something wasn't right. They were terrified that the illegal activity was far worse than they knew, but they rarely caught their husbands doing anything suspicious. (No wife can watch her child molester husband 24 hours a day, seven days a week, even if they believe they can.)

They lived in constant fear they would be humiliated and have their reputations destroyed. They confronted their husbands and demanded answers—and got lies.

The wives I interviewed for this book had divorced and were much

---

to Child Stimuli in Pedophiles," ***Arch Sex Behav*** 45, no. 7 (10/16): 1863-7, accessed 08/20/19, https://www.ncbi.nlm.nih.gov/pubmed/26585168.

42 Michael Neuman "Pedophilia: An Overview," ***Science Direct*** (2015), accessed 7/9/2019, https://www.sciencedirect.com/topics/medicine-and-dentistry/pedophilia.

43 This quote was from a forensic psychological evaluation I was only allowed to see under condition of anonymity.

happier, no longer living in fear and turmoil. Some changed back to their maiden names to avoid the shame. Several remarried and now have loving husbands.

As a psychologist who has spent over 20 years working with and studying victims and sexual offenders, Dr. Anna Salter says that "many offenders report that religious people are even easier to fool than most people."[44]

Some people of faith confuse the concept of *justification* with *sanctification*. God does save any truly repentant sinner, but he does not promise to fix people in this lifetime. Even Jesus didn't fix everyone around him. Judas was with Jesus constantly for three years and still betrayed him. If Jesus "failed" to fix Judas, why do we think we will succeed?

When your spouse molests children, has lost jobs due to porn consumption, abuses you and others, or commits adultery, it is not your fault. The choice is up to you, but if you want my recommendation: Don't stay. Run, run, run!

Myth Eleven: It Is Your Fault They Abused You, Because You Deserve Punishment

This myth says you are to blame if your spouse abuses, hits, slaps, mocks, punishes, or ridicules you; calls you names; denies you food, clothing, or basic needs; acts indifferently toward you; withholds things you enjoy; or monitors or controls you. Some people who feel guilty about a past sin (often sex, youthful rebellion, abortion, criminal behavior, etc.) come to believe that the abuse is God righteously punishing them. In the story in Chapter 4, Priscilla felt John's abuse was punishment for sleeping with her college boyfriend years before.

This is not a right understanding of God.

The Bible promises that "If we confess our sins, he is faithful and just and will forgive us our sins and purify us from all unrighteousness" (1

---

44 Kim Harris, "Sex Offenders Groom Churches Too: How predatory behavior goes undetected in congregations," ***Christianity Today*** (6/8/18,) accessed 7/9/19, https://www.christianitytoday.com/ct/2018/june-web-only/sex-offenders-groom-churches-too.html.

John 1:9, NIV). Jesus has taken the punishment for our sins on himself, on the Cross. The debt has been paid. We have been washed clean because Jesus paid the penalty for our sins.

In this world, we all may still have the natural consequences of bad behavior (such as needing to apologize and make things right when we say something unkind to a friend).

But God doesn't get revenge on us or punish us with abusive marriages to teach us a lesson.
That is not the kind of God he is.

For example, when religious authorities wanted Jesus' permission to kill a woman caught in adultery, Jesus told her he did not condemn her. He let her go free (John 8:1-11). Our God is a God of mercy, forgiveness, and love.

You aren't supposed to die for your own sins.
That's Jesus' job.
God loves you and forgives you.
And if God has forgiven you, maybe it makes sense to forgive yourself.

Jesus' Great Commandment calls his followers to love one another. Abusive behavior is certainly not love. Three times in Ephesians 5, husbands are called to love their wives. Abuse and neglect are not signs of love.

If anyone does not provide for his own,
and especially his own household,
he has denied the faith and is worse than an unbeliever.
—1 Timothy 5:8 (BSB)

Myth Twelve: It Is Your Fault Because You Didn't Submit Enough

This myth, used almost exclusively against women, says your marriage is in trouble because you aren't a submissive wife. If you did everything your husband wanted, your marriage would be great.

Women who have been taught this myth and internalized it often become trapped in dangerous marriages; they believe that the Bible says women must submit to their husbands in everything and always put his preferences and desires first, obeying him no matter what. Some wives have been taught that headship means that only the husband can make major decisions—or in some cases, all decisions.

One woman had been taught to "submit in all things" and handed over *all* responsibility to her husband—

I was better with money than he was,
but I still didn't give my opinion about all of the financial decisions,
because I thought it was my role to be submissive.
We got into financial trouble. He was desperate for my advice,
but my [faith tradition's] teaching didn't allow me to give it.
I made him decide. Only his vote for restaurants mattered.
I gave up having an opinion.
[We were taught that godly wives] make their husbands
make all the decisions and then blame him for the results.

She was taught that her husband must make all decisions, and that this was the best way to show him respect. So, when the husband makes a bad decision, wives are taught they cannot advise, correct, or contradict their husband, and that it is godly for a husband to bear all the responsibility for bad decisions.

Under this myth, it's the husband's fault when his ideas make the family go off the rails. Wives are powerless to stop train wrecks that hurt the family; they have no control over their own life, no voice, and no veto ability that allows them to say "Stop!"

The truth, however, is different. What the Bible teaches is *mutual* submission, cooperation, love, and partnership, in which both the husband and the wife have an important say in the marriage and family.

Many Christians don't realize that Ephesians 5:22 *does not* use the word "submit." The Greek wording in this verse literally reads, "Wives, to your husbands as to the Lord."

"Submit" only appears in verse 21, where *all* believers are commanded to submit to one another (not just wives to husbands). Even here, the word *submit* is not the same Greek word as the word for *obey*. And the Greek word *kephalē* ("head") is never used to mean leader, chief person, or authority. It means "origin, beginning, or source."[45]

In addition, there is—

- nothing about the husband leading and the wife following
- nothing about the husband making all the decisions or having the final say
- nothing about wives obeying (in contrast, in the next part of Ephesians, *children* are told to obey)
- nothing about the husband speaking for God
- nothing about God always supporting or defending a husband's decisions[46]

Most importantly, just one verse before, the Scripture says, "**Submit to one another** out of reverence for Christ" (Ephesians 5:21, NIV). And Ephesians 5:1-2 says that all followers of Jesus should *love.*

Submission isn't just for wives.
Submission is a behavior for all Christians.

As one scholar put it, "Sacrificial love isn't just for husbands (Ephesians 5:1-2, 21)."[47] How can anyone talk about submission without mentioning verses like these, which show a two-way street?

Jesus and Paul also teach—in two passages—that their followers are not to "lord it over" one another, meaning not wielding authority over others and controlling people (Matthew 20:25 and 1 Peter 5:3).

So whom do we obey in life? We obey God!

We ought to obey God rather than men.
— Acts 5:29 (NKJV)

For there is one God and one mediator between God and mankind,
the man Christ Jesus...
—1 Timothy 2:5 (NIV)

---

45 Marg Mowczko, "Kephalē and 'Male Headship' in Paul's Letters," ***MargMowczko.com*** (9/18/11), accessed 08/13/19, https://margmowczko.com/kephale-and-male-headship-in-pauls-letters/. Mowczko's article goes on to say that if ***kephalē*** ("head") did mean leader or chief person in Eph. 5:22, why does the Apostle Paul talk about husbands sacrificing and loving their wives rather than leading them? Also of note: 1 Corinthians 11:3 is not about marriage or husbands and wives.

46 Ibid.

47 Ibid.

We are always to put *God* first. We are to have "no other gods before him," as the Ten Commandments say—and that includes a husband.

Most of the time, husbands and wives support and love each other. But when one spouse does not—for example, when a husband wishes to do something that is sinful and destructive to his family and to himself—it is the other spouse's duty (in this case, the wife's duty) to protect themselves and their children.

If a woman chooses to marry, it's her job to be a good partner and companion, mutually following Christ together with her husband. Throughout Scripture, we see wives advising husbands, and (in the case of danger) wives courageously taking initiative to protect the family.

Examples:

- Zipporah, the wife of Moses, took action to save his life when he did not know what God wanted him to do (Exodus 4).
- Deborah, a prophet of God and a judge in Israel who the Bible says was leading the country, commanded the military to protect her people (Judges 4).
- Abigail saved the lives of her family and servants by disobeying her husband, Nabal. She was rewarded for her wisdom. She is the only woman in the Bible called both beautiful and intelligent (some Bible translations say "clever") (1 Samuel 25).
- Samson's mother was visited by an angel who announced her son's birth. Samson's father didn't believe it and wanted the angel to tell him directly. The angel repeated everything and said, "Your wife must do all that I have told her" (Judges 13:13, NIV). Later, Samson's father made an incorrect statement about the angel who visited him. His wife gave him a wiser interpretation (Judges 13:23).
- Ruth told Boaz he should redeem her and the land (Ruth 3).
- Abraham was told by God to listen to his wife, Sarah (Genesis 21:12).
- Esther's husband, the King, wanted to kill her people, but she knew she must risk her life, be brave, and concoct a plan to persuade him to change his mind.

One abused wife said —

I put my husband above God. I shut God out for 8 years. God would tell me to share [my situation with others], but I didn't. Doing this made me not responsible for my own choices. We went to a conference together, and I repented that I put my husband above God as I had been taught by Bill Gothard. I started hearing from God again.

I turned myself into a doormat.

In the words of a woman who was homeschooled and raised in the Mennonite culture:

> *I read a book that said if the woman does her part, her husband will eventually come around and everything will be OK. I also read the "love and respect" book. That taught me that if I just respected my husband more, he would love me more. It taught my husband that if I just respected him more, he would automatically love me more. These false teachings were devastating to our marriage.*
>
> *I believed so strongly in submission that in many ways I feel like I created a monster. Here I had done the right thing, and God's promises didn't happen. My husband slept with prostitutes, he went to strip clubs, he got lap dances, and he physically abused me.*
>
> *I was so angry with God. It's like God said to me, "You're angry at me; go get angry at your husband. I'm not the one who screwed up; he is the one that screwed up. Go get angry at him." I felt that God had just had enough of it.*
>
> *I moved in with my parents. My siblings were all completely on board. They thought it was completely the right thing to do to leave and divorce my husband. But it was tough on my mother… I realized I had to let my mother have her own feelings.*
>
> *For people from conservative faith backgrounds, nobody expects to go through divorce. My parents do a lot of pastoral care counseling, but they are not trained counselors. The funny thing is, now that they have a daughter who is divorced, they have people coming up to them asking them how to handle situations… [One] pastor called my dad and said, "There is a person in our church, and we just don't know what to do." So my dad is giving them some advice on how to handle it. When your book comes out, I would like for them to be able to give it to people.*

Ephesians 5:21-33 describes the responsibilities for marriage, love, and submission. For believers, there is to be *mutual* submission (v. 21), with wives and husbands showing each other this submission as to the Lord, sacrificially, as Christ does for the Church (vs. 22, 25). *Many times* husbands are called to love their wives (vs. 25, 28, 33), feeding and caring for them like the husband cares for himself (vs. 28-29), and the wife is called to respect him (v. 33).

Another woman pointed out that her Christian counselors demanded that wives obey this passage, but they did not hold the husbands' feet to the fire. How is that biblical? Where is the man's love and his sacrifice like Christ? Where is the caring at the same level that he cares for himself? She said:

> *We were taught at church that men wanted respect and women wanted love. I tried to be agreeable. I tried to be more compliant and let him have his way. I tried to be more submissive. He insisted that I make coffee for him early in the morning, long before the kids needed to get up for school. To him this was small, but for me, if I didn't get any sleep the night before, I wanted to say, "Make your own coffee today." Where is the compromise? Isn't that what we are supposed to do?*
>
> *I would try to bend over backward not to disturb him if I went to bed late. But when he got up early in the morning when I was asleep, he turned on all the lights and turned on the music loud while he showered. The message I got was, "Roll out the red carpet for me, but I can't be bothered to be considerate for you."*
>
> *Our entire Christian marriage ethic and teaching just encourages extreme laziness and selfishness on the part of men.*[48] *We are teaching them not to be considerate or mature or wise, or to show sacrificial love. We are teaching them to do what they want.*
>
> *I finally said, "If there is an issue and we don't agree, we need to accept that God gave us to each other. So if we don't agree, we should wait to make a decision."*

---

48 Pete Briscoe, "Awkward: Uncomfortable Conversations about Marriage, Part 2: Submission," ***Bent Tree.org.***, accessed 12/13/19, https://benttree.org/sermon/part-2-submission/. One of Pete Briscoe's sermons at Bent Tree Bible Fellowship, in the "Awkward: Uncomfortable Conversations about Marriage" sermon series, discusses submission and touches on this topic of how we are training men to indulge their selfishness.

I love the Lord, but it was just lip service about men laying down their lives.

The Bible says both spouses need to submit to each other. Each should care about the wellbeing of the other. That's what love is. Their life together should be considerate and have mutual involvement and input.

Neither should be threatened or live in fear from their spouse. Together they have input on the decisions that affect them, and they are to work in good faith side by side to find a solution. Both should have access to spending money and opportunities for leisure time and activities, because the husband is to care about his wife just as much as himself.

Selfishness, threats, and dominance have no place in godly Christian marriages.

Myth Thirteen: The Person Who *Files* for Divorce Is the One Who Caused the Divorce

"Divorce is not the innocent party ending a marriage.
Divorce is the innocent party obtaining legal recognition
that the guilty party has destroyed the marriage."
—Rebecca VanDoodewaard[49]

Many people live with this misconception. They believe that only an unfaithful or badly behaving spouse wants to get out of the marriage and file for divorce.

The reality is often the reverse: the cheating, addicted, or abusive spouse wants to stay with the other spouse as long as they can benefit from it.

The lying, cheating, selfish, or abusive spouse wants the invested spouse to earn the money, pay bills, make the food, clean the house, do the laundry, care for the children, help with homework, support them emotionally, and offer them a warm bed. In fact, often the bad spouse will not leave. They fight to block or delay the divorce, demanding their spouse reconcile because "God hates divorce."

---

49 Rebecca VanDoodewaard, "A High View of Marriage Includes Divorce," ***Gentle Reformation*** (7/20/17), accessed 6/6/19, https://gentlereformation.com/2017/07/20/a-high-view-of-marriage-includes-divorce/.

This is common in abusive relationships. The abuser refuses to discuss custody, living arrangements, money, and options on how to divide the assets. They don't cooperate. They ignore the attorney's letters. They make unreasonable demands, or they go silent and make no counter-offer at all.

Sometimes the cheating spouse is not loving, honoring, and cherishing—rather, they are leeching, disrespecting, and exploiting.

It's a one-way street, with one spouse sacrificing their health and wellbeing, and the badly behaving spouse doing all the taking (though often telling others they are doing a lot). What selfish person wouldn't want a one-way relationship?

But this is human nature unchecked. We all start out this way as toddlers, taking without giving back, thinking primarily of ourselves and our own interests.

In an adult, however, that behavior is not acceptable.

And it has disastrous, harmful consequences to families and partners. To let someone's sin nature run rampant, unchecked, is not loving.

- Love says *No.*
- Love says *You may not treat me this way.*
- Love sets consequences for bad behavior.

Many badly behaving spouses do not cooperate with or listen to the abused spouse's protests and needs. They will not stop unless you force them out of your life. They may try to block the legal process of divorce by refusing to discuss the terms.

So, for some women (and, more rarely, men), bifurcating the divorce (ending the marriage now, and figuring out the financial terms later) is the only way they can get away and force their spouse to face the truth: *The marriage is over, and there's nothing you can do to force us to stay together.* (Note: Ask your own attorney about bifurcation if you have a spouse who stonewalls; professional legal advice is outside the scope of this book.)

Myth Fourteen: Divorcing Bestows a Curse on Your Family

This false belief teaches people that getting divorced bestows a curse on your family. It says that a divorced family is a *broken* family, and a black cloud will be with them forever—the members of that family will never do well in life, never mature, never thrive, and never become respectable people.

In reality, a family with a parent who indulges in long-term immoral behavior is *already* broken. Far from bestowing a curse on the family, the divorce brings God's freedom into the family. It frees the innocent spouse and children from bondage to this toxic system forever.

> "In some cases, divorce may be the best option for husbands and wives in a difficult or dangerous marriage. Domestic violence, drug and alcohol abuse, and infidelity—among other things—are certainly legitimate grounds..."[50]
> —W. Bradford Wilcox, Institute for Family Studies

Myth Fifteen: God Will Heal Your Marriage If You Pray Enough

Many women have been influenced by a Christian book called *Lies Women Believe,*[51] in which the author makes this comment: "There is no marriage God cannot heal. There is no person God cannot change."[52]

The author's statement is partially true: God can do anything! Nothing is too big for God. God is a powerful God. *But that's not the message she is giving.* Her real message (quoted from the same page) is that if you are hurt by your spouse's behavior and you justify your decision to divorce, she says you have a hard heart, and you've "fallen into the Deceiver's trap and have been ensnared by his deception."

To me, this clearly doesn't apply to spouses who have been abused or cheated on. A woman who stays, prays, and tries harder has already proven her dedication to her marriage over and over. Wives who endured, in the face of betrayal or abuse, do not have a hard heart. Their husbands do. These wives did not fall into the Deceiver's trap. Their husbands did.

I Believe in the God of Miracles

I've seen miracles. My own mother had a miraculous healing when I was a teenager.

But the implication that God *will* heal every time if you are faithful enough is wrong.

- God can—but does not—heal all cancer.

---

50 W. Bradford Wilcox, "Three Reasons Not to Make This January Your Divorce Month," ***Institute for Family Studies*** (1/11/17), accessed 9/2/19, https://ifstudies.org/blog/three-reasons-not-to-make-this-january-your-divorce-month.

51 Nancy Leigh DeMoss, ***Lies Women Believe*** (Chicago: Moody Publishers, 2001).

52 Ibid., 159.

- God can—but does not—heal all car accident injuries.
- God can—but does not—heal all childhood birth defects.
- God can—but does not—keep good people from suffering.

Will God Magically Fix My Marriage?

My parents had elderly friends at our church who were an amazing, born-again Christian couple. They were loving and volunteered for everything at church. They were loving believers and were devoted to prayer. They were wonderful models of Christian living and sacrificed their time and effort for others. They had no children, so they gave all their money to Christian causes.

The husband got very ill, and the church gathered to pray for him. The pastor and elders laid hands on him. The couple traveled to a revival where a faith healer invited people to come forward for healing.

Many people claimed to be cured, but our elderly friend wasn't. They were told they didn't have enough faith, that there must be hidden sin, and they hadn't given enough money.

They were devastated and wondered what they did wrong.

They prayed, examined their lives, and went over and over to the revival meetings, but he still wasn't healed. It was painful to watch this devout couple beating themselves up.

This story shows a toxic misunderstanding of God and his power, and it's a shame these dear saints suffered from this false teaching.

In John 9, Jesus corrected this lie. His disciples asked him why a certain man had been born blind. Was it because of the man's sin, or his parents' sin? Jesus said, "Neither." It was not punishment from God.

The Prosperity Gospel and Marriage

In the story above, I showed the difference between Jesus' teachings and the prosperity gospel mindset.

The False Logic of the Prosperity Gospel:

- God blesses all people who are good.
- God curses all people who are bad.
- God's sign of blessing is a loving marriage, money, and health.
- If you do not have a good marriage, money, and health, you must be a bad person (even if you **think** you are good).

Jesus rejected this false belief. He taught that bad things happened to good people. The Bible says that God "sends rain on the righteous and the unrighteous" (Matthew 5:45, NIV). Sure, there is a principle of reaping and sowing, but that doesn't mean only good people get rich, and only bad, lazy people get poor. We all know godly people who are poor and evil people who are rich.

Just because some people say they were healed doesn't mean *all* people will be healed. Don't be like the false faith healers who say you're doing something wrong if God doesn't heal your marriage right now.

Unanswered prayers may not mean you don't have faith in God. You just don't have the answers yet. And you may never know the *whys* in this life. But you can be sure God weeps with you, and he is growing in you the courage to protect yourself and your children.

A STORY OF UNANSWERED PRAYER

A churchgoing Christian woman, whose husband had a series of affairs, prayed and hung on for years.

In her own words—

[My husband] moved out, and for the next several years I tried everything to win him back. We had pastoral counseling because I believed God hated divorce, and I refused to give up on the marriage.

Our pastor interviewed us separately and finally told me, "This man is determined to leave; let him go." That's not what I wanted to hear. I wanted the pastor to fix him. I wanted my husband to be changed magically. I wanted him to come back to me and to God. I was destroyed.

To make matters worse, my husband found a fourth woman [after his previous three affairs] and moved into her house right across the street from us. Every morning the kids and I could see him kissing her and going off to work. It devastated me. At the same time, he was coming over, hanging out with the kids, and occasionally acting as if he wanted to reconcile.

I was in a fog of confusion. I didn't know what was happening. He said we would get back together soon, in time for our upcoming tenth anniversary. I wanted to believe him and took any positive comment or act of kindness as a sign of hope. He just kept stringing me along, and I fell for it.

This made me literally insane. I gave up hope and figured out a way to kill myself. I didn't want to leave a note. I wanted it to look like an accident and planned it carefully. The day I decided to die, just as I was walking out the door, my three-year-old daughter said, "Mommy, you're not going to leave like Daddy, are you?" That stopped me in my tracks. How could I abandon her? I turned around, went back into the house, and knew I had to stay alive for my children.

The counselor asked me every week, "Is your marriage over?" (It was obvious to everyone else but me.) Each time I said no. I kept hanging on.

One evening, I went to pick up the kids from his house. His girlfriend and my daughter were playing on the bed. Suddenly the truth hit me: My husband is sleeping with this woman. They are living together. I shook myself, asking, "What am I doing?"

Later I went for a drive. I needed to be alone and pray. I felt an overwhelming need to pull over and let God overcome me. I felt the Holy Spirit free me from the spiritual obligation to continue trying to save my marriage.

I knew God hated divorce, but I also knew God had taken the burden off my shoulders. I was free and felt God's blessing. The next week I found a paralegal and filed for divorce.

When you're focused on holding a marriage together, you don't realize how that desire overcomes rational thought and can become an obsession.

Myth Sixteen: It's God's Will for You to Suffer: "Holiness Over Happiness"

This myth is usually wielded against women (but sometime against men). It says they should suffer silently in order to be seen as godly Christian spouses who value "holiness over happiness," believing that suffering is refining them and knocking off the rough edges.

And while it is true that learning to give and take, to fight fairly, and to solve problems with our spouse can mature us, this myth takes it a step too far. It says godly spouses should sacrifice their wellbeing, health, and safety, and put up with marriage-endangering sin because it will somehow make them holy. They are pressured to uphold the image of a perfect family that represents a cheerful Christianity to the world.

The myth also suggests that any suffering you're experiencing is your fault for picking a bad mate, saying, "You made your bed; now lie in it."

But is that fair? Only God knows people's thoughts. And even if you saw a red flag, you had no idea how unbearable and extreme it would become. You are not responsible for being deceived by someone who presented themselves in the best light, or for praying and believing that the Lord brought you two together.

Abuse is not what God wants for you. And it is bad for your spouse as well. It is immaturity and selfishness run amok. When we read Scripture, we see that God's will is not for his people to cover up marriage-destroying sin, but for justice and love to triumph and be lifted high. God is against abuse and oppression, and his will is to deliver those who are being oppressed.

And by the way, no one has the right to demand your reasons for divorcing. Not a stranger, a friend or parent, a pastor, or a random person on social media. You do not need to try to convince others of the rightness of seeking safety. God gave you the instinct for self-preservation.

For Christian men, usually this myth takes the form of "loving sacrificially," "laying down your life" and "dying to self," even if your wife is the one who is manipulating or abusing you.

In secular circles, sometimes the myth takes the form of the "happy wife, happy life" idea—that if you keep your wife happy by any and all means, your marriage will thrive.

So as we read these verses, keep in mind that these principles also apply to women who abuse their husbands. (For more on male victims of abuse, see Chapter 9.)

The Apostle Peter says abusive spouses do not get their prayers answered by God:

> ***Husbands, in the same way be considerate as you live with your wives, and treat them with respect as the weaker partner and as heirs with you of the gracious gift of life, <u>so that nothing will hinder your prayers.</u>***
>
> ***—1 Peter 3:7 (NIV, emphasis mine)***

This verse has two interesting insights. First, when a husband continuously sins against a wife (and likely vice versa), it leads to having his prayers hindered. It is not biblical for the wife to stay silent in this case. (See the list of biblical women in Myth Twelve who wisely advised their husbands to do the right thing.)

Second, the word honor in that verse is the same word used in Romans 13:7 for the honor you show to the authorities that God put in place.

... for the authorities are God's servants, who give their full time to governing.
Give to everyone what you owe them: If you owe taxes, pay taxes; if revenue, then revenue; if respect, then respect; if honor, then honor.
—Romans 13:6b-7 (NIV)

Show proper respect to everyone, love the family of believers, fear God, honor the emperor.
—1 Peter 2:17 (NIV)

God wants us to honor our spouses, just as God wants us to show honor to all people and to the authorities. And God commands men to be understanding to wives, otherwise their prayers are hindered. God demands that all believers, regardless of gender, show one another understanding, love, respect, honor, and kindness. It is a sin for a husband to treat his wife harshly.

Husbands, love your wives, and do not be harsh with them.
—Colossians 3:19 (NIV)

God is against those who are violent. He sides with and saves the oppressed and the underdogs.

Put away violence and oppression and do what is just and right.
—Ezekiel 45:9a (HCSB)

Do not envy the violent or choose any of their ways.
—Proverbs 3:31 (NIV)

An angry person stirs up conflict,
and a hot-tempered person commits many sins.
—Proverbs 29:22 (NIV)
Rescue me, Lord, from evildoers;
protect me from the violent,
who devise evil plans in their hearts
and stir up war every day.
—Psalm 140:1-2 (NIV)

The LORD works righteousness and justice
for all the oppressed.
—Psalm 103:6 (NIV)

Do not take advantage of a hired worker who is poor and needy,
whether that worker is a fellow Israelite
or a foreigner residing in one of your towns.
—Deuteronomy 24:14 (NIV)

God does not accept the sacrifices of men who betray their wives.

Another thing you do:
You flood the LORD's altar with tears.
You weep and wail
because [the LORD] no longer looks with favor on your offerings
or accepts them with pleasure from your hands.
You ask, "Why?"
It is because the LORD is the witness
between you and the wife of your youth.
You have been unfaithful to her, though she is your partner,
the wife of your marriage covenant.
...So be on your guard,
and do not be unfaithful to the wife of your youth.
—Malachi 2:13-14, 15b (NIV)

God does not look away when people are exploited.

Each of you must know how to control his own body
in a holy and honorable manner,
not with passion and lust like the gentiles who do not know God.

Furthermore, you must never take advantage of or exploit a brother in this regard, because the Lord avenges all these things, just as we already told you and warned you.
—1 Thessalonians 4:4-6 (ISV)

These verses show us the heart of God and his will for us: not to suffer quietly to make Christianity look good, but to display his love and his passion for justice, even in our marriages. Sometimes, this means putting an end to abuse by getting out of a dangerous marriage.

Many people say, "God wants loving marriages; Satan wants divorce." But in reality—

God wants loving marriages.
Satan wants cruel marriages.

Satan loves the fact that innocent spouses and children are bound to someone who devastates them, humiliates them, betrays them, and treats them treacherously. He loves when Christians suffer abuse quietly, over and over again, for years.

Jesus isn't like that. Jesus came to set people free.

Myth Seventeen: Marriage Is God's Best Way to Mature You Emotionally and Spiritually

This myth says that marriage is God's greatest tool for making people mature. Many pastors preach that the highest calling for Christians is marriage and children; and as a corollary to this, they warn believers that to divorce is to walk away from God's best plan for your life.

Although this sounds good, there's no biblical basis to the idea that marriage matures a person more than other influences in life. Jesus wasn't married, and the Apostle Paul was single. Certainly, they matured without being married. They also both taught that singleness was an honorable state of being, despite pressure from others.

It's important to remember that, about the time of Jesus, in the Roman Empire under Caesar Augustus, it was *illegal* for a widow to stay single more than two years or for a divorced woman to stay single more than eighteen months.[53] In the ancient world, including Judea at the time of

---

53 "Marriage, Weddings and Love in Ancient Rome," Facts and Details (2018), accessed 9/2/19, http://factsanddetails.com/world/cat56/sub369/item2074.html.

Jesus, it was almost unthinkable that a person would remain single after a divorce or widowhood. It was their fundamental right and obligation to remarry. [54]

So when we see in the Bible that Jesus and Paul taught that singleness and marriage are both options (Matthew 19:10-11; 1 Corinthians 7:6-7), we recognize what a radical concept this was at their time. Paul even put singleness *above* marriage. Many early church fathers did, too.

A lot of people develop maturity and character from their jobs, their friendships, good parents, teachers, pastors, platoon leaders, and supervisors.

God has many ways of maturing us, and marriage is just one of many.

When it comes to an abusive or dangerous marriage, sometimes getting out is the path to maturity in Christ!

Myth Eighteen: God Forbids All Divorce; All Divorce Is Sin; Divorce Is the Unpardonable Sin

In my interviews with Christian divorcees, I've often heard that they stayed in an unfaithful or abusive marriage for decades because they were taught that "God hates divorce," and the Lord will judge them.

This myth says that all divorce is forbidden by God, sinful, and unpardonable in God's eyes—or, similarly, it says that Jesus or Paul never mention abuse, so it must not be a biblical reason for divorce.

In reality, Scripture shows us God's permission for divorce in several places. Emotional and physical abuse and neglect are mentioned in the Old Testament and repeated in the New Testament, but we've never seen it because we aren't looking for it. (See Chapter 6 on biblical reasons for divorce for abuse).

Jesus allowed divorce for **infidelity:**

Matthew 19:9 (ESV)	And I say to you: whoever divorces his wife, except for sexual immorality, and marries another, commits adultery.

54 David Instone-Brewer, Divorce and Remarriage in the Bible (Grand Rapids: Eerdmans, 2002), 299.

The Apostle Paul allowed divorce for **abandonment:**

1 Corinthians 7:14-15 (NIV)	For the unbelieving husband has been sanctified through his wife, and the unbelieving wife has been sanctified through her believing husband; for otherwise your children would be unclean, but as it is, they are holy. Yet **if the unbeliever leaves, let it be so.** The brother or the sister is not bound in such circumstances; God has called us to live in peace.

The Law of Moses allowed divorce (and actually commanded divorce) for breaking any of the **three marriage vows** in Exodus 21:10. Marital rights, in this verse, can be defined as material care and "love," as we read in the New Testament passages Eph. 5:25-33 and 1 Cor. 7:33.

Exodus 21:10-11 (ESV)	If he takes another wife to himself, he shall not diminish [the first wife's] **food, her clothing, or her marital rights.** And if he does not do these three things for her, **she shall go out** for nothing, without payment of money.

In the Book of Exodus, if a man took a second wife, it was against God's command to reduce the first wife's food, clothing, or marital rights (love). He was not allowed to demote her to slave status. If he was unwilling to treat her as a wife, he had to let her go so she could marry someone who would treat her properly.

The same was true for a prisoner-of-war wife who was captured during a battle. If a man took a captive as his wife, he had to do her the honor of letting her mourn a month before sleeping with her. As his wife, she must be treated properly.

The Law of Moses required divorce if that man **reduced his wife to a slave or tried to sell her.** He had to let her go and give her the freedom to marry someone else. The husband could not treat this woman any way he wanted. She was either a wife with rights, or she had to be set free.

Deuteronomy 21:11-14 (NIV)	...if you notice among the captives a beautiful woman and are attracted to her, you may take her as your wife. Bring her into your home and have her shave her head, trim her nails and put aside the clothes she was wearing when captured. After she has lived in your house and mourned her father and mother for a full month, then you may go to her and be her husband and she shall be your wife. **If you are not pleased with her, let her go wherever she wishes. You must not sell her or treat her as a slave,** since you have dishonored her.

This sounds like abusive marriages today where a woman has no voice and no power. All she can do is obey, like a slave. Read more about this in Chapter 6, which looks at many Bible verses on divorce (including verses you may never have read before).

"When a man chooses to be abusive, he breaks the covenant.
An abusive man forfeits the right to remain married..."
— Justin and Lindsey A. Holcomb[55]

Myth Nineteen: Your Divorce Will "Shatter the Image of Christ and the Church."

Nowhere in the Bible does it say a divorce will shatter the image of Christ and the Church. No human being is powerful enough to do that, because image of Christ and the Church is eternal and holy. And, as we saw in the prior myth, the Bible allows divorce in five passages (Ch. 6). In fact, even God divorced his own people. In Jeremiah 3:8, he explains he had "given her [Israel] a certificate of divorce," because of Israel's unfaithfulness.

People who teach this base their views on Ephesians 5:25-32, written by the Apostle Paul.

55 Justin Holcomb and Lindsay Holcomb, "Does the Bible Say Women Should Suffer Abuse and Violence?" JBC 28, no. 2 (2014), accessed 12/13/19, http://justinholcomb.com/wp-content/uploads/2014/09/Does-the-Bible-Say-Women-Should-Suffer-Abuse-and-Violence-Holcomb.pdf Justin is a frequent contributor to The Gospel Coalition blog.

Husbands, love your wives, just as Christ loved the church and gave himself up for her to make her holy, cleansing her by the washing with water through the word, and to present her to himself as a radiant church, without stain or wrinkle or any other blemish, but holy and blameless. In this same way, husbands ought to love their wives as their own bodies. He who loves his wife loves himself. After all, no one ever hated their own body, but they feed and care for their body, just as Christ does the church— for we are members of his body. "For this reason a man will leave his father and mother and be united to his wife, and the two will become one flesh." This is a profound mystery—but I am talking about Christ and the church. However, each one of you also must love his wife as he loves himself, and the wife must respect her husband. (NIV)

This passage calls husbands to imitate Christ's example. (By the way, notice that nowhere do these verses say that divorce *harms* Christ and the Church.)

The husband is called to **feed, care for, and love** his wife as Christ does the Church. Does this ring any bells? If you read Chapter 6 on biblical reasons for divorce, you'll learn that Paul is repeating the biblical Law of Moses in Exodus 21:10-11, about the basic standards of care for a wife. If this standard was broken, the innocent spouse had the option of leaving. An injured spouse was free to divorce and remarry someone who would care for them.

Notice that in this passage, Paul says *nothing* about the husband exercising authority over his wife; just the opposite, in fact. In this passage, he tells the husband to "give himself up" for her.

A valid divorce doesn't dishonor the Lord;
chronic treachery, abuse, and mistreatment of a spouse does.

When one spouse withholds food, care, and love, while benefitting at the expense of the other, they violate God's desire for Oneness in a loving marriage. We are to imitate Christ's example, and that example is all about giving and caring and Oneness. We're supposed to be a team, a partnership. As Rebecca VanDoodewaard writes:

"While God created marriage, loves marriage, and says that
it is a picture of Christ's relationship with the church,
Jesus didn't die to save marriage. He died to save people." [56]

Myth Twenty: If You Are Godly, You Can Marry Any Christian and It Will Work

This false teaching is often foisted on both young men and women. For guys, it's another prosperity gospel formula: If you are a godly spiritual leader, you can marry *any* Christian woman, regardless of her personality and character, and your life together will be happy. Put her on a pedestal, and everything will be smooth sailing. What could go wrong?

The truth is that character matters, and cultivating a healthy marriage takes two people's efforts, not just one. In my interviews, I find loving, godly men and women who marry selfish, manipulative people; one spouse's godliness doesn't magically make the marriage work.

Marriage Vows Are about the Basics

Naturally, married life comes with challenges. Often, marriage requires more faithfulness, commitment, and mutual loyalty than our newlywed selves knew to expect. The Apostle Paul reminds singles that marriage comes with *new priorities,* such as pleasing your spouse —

I would like you to be free from concern.
An unmarried man is concerned about the Lord's affairs
—how he can please the Lord.
But a married man is concerned about the affairs of this world
—how he can please his wife—and his interests are divided…
—1 Corinthians 7:32-34 (NIV)

As people mature, some do become better spouses who meet the basic responsibilities of the household and marriage:

- They earn money for food and clothing, and they keep a roof over their heads.
- They do the dishes, laundry, cooking, child raising, car repair, grocery shopping, and clothing purchases.

56 VanDoodewaard, "A High View."

- They are loyal and supportive of each other in tough times.
- They are faithful sexually, and they generally treat each other as they would want to be treated. They view sex and physical affection as important to the marriage.

We are talking basic standards, the level of food, clothing, housing, respect, kindness, and care that would be expected in decent society.

It is not about keeping up with your friends and neighbors. It isn't about the type of house or car you have, or your career success. This is not about getting rich, finding your soulmate, healing all your emotional wounds, or winning the "wife of the year" or the "husband of the year" award.

It's just the basics.

But some people either cannot or will not keep their vows.

- They break those promises over and over.
- They resist the responsibility.
- They misuse the family's resources: time, money, and energy.

People who can't manage the basics are not safe to marry.

Rather than treating their spouse fairly, they treat them like the enemy. They aren't faithful or supportive. They refuse to meet the basic needs of their spouse for food, clothing, and affection. They show disrespect and disdain, and they do violence. Their selfish desires trump their marriage vows.

A marriage is a partnership, and like any partnership, betrayal can destroy it. Picture marriage as a two-person canoe—it cannot get where it's meant to go unless both people are paddling. If one person paddles while the other one drags the anchor, or only one person is making loving, cooperative efforts, while the other is cheating, abusing, lying, or behaving dangerously, the marriage cannot work.

Myth Twenty-One: Divorce Will Destroy Your Children. You Should Stay for the Sake of Your Kids.

This myth is often used to terrify spouses that their divorce will destroy their children by causing irreversible harm emotionally, making them fail in school, and causing them to have more drug and alcohol problems. It says that a two-parent home is *always* better than a single-parent or stepparent home.

But this is not true. Often, abusive two-parent homes are worse.

A safe home where two married parents have little conflict is indeed best for children. Warm, accepting homes are very important to children's outcomes. But this isn't the case in abusive homes.

In high-conflict married homes, where the parents fight, or destructive behavior causes tension, children have higher likelihood of dropping out of high school, earning poor grades, smoking, binge drinking, early sex, out-of-wedlock pregnancy, and divorce. Children raised in these poor quality homes are no better off than those brought up in divorced single-parent families.

In fact, kids from high-conflict married homes are *more likely* to binge drink and have poor grades than kids from single parent or step-parent homes.[57]

But the biggest factor is the damage that high-conflict married homes do children's wellbeing. The trauma from these tense homes is significant. In Chapter 7, we'll see that kids rescued from these "very high-discord" homes had ten times better wellbeing than kids whose parents stayed together.

So the message that divorce is universally detrimental to children is simply wrong. Is divorce hard on kids? Yes, it is. But even the most pessimistic major researcher of the past 30 years, Dr. Judith Wallerstein, reported that 7 in 10 children of divorce turned out "average," "very well," or "outstanding.

As Dr. Mavis Hetherington summarized:

> "In the short run, divorce is brutally painful to a child. But its negative long-term effects have been exaggerated...
>
> "Twenty-five percent of youths from divorced families in comparison to 10 percent from non-divorced families did have serious social, emotional, or psychological problems. **But most of the young men and women from [the study] looked a lot like their contemporaries from non-divorced homes.** Although they

---

57 K. Musick, A. Meier, "Are Both Parents," Social Science Research 39 (2010): 823-26. See also: Paul R. Amato, "Reconciling Divergent Perspectives: Judith Wallerstein, Quantitative Family Research, and Children of Divorce," Family Relations 52, no. 4 (10/03): 332-339. And Judith S. Wallerstein, *The Unexpected Legacy of Divorce* (New York: Hyperion, 2000), p. 333

looked back on their parents' breakup as a painful experience, most were successfully going about the chief tasks of young adulthood: establishing careers, creating intimate relationships, building meaningful lives for themselves."[58]

In most cases, divorce does not ruin kids' chances in life or traumatize them forever. But being exposed to substance abuse, criminal behavior, violence, psychological and conflict for years on end could very well do just that!

Kaiser Permanente did a large study in 1998 that showed the health effects of adults who, as children, were abused or had witnessed their mother being abused, or had lived in a household with substance abuse.

They found that children who've been abused or exposed to abuse are at a higher risk when they become adults for major diseases such as ischemic heart disease, cancer, chronic lung disease, skeletal fractures, and liver disease. If children had been exposed to **four or more** of following seven categories, their health as adults was likely to be affected. The more categories they had been exposed to, the higher their risk, including increased health risks for alcoholism, drug abuse, depression, and suicide attempts.

The Seven Adverse Childhood Events (ACEs in 1998):

- psychological abuse, physical abuse
- sexual abuse
- violence against mother (later changed to include all violence against people in the home)
- living with household members who were substance abusers, mentally ill or suicidal, or ever imprisoned

To ask, "Is divorce good or bad?" is like asking, "Is pulling this fire alarm good or bad?"
If there's a fire—pull it! That's what it's there for.

Myth Twenty-Two: It Takes Two Parents to Raise Good Kids

This myth says divorced men and women can't raise healthy kids by

58 Hetherington and Kelly, *For Better*, 7.

themselves—that children need a married father and mother in the same home in order to turn out all right. In reality, single parents and stepparents can do a great job of raising healthy, well-adjusted kids.

When homes are unsafe, filled with anxiety, and children are exposed to a parent's dangerous, harmful behavior during their developmental years, kids truly suffer.

This is a hot-button issue, and a lot of people may misunderstand what I am saying. Some will accuse me of being anti-men. I am not.

I am saying research shows us that abusive spouses who torment their spouse and/or children are very destructive to the kids in the home.

According to a major study, fathers with antisocial behavior (lying, impulsivity, aggressiveness, lack of remorse, etc.) can be harmful to children, and some kids may develop conduct disorders themselves if they live in the same home. See chapter 7.

Myth Twenty-Three: You Can't Divorce Your Spouse; They Don't Know Any Better

Often even the person being abused falls victim to this myth. We find it hard to believe that people can be cruel; it is hard for us to face the reality that someone we love is abusive, and we want to continue to see them as worthy of love. We want to think the best of them.

So we ask ourselves, "Does my spouse really intend to be abusive? Do they *know* they're being abusive? If I could just make them understand, surely they would stop!"

Though these questions can torment us for a long time, in the end, they are beside the point. Maybe the abusive spouse understands perfectly, and they're causing that pain anyway. Maybe they don't understand and are blind to their own behavior; maybe they came from an abusive home themselves, and this is all they know.

Either way, the abuse is real—it's happening—and it is completely unacceptable.

That is what matters. That is why a life-saving divorce is necessary.

For some of us, it is important to believe the best of our spouse, and we don't want to consider that they are being deliberately, knowingly cruel, so we cling to this myth: Because our spouse doesn't "get it" and "doesn't know any better," we are not allowed to divorce them. We have to stay, letting them abuse us, and trying to make them understand. Leaving, we think, would be unloving. It would be "giving up" on them.

But that's not true. And we don't have to choose between leaving and loving. We can do both. We can still believe the best of them, giving them the benefit of the doubt, *and* get a life-saving divorce. Why?

Because sometimes people are doing their best, and their best is still *dangerous.*[59]

Abusers are as worthy of love as all the rest of us—after all, we are each made in the image of God. But when you are being abused, getting yourself out of your abuser's power is not unloving, and it doesn't mean that your spouse is unworthy of love. It also doesn't mean that you need to blame or hate them, or that you need to believe that they are a monster or an evil person.

It just means that your marriage together has turned dangerous and needs to end.

You can have compassion for your spouse and still leave a destructive marriage. In such situations, love says a loud, resounding *NO*, and gets out of there!

Myth Twenty-Four: If You Stay and Suffer, You Might Save Your Spouse, and You Will Glorify Christ

Your spouse is not abusing you because of your faith, and Christ is not glorified by your anguish. Staying and suffering is no guarantee that you'll win an abusive spouse to Christ. Christians are familiar with the biblical concept of redemptive suffering and of suffering persecution for Christ's sake. Christians may believe they "are to suffer grief for a little while" on the basis of 1 Peter 1:6.

This verse, combined with verses like 1 Peter 3:1-2 or James 1:2-5 about enduring hardships and becoming godlier, are misused to imply

---

59 I am indebted to Dr. Brené Brown in her book *Rising Strong* for the concept that sometimes even people who are doing their best can be dangerous, and we are allowed to protect ourselves or separate ourselves from them.

that believers should stay in abusive relationships. Some people say believers should suffer like Jesus suffered on the cross. They were to "count it all joy when they encounter various trials."

We know this idea by heart, and we want to model our lives after Jesus, who himself suffered for our sake, to reconcile us to God.

*But this myth takes this beautiful idea and misapplies it to people who are suffering **needlessly** in destructive marriages.*

Similarly, many devoted Christians feel it is their duty or calling to convert their abusive spouse to Christianity, and they believe they can do this by staying and submitting to abuse over and over.

In the face of this powerful myth, we must recognize a few truths.

First, a spouse who is abusing, extorting, threatening, or terrorizing you and/or your children is *not* persecuting you because you are a Christian (which is what those Bible verses are talking about).

They would behave this way with anyone who has less power than them, regardless of that person's faith. Their behavior is not triggered by your belief in Jesus but by their own poor emotional regulation, bad coping skills, dangerous habits, past trauma, or any variety of things that drive abusive patterns in their life.

This is why this myth is a misapplication of verses like 1 Peter 1:6. Back in the first century, there was persecution of Christians, and their lives were in danger from the governmental and religious authorities (both Roman and Jewish). Christians were being hunted down and killed. "Hardships and suffering," in this context, was political persecution—not spousal abuse.

Many New Testament writers (like Peter, Paul, and James) tried to bring comfort to Christians who were being persecuted by telling them it would all turn out for the glory and honor of Jesus Christ. Peter told people they would be persecuted and there would be a good outcome: genuine faith worth more than gold.

In this world, there is certainly suffering that is unavoidable. But the Bible doesn't call us to tolerate violence when it can be avoided, or to suffer when we could use our God-given gift of self-preservation and exit. As Justin and Lindsey Holcomb say: "We are not called to passively accept every form of pain that comes our way."[60]

Sufferings that we cannot control (cancer, natural disasters, birth defects, illness, etc.) do teach us patience and faith. But there's nothing virtuous about violence or subjecting yourself to injury when you can avoid it. There is nothing especially holy about suffering when you do not need to. Enduring, rather than getting to safety, endangers you and your children.

Jesus doesn't want you to be beaten by your spouse to bring him glory.

As one Twitter user says: "It's so easy to find [Bible] verses about persecution and suffering and make them fit your situation. I recommend reading verses about evil and what the Bible says we are to do in the face of it."

And what *does* the Bible say?

The Bible contains many examples of great people of faith who avoided suffering and violence and sought safety:

- Noah and his family avoided the flood (Genesis 6:9-22)
- Abigail defied Nabal and saved her family (1 Samuel 25)
- Rahab escaped the destruction of her city by allying herself with the Israelite spies (Joshua 2)
- Paul used his Roman citizenship as a way of avoiding being killed by a mob (Acts 22:22-29)
- Paul fled the city when he learned of a plot to kill him (Acts 9:24-25)
- Jesus himself eluded the Pharisees who tried to kill him (Matthew 12:13-15)
- David fled two times from King Saul, who threw a spear at him (1 Samuel 18:10-11)

We don't get spiritual points for suffering when we can avoid it. God told people to leave dangerous situations, in the cases of Noah, Abraham, Isaac, and Jacob. He did not miraculously fix their circumstances. He told them to act, and to get out of harm's way.

God has made us with an inborn instinct for self-preservation, and he wants us to listen to it!

---

60 Holcomb, "Does the Bible."

Furthermore, staying in a marriage with someone abusive is very unlikely to convert them to Christianity. The Bible itself says in 1 Corinthians 7:16 that you cannot know if you will save your unbelieving spouse. A person comes to accept Jesus by the power of the Holy Spirit.

And for many believers, their abusive spouse *is* a regular churchgoing Christian, perhaps even a leader in their church. In fact, many Christian men who turn to abuse do so using extreme, twisted Bible verses as rationale for their terrible behavior. They use the name of God to justify their wielding of power over vulnerable people in their care. Such behavior betrays the way they are using this belief system as a weapon for their own gain.

"Biblical patriarchy," or the teaching that men are designed by God to have all the power and control over women, is just another symptom of the fallenness of humanity. It is not God's original design. (You can read more about the problems of so-called "biblical" patriarchy in Chapter 2.)

But whether your spouse claims to be a Christian or not makes little difference. Even if they are unsaved, you can be a good spouse, but the Bible makes no guarantees about your spouse's salvation. In fact, the Apostle Paul says if that person abandons you (no longer providing material goods, shelter and love mentioned in Exodus 21:10-11), let them go. Paul also says, "How do you know, wife, whether you will save your husband? Or, how do you know, husband, whether you will save your wife?" (1 Corinthians 7:16, NIV).

As a kid, I believed God heard my prayers, and God would never put someone bad into my life, but if I allowed a troubled person to enter into my life, then I'm supposed to save him. So I met my husband, dated six months… He was not a Christian, but I could change that!

Now looking back at twenty-five years of serial infidelity and physical abuse, I had thought my husband and I were brought together so I could save him… and make him a Christian, but God's plan was totally different.

Additionally, it's illogical to compare a woman or a man enduring their abusive spouse to Jesus carrying the sins of the world on the cross and taking the punishment for all time and eternity. Jesus died to take away the penalty of sin and redeem humanity.

A woman cannot take away the penalty of her husband's sin, and vice versa.
Her suffering doesn't redeem his sin.
He alone bears his own responsibility for his sin.

It is tempting to imagine a future in which your silent suffering of abuse transforms your spouse's heart from the inside out, makes them see their bad behavior, repent, and change. This is promoted by Christian romance novels where the heroine quietly sets a good example, thus winning over a "bad boy." But in the Bible, Christians are called to stop associating with abusive, sexually immoral, selfish, or addicted people (1 Corinthians 5:11). In fact, never experiencing consequences for abusive behavior usually has the opposite effect: it keeps the abuse going.

After all, why should the dangerous spouse be motivated to make any changes? They have learned they can act out in horrible ways, and they still get to stay married to someone who keeps the household running, takes care of the kids, supports their career, picks up all of their slack, and helps keep their reputation squeaky clean in their community.

They are getting all the benefits of a committed, mutual partnership with none of the responsibilities and effort required.

Their best chance of seeing their bad behavior, repenting, and changing isn't to have you keep putting up with abuse, absorbing the devastation, and never protesting or taking a stand.

No, their best chance is to get a loud, firm wake-up call: *If you keep doing this, you will lose your marriage, your family, your social standing, and the respect of your community.*

That behavior is unacceptable, and if they want to keep what they have, they need to make major changes and take responsibility for their actions, just like all the rest of us.

One pastor rejects the myth that you should just endure:

"As a young pastor I would hear stories of women being told, 'Your black eye is your cross to bear. I wish that hadn't happened to you, but you are not free to leave your relationship because God is trying to soften your husband's heart with your faith.' I was [thinking]: That's sociopathic. This is a disease.

"Listening to their stories, I knew these women were more precious than anyone's theology or ideas about marriage. To the living God, people are infinitely more valuable than principles. In Greek, the term 'sound doctrine' means 'healthy doctrine.' If your doctrine is healthy, then the people living by it will be healthy, too."[61]
—Pastor Steve Daugherty

Abusive marriages are not healthy.

Myth Twenty-Five: You Can Only Divorce If They Hit You; Emotional, Spiritual, Financial, and Verbal Abuse Don't Count

Some Christian leaders don't consider other forms of abuse to be real abuse because they leave no visible scars or broken bones. It's the old lie, "sticks and stones will break my bones, but words will never hurt me."

However, this is not supported biblically, legally, or morally. The Bible says words matter—

- Cruel words are like stabbing someone with sword thrusts – Proverbs 12:18
- A lie is like a war club, sword, or arrow – Proverbs 25:18
- The words we say have the power of life and death – Proverbs 18:21
- Words defile a person more than physical things, such as food – Matthew 15:10-11

The Bible says words are deadly and likens them to weapons of war. In today's justice system, weaponized words and "malicious harassment" (making threats) can land a person in legal trouble.

Bribery, extortion (coercing someone to give them money), blackmail (demanding money in exchange for withholding damaging information), perjury (lying under oath), and defamation (making false accusations) are illegal. Financial abuse—such as identity theft and stealing money or property—won't give you a black eye, but it is illegal and can destroy a person. It is a crime and a violation of the commandment "Thou shalt not steal."

My husband opened accounts in my name online using my Social Security number and driver's license.

---

61 Interview with Steve Daugherty, teaching pastor at Crosspoint, Cary, NC, author of ***Experiments in Honesty.*** Host of the podcast "Noises from the Attic."

He slept with a bank teller to get an ATM card for my savings account and took everything.
He forged my signature on the checks.

The emotional pain from a cruel mother, father, teacher, or spouse hurt a long time. Verbal abuse of children or elders is a criminal offense. Malicious harassment (making threats) is a crime.

All of these do damage, and some of it can be more devastating and longer lasting than physical injury.

Evildoers and impostors will go from bad to worse, deceiving and being deceived.
—2 Timothy 3:13 (NIV)

Myth Twenty-Six: Husbands Must Cleanse and Sanctify Their Wives

This false teaching says a husband is responsible for the spiritual growth of his wife, making her holy, presenting her to God, and acting as an advocate or mediator, just like Christ does for the church.

This idea turns the wife's "cleansing" and "sanctification" into the husband's task (Ephesians 5:26-27). Some versions of this myth include:

- "You're the priest of your house."
- "You represent your wife before God."
- "The man is responsible for the spiritual life of his household."
- "The man sets the spiritual tone of his relationship."

The truth is that a husband cannot (and should not!) take the place of Jesus Christ as his wife's savior or take on the role of the Holy Spirit to sanctify her.

Each person stands before the Lord on their own.

Their decision to call upon the Lord and believe in him is their own responsibility, as is their spiritual growth. A husband is not called to do Christ's work of cleansing his wife from sin. Nor is it his job to present her to Christ. One day Jesus will present all of us (the Church) to himself.

"The moment we make the decision to trust and follow Jesus Christ as Saviour and Lord, we are sanctified, set apart as a child of God. But a process of sanctification and spiritual growth continues, aided by the Holy Spirit.
The goal of this process is that we become mature in our faith. And the ultimate role model and the pinnacle of that maturity is Jesus. *It is not our spouse.*"[62]
—Marg Mowczko (emphasis mine)

Myth Twenty-Seven: You Cannot Divorce; You Are One Flesh and Have a Soul Tie to Your Spouse

Some Christians teach that you are eternally bound to your spouse (or anyone you've had sex with) due to the Bible passage 1 Corinthians 6:13-20.

These verses were written to the church in the city of Corinth. There was a lot of sexual immorality in the church, including a case of incest in 1 Corinthians 5 and the mention of prostitution in 1 Cor. 6. This passage is warning believers in the new church in Corinth about rampant sexual immorality.

It warns that if you have sex with a prostitute, you are "one in body," and in the next three verses (18-20) it gives the remedy for this:

- "Run from sexual sin!" (Running away, or "fleeing," breaks the oneness)
- "Unite yourself with the Lord!" (Meaning drawing close to God)

In other words, the act of leaving breaks the "one flesh" bond. We turn to Christ, because our bond with the Lord is eternal and cannot be ended. You aren't bound to your spouse once you leave. Your bond to the Lord is eternal; the bond to any human being is not eternal—not even to a good spouse. After their death (or a divorce), a person is no longer bound.

Summary

As a child, I thought there was only one way to interpret Bible passages: my first pastor's way. As I read the Bible for myself and listened to a

---

62 Marg Mowczko, "The Responsibility of Husbands in Ephesians 5," ***MargMowczko.com*** (6/16/16), accesssed 10/29/19, https://margmowczko.com/responsibilities-of-husbands/.

variety of godly pastors, I came to realize they did not interpret every verse the way he did.

I believe the Bible sets a standard for the care of spouses. And abuse is not an acceptable part of that standard.

People in dangerous marriages need support, encouragement, and assurance that they've tried their best—and that there's hope for a safer, healthier life on the other side of a life-saving divorce.

Christians in this position often turn to their churches, their pastors, or other spiritual leaders for support and help—and instead, they receive shame and judgment from other Christians who believe in these destructive myths. Years later, when the truth comes out, pastors shake their heads and wonder, "Why did she put up with that for so long?"

And I reply, "Because you told her to."

Eventually, these struggling believers shame and judge themselves, becoming captive to these false beliefs. Self-doubt haunts them. They stay for years, even decades, in horrific situations, desperately trying to make it work.

And the devil, who loves cruel marriages, rejoices.

But our God is a God of freedom and life, not cruelty and captivity.

His love casts out all fear, and his power breaks us from bondage. By his Spirit, we can release the hold that these dangerous myths have on us and on the church. And the way to do that is with God's truth.

MYTH 1 : *You just fell out of love.*
TRUTH : No. Many divorces are life-saving.

MYTH 2 : *You just don't take God-ordained marriage seriously.*
TRUTH : Life-saving divorcees took marriage very seriously. Their *spouse* didn't—with their actions, not just their words.

MYTH 3 : *You just didn't try hard enough.*
TRUTH : People in the most destructive marriages try harder, and longer, than most spouses.

MYTH 4 : *You didn't attend church enough.*
TRUTH : Churchgoing doesn't make dangerous marriages safe, and it doesn't make dangerous spouses magically change.

MYTH 5 : *Christians have to forgive over and over again, forever.*
TRUTH : Christians can forgive and get out of a destructive marriage.

MYTH 6 : *You're exaggerating! We'd all know if your spouse was* that *bad.*
TRUTH : It is almost impossible to spot dangerous spouses from outside of the marriage.

MYTH 7 : *It's your fault, because "it takes two to tango."*
TRUTH : It only takes one destructive spouse to make a marriage dangerous.

MYTH 8 : *It's your fault, because you're not perfect, either.*
TRUTH : We don't have to be perfect before we call for a stop to abuse and cruelty.

MYTH 9 : *You can't demand good treatment. Christians have no rights.*
TRUTH : It is godly and biblical to call for justice and loving treatment, for ourselves and others.

MYTH 10: *It's your fault, because you didn't give your spouse enough sex.*
TRUTH : Cheating or sexual abuse is never justified. Your spouse's sexual addiction or deviance can't be fixed by giving them more sex.

MYTH 11: *It's your fault, because you deserve punishment.*
TRUTH : No one deserves abuse or cruelty—ever. God calls us to love one another, not mistreat and betray each other.

MYTH 12: *It's your fault, because you didn't submit enough.*
TRUTH : Submission doesn't prevent abuse. If there is abuse, commanding more submission makes things worse, not better.

MYTH 13: *The person who files for divorce caused the divorce.*
TRUTH : The person who betrays, abuses, and breaks the vows is the one who caused the divorce.

MYTH 14: *Divorcing bestows a curse on your family.*
TRUTH : A life-saving divorce brings God's freedom to the family, not a curse.

MYTH 15: *God will heal your marriage if you pray enough.*
TRUTH : God does not promise to heal all marriages in answer to our prayers. Sometimes, he answers our prayers by helping us get out of a marriage when it turns dangerous.

MYTH 16: *It's God's will for you to suffer: "Holiness Over Happiness"*
TRUTH : God's will is for justice, love, and truth to be lifted high—not for his children to live in silent suffering and bondage.

MYTH 17: *Marriage is God's* best *way to mature you.*
TRUTH : God matures us in many ways, not only through marriage. He can mature us through a life-saving divorce and through rebuilding our lives afterward.

MYTH 18: *God forbids all divorce; all divorce is sin; divorce is the unpardonable sin.*
TRUTH : Scripture shows that God gives permission for divorce.

MYTH 19: *Your divorce will shatter the image of Christ and the church.*
TRUTH : No human being is powerful enough to shatter the image of Christ and the church. Abuse and betrayal dishonor Christ, not life-saving divorces.

MYTH 20: *If you are godly, you can marry any Christian, and it will work.*
TRUTH : It matters whom you marry, because a healthy marriage takes two to build, not just one.

MYTH 21: *Divorce will destroy your children. You should stay for the sake of your kids.*
TRUTH : Dangerous marriages harm children by making them victims of cruelty, or witnesses of it. Life-saving divorce can get them to safety and help them to thrive.

MYTH 22: *It takes two parents to raise good kids.*
TRUTH : Emotionally healthy single parents and stepparents can do as good a job of raising healthy kids as anyone else.

MYTH 23: *You can't divorce your spouse, because they don't know any better.*
TRUTH: We can put a stop to abuse even when the abuser doesn't "get it." We can love someone, and leave our dangerous marriage to them, at the same time.

MYTH 24: *If you stay and suffer, you might save your spouse, and you will glorify Christ.*
TRUTH: Your spouse is not abusing you because of your faith, and Christ is not glorified by your anguish or by the danger you or your children are facing. Staying and suffering does not guarantee you will win an abusive spouse to Christ.

MYTH 25: *You can only divorce if they hit you.*
TRUTH: Emotional/verbal abuse, financial abuse, and spiritual abuse are all unacceptable forms of treatment and are grounds for divorce, both from a biblical and legal perspective.

MYTH 26: *Husbands must cleanse and sanctify their wives.*
TRUTH: Jesus cleanses and sanctifies us, not our spouses. Husbands cannot and should not try to take the place of Jesus in their spouse's life.

MYTH 27: *You cannot divorce because you are one flesh and have a soul tie.*
TRUTH: Biblically, the one-flesh bond is broken simply by leaving and walking away. Only our bond with the Lord is eternal.

So if these myths torment you, making you second- and third- and fourth-guess yourself, cling to God's truth.

The abuse, neglect, infidelity, or other immorality is not your fault.

You tried hard enough—and then some! There is nothing more you can do. Your kids are not likely to be ruined forever if you get a life-saving divorce. God will not punish you for divorcing. On the contrary, he will help you through, and he will help you heal afterward.

Don't live in silent suffering, captive to the bad behavior of your spouse, mired in perpetual disrespect, contempt, or misery. You are valuable to Jesus.

Let God's truth set you free.

And if you are reading this as someone in the church—a pastor, a Bible study leader, or just a friend—and someone you love is in a dangerous marriage, don't speak any of these myths to them and contribute to their ongoing bondage. Instead, cling to God's truth, and just say a few simple, powerful words:

I believe you.

I see your pain, and I am so sorry this is happening to you.

It's not your fault.

Only you know what's going on behind closed doors.

I support you.

You can love Jesus AND get a life-saving divorce.

I care about you.

If you ever need to talk, I'm here.

God cares more about **you** *than he cares about your marital status.*

AM I BEING ABUSED?

I love this Psalm from the Bible. In it, the writer says that God sees our troubles and our tears. He hears people who are afflicted. He supports them and listens to them.

But you, God, see the trouble of the afflicted;
you consider their grief and take it in hand.
The victims commit themselves to you;
you are the helper of the fatherless...
You, LORD, hear the desire of the afflicted;
you encourage them, and you listen to their cry...
—Psalm 10:14, 17 (NIV)

Perhaps you are in trouble—a difficult marriage. Perhaps you have shed tears of grief, been afflicted, and felt alone. And I'm sure you too have cried out to a loving God who cares about the afflicted.

As Chapter 6 discusses, in the Bible, marriage was created for companionship, not just for sex and having children. God required the husband to provide material care and love to the wife, and if he didn't, she was free to go, get divorced, and find someone who truly cared for her.

One Christian counselor who specializes in sexual addictions put it this way:

"A marriage must be **safe** and **loving**, or at least respectful,
otherwise it's not a marriage.
It could be kidnapping, incarceration, or servitude.
But it is not a marriage."[63]

63 Michael Alvarez, MFT, personal conversation.

In other words, both people must invest effort to make sure the marriage feels safe and loving to both spouses, not just one.

In an abusive marriage, only one spouse's feelings matter.

Everyone else makes that one person feels safe and loved. No one else matters, apart from their utility to the abuser.

An abuser can be defined as: A person who feels deeply *entitled* to wield power over their victim, believing themselves *justified* in using a wide variety of methods, including fear, obligation, guilt, and threats, to maintain their control of their victim.

In other words, the abuser feels entitled to control you and mistreat you and will use many different tactics to do it. He or she will look for any excuse to coerce you to comply. This is different from a spouse simply speaking up and asking for their needs to be met.

In a good marriage, *both* spouses work to make sure the other feels safe and loved, and both show gratitude for the other's capabilities.

But where there is abuse, one spouse carries the burden for the problems in the marriage. They are viewed as have no worth or value other than the benefits they provide to the abuser. In an abusive marriage, the abuser gets off scot-free.

For example:

- Do you feel it's your responsibility to fix your spouse, to change their mood from sullen to happy, or to make sure they feel loved?
- Do you feel that your spouse's emotions are the only ones in the family that matter?
- Do you feel you should sacrifice your wellbeing for your spouse's career, hobbies, and goals?
- Do you feel if only you were sexually available enough, you could keep your spouse from viewing porn or being unfaithful?
- Do you feel that if you were only quiet and submissive enough, your spouse would automatically feel more loving toward you?
- Do you make excuses to your friends and family for your spouse's rudeness at birthday parties or last-minute absences from family gatherings?
- Does your pity for your spouse's bad childhood drive you to try to fill the empty hole in their heart with your generosity and self-sacrifice?

- Do you feel responsible for keeping up an act, putting on a composed demeanor or a happy face, to cover for your spouse's behavior?
- Do you feel you have to keep up appearances in order to keep your family's reputation in the community?
- Do you feel that you are starting to doubt what you saw or heard, to wonder if your perceptions were really true, and to question your experiences, because your spouse tells you you're crazy, stupid, or incompetent?
- Do you feel that you are only valuable and beloved if you are doing exactly what pleases your spouse?

If you are carrying the responsibility for your spouse's behavior, that is a sign of abuse.

If you and the children often walk on eggshells to avoid setting your spouse off, that's a sign of abuse.

When you feel that it's all your fault, even though other people disapprove of your spouse's behavior, that is a sign of abuse.

When your spouse blames you for *making* them cheat, lie, drink, or hurt you, that's a sign of abuse.

When your spouse treats you as if your time, energy, talents, interests, health, or loyalty are unimportant, that is abuse.

When your spouse brings gifts and says "I love you," yet treats you disrespectfully, that's not love—that's abuse.

Recognizing Abuse

For most of us, the hardest thing to do is to recognize that we have been abused and perhaps are still being abused.

Sometimes it can feel scary, intimidating, or wrong to call it "abuse."

We tend to think of abuse as something that happens to other people, something that only totally depraved monsters do—not something that can happen in a marriage we chose for ourselves, where there have been good times, and with a spouse we once loved very deeply (and maybe still do).

If this is you, please know that you are not alone—this happens to many, many people—and you are not crazy.

You also do not have to call what is happening to you "abuse" yet, if you are not ready for that. You can try something that feels easier:

- *This is not okay.*
- *This is not acceptable.*
- *This is hurtful behavior.*

In this chapter, and in the rest of the book, I use the word *abuse* to describe behaviors that make marriages dangerous. But if that word is hard or impossible for you to apply to yourself and your situation, you can substitute something that feels easier to grasp.

When a marriage turns dangerous, sometimes the pain is so intense and so constant, and the struggle to just survive each day is so all-consuming, that it can be next to impossible to take a step back from the situation and truly understand what is happening.

When you're in it, it feels inescapable and inevitable, and you can't imagine that a safer, happier life is possible. Maybe you tell yourself this is just how marriage is, and this is just what it looks like to love someone and be loved by someone. Marriage is hard work—right?

But somewhere deep inside you, a still, small voice says, *Surely it's not supposed to be* this *hard.*

Something's wrong here.

In that still, small voice, we hear Jesus calling us into greater freedom and release from bondage, though the road to that freedom may be long and challenging. We take one small step at a time, as we are able, and God walks right beside us, leading and guiding and strengthening us to face the next step.

In this chapter, we will work on one important step in particular: learning to see and name the wrong behavior as *wrong*.

Abuse and betrayal are not how marriage is supposed to be, and it's not the way God designed love to work between a husband and wife. It really *shouldn't* be this hard! Something really *is* wrong!

Furthermore, it's important to realize that spouses who behave dangerously and abusively in their marriages tend to do so in predictable ways. Your spouse is not the first or only person using these tactics—far from it! In fact, these behaviors are so common that they have names and can be identified.

Victims of abuse often gain immense confidence, validation, and freedom through understanding what abuse looks like and how it works, and that is what we are going to do in this chapter—together.

5 Types of Control and Abuse

- **Physical/sexual** abuse is the willful infliction of physical pain or injury, such as slapping, bruising, sexually molesting, or restraining. More covert methods also constitute abuse, such as blocking your way, sleep deprivation, physical abandonment, displaying weapons, or giving you drugs or medicine without consent.
- **Verbal/Emotional/Mental** abuse is the infliction of mental or emotional anguish, such as humiliating or threatening language and treatment. More covert methods also are abusive, such as lying, accusing, isolating, blaming, denying, demeaning, ignoring you, or demanding to know where you go and whom you've spoken to. *Gaslighting* also falls under this category. (The term *gaslighting* comes from a 1944 movie and is now used in psychology to mean chronic manipulation in which the gaslighter (the abuser) causes the victim to question their identity, their judgment, their self-worth, and their perceptions of reality.)
- **Financial** or material exploitation is another form of abuse, in which the money, credit, or belongings of a spouse are used—or withheld—without their consent. This also includes running up debt, making major purchases, and withholding information about joint taxes, banks, and credit card accounts.
- **Neglect** is the failure of a caretaker to provide goods or services necessary to avoid physical harm, mental anguish, or illness:[64] things such as food, water, clothing, shelter, or medical care. Indifference to your wellbeing falls into this category.
- **Spiritual** abuse is the willful use of religious beliefs to manipulate or shame one spouse into giving control to the other spouse, who "lords it over" their partner, rather than giving each spouse the

64 "Elder or Dependent Adult Abuse," ***Psychology Today*** (4/2/19), accessed 6/29/19, https://www.psychologytoday.com/us/conditions/elder-or-dependent-adult-abuse. The first four types of abuse are adapted from this article.

responsibility to follow a loving God above any other person. It is also spiritually abusive to use religious sayings, scriptures, threats of divine punishment, threatened withdrawal of divine favor/ blessing, or negative spiritual judgments about your character to make you remain in a dangerous situation. People who claim prophetic authority to tell you what to do with your life, or who claim special knowledge about God's mind and will that "people like you" don't have (rather than recognizing your ability to hear from God directly) are also being spiritually abusive. Note that spiritual abuse can be perpetuated by one spouse against the other, but it can also be perpetuated by a pastor, religious leader, or an entire religious community, against an individual whose wellbeing is at stake.

ABUSIVE BEHAVIORS

This is a list of examples, not a complete list.[65]

Physical Abuse, Sexual Abuse, and Neglect

Much of physical violence and sexual abuse is a felony, misdemeanor, or criminal behavior. It is illegal in many states. These behaviors are abusive when directed against an adult spouse, and also when directed against children.

- Throwing knives, stones, or other objects at you or near you. Spitting at you.
- Slapping, hitting, kicking, punching, burning, dragging, shaking, kicking, choking, shoving, or "accidentally" knocking into you. Breaking bones or twisting joints.
- Stalking, repeatedly following you, or harassing you, in a way that would make you fear injury. This is a crime in many states.

---

65 "Domestic Violence," ***The United States Department of Justice*** (6/16/17), accessed 4/9/18, https://web.archive.org/web/20180409111243/https:/www.justice.gov/ovw/domestic-violence. The Department of Justice definition of domestic violence includes physical, emotional, economic, or psychological actions or threats of actions. "We define domestic violence as a pattern of abusive behavior in any relationship that is used by one partner to gain or maintain power and control over another intimate partner."

- Waving a gun or displaying a gun—or any other weapon, such as a baseball bat or knife.
- Holding down, tying up, kidnapping, locking up, or restraining you against your will.
- Threatening to hurt you, your pets, your children, your possessions, your heirlooms and valuables, saying, "You deserved it because you were _______." Frightening you with dangerous behavior: for example, fast driving, holding you or your child or pet over a ledge.
- Withholding food, water, clothing, heat, electricity, or other basics.
- Towering over you, pinning you against the wall, blocking your way, or invading your space.
- Giving you drugs or medicine without consent. Hiding, removing, or tampering with contraceptives. Deliberately having sex without contraceptives with the goal of spreading disease or impregnating you against your will.
- Sleep deprivation. Frequently waking you up in the middle of the night for non-emergency issues, to have sex, or to criticize you.
- Sex without your consent. Unwillingness to accept your "no." Unwanted sexual contact, molestation, fondling, or brushing up against you without consent. Marital rape.
- Abandonment: Either temporary (for example, leaving you alongside the road and driving away), or long term, by leaving for weeks or months without any significant support or communication, relying on you to hold things together.
- Neglect during medical situations: Surgery, delivery of a baby, or times you cannot handle basic life functions (using the bathroom, feeding yourself).
- Wife "spanking" for disobedience (also known as Christian Domestic Discipline),[66] which is coercion to establish control.
- Pressuring you to have sex in trade for something, perhaps their cooperation or good mood.

---

66 Julie Ann Smith, "The Christian Patriarchy Movement's Dark Secret of Wife Spanking," ***Spiritual Sounding Board*** (1/3/14), accessed 1/3/20, https://spiritualsoundingboard.com/2014/01/03/the-christian-patriarchy-movements-dark-secret-of-wife-spanking/. For more on the topic of wife spanking, see the article above, or go to thelifesavingdivorce.com/links.

- Exhibitionism, voyeurism (watching people through the window, or other situations where people would reasonably expect privacy), or exposure to pornography against your will.
- For children: Exposure to pornography, taking photos of children in a sexualized situation, having sex in front of children, incest, or attempted sexual contact.

Definition of Battery

The crime of battery is "the intentional touching of another in an angry manner, or the intentional use of force or violence against another. Grabbing someone's arm, pushing or punching a person, or striking a victim with an object, all are crimes of battery." This applies to adults and to children.

Definition of Assault

In some states, "assault does not involve actual physical contact, and is defined as an attempt to commit a physical attack or as threatening actions that cause a person to feel afraid of impending violence."

https://www.criminaldefenselawyer.com/crime-penalties/federal/felony-assault-battery.htm

Verbal and Emotional Abuse

Mental abuse (sometimes called psychological aggression and control) causes the survivor to question their own reality, sanity, judgment, and worth. It makes them feel they deserved or caused the abuse. An occasional incident (a snarky comment, a grumpy eye-roll, a flare-up of temper) may not be emotional abuse. Watch for a pattern: repeated incidents combined with an attempt to control.

- Having a chronic pattern of criticism, belittling, blaming, and telling you it is for your own good, so you become a better person.
- Shaming/sarcasm: for example, "You can try, but you'll never be very good at it."
- Having a pattern of name-calling, slurs, put-downs, screaming, or yelling.
- Cyber-stalking, demanding to know where you are at all times, tracking you via GPS, or installing cameras, spyware, or a keystroke

logger (recorder) on your computer to capture your passwords and read your messages.

- Using location-sharing apps or "find my phone" apps to monitor you.
- Downloading apps on your phone to track you without your permission.
- Hacking your email, looking at your email account without permission, hacking your social media, having unwanted access to bank, music, messaging, or other online accounts. (Hacking your email is a felony.)
- Giving you a mobile phone, computer, or tablet they've set up for you (which is capable of collecting information about you, listening to your conversations, your calls, and tracking your location), especially if they are known to be good with computers.
- Sending you dozens of texts a day to ask where you are, who you're with, or what you're doing.
- Making verbal threats of harm, leaving, divorce, or suicide: Anything that makes you live in fear.
- Demanding that you keep secrets, staying silent, not telling anyone what happened.
- Requiring that you report back to them the details of your conversations with others.
- Professing love often, but words and actions don't match.
- Listening to and recording your private phone calls routinely. Installing listening devices and cameras, or using software to monitor you.
- Refusing to talk, but expressing moodiness, sulking, and self-pity. Forcing you to guess what's wrong. Saying "If you loved me, you would know why I'm mad."
- Chronic false accusations of infidelity, stealing, cheating, or lying.
- Blame shifting: "I wouldn't have done _____, if you hadn't ______." "I went to the bar because you're in a bad mood all the time." "You drove me to do that because of your nagging." "You made me do it." "I would have gone to your mother's birthday party if you hadn't ______." "I wouldn't have seen prostitutes if you had been meeting my sexual needs."
- Backing out of commitments at the last minute. Or stonewalling: Never making the commitment, leaving you hanging, or coming too late to the event.

- Making demands of your time, energy, or money, but allowing you no voice, vote, or veto.
- Interruptions: Frequently interrupting you during phone calls, at work, naps, bathing, prayer, or a planned event, for something that is not an emergency. Taking non-emergency phone calls while you are together in the middle of an important event or discussion.
- Blaming you for things that happened to you. "If you weren't wearing that, you wouldn't have been raped."
- Suicide threats. "If you don't do what I say, I can't go on living." "If you leave me, I'll kill myself, and it would be all your fault."
- Silent treatment (punishing you by pretending you don't exist). Not talking to you, not acknowledging your presence, or ignoring your attempts to communicate.
- Stonewalling (refusing to talk, discuss important issues, or make decisions in a reasonable timeframe). "I don't have time for your drama." "I'm busy right now." "I can't do that now." "I won't sign that."
- Humiliating you in public, in front of friends, children, etc. For example, saying, "You're crazy. You need to see a psychologist."
- Undermining your reputation, smearing your character to friends, family, children, bosses, and pastors. "She's a weak person." "You can't trust everything he says." "She doesn't know what she's talking about." "He's not the sharpest guy."
- Finding people to enlist as allies in their cause to discredit you and make you look bad in your workplace, school, social media, neighborhood, organizations, or church. By convincing others that you are the problem, they keep their hands clean. These allies are often called "flying monkeys," who show their loyalty to the abuser by looking for ways to target you.
- Threatening with injury, and claiming it is fair due to your bad behavior. "If you fall, you're only getting what you deserve." "If you do that again, I'm going to snap, and who knows what I might do when I get angry." Or showing no concern for your wellbeing when you are injured: "If you fall, you're only getting what you deserve."
- Threatening you with revenge porn, posting your texts and/or photos in order to get revenge or to blackmail you back into the relationship.
- Body-shaming. Saying that if you were prettier, skinnier, more

sexually appealing, or more sexually satisfying, your marriage would be better.

- Claiming you will never see your children again if you don't do as you're told. "If you divorce me, I'll take everything." "The judge will see you're a horrible parent."
- Lying. Changing the story. "I didn't do that." "How can you say that? You were there." "You're just making that up." "They're lying because they don't like me."
- Turning the tables and accusing the victim of being judgmental and unforgiving. "You're just a hypocrite."
- Provoking you in public so you react in front of others, making it appear that you are the aggressive spouse.
- Causing a fight and forcing *you* to apologize.
- Acting helpless to avoid responsibilities.
- Justifying crossing your boundaries by questioning your decision-making ability. "You've got mental problems." "You're overly sensitive." "Sure, I did, but what about when you did this?" "You've got issues." "You always gripe about the same thing." "You're always nagging."
- Giving a gift to force someone to extend forgiveness, while pretending the abuse never happened, making no amends, and doing nothing to change the problematic behavior pattern. (For example, a father exploding at his young son one day, then buying the boy a bicycle the next without ever referring to the explosion, as though the gift settles the "score." Often abusers who do this grow enraged if their victim brings up the abusive event. "I bought you a bike! Stop complaining!")
- Minimizing or explaining away bad behavior. "You're angry over nothing." "That's not true; you're just over-reacting." "That's not how it is."
- Threats, if you say no to requests for sex: "I can get sex elsewhere."
- Seducing you and then rejecting you.
- Mocking your looks or your clothes: "You are ugly." "That outfit is ugly." "No one would want to have sex with you."
- Degrading you sexually: "I saved myself for you, but you've had other partners. You're dirty." "You're no good in bed. I've had better sex." "You've got a long line of sex partners coming around. You're just a ____."

- Criticizing your hobbies, interests, or sports. Resenting time and effort you spend on things you enjoy, often in the face of their time/money use for their leisure activities.
- Degrading your capabilities: "You can't make it without me." "You're weak."
- Bribing you to stay silent about the abuse by giving gifts, vacations, or other things valuable to you.
- Saying you are crazy or stupid, then excusing it. "Hey, I was only joking." "Can't you take a joke?" "I never said that." "You're just imagining things." "That never happened." "I never said that. I said this." These are classic examples of gaslighting.
- Saying you're incapable of living without them. "You'd never make it on your own." "No one would hire you." "You're too stupid." "No one else could possibly love you."
- Claiming you have no worth apart from them. "Without me, you'd be nothing." "Shouldn't I get first priority in your life?"
- Refusing to be pleased by your efforts to be a good spouse. Saying you ought to be grateful for even the smallest amount of respect, care, affection, or appreciation. Belittling your looks, your mannerisms, or your values.
- Using "always" and "never" to describe your behavior. Exaggerating your behavior to smear your character.
- Walking out of a party or gathering in a way that would draw attention. Eyes turn to you, and you are left to make explanations.
- A pattern of refusing to discuss a major issue fully, explore various options, list pros and cons, and weigh the risks and rewards of each. Failure to listen well.
- Claiming you deserve nothing good and your opinions are worthless. "That's just stupid. No-one thinks that."
- Condescending and patronizing: "I know you try hard to be a good wife, but you'll never be a real gem." "You can work out at the gym, but you'll never be attractive to me." "You can read all those books and take classes, but you're not smart enough to live without me."
- Predicting you will fail at anything you attempt on your own. "You're a failure." "That might be a good idea, but you'd never be able to pull it off." "You're not good at figuring this stuff out like I am. You should let me do it for you."

- Claiming that *everyone* knows you are the problem, and that *everyone* sides with the abuser. "No one believes you."
- Making major decisions unilaterally that they know would affect you: Calling your boss or coworkers, opening a new credit card account, making a major purchase, or taking on new debt.
- Lecturing you about mistakes you have made or might make, talking on and on about their experience and knowledge, and generally treating you and others as if you are beneath them.
- Unwilling to listen to your goals and find the best way to meet them.
- Treating you like a child. Stooping to threats or bribery to get your cooperation rather than using respectful means.
- Using social media to bully, stalk, threaten, or intimidate you.
- Changing the rules so they always apply to you, but never to them.
- Threatening to turn people against you and tarnish your good name (your kids, family, friends, coworkers, boss, etc.). "No one will ever believe you." "Sure, go to the police. They won't believe you."
- Isolating you from family and friends. Prohibiting communication with family or friends.
- Coercing you to do their wishes by blackmail: "If you don't do what I want, I'll tell everyone what you did." Or by extortion: "If you don't do what I want, something bad will happen to you [your loved ones, your possessions, your business, etc.]."
- Making false accusations with no evidence (defamation).
- Making hateful or demeaning glances and gestures. Rolling their eyes, smirking, or raising an eyebrow when you speak to indicate that your opinions are invalid or ridiculous. Hand signals or gestures to indicate you are beneath them.
- Blaming strangers for coming up and starting flirtatious conversations with them. Claiming to be innocent and passive in sexual encounters. "I can't help it; she came on to me."
- In contrast, blaming *you* for unwanted attention, flirtation, or sexual harassment you receive. "He wouldn't have hit on you if you weren't dressed that way." "You aren't modest enough." "You're a slut / whore / asking for it."
- Indifference toward you and your wellbeing. Ignoring basic needs.

- Giving the silent treatment or cold shoulder.
- Insisting on knowing your passwords, suggesting you would let them have your passwords if you had "nothing to hide." Keeping control of your passwords.
- Demanding to know where you were, what you did, and who you talked with. "Why did you go there today? What were you doing?" Giving you a curfew.
- Telling you they have the right to go through your purse, billfold, briefcase, or phone. Asking to see your mobile phone or taking it from you.
- Excusing their hostile treatment by saying they do it only to make you stronger or better, or to teach you a lesson.
- Threatening to destroy you legally or professionally, and to drag your reputation through the mud.
- Demanding proofs of your love or loyalty: "If you really loved me, you would _________." "If you truly care about me, you would sign this."
- When you confront them, immediately turning the tables to accuse you of being un-Christian: unloving, judgmental, and unforgiving. "You claim to be a Christian, but you aren't loving at all. You're a hypocrite." "If you were a Christian, you would forgive me and give me another chance."
- Not allowing you to visit friends or family. "They are always against me. I don't want to be around them." "You like them more than me." "Shouldn't I come first in your life?"
- Confessing to a minor betrayal in order to appear honest, and demanding forgiveness, when in reality there's a larger betrayal yet to be revealed.
- Excusing and minimizing seductive behavior as "boys will be boys." "Sure, I think our babysitter is cute. Any guy would." "This is just how guys are."
- Excusing their porn addiction. "Well, if you just _______, I wouldn't watch porn."
- Acting smug or superior.
- Muttering things under their breath. Sighing. "Here we go again." "Why is that not a surprise?"

Financial Abuse

Some of the examples that follow constitute criminal behavior and are illegal on state and/or federal levels.

- Stealing money from your purse or bank account.
- Stealing valuables and pawning or selling them, or using them as blackmail.
- Using your ID to open new accounts and change addresses.
- Refusing to give you access to bank accounts or credit cards used for routine essentials, such as food, clothing, transportation, utilities, fuel, and supplies.
- Storing, keeping track of, and using your user name, passwords, and account IDs without your permission on your electronic devices, including computers, phones, and tablets.
- Opening new credit cards that bill to your bank account without your agreement or without discussing it with you first.
- Running up credit card debt and taking out loans without discussing it.
- Demanding loans for friends and relatives that actually are used in another way.
- Lying about missing or damaged valuables.
- "Accidentally" losing or breaking things of sentimental or monetary value to you, especially after a fight, as a passive-aggressive way of punishing you (often while denying they are upset or did it intentionally, which is gaslighting).
- Removing your access to essential funds as a penalty for making small accounting mistakes or a late payment.
- Demanding to be added to the title (ownership) of a house or real estate they didn't buy with you.
- Demanding you refinance the house and give them the cash.
- Selling your family home, car, or other marital property without your consent.
- Making major decisions unilaterally that they know would affect you: for example, telling your boss you are quitting; prohibiting you from earning money; opening a new credit card account and making a major purchase; or taking on new debt.
- Without your agreement, using their own paycheck for their own

pleasure, leisure, recreation, sports, and other activities, while demanding you pay for all essentials (housing, food, medical insurance) for the family.

- Blackmail. "If you don't give me money, I'll tell the police, your boss, or your pastor what you did."
- Extortion. "Something bad will happen to you if you don't give me money."
- Refusing to help support the family in terms of money, time, effort, or priority.

Spiritual Abuse

Forced obedience is forbidden by Jesus, who says Christians must not exercise authority or "lord it over" others (Matthew 20:25-26), but many people try. The same people who quote these verses don't recognize that basic material care (food, clothing, shelter, etc.) and affection are the minimum standards the Bible requires of a spouse, as is discussed in Chapter 6.

Note that spiritual abuse can be a tool of control that one spouse uses against another, but it can also be something perpetuated by a pastor or other spiritual authority—or even an entire church community or denomination—to dictate and control the way an individual believer lives his or her life. In contrast, Scripture gives a believer the freedom of conscience on topics such as money, marriage, and religious observance.

- "You must submit and obey me in everything… because the Bible says so." Ignoring the passages that say submission is for *all* believers, not just wives, as well as the passages that say husbands must love their wives, be sacrificial, and give wives the same care and treatment they get.
- "You must give me sex whenever I want. I have a right to your body. You cannot deprive me."
- "You must stay at home and care for the kids and the house all your life, regardless of your own talents, skills, or desires."
- "You must be silent because you're a woman, like the Apostle Paul says. Know your place."
- "You are a sinner and have no right to claim you deserve good treatment. You deserve nothing more than the privilege of being a slave."

- "Your suffering in this marriage brings glory to God and makes you holy."
- "You claim to be a Christian, and therefore you must forgive me and get together again."
- "You owe God everything. Jesus paid the price for your soul. So every choice you make must serve God through ministry. You cannot have fun, pleasure, hobbies, friendships, possessions, pets, or fun activities."
- "You have no rights. You cannot claim to be a victim, because Christ was a greater victim. If you are angry or want restitution, you are in sin."
- Telling you that you must ignore your own God-given instincts for self-preservation and instead that you must obey what the church or person in spiritual authority thinks you should do.
- Claiming to have special knowledge about what God's will is for your life—knowledge that they say you can't access by going to God directly. Claiming to have heard from God about what is right for you and what choice you need to make in a given situation.
- Threatening you with the wrath of God or with the loss of God's favor if you don't do as they say and make the choices they are telling you to make with regard to your marriage.
- Promising special, exclusive access to God (God's power, God's blessings, the knowledge of God) if you support their ministry and follow their marriage advice.
- Threatening you with separation from God and divine punishment if you try to leave their church or ministry. Telling you you're not a real Christian if you don't follow God the way they think you should.
- Telling you that leaving your marriage and/or leaving one specific church is the same thing as leaving Jesus (sinning, being disobedient to God, being apostate, or going to hell, etc.).
- Using scriptures or church language to shame you for having feelings of anger, desperation, fear, or rage in response to abuse or betrayal.
- Telling you if you were a better Christian, loved God more, prayed or read your Bible the right amount, went to church more, or gave more money or time to church endeavors, that: you would have

constantly positive emotions, your struggles would be resolved, the abuse would stop, and/or your marriage would be fully healed.

THE DULUTH WHEEL OF POWER AND CONTROL

This helpful diagram, the Power & Control Wheel,[67] shows the tactics abusive husbands use to ensure power and control over their wives when they have already used **physical violence**.

On average, nearly half of the men who batter their wives do so three times a year.[68]

Note: Though it is rarer for the female spouse to be the abuser, it does happen; this chart uses female pronouns for the victim, but anyone can be a victim of abuse, not just women.

A divorce attorney, whose practice includes a lot of people of faith, said, "My clients often describe abusive behaviors, but often don't see themselves as abused. Then I show them the Duluth Wheel. I try to do it gently. They start to cry."[69]

The next wheel, the Duluth Wheel of Equality, on page 144, is the counterpart of the Power and Control Wheel. It shows what a godly, loving, mutual marriage should look like.

(For some Christians, the word "equality" makes them skittish, because they think it is a liberal idea and therefore not biblical. If this is how you feel, you can replace the word "equality" with a word like "mutuality" or "godly love." The concept is the same, regardless of what you choose to call it.)

---

67 "The Duluth Wheel of Power and Control," and "The Duluth Wheel of Equality," *The Duluth Model*, Domestic Abuse Intervention Programs (Duluth, MN, © 1982, 2019). Used by permission. Retrieved 1/7/19. For more information, including FAQs and gender-specific wording, go to www.theduluthmodel.org.

68 Anne H. Flitcraft and Susan M. Hadley, et al., "Diagnostic and Treatment Guidelines on Domestic Violence," ***American Medical Association*** 6 (1992): 6, accessed 1/3/20, http://www.ncdsv.org/images/AMA_Diag&TreatGuideDV_3-1992.pdf.

69 This divorce attorney gave me a private phone interview, under condition of anonymity.

© 1982, 2019 Domestic Abuse Intervention Programs (Duluth, MN). Used with permission.

Warrior reborn @Elizabe43906267 · Sep 8, 2019
Replying to @GGBaskerville
Oh the **Duluth** Wheel! **Terrified** me when my domestic abuse worker first showed it me, but it was a big aid in beginning to acknowledge that I was a victim, and that the man who I promised to love forever had done nothing but abuse me.

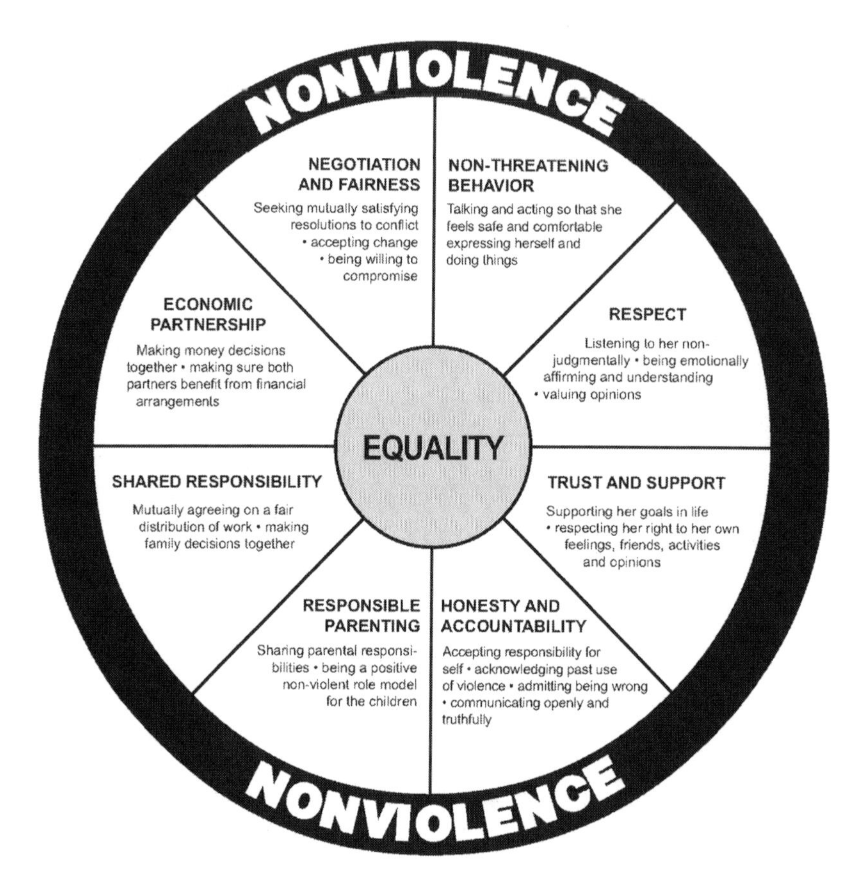

© 1982, 2019 Domestic Abuse Intervention Programs (Duluth, MN).

THE ABUSE CYCLE

I'll never forget the day that one of our pastors came to my divorce recovery group and explained the abuse cycle. It was so powerful and eye-opening. Those of us in recovery finally had an explanation of how abuse works.

In this next section, we will address the Abuse Cycle and look at a few helpful systems that enable people to identify and recognize abusive behaviors.

The cycle of domestic violence includes three parts:

- Abuse/Violence – the abusive event itself.
- Honeymoon Phase – a deceptive period of calm, harmony, and even intimacy, following the abusive event; a dramatic, temporary display of remorse in which manipulation still continues. (These are the sweet times that keep many abused spouses in the relationship.)
- Building Tension or Agitation – the gradual increase in strain when you sense your spouse is getting upset; "walking on eggshells," waiting for the inevitable explosion.

The Abuse Cycle helps victims understand why there are "good times" in their marriage. Experts now emphasize that the Honeymoon Phase is still abuse, but with different tactics. They argue that calling it a *honeymoon* makes it seem like a break from the abuse, a change in behavior, or a sign of true remorse and understanding of harm done—when in reality it is just as abusive, manipulative, and deceptive as the other phases. We can more accurately call it "Manipulative Kindness."[70]

This is important to understand, but I also see a lot of value in learning about the Honeymoon Phase. Why? Because after looking at the examples of physical, emotional, and spiritual abuse, spouses often say, "That's not me. Life with my spouse is not filled with conflict *every* day. We've had good times, some good memories."

The truth is, *most* abusive households do not appear abusive every day.

But sadly, abuse is often hidden and inflicted on the victim in covert ways. The abuser deliberately switches tactics, using gifts, tearful repentance, and promises to change. Behind the scenes, the manipulation, deceit, and control are the same.[71]

The thing to recognize here is that *abuse has nothing to do with the victim*. It is the abusive person's own problem—their inability to emotionally regulate themselves and respond safely, appropriately, and maturely to the many frustrations and difficulties of life.

In this world, each of us must learn (hopefully at a young age) how to manage our emotions and our behavior when we aren't getting what we want, not blame everyone else.

---

70 Julie Owens, "The Myth of the 'Cycle of Abuse,'" ***Julie Owens: Violence Against Women Consultant*** (5/9/18), accessed 9/19/19, **https://www.domesticviolenceexpert.org/newsletter/2018/5/9/newsletter-may-2018**. Julie Owens does church training programs on domestic violence.
71 For more on this, see Julie Owens' book.

Abusive people never learned how to do this well.

Instead, they attack, bully, intimidate, threaten, humiliate, shame, and in a whole host of ways try to force other people to do exactly what they want, whenever they want it.

Their temporary remorse and apologies right after the abusive event also have nothing to do with the victim, and their emotional display is not a sign that the abuse is going to stop. In fact, it's just a part of the cycle, because the abuser has still not learned how to self-regulate in the face of frustration and to treat others with respect and consideration.

Even their show of remorse is still about *them*: they fear losing the benefits they are getting from their victim, and sometimes they also want to keep their image of themselves as a good person. So they buy gifts, make promises, and give speeches about how much they have changed.

None of this is evidence that the abuser is a sweet, loving person who just gets under stress from time to time; it is, instead, yet another tactic to make sure that they keep getting their own way and do not have to face any uncomfortable emotions—especially the discomfort of seeing how their actual behavior doesn't line up at all with their image of themselves.

They want to feel instantly good again without doing any work to heal the damage they have done to their spouse and family and the people they have hurt.

And they want to make sure that they do not lose their spouse, whose labor, sacrifices, and enormous expenditure of energy to keep the marriage working is all making it possible for the abuser to get their own way without having to do their share of the work in the relationship.

The victim holds the relationship together at great personal cost; the abuser gets all the benefits.

But life with other people is never going to be without difficulty, requiring no compromises or cooperation, and allowing us to always have things go our own way. And experiencing momentary remorse has not taught the abusive person how to self-regulate or how to properly respect the rights and wishes of others.

It is only a matter of time before their ingrained, established pattern of abusing others when they're upset by something bursts onto the scene again. And the cycle continues.

The violence may not be obvious before you marry. It may start after the abuser "has you." Many people report abuse on the honeymoon, or within the first six months. Sometimes it starts when you're vulnerable, perhaps pregnant or going through a health crisis.

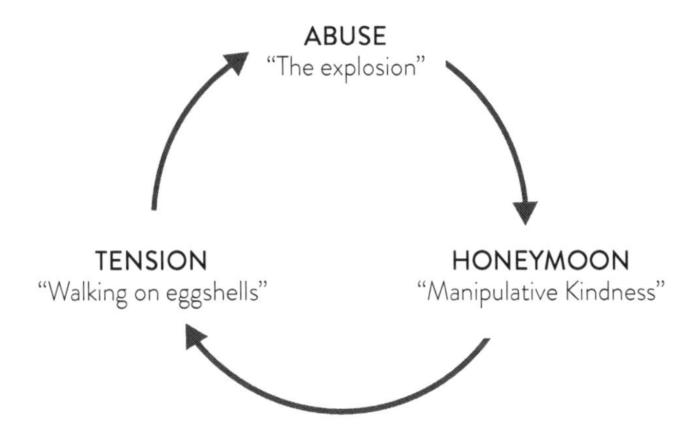

Abuse/Violence Phase – The Explosion *Explosive rage used to dominate through force, threats, violence, isolation, or intimidation.*
Abuser: Acts out aggressively through rage, sarcasm, physical violence, intimidation, locking spouse in a room, smashing things, rape, accusations, put-downs. May abuse children and pets, damage property, discard sentimental items of value to the spouse. May try to make them lose their job. The abuser's goal is to show who is in charge. This is the bullying phase.
Victim: Fights back, argues, tries to get away, leaves, protects self and kids, calls the police. May try to reason with abuser, calm them down or pacify them.

One woman used sex to keep herself safe during the abuse phase—

I was scared of him. He was angry. He pushed me, but I couldn't leave. If I left, I was afraid he would retaliate. So I snuggled with him that night. I told myself, "Keep your enemies close." I didn't want him to know I wanted to leave him. His family accused me of giving him mixed messages, but sometimes women have sex because they are scared of what will happen if they don't.

Honeymoon Phase – "Manipulative Kindness" *Manipulation continues in the form of repentance, confession, tears, apologies, promises, and sweetness. The abuser needs the victim, so abuser acts sweet to get them back. As the old saying goes: They are not sorry for trying to intimidate you; they are sorry for getting caught.*
Abuser: Shows remorse, acts repentant, apologizes, and gives gifts. Gifts are designed to bribe you to stay silent, or to coerce you to forget about the abusive treatment. Brings flowers, jewelry, promises of vacations, or other things you want. Claims that the gift erases all mistreatments of the past, therefore you must forgive and excuse all destructive behavior. Abuser wants you to stay silent by saying you can't tell anyone now that you have accepted their gift. Explains away, denies, or minimizes behavior while apologizing. Promises of change: To do better, to go to counseling, to be kind and generous. Abuser calms down for a while. Acts sweet, apologetic, and attentive.
Victim: Forgives, agrees to stay, tells the police there was no injury, stops legal proceedings, starts to hope again, sets up counseling appointments, tells themselves everything will be okay.

"What used to be called the honeymoon phase of the cycle is actually just more abuse—a very purposeful, deceitful, manipulation by the abuser to prevent the victim from leaving him, reporting him to the police, or doing anything else that might make things hard or result in consequences for him. It is not about his partner at all, and it is not about love. (Note: I use the terms him & her for simplicity, although that's not always the case.) The so-called Honeymoon phase is much more appropriately referred to as a period of 'manipulative kindness.'"
—Julie Owens[72]

72 Owens, "The Myth."

One wife shares her experience with an episode of "Manipulative Kindness"—

> *My husband and I had agreed to live separately so we could decide what to do. One day I got an eviction notice from my landlord. I called my husband. He said he had not paid my rent because he "wanted me to know how it feels to be a single mom." He later denied having said it and bought me a $100 bracelet for Valentine's Day (it had a bride and groom on it). It meant nothing to me. Now his family was upset at me because I wasn't appreciating the efforts they could see him making.*

Rather than requiring real, long-term proof that he had changed and sought to regain his wife's trust, the husband's family turned their anger at the wife for not being grateful for the gift or the effort.

Sometimes the abuser ropes in others to help them put pressure on the victim. In this instance, notice the husband's gaslighting, saying he never said what he said.

The family in this story is out of line in being angry with the wife. It was her decision whether she could trust him, not theirs. She alone had the responsibility to keep herself and her children safe.

Tension Phase – Criticism Starts Again *The rage is forgotten. Now the irritations increase. Tension builds. The victim does everything to avoid the next volcanic explosion.*
Abuser: Pretends nothing happened. Nit-picks, criticizes, excuses own behavior, withholds money, blames spouse for provoking them, uses name-calling or disrespect, comes home late without advanced notice, makes threats, stops being affectionate, uses hateful or mocking glances and gestures, says spouse isn't perfect either, tells a wife she's not submissive, breaks promises, makes suicide threats blaming the spouse, denies abuse, denies bad behavior, refuses counseling, humiliates spouse publicly or privately, coerces spouse or kids to do illegal things, makes accusations and looks for ways to justify hurting spouse again.

Victim: Walks on eggshells, tries not to do anything that would upset abuser, tries to make themselves small and invisible to protect self and children, doesn't stand up for themselves or children, avoids conflict, disappears emotionally, leaves the room or the house to avoid contact, keeps kids quiet, feels guilty and responsible, tries to please or distract attention in other ways.

After separating for a while, one wife tried again to make her marriage work and allowed her husband to move back in. He came back and started "love-bombing" her: the first part of the cycle of emotional abuse. She describes the tension—

He was acting very passionate. That evening his mom made a comment that she wished her husband would look at her like that. It made me afraid. He was idealizing me again, and I knew the abuse was about to follow. I could recognize the cycle by now.

After the cycle has occurred several times, you get beaten down. Negative messages such as "I can never make it on my own," or "My children will be destroyed," or "I don't want to go through divorce," put pressure on you to stay.

If you spend your life walking on eggshells,
you might be in an abusive relationship.

Over time, the honeymoon phase decreases and finally disappears. It is replaced by more agitation and more violence.

The person seeking control is very insecure. They squeeze the life out of the relationship. Abusers are very scared, because the faithful person is the *anchor* in the relationship.[73] If they stop doing their part (of fixing everything and absorbing all bad treatment), the abuser falls apart.

When the victim establishes boundaries, the abuser gets angrier and attacks at any point of weakness. The abuser goes into shock.

In these situations, the best thing for the victim to do is *refuse to work on the relationship* and get to safety.

---

73 I first heard the concept of an anchor spouse in a talk by Pastor Nate Aanderud.

Don't try to patch things up when the abusive spouse gives the silent treatment or plays the victim. Part of the manipulation cycle is going into a "puppy-dog mode" of intense remorse. The abuser begs and promises not to do it again.

But it's like quicksand: the more you fight, the more you sink. Instead, find solid ground and stay there. Make it clear you're not going to jump back into the quicksand. (For more on responding to abusive situations, see Chapter 9.)

RECOGNIZING ABUSE: THE STORIES OF VICTIMS

Sometimes, it takes hearing someone else's story to finally recognize the truth about your own.

In the following true stories given by some of the people I interviewed who suffered in dangerous marriages and at last sought out a life-saving divorce, we can see many of the abusive behaviors we have been discussing—in action, and in the real lives of real people.

As you read, see if you can identify those behaviors. See if you can identify the "not okay" things that were done or said to these victims of abuse.

- *What* was wrong about it?
- *Why* was it wrong?
- *How* should that person have been treated instead?

Can you see what abuse looks like, and the effect it has on the victim, to keep them questioning themselves and stuck in the dangerous marriage?

Priscilla's Story

I was a nice Christian girl from a good home. My parents were married, and we had a big, happy family. So my expectation of marriage was that I would marry someone kind, loving, and understanding. If you're going to live with someone the rest of your life, you want a love as described in the Bible: Love is patient, love is kind, it is not self-seeking, not easily angered, and so on.

When I was introduced to John, I really liked him. But after we married, he became controlling. Financially, we were both working and had good jobs. But he doled out money only when he thought

I needed it. Just enough for groceries. Anything I bought for myself, even if it was small, would make him irate.

Yet he would buy anything he wanted. One day he brought home a boat. He never asked me if I wanted one or if we could afford it. The first time we used it, I spent two hours cleaning the boat seats using a toothbrush. He told me, "If you don't finish the job, you aren't riding in the boat." It was a humiliating to be treated like a child.

And he liked to show contempt. On a family vacation, we drove across the country. At one stop, we switched places. John went to sleep, and I continued driving for about 40 minutes. When he woke up, he said, "Why aren't we in Knoxville yet?" He took the wheel, did a U-turn, and drove all the way back to the place we had switched. At every exit along the route, he pulled over and took a photo of the highway signs. He had to "teach me a lesson." He wanted to humiliate me and have proof. I thought it was my fault and thought I deserved this kind of embarrassment. He manipulated it so I accepted that everything was my fault.

It was like the movie, "Sleeping with the Enemy." I did the yard work, groceries, everything. Yet he criticized me constantly. There were so many picky rules. I wasn't even allowed to put any decorations or hang any picture on our walls. All he did was eat, run, work, and sleep.

One evening, just after our daughter was born, he came home, and the dog's water bowl was low. "How do you think you can take care of a child, if you can't take care of a dog?" he said.

I was not treated with love and kindness. I did everything I could to be loving and kind and not fight. But he told me everything was my fault—and I believed him. He talked down to me constantly. He insisted I cater to him in every way. But in return, he was mean and hateful.

You might wonder why I accepted this. Down deep inside, I told myself I deserved to suffer. I believed God was punishing me for sleeping with my college boyfriend.

Our daughter would shut the door when we fought. It was too traumatizing to her. So I promised myself I would not fight with John anymore. I didn't believe in divorce, but I couldn't watch my daughter go through this.

My husband attended the Promise Keepers conferences. This was a Christian ministry that focused on being a man of integrity. I told John we had to work on our marriage. And I went to our pastor to ask for help.

John was part of a church men's group, and part of their homework was putting together a Manhood Plan. It was supposed to be a reckoning of his own successes and shortcomings, and a list of his personal goals. In it, he blamed me for everything. He stated that one of his life goals was to be able to forgive me. He wrote: "I'm praying God will help me forgive you."

It was the 25th year of marriage. Our daughter had just gone to a nearby college. John was trying to control her, too. She didn't want to come home and be around him. He humiliated her, too.

Finally, I was desperate. I could survive John's meanness, but I didn't want my daughter treated that way. I wanted John to be a good Christian husband.

I put together a three-page list of problems and ugly incidents and went to my pastor. He asked me to read it aloud in his office. Calmly I read line after line. To hear it, in my own voice, was eye-opening. I realized I had allowed myself to be abused for 25 years.

My pastor met with us and asked John to move out for a while, but John refused. John threatened me: "If you divorce me, I'll keep our daughter, and you won't get anything."

I called out to God. I felt God's presence like I'd never felt it before. I had this calming peace about me: "I know what I'm going to do." I felt God's hand on me. "John has to go. It's over." From that moment, I became a different person.

I didn't believe in divorce, but I needed to be away from him. I filed for legal separation, hoping for him to change. He filed for divorce in response.

As I look back, I am grateful to God for helping me and giving me peace in the decision.

And my life now? It is so amazing, it's hard to believe. Now I know what happiness is! I have no regrets.

Listen to Priscilla's words—

- He never hit her. It was all words, actions, and demands. *It was still abuse.*
- She felt hated, disrespected, unimportant, humiliated, and embarrassed.
- She felt like she was being controlled ("you can't go in the boat if you don't finish the job") and treated like a child.
- She was desperate and wanted to protect her daughter.
- She looked inward and doubted herself: Was she really being loving enough?
- She believed his criticism.

The Wake-Up Call

She read her list aloud and—for the first time—realized she was being abused. Her pastor was just the audience in this story. After 25 years, Priscilla was the one who saw her husband's behavior and identified it as abuse.

Now she had clarity, so she put up boundaries. Her pastor supported her decision and was with her when she told her husband to leave and get help for his abusive attitudes and behaviors.

Her husband refused to comply and responded with threats. Priscilla didn't feel comfortable filing for divorce due to her Christian beliefs, so she filed for separation, and he responded by filing for divorce.

Priscilla was in her fifties, and she decided to start over and embrace a new life. She had not worked much outside the home during her marriage, but she jumped into a new career. When we discussed including her story in this book, she wanted me to add: "I have a wonderful life now!"

Martina's Story

> *Thank you for asking about my life experiences. Somehow, they don't seem so remarkable to me… I suppose my culture shaped some of that perception. We often tend to use the phrase, "That's okay," to deflect and bury painful moments.*
>
> *I have now retrained myself to say the words, "No. That's* **not** *okay with me." It was the hardest lesson of my life. But that comes much later in the story.*

Before I share much about my marriage and divorce, I would like to introduce myself and tell you a little bit about my childhood. I want to ask a favor, though. Please don't allow yourself to feel sorry for me. You'll be tempted, I know. I just want you to know beforehand that this more than difficult beginning has a wonderful outcome. You may come away with more faith and hope than you ever thought possible.

I certainly did.

I am the oldest of three children. I really functioned as the mom to my siblings for most of our childhood. Our father was married to someone else when we were all conceived, so he was never around us. We didn't really "belong" to him, so there seemed to be no need for a relationship.

We lived a very rough life. My mom was single and had a hard time finding work. And because my mom worked, we stayed with other family members. We were always running and moving around. I was in fifteen schools before I was a teenager. It was very hard for young children, and there was no chance for a normal life. I lived with a lot of fear and depression during my life.

[When I was fifteen, my mother] left us with her sister, who was married to the man who sexually abused me. My uncle was a mean person. He would come to my bed at night and kiss me, touch me, and do other things. He would tell me he knew I needed to have food and clothes, and he would give me money if I would let him do whatever he wanted. My bed was by a window, so I just looked up at the sky to see the stars. I would be very still and think about the day I would be able to get away from him.

When I was 18, I met my husband, Mateo, through people who were friends of one of my aunts. He was 26. We begin to date and quickly developed a relationship. I was so shy and untrusting. He had already been married and had a child. So there I was, eighteen years old, and I didn't know anything. About anything!

I don't know why, but from the way I grew up and what I saw with my mom, I just learned that no matter what happened to you, [you have to shrug it off and say,] "It's OK. Everything is OK."

Someone hurts you? "It's OK; I can take it."

People can hurt you like that, and "it's ok."

In my eighteen years, that was my experience, and it was normal. Experience is truly a teacher—even when the lessons are wrong.

Mateo was very immature—and I wasn't like that. I'd seen too much of life already. But honestly, I thought this could be how people have a stable and happy home. With nothing to use as a comparison, I didn't know what I didn't know.

It was totally my choice to stay, and I was beginning to think my dream was coming true. Mateo was going to be my husband; we were going to have a wonderful marriage; and we were going to have a beautiful home together. That life and dream had never been within my grasp, so I was clutching at it and holding on tight.

Consequences never crossed my mind—not one time. In my mind, this was going to be the way to my happiness. I was determined to do everything possible to make this relationship work and to finally have a happy family.

During the summer, I became pregnant, and I was starting to like him more. About three months after we discovered we were having a baby, he lost his job… no job, and I had no job: what were we going to do?

Truly, for about two years, everything was okay. At least, I thought it was okay. He would leave the house and not come home until very late. Okay. He would come home drunk. Okay. Doing very bad things. Okay.

It was okay because I had a home and a baby. When I looked at baby Virginia, I would talk to her and promise that she would have a future. I told her, "You are not going to be like me. You won't have the kind of life I had. I will make sure of it."

I thought we would always be a family. No matter what it took.

And for two years, we were okay. Then things started going wrong.

The beginning of the end started after we returned home from a trip. We had gone to Mateo's daughter's (my step-daughter's) birthday party. I bought a little necklace, a small cross, to give to her. I wanted her to be happy, and I understood what it meant to not have a father around.

After the party, we came back home. He left that night, a Thursday, and didn't come back home until Saturday. The next day, he told me, "I don't love you; I'm with someone else. I'm out of here." A meltdown happened as I completely freaked out and told him, "You can't do this—you can't leave—it isn't right!"

Up to this point in my life, nothing could be allowed to impact my emotions, because I had learned not to acknowledge them. Everything was going to be okay. But this time, I was devastated. I couldn't believe he would do this to me or to our daughter, Virginia. I begged him to stay and assured him that things would be better.

He had another job and became friends with a lot of the people in his office. He started having parties at our house with guys and girls. I was so incredibly naïve and so desperate to keep my family together.

He began having an affair with an eighteen-year-old girl, who became his girlfriend. He would bring her to our home and, while I was asleep, they would have sex in our house. Then, she would be at our house as a guest. I'm still saying, "It's okay."

We had a Christmas party at our home for his friends in the office. Some people drank too much; [there were] a couple of fights. After everyone left, he blamed me and said those fights were my fault. He hit me and told me he was leaving. This time, he really did it.

When I found myself in that situation, the bottom fell out of my world. I couldn't recognize myself. I was lost. I couldn't think, couldn't feel, and my life was spinning out of control. Only one thing was operating at full capacity: survival.

My dream family is shattered; I have a baby daughter; an eighteen-year-old girl has entered my life as my husband's girlfriend, and her picture is on our dresser. Now, he's made good on his threat to leave, and I am left holding all the broken pieces.

Somehow, I kept convincing myself it would be better at some point (I have no idea why we truly think that sometimes). My self-talk was about how I could handle this—I could take anything—it's going to be okay.

It wasn't. Not for a long time.

I let him come back three or four times during those years. It was the biggest mistake but the only thing I knew to do. I was determined to keep the cleanest house, have the prettiest hair, be the thinnest and best-dressed woman he knew... it was a never-ending performance cycle. Cleaning the house at 3 am still resulted in being hit multiple times and verbally abused. It wasn't good enough. I wasn't good enough. I was completely obsessed with making him stay.

My depression was in full swing. The voices of all the past kept crashing into my mind. I just wanted to talk with someone who would be kind and listen to me. I called 911 in a panic and talked about suicide. A Christian police officer answered my call that night. He was so compassionate and gave the information for a hospital that had people who could help me and where I could have time to think.

I was having a breakdown of some sort... I knew God had me there to bring me back to myself. This was the experience that caused me to know that my marriage, the life we had been living, and all the drama had to stop. I had to make the decision to stop it for me and my children.

Things were now crystal clear. It was at that point when I decided I would no longer live in this manner. I didn't have a plan but was trusting God to direct me.

*For the first time in my life, I said, "**This is not okay**."*

[It still took a while for me to finally leave.] Several months later, my second baby was born. My husband came to the hospital for the birth after my cousin phoned him. When I came home from the hospital, it was Halloween.

All my family knows that I have a recipe for a great salad with apples and a lot of special things. Everyone loves this salad! Halloween Day, I came home with our baby, and my husband asked me if I would make the salad for him to take to the party with his new girlfriend. Now, I had just gotten out of the hospital that day after giving birth to his son.

Make a salad for the party? Really? I cried my heart out—it was so very painful. It hurt me so much. The realization finally set in that he loved his girlfriends more than his wife.

All things culminated that night. This, after this, after this, after this... it was too much for me to handle anymore.

With two babies and a full-time job at Chick-Fil-A, I had more than my share of things to manage. I had become two people: The work person who was happy and competent, and the home person who was fearful, still dealing with all the pain in my life, and trying to determine next steps.

One afternoon, I came home from work, and my husband began yelling, "Why did you call her?" He accused me of calling his girlfriend (I didn't know who she was) and revealing to her that he had a wife and two children. His big question was, "How could you do that to me?"

Seriously?

[When I finally left,] it was a Monday night. I went to the bedroom and began packing all my clothes. I told him I was filing for a divorce on grounds of abandonment and for child support. He continued to tell me I was weak, that I wasn't going anywhere... He threatened to call my mother and tell her I needed to go back into the hospital for crazy people where I belonged.

"You will come back. You can't survive without me. You are too ugly," he said. On and on and on with the belittling, the criticism, the verbal assault.

I kept packing.

This time, I got my things together, and I finally walked out the door. A decision had been made, and I was not going to do this anymore.

It was not okay anymore.

There was a history with him of getting girls pregnant. The first girl got pregnant twice and had two abortions. My husband took my credit card from my purse and paid for both abortions. I had no idea of what he had done until the bill came.

Now, one last time, he tells me he needs my help. The girl he has been with is now pregnant, and she is only seventeen.

I can't help you.

His life was so very sad. I wanted him to be the right kind of husband, a father to his children, and for us to have a happy and stable home. But it wasn't possible. It was too much. The impact on the children was awful. My daughter cried each time he left, and it would break my heart. She was lonely for her father.

But finally, ***it was not OK. None of this was OK.***

My children and I were settled in our home. I began to see a counselor and started rebuilding my emotional and spiritual life. I learned to feel, to think, to know what is right, and to be respected in my own eyes. I began to grow as a woman… as a person. I now believe in myself and that everything has a purpose.

People can take things from you if you let them. They can take your dignity and security.

They can make you feel unworthy and at fault for everything.

Everything becomes about survival, so you can't focus on loving. Not yourself or others. You just focus on breathing and taking the next step.

But there comes a time where you must stop scrambling and start loving—focus—decide you can do it. And then go do it. You may be hurting, and you may be suffering, but there really is a good tomorrow. It's all about you what you decide—not what others tell you. Learn to understand yourself, [and then you will be able to] to understand others.

If you really believe in God and believe there is a better tomorrow, a better tomorrow will come. I try to find the best in every situation and learn any lesson that is contained. We work hard as a family to be positive and supportive of one another. I'm very happy today with my life and with myself.

Both of my children are happy and successful. They love each other, and they know how to share love with others. They are not selfish or self-centered. I am never afraid of them making bad choices, because we walked together through difficulties. We know each other and are committed to each other.

There have been many tears in my life. But my family is good; we are stable; we make memories and traditions together. I'm very peaceful about my life now. It has only come from God. He has given me everything I have always wanted.

Listen to Martina's words—

- She saw herself as a survivor: No matter what life handed her, she said "It's okay"—until it wasn't okay any longer.
- She felt belittled, used, unworthy, uncared for, neglected, unimportant, ugly, inadequate, unappreciated, controlled, and unfairly accused.

- She said when you focus on survival, you can't love yourself or others.
- There were two Martinas: Work Martina was happy and confident; Home Martina lived in fear.
- She wanted Mateo to be a good husband and father, but she recognized it wasn't possible.
- She didn't know how she would get free, but she knew God had a plan.

The Wake-Up Call

Her depression and suicidal 911 call led to a hospitalization that gave her time away from the home, and time to think. She saw God's hand in this: helping her get clarity and bringing the drama to an end.

She realized she had to stop the nightmare for her and her children.

Now she had clarity. She wanted love in her family, not just survival. When her husband didn't care for her during the labor and delivery of her second child, and then asked her to make a special salad for him and his girlfriend, it was the last domino to fall.

So many of my interviewees were saved from severe depression by going into a hospital or psychiatric facility. Up until then, they live in a fog of making it through each day, which means they are so focused on surviving, walking on eggshells, they have no mental energy to plan a path out of the turmoil. They are emotionally exhausted and often suicidal. They don't feel safe until they enter the hospital and get help.

In many cases, getting professional help means the difference between life and death.

LIVING ON "PLANET ME" OR "PLANET WE"?

Living on "Planet Me"

Martina told her story about coming home from the hospital with a newborn baby, and her husband demanding she prepare food for a party with his new girlfriend.

In spite of ourselves, we can't help but laugh at the absurd self-centeredness of her husband. But his unrealistic expectations didn't develop overnight. Like many chronic abusers, he had a pattern of wearing Martina down by his selfishness. His background told him that he was the center of the universe, not God.

When one spouse points out your shortcomings and rarely admits theirs, they are living on "Planet Me." On Planet Me, most of their actions are okay. Everything *you* do that they don't approve of, is not okay.

The rules never apply equally.

There's always a reason why the same rule doesn't apply to them. When you live on Planet Me, the abuser gets to define reality.

They have their own standard of justice, and that standard favors them at all times. They make the laws. They are the umpire. They are the referee. They are the judge and jury, and they are *always* right.

On Planet Me, they make the rules.

It makes no sense. You won't be able to convince them of the double standard. Often the abuser brainwashes the victim to living by the rules of Planet Me, too. You start to wonder about your own observations:

- Did he really leave this bruise, or did I fall?
- Did he really lie, or did I mishear him?
- Did he disappear without telling anyone, or did he leave a note that somehow got lost? He says that never happened or that I just misunderstood it.

After a while, you've been gaslighted so long, the feeling that you are *always* wrong becomes the new normal.

On Planet Me, you will feel that you haven't given enough or been a good enough spouse, even though you know you have sacrificed your safety and your health to follow these lopsided rules.

Living on "Planet We"

We know what a good marriage looks like:

- The spouses are friends who are also lovers, companions, and partners who build their own shared life together.
- They both need, and both get, safety and love from each other.
- They have a Oneness, as the Bible says; they are on a journey together.

- They each can come to each other for comfort and support.
- They go through ups and downs together.
- They brush off slights, forgive one another, and figure out how to solve their problems with understanding. It's not a one-way street.
- They each bring precious assets into the union: their time, energy, skill, intellect, valuables, and their loyalty.
- They are a team.
- Each one of them matters, and each has choices, a say in how the marriage and family work, and responsibilities that they faithfully uphold.

Sure, there is sacrifice, but it is due to circumstances beyond their control: health problems, accidents, or job losses—not due to a pattern of selfishness, disrespect, or betrayals by the other.

An abuser can be either spouse, although most abuse is men on women. There is, however, plenty of evidence that wives can be physical batterers or emotional abusers who exert control and power over their husbands and children.[74]

Anyone who doubts this should to look at the many books written by psychologists and adult children of narcissistic mothers. Many adults raised in these families say they wish their father had divorced early and taken them away to safety.

In Andrew's story, we see exactly that: A daughter's comment is indelibly imprinted in his mind.

Andrew's Story

> *One of my best memories as a kid was when I walked into the kitchen one day, and I saw my parents kissing. And I was thinking,* Yes, Dad, kiss Mom more. She needs that. I want her to feel that she's loved and she's special.
>
> *And that was right before their divorce. Even as an eight-year-old, I knew it was coming.*
>
> *I've always been a hopeless romantic. And when you think*

---

74 "Statistics," ***National Coalition Against Domestic Violence,*** accessed 1/3/20, https://ncadv.org/statistics. It should be noted that "domestic violence" technically includes a wide range of abuse, including physical, emotional, and verbal. This site gives information on all types of abuse.

about marriage… you hear all the love songs on the radio. This is gonna be great. I'm gonna find my soul mate, and everything's just gonna be awesome.

It was a real shock when I didn't get that.

I'm a very affectionate person, but it's taken me a long time to know how to act in a relationship. I'm kind of like a puppy dog. I was a nerd in elementary school and high school, and I was the chubby kid. But then when it came time for me to go to college, I dropped a lot of weight. And when you didn't have all that extra weight to look through, a lot of girls were like, this guy's really sweet.

When I met my ex, she was just so together. She was so organized. She was fun, but I knew by looking at her I could learn so much from her about how to get through college, about how to be a better person, about how to be a more respectful partner, and everything. I just felt that from her.

I was so taken by this woman. We met at a Halloween party; I walked her home that night, and I got the guts up to kiss her goodnight right there on the front step of her dorm. And I was hooked.

I did the gentleman thing, and I tried to do everything right: brought the flowers, the presents, and everything. But even in the beginning she was really picky about my appearance, because I was the hippie kid.

I was just so crazy about her. Within six months after we met, I asked her to marry me. It just kinda fell out of my mouth.

Early in the relationship, she got in a huge fight with her mother while I was visiting, and her mother said to her face, with me there in the house, "He's too good for you. You don't deserve him." She was upset with me because I didn't defend her.

I remember when we were still engaged, I had a few twinges of, "Get out now!" But, at that point, you don't know it's a disorder. You think, it's just my imagination, right? [B]ecause of all the "love bombing," [the feeling I had that] there's so much good, [I told myself that] she can't be that crazy, right? All relationships have their down sides. This is just one of them. We'll be fine.

But I stayed because I didn't know how I was going to get out of my lease. (We had just signed a lease together.)

[Our first Christmas as a married couple,] I got her a Christmas present that was very special to me. It was a nice clock, and every time I looked at it, I thought of home… and of family. It was a new tradition I wanted us to start.

She opened the present and started screaming at me. "You bought this for you. You did not buy this for me. You got this for you." Her explosion of temper was so quick, I didn't get the chance to explain it. And I started bawling because I felt I had hurt her that deeply… We went out and exchanged it for a jewelry box, and I felt totally humiliated.

I reminded her of that several times during our marriage and how much that hurt me. And I remember one time she gave me the stereotypical narcissist response and yelled, "Well I said I'm sorry, what more do you want?" No, if you're still yelling at me, you're not sorry. That was a big red flag.

It was just like everything else you read from everyone else who deals with narcissism. It was almost [as though she was saying], "I'm sorry you feel that way. It's not about my actions. It's about your overreaction. I'm gonna gaslight you. I'm gonna pin it on you."

I had a good foundation in faith. We both did. But her family was a lot more conservative than mine. One thing she really didn't like was that I wasn't a virgin when we met. That was pushed in my face several times. It was one of the worst things she ever said to me. "I saved myself for the person I was going to marry, but you can't say that. And I know you can't change that now, but I remember that every time you lay down next to me." I just felt so filthy.

The next big red flags didn't come until our kids were born.

When our daughter came along, things got really rough. Another part of her controlling was homeschooling. We were both public school teachers. I still am a middle-school teacher.

In the beginning, homeschooling was great, because I thought, "I'll know everything that's happening with my kids, because my wife's doing it." So, she said, let's homeschool them, and I was like, of course, that's wonderful.

And it was wonderful until my daughter started catching on to how controlling her mother was. My daughter wanted to come to middle school with me. My wife said, no way. My daughter got really angry.

My wife also controlled our diet. She insisted on us being vegan, even though we didn't want to be vegan, and she inflicted that lifestyle on us through shopping. I was a vegetarian for twenty years. I have no problem with changing your diet, but when someone says, "I don't want to do this," and the other person says, "Forget you, you're going to do it anyway," that's when it becomes abusive.

They had to move to another state for work, and they got involved in a church that had multiple sexual and staff scandals. They had been team-teaching Sunday school and kids' club, but they got burned out and walked away. Finally, a job opened up in their home state.

So, after we moved back to our home state, she started going to church again. And I went too because she wanted it. I didn't want to go, but I'm like, "She's going. The kids are going. I should do this just to make her happy." But, at that point, I knew what narcissism was. I had been telling her for a couple of years, "You're abusing me. You have to stop." But I went back to church because I just wanted to give her something, because moving was tough.

We'd had so many face-to-face conversations that I started to write her letters instead. I wasn't interested in having face-to-faces anymore, because I was just going to be shut down. My wife accused me of being the troublemaker when I told her how she hurt me and our daughter.

It was as if she was saying, "Please stop saying these true *things about me because they make me feel guilty." (She would just explode.) It would be the equivalent of the husband that says to his wife, "Don't tell me how much it hurts when I beat you, because that makes me feel guilty, and that's mean." Or like the husband who stands over his kid with the belt in his hand and says, "This is gonna hurt me more than it hurts you." [Nonsense,] it's not. The abuser's the problem, period.*

And at least with a letter you can take two days to write it, you can edit, you can say exactly what your emotions are, and you know you won't be interrupted.

We had another baby, a son. I was totally putting myself into work, because I work in a field where they expect you to give a bajillion hours. And the biggest mistake I made was working sixty hours a week, and not spending enough time at home…

She said something that was absolutely true: "I have been a single parent for the first year of our son's life. I'm not going to leave you. I'm not going to divorce you. But I need you to divorce your job and come back to me."

And of course, when she said that, I wept tears all over again. I couldn't believe I'd hurt her so much. So I changed my work hours, because if I hadn't, I might not have known my son until after it was too late.

The thing that really led up to me knowing that it was time to get out of the marriage was when I continually told her, "You're abusing our daughter. You have to stop." And her saying, "No, no, no." I remember the year before, my daughter would pull me aside and say, "Hey, we have to talk about Mom. She's driving me crazy. I can't stand her. I do not want to be homeschooled. I need to go to public school. Get me out of here."

My wife said, "Okay, we'll do that." But she met with the guidance counselor in secret. She didn't tell us about any of those meetings, and she only set my daughter up for a half day so she could still be homeschooled for a half day.

I threw an absolute fit, and so did my daughter. I told my wife, "You are doing this totally all on your own, and you're telling two of the three people involved that what we think doesn't matter at all."

I wanted to stay married until my daughter graduated. But that spring I started looking for a divorce attorney… I've never been cheated on. I've never been beaten. I've never been sexually assaulted. I've never dealt with so many of the things that so many of my friends have. I just had the weird emotional stuff.

One of my turning points?
When my daughter said to me: "I love you, Dad.
I wish your wife did."

I was afraid that I would lose my kids. I was worried she and her mother would start a smear campaign. And that was her first counter to me filing for divorce. She threatened me: "You're going to lose all parental rights."

My attorney said, "No way. This guy has been a schoolteacher for twenty years. He's loved. He has a tight relationship with his kids. There's no way that his kids should be totally taken away from him." She had to bring that up once, and it was never mentioned again.

I asked this man if he had any words for men in his situation, and he said:

Take care of your kids. Don't fear that a broken home is going to break your kids. Because keeping your kids in an abusive relationship will break them more.

You're still a man. You are in no way less masculine because this is what's being done to you. As a matter of fact, in my case, this was being done to me because *I was trying to follow what the Bible said. I mean, I'm big into "Love your wife as Christ loved the church, laying down his life for her." That was a big passage for me because we love to talk about the women submitting, but we never talk about how the men are supposed to do it.*

And I've changed so much because I loved her so deeply. I changed the way I groomed. I changed the way I walked in the house. I changed the way I went to the bathroom. I mean, there was so much.

But just because you're being attacked by someone who can't feel, you are no less of a man. As a matter of fact, I think you're more because of it. Because you have enough tenderness to listen [to your wife] instead of just saying, "Shut up, woman, we're gonna do it my way." Because that's not what masculinity looks like.

I'm so grateful now. I mean, it's only been a year. It's so much different, and it's so much better.

Listen to Andrew's words—

- He saw himself as needing help in life. He was attracted to her abilities.
- He felt manipulated, misunderstood, unheard, dismissed, filthy, controlled, deceived, and attacked.
- He set boundaries, and his wife was defensive and went on

the attack. To protect himself from face-to-face anger, he wrote detailed letters instead.

- He felt ignored and controlled about food, grooming, and education choices.
- After 29 years, he filed for divorce.

Is There a Test I Can Take—For Myself, or for Someone Else's Situation?

There are many free online tests to determine whether you are in an abusive or unsafe situation, for example, the MOSIAC Threat Assessment. See also www.lifesavingdivorce.com/selftests.[75]

MOSIAC is a 30-minute online test. You'll need to give a valid email address, because they send an access code to that email. (You might want to do the test at someone else's computer or at a library.)

It asks more than 40 questions. Most are very quick and easy: age, marital status, child custody status, etc. It gives you very clear instructions. In case you cannot decide between the multiple-choice answers, you can add explanations to your answers if you wish. At the end it gives a full written report and a score of 1 to 10 on your situation.

CONCLUSION: AM I BEING ABUSED OR CONTROLLED?

Are you being controlled? Do you feel your choices have to meet your spouse's approval? Can that person pull a trump card and overrule your clothes, your hair, your work, your time, your food choices, or your looks? Have you been coerced to do something you would rather not do?

The Bible says that even leaders shouldn't be controlling. They

75 "MOSAIC Frequently Asked Questions," ***MOSAIC Threat Assessment Systems,*** accessed 8/26/19, https://www.mosaicmethod.com/?page=faq. I have no affiliation with MOSAIC. MOSAIC Threat Assessment is free. The company that created it specializes in workplace violence, school/university harassment, and threats to public officials or judicial officers. There is a free version for people who wish to evaluate their own (or someone else's) personal situation. The organization claims: "Everything you enter is completely private. This online system allows you to answer questions and enter information, then print a report. When you delete the assessments you do, they are gone. Nobody other than you ever has access to the information you enter."

should set an example, "not lording it over those entrusted to you, but being examples to the flock" (1 Peter 5:3, NIV).

People fall prey to the control of others through physical, mental, verbal, financial, or spiritual methods—or a combination of several of them. Usually it happens slowly over time.

It makes sense, right? Because if you're in a painful marriage, it usually didn't start that way. You gradually put up with more control, more disrespect, and more conflict over time. You stayed because you were committed, because you believed in the sanctity of marriage, because you were going to solve this, and because you wanted your marriage to work. Your marriage became the most important thing in your life. Your desires—to be safe, loved, treated with respect, heard, etc.—were gradually worn down.

Abusers secretly want a one-way street where only their desires and emotions matter.

They might talk about their love for the family or for God—they may even tell you they love you—but it's a smokescreen. Everyone else must give up what they want to meet the abuser's demands. There is no mutuality, no caring for the other spouse at the same level that they care for themselves.

As the Abuse Cycle shows us, one very common tactic of abusers is to cycle between hot and cold: explosive and vindictive at one point, and full of remorse and loving attention later, over and over. This is what therapists believe causes trauma bonds that keep you in the relationship, that feeling of love for a spouse who has a pattern of hurting you.

In a nutshell: An abuser's goal is to keep you captive in the relationship and to wear you down to go along with their view of life. To do this, they must get you to believe you are no longer important, sensible, intelligent, or worthy of decent treatment, and they must ensure that you don't tell others about what's really going on, get support for yourself, or make it possible for you to get out from under their control and live a stable, fulfilling life without them.

As you look back at Priscilla, Martina, and Andrew's stories, you see how their spouses applied pressure to get what they wanted, using a variety of tools: lies, humiliation, disrespect, and bribes.

There's nothing wrong with trying to persuade your spouse to do something or to change their mind, but the methods cannot be demeaning or coercive. Marriage was meant to be caring, loving, and lifelong, but instead of being treated as full partners in the marriage, where two adults mutually agree to major life decisions, one spouse was pushed aside.

Instead of two people supporting each other in their goals in life, being honest with each other, and taking the other person's desires into consideration, one person lied to get their way, regardless of the other's wishes.

Instead of having a marriage based on trust and love, where each had the ability to have their own feelings, friends, and activities, one spouse indulged their whims, while the other stayed at home and held everything together.

This is not fair, right, or godly.

In Scripture, we see that God desires for men and women to be loving partners, who treat one another with consideration, respect, and affection. In a loving, godly marriage, we would expect:

- a willingness to cooperate and compromise
- speech and actions that help everyone feel safe
- openness about finances, making financial decisions together, and making sure each spouse has access to the family's financial resources
- listening, showing respect, and valuing the opinions and feelings of the other
- mutual, intimate, and pleasurable sex for both, without coercion or pressure
- mutual agreement on how to divide up the work that goes into running a household
- making big decisions together
- honesty, reliability, and healthy boundaries
- support for each spouse's goals in life
- room for both spouses to have their own feelings, opinions, interests, friends, and beliefs, and respect when these are different
- respecting the other spouse's privacy, history, and dignity
- accepting responsibility for one's own actions, admitting personal

fault, and committing to make amends and change behaviors that are hurting the other spouse[76]

In your own marriage, you alone know what's happening behind closed doors. Only you can determine if this is a loving, mutual relationship or a lopsided one. Only you can decide if you are an *anchor* person, the one who fixes everything and holds it all together.

It's not easy to admit to your friends and family that you are being abused. Those who are being abused often keep it secret for years, if not decades. You are not alone in feeling scared of the consequences of standing up for yourself, or doubting yourself and your abilities, or feeling convinced that you are to blame for what is happening.

But the abuser's sin is not the victim's fault,
and the best way of ending it is to get out.

Only you can decide if it is time to put up boundaries and say, "No more. I want to be treated with respect, as a full partner in this marriage."

---

76 This list is compiled with help from the material on Tom Graves' website, www.batteredmen.com.

TO STAY, OR TO GO?

If you are struggling with the question of "To stay, or to go?" believe me, I understand. I've walked in your shoes.

I found out my marriage was in serious trouble seven years before I asked my husband to leave. It was a shock—a wake-up call. There had been incidents, which I had forgiven and forgotten. He promised to get counseling. We reconciled.

As a committed Christian, marriage was very important to me, and I was going to give it my all. And frankly, I loved my husband. But this particular revelation, while I was pregnant, hit me when I was least able to walk away.

I decided to stay.

Three years later, another baby and another shock. I met with a divorce attorney with a newborn in my arms. That attorney walked me through the process and explained the steps. Then he looked at me with compassion in his eyes and said, "Are you up for this?"

My mind was swirling. The baby wasn't sleeping much, and I was sleep-deprived. I was already exhausted from keeping up with my toddler. I couldn't handle any more.

I said no.

But I kept the attorney's phone number. Four years later, though I *still* wasn't completely ready, I called the number.

Later in this chapter, you're going to hear people's stories, in their own words. They too struggled with this question—should I stay, or should I go?—but in the end, it was *their* decision and *their* timing.

This is your decision. Not your pastor's, not your parent's, not your Bible study leader's, not your children's, and not your friend's.

You are the one living with the marriage.
You are the one who decides if you stay or go.

Jesus Sets the Captives Free

In the previous chapter, we looked at ways people may try to control us, manage us, and pressure us to do their bidding—even if it is not good for us or our children!

There is a fascinating story in the Bible about control: spiritual control.

This is the story of Jesus healing a disabled woman on the Sabbath. You may have heard it before, but this time, focus on the areas I have underlined.

> ***Now [Jesus] was teaching in one of the synagogues on the Sabbath. And behold, there was a woman who had had a disabling spirit for eighteen years. She was bent over and could not fully straighten herself. When Jesus saw her, he called her over and said to her, "Woman, you are freed from your disability." And he laid his hands on her, and immediately she was made straight, and she glorified God. But the ruler of the synagogue, indignant because Jesus had healed on the Sabbath, said to the people, "There are six days in which work ought to be done. Come on those days and be healed, and not on the Sabbath day." Then the Lord answered him, "You hypocrites! Does not each of you on the Sabbath untie his ox or his donkey from the manger and lead it away to water it? And ought not this woman, a daughter of Abraham whom Satan bound for eighteen years, be loosed from this bond on the Sabbath day?"***
>
> ***—Luke 13:10-16 (ESV)***

Jesus healed a woman who was trapped by a disabling spirit. It was a hostile spirit, one that wanted to control her so she would live a life of infirmity. That was the spirit's goal. Jesus said he came to set the captives free—free from the bonds of torment.

Jesus was willing to stand up to the leaders of his day to rescue people and release them from bondage. Jesus defied the religious leader's attempt to control him, and he healed the woman on the Sabbath, an act that leader considered a violation of the Ten Commandments.

But Jesus said it was good and right to release her from bondage. Look closely at this story. The woman in this passage had been disabled for many years. The Bible says she lived a miserable life brought on by an evil spirit that wanted her to suffer. Jesus said Satan had bound her.

Jesus set her free.
She straightened up and glorified God!

Setting people free brings glory to God.
Keeping people in bondage brings glory… to Satan.

The ruler of the synagogue was incensed. He was a strict legalist and was angry at Jesus. He said Jesus should have waited, should have healed the woman on another day of the week.

Of course, Jesus could have healed her on another day, but he was trying to make a point:

Rescuing people comes ahead of legalism.

Then it was Jesus' turn to be incensed at the ruler of the synagogue and at others who believed as he did—

"You hypocrites! Doesn't each of you on the Sabbath untie your ox or donkey from the stall and lead it out to give it water? And ought not this woman, a daughter of Abraham <u>whom Satan bound for eighteen years,</u> be loosed from this bond on the Sabbath day?"
—Luke 13:15-16 (NIV)

That leader did not recognize the woman as a person of worth, as a valuable daughter of Abraham. He didn't even consider her to be as valuable as an animal.

Jesus saw her as valuable. Jesus sees you as valuable. You are were made in the image of God. You are precious, and you should not be treated this way.

You, like the woman, can defy other people's spiritual control, walk over to Jesus, and be set free.

TEN COMMON TURNING POINTS

People of faith stay longer and endure worse treatment in these painful marriages than most people.[77] They often prefer a bad marriage to a divorce. And if they are surrounded by friends and family who value marriage at all costs, they are very hesitant to leave unless their lives are miserable… very miserable.

I feel honored when a person tells me their divorce story. It requires trust. If they are Christian, it is likely I'm going to hear a story of tremendous pain.

Most stories follow a similar pattern:

- *I liked this person. They liked me.*
- *We prayed. We fell in love. We got married.*
- *No one saw any red flags; or I saw some red flags early on but had no idea how bad it could get; or I ignored them, excused them, or minimized them because my fiancé had so much potential for good.*
- *When it got worse, we tried to get counseling (maybe) or talked to the pastor.*
- *Eventually it was evident that our marriage was in trouble.*
- *I didn't want a divorce, so I stayed and stayed and stayed.*
- *And then something happened.*

And that *something* is different in every story.

What was your turning point? What was that *Aha* moment that made you realize your marriage was over and it was time to go?

These are the ten turning points I hear the most.

1. Fear: I Escaped and Never Came Back

A wife of a charming man, who was a handsome serial adulterer, wanted to separate from her husband so they could work individually on their marriage—

---

77 Two studies discuss this: Michal Gilad, "In God's Shadow: Unveiling the Hidden World of Domestic Violence Victims in Religious Communities," ***Rutgers Journal of Law & Public Policy*** 11, no. 3 (Spring 2014); and Leonie Westenberg, "'When She Calls for Help'—Domestic Violence in Christian Families," ***Social Science*** 6, (2017): 71.

I gingerly recommended we should separate. I knew nothing about abuse... nothing about how abusive men behave. And all of a sudden, he realized what I was saying.

He said, "Wait a minute. Separate? Are you talking about separating?"

[She replied,] "Oh, just temporarily, so we can sort things out."

"Absolutely not! We are not separating!"

To make a long story short, I watched this man—he got a blank stare in his eyes. A switch went off with him. All night I did mental gymnastics and tried to figure out how to survive the night. He just snapped. [It was] the scariest thing I have ever experienced in my life. [We had guns in the house.] I really thought it would be a murder-suicide situation.

He went to work in the morning, and I ran out the door and left—with only the clothes on my back. I even left my dog, whom I loved to pieces. I was just so scared I left, and never came back...

Narcissistic sociopaths are all about image. I was going to blow his carefully set-up image. And that's what upset him. It wasn't about losing me at all, in my opinion—it was about his image being threatened.

2. *Protecting My Children from Direct or Indirect Abuse*

Many parents feel they can "handle" abuse directed at themselves, but they won't tolerate abuse directed at the children. That's their line in the sand.

I watched my son slowly start getting more nervous about Daddy coming home. We had to be quiet in the car and at home.

[My husband] spanked her [with a rubber tarp strap] at least 25 to 30 times. He told her, "Mom and I have decided this is what needs to be done." She was covered with bruises.
I never knew about it.
And she said, "Well, don't you remember the time Dad spanked me so much?"

I'm like, "Honey, what are you talking about?"
She said, "Dad said you guys were in agreement about it."

Two very large studies of the effects of adverse childhood experiences were published in 1998 and 2019. They showed that children who are abused, who observe a parent being abused, or who live in a household with substance abuse or mental illness may suffer health effects in their adult years.[78] And if they experience or observe multiple types of abuse, violence, substance abuse, or other factors as they grow up, they will likely have more health problems as adults.[79]

"Witnessing a parent being victimized
is often more psychologically damaging to children
than injuries from direct child abuse."[80]
—Steven Stosny, Ph.D.

Finally, the day came as I… told my husband the marriage was over, and that I would never allow him to beat me again. Before that moment, I never really knew my own strength. I knew God was with me because of the peace that I felt. My husband shed tears and made promises, but the decision was made. I would never be hit again, ***and I wasn't going to allow my daughter to witness that kind of behavior for one more day.***

Your kids are victimized by watching you be humiliated. Sometimes they see the abuse more clearly than you do, and they want you to get

---

78 Felitti and Nordenberg, "Relationship."

79 Ibid.

80 Steven Stosny, "Emotional Abuse in Committed Relationships: Effects on Children," ***Psychology Today*** (1/28/11), accessed 1/6/16, https://www.psychologytoday.com/us/blog/anger-in-the-age-entitlement/201101/emotional-abuse-in-committed-relationships-effects-children.

away! Watching you being treated without respect damages them. (But the kids' healing starts the day you walk away.)

My daughter said, "Mom, you have taken him back so many times in the past 21 years of my life, and he keeps treating you badly and doing the same thing. Mom, my biggest fear is that you'll take him back again."

Then my thoughts went to my two young sons and that I didn't want them to repeat this behavior on their wives when they grew up, or on me, if they ever got angry. So I turned to my daughter and said, "Honey, you will never have to worry about me taking your dad back again."

3. I Can't Take it Anymore: Depression, Suicidal Thoughts, Medical Issues

These spouses have grown desperate from the abuse, addictions, or infidelity. They can't live another thirty years this way. They've tried everything. They feel trapped and fear there is no way out. They cannot go on. The depression is so deep they are close to suicide.

They end up going to the hospital or a psychiatrist.

One man had a wife who was so emotionally abusive and manipulative, he was deep in despair. (His full story is in Chapter 9.) His church had taught him not to go to professional licensed counselors, only to pastoral counselors (also called nouthetic counselors or biblical counselors). The man's pastor had told him to live with it. The man felt trapped and started weighing his options—

"How do I get away with suicide, so the kids don't know? This is the only way I can get out of my vows without burdening my children."

His situation got so bad, he was forced to get in-patient treatment with professional, licensed counseling. The counselors caught onto the problem and helped him realize that the messages he had gotten from his home church and Christian books were destroying him.

How Cancer Saved Me!

Many people report that being in a physically or emotionally destructive relationship leads to poor physical health. As trauma expert Dr. Bessel van der Kolk, MD, explains:

> "Research… has revealed that **trauma produces actual physiological changes…**
>
> "After trauma the world is experienced with a different nervous system. The survivor's energy now becomes focused on suppressing inner chaos, at the expense of spontaneous involvement in their life. These attempts to maintain control over unbearable physiological reactions can result in **a whole range of physical symptoms, including fibromyalgia, chronic fatigue, and other autoimmune diseases**…"[81]

Paradoxically, that vulnerability and realization that you cannot trust your spouse to care for you if you get sick or injured sometimes gives people the wake-up call they need to see the abuse for what it is.

After many years in an abusive marriage, one woman developed an intense fear of cancer. She developed orthorexia, an obsession about having a healthy diet. She changed her diet dramatically in an effort to avoid cancer. Then one day she found a mole…

> *I had a mole removed, and my doctor was concerned. "You have to come in." Of course, my husband is not available, so my dad goes with me. And this is the story of my marriage: my husband is*

---

81 Bessel van der Kolk, ***The Body Keeps the Score*** (New York: Penguin Books, 2014), 2-3, 53 (emphasis mine). According to his website, in 1984, Dr. van der Kolk "set up one of the first clinical/research centers in the US dedicated to study and treatment of traumatic stress in civilian populations, which has trained numerous researchers and clinicians specializing in the study and treatment of traumatic stress, and which has been continually funded to research the impact of traumatic stress and effective treatment interventions."

not available, and my parents step in to either build me back up emotionally, support me, or (in this case) go to the doctor with me.

And it turned out to be a melanoma. Which is funny, because my biggest fear just came true, and God used it to do the biggest work in my life. It was the best thing that has ever happened to me.

But at the time, I didn't know what stage it was. It was Thanksgiving, and we were at my parents'[house]. I was crying pretty much the whole day, because my worst nightmare had just come true, and I just didn't believe it.

That night, my husband came over and said, "Don't you think you're being a bit selfish by ruining Thanksgiving with all your crying?"

That was the trigger when I finally… when the scales just lifted off my eyes. And that's when I left.

Intense Pain Drove Me to Get Help

One homeschooled missionary woman got married to an American she had met in another country. They became missionaries together.

She endured years of her husband's emotional abuse, porn addiction, and hiring of prostitutes. She had been heavily influenced by Bill Gothard and Debi Pearl's toxic teachings that had led her to put her husband above God in her life —

> *My clothes had holes in them. My husband was spending our money at strip clubs. I was so depressed. I was diagnosed with fibromyalgia. The physical pain in my body was so high every day, I just couldn't function. I finally went to another state to a Christian therapy center. They have nutritionists, doctors, counselors, everything.*
>
> *Several months after the divorce, I stayed with my ex-in-laws. They asked, "Why are you doing so well now? How did you get healthy?"*
>
> *"I let go of your son. I prayed and prayed to God. I forgave him, and I let him go. I pray now that he comes to God."*

Getting Out—And Finding Relief

Finally, many of the people I interviewed for this book mentioned they had developed a wide variety of health problems during their marriage that improved dramatically (some, but not all, went away completely) after the divorce. In an informal poll conducted in my online group for separated and divorced Christians, 8 in 10 respondents said their health improved after separation/divorce. One in 10 said it stayed the same; 1 in 10 saw a decline.

Even conservative pro-marriage researchers say that once the stress of the divorce process is over, most adults (7 in 10) turn out emotionally and socially the same or better after divorce.

> "20% of divorced adults find their lives enhanced, and another 50% seem to suffer no long-term ill effects."[82]

Three in ten people go significantly downhill emotionally and socially after a divorce. Some of it is due to the trauma from years married to an abuser, or even earlier trauma from childhood. Some is due to high conflict with their ex-spouse during and after the divorce process.[83] Some is due to the normal stress of divorce: handling legal expenses, moving homes, childcare, managing the children's stress, switching schools, custody issues, conflict with the ex-spouse, financial pressure, and loss of social standing in their community and church.

Nevertheless, seven out of ten people reported feeling the same or better after divorce. Some people even see improvements in their physical condition.

One ex-wife of a pastor who had been married 25 years relates—

> *I was a conservative homeschool mom and a supported Southern Baptist Convention pastor's wife. [My husband left me, but] I should have left him years ago… My heart palpitations stopped one-and-a-half weeks after he left.*

---

82 W. Bradford Wilcox, "The Evolution of Divorce," ***National Affairs*** (Fall 2009), accessed 1/3/20, https://www.nationalaffairs.com/publications/detail/the-evolution-of-divorce. This is according to E. Mavis Hetherington, landmark researcher in the field of divorce for more than 40 years, as quoted by Wilcox.

83 David A. Sbarra, "Divorce and Health: Current Trends and Future Directions," ***Psychosomatic Medicine*** 77, no. 3 (Apr. 2015): 227-236.

A wife who has been separated from her abusive husband for several years reports—

> *It's really amazing how much my health—even my mental and emotional health, as well as my physical health—has improved since separating, which is exciting and also sad, because I think the stress and abuse of the relationship was impacting my health pretty significantly. And I think that's fairly common for survivors. I literally grew an inch of measurable height after I separated from my husband. No idea how that happened in my middle-aged years. I'm standing taller both figurative and literally.*

Another wife, this one married more than 30 years to a serial cheater and emotional abuser, said, "I still do have some really serious health issues, which is very typical when you're in an abusive relationship long term..."

Another woman reported, "My personal experience is far fewer stress-induced issues. My autoimmune issues significantly reduced post-divorce."

Stories of improved health after a life-saving divorce are common, as leading researcher Dr. Mavis Hetherington notes:

> "The one striking exception to the otherwise general rule about post-divorce decline in health were women who had been in distant or hostile marriages."[84]

And of course, it's not just women who see improved health after a divorce from a distant or hostile marriage. Men say the same thing:

> *My health got better after divorce. I took care of myself instead of walking on eggshells and worrying what was going to blow up next. My kids and I ate better, and I got involved in sports leagues. Climbed Half Dome. Twice!*

---

84 Hetherington and Kelly, ***For Better***, 59.

I dropped 15 pounds. My [blood pressure] and cholesterol are normal. They were not when I was married...

4. Help! I Am Alone with the Abuser

Priscilla's story in Chapter 4 is not unusual. Empty nesters wake up to discover that the kids have grown and left. The children had been distractions in the home. They were also witnesses to what was happening.

Once they left, the spouse realized they were alone with a person who treated them with disdain—sometimes feeling trapped in a house with someone indifferent as to whether they live or die—and they finally realize, "I can't live the rest of my life with this person."

As Baby Boomers come into their retirement years, news stories about "Gray Divorce" have popped up everywhere. Roughly 1 in 4 divorces in 2010 occurred to persons aged 50 and older. And the gray divorce rate is expected to rise,[85] even though the overall U.S. divorce rate has dropped and is expected to continue to drop.

These Boomer couples frequently divorce after long marriages: twenty-five or thirty years, often telling the researchers about a breaking of marital promises, not usually boredom or unfulfillment. In addition to infidelity and mental health issues, women's reasons included: addictions to alcohol, drugs and pornography; and verbal and emotional abuse. "[T]hey frequently endured years of this treatment—desperately hoping for change—before finally pulling the plug on their marriages."[86] In addition to infidelity and mental health issues, men pointed to their wives' excessive spending and not working, and disagreements on how to treat their adult children.[87] Loneliness and economic instability seem to be the biggest challenges after a grey divorce.

---

85 Susan Brown, "The Gray Divorce Revolution: Rising Divorce Among Middle-Aged and Older Adults, 1990-2010," ***The Journals of Gerontology Series B Psychological Sciences and Social Sciences*** 67, no. 6 (Oct. 2012): 731-41.

86 J. E. Crowley, "Gray Divorce: Explaining Midlife Marital Splits," ***Journal of Women Aging*** 31, no. 1 (Jan-Feb 2019): 49-72, accessed 1/3/20, **https://www.ncbi.nlm.nih.gov/pubmed/29210619**.

87 Crowley, "Gray Divorce." See also her article: "Baby Boomers Are Divorcing for Surprisingly Old-Fashioned Reasons," ***Quartz*** (5/8/18), accessed 9/11/19, https://qz.com/1272362/baby-boomers-are-divorcing-for-surprisingly-old-fashioned-reasons/. Crowley is Professor of Public Policy at Rutgers University, where she specializes in family law in the United States.

When I interviewed people of faith who divorced over age 50, I saw men and women who endured infidelity and abuse for decades, "for the sake of the children."

Why didn't they divorce earlier? Because of the messages they got in church, and because, in most cases, they were so busy caring for their children that they lived in a distracted fog, running at a hectic pace for years, unable to stop and identify the abuse.

They knew something was off, but they couldn't place it.

In this woman's story, as she and her husband became empty-nesters and downsized, she realized that the man who told her he loved her every day in reality had disdain and contempt for her.

> *I was a shell of a person by this point, but we moved to a different house when the last kid left, downsized, and I really noticed it when the kids left. We had homeschooled, and I had no idea what an emotional buffer they were.*
>
> *Without kids providing emotional zest and distraction, the emotional barrenness of the relationship became starkly apparent. My husband's disdain and contempt became impossible to overlook.*
>
> *And this is the man who prayed with me almost every night, regularly read his Bible and said he loved me almost every day. So those times when it says you have a .03% chance of getting divorced if these things are present in your life, well, I'll let you know that I'm the .03%. He looked so [morally] good; he was an elder in the church.*
>
> *I did not realize that he had started a smear campaign behind my back for years. My daughter said, "Mom, Dad so undermined, devalued, and invalidated you our whole growing up that if we hadn't homeschooled, I don't think we would've given you any credence."*
>
> *I had no idea I was sleeping with the enemy.*
>
> *It seems in retrospect he did everything he could to make me leave the marriage he didn't want and then blamed me for divorcing him. He told me how miserable he was, but he would "never go through the public humiliation of a divorce."*
>
> *When he was able to present himself as the victim of a crazy*

> *wife, I got to bear the shame and blame while he received sympathy [thanks to] the smear campaign I did not realize he had been waging for many years to our children, family, church, and community…*
>
> *This man is so smooth. I don't know how to describe it to you…*
>
> *[Now] I feel far less lonely than when I was married. There's something horrible about living every day with someone who has contempt for you.*

It is more common than you might think to have an abusive spouse who frequently proclaims their undying love. At the end of this chapter, you'll hear from a woman married to a serial cheater who told her literally fifty times a day he loved her. It is part of the masquerade to cover up their true identity and behavior behind the scenes.

But when the kids have left home, sometimes the mask slides off, and the truth is revealed.

Some empty nesters use their newfound freedom to go to counseling and get better at problem-solving and conflict management. For some people, this saves their marriage. By learning to set boundaries and speak in a way that they will be heard, the victim communicates in a way the abuser finally understands. The abuser doesn't call the shots anymore. Their spouse no longer lives on Planet Me. In some cases, the abuse stops.

As this woman's story shows, finding her voice and (for the first time in more than thirty years of marriage) asking questions, led her to realize her boundaries had been violated and trampled, and she was no longer willing to look the other way and ignore the evidence of her husband's many affairs. Without children at home, it was easier for her to leave.

> *[For a while I told myself,] I'm just going to pretend like nothing's happening, and I'm just going to carry on and have a happy marriage. I had learned to protect myself by disassociating and never confronting him, so we actually got divorced never having had one fight…*
>
> *I think because of my therapy, and [because I was challenging] him, he started coming home at a normal time; he started taking me out on walks and things; he started paying attention to me, so I think he was doing that whole thing that abusers do to try to keep you hooked.*

[He started confessing his long string of infidelities, some of which were recent,] and he thought that would appease me… All of a sudden I was sitting there, and I realized I had no clue who I was married to. And that was frightening. That was very *frightening. I just realized I did not know who this man was…*

[The] night that he told me, I lost it. All I could think of was committing suicide…

[We were out of town and] we faked our way through the weekend. I was just out of my mind, I was so shocked and so overwhelmed. I said if I hear anything more that he's done to me, it'll crush my soul. I can't… I can't hear it, and I'm filing for a divorce.

She left. Today she has found happiness and peace, and she ministers to other Christian women who are married to serial adulterers.

5. This Really Is Abuse!

A lot of people don't identify what they are going through as "abuse." They do not see the pattern of indifference, threats, control, and put-downs as abuse. They call it a "difficult marriage." They blame it on themselves for not being good, submissive, or obedient wives (or in the case of men, on not being godly spiritual leaders).

Not until they read a book—or a pastor or counselor calls it abuse—does the light turn on.

Abuse victims sometimes benefit from seeing a list of examples of abuse, such as the ones in Chapter 4. For some, they discount emotional abuse because it's "just words," not fists. They may not identify physical intimidation (blocking exits, towering over you, pinning you to the wall) as abuse.

For me, counselors, advisors and others using the word abuse was what gave me the freedom to start seeing the way things were as not being okay, and not something just wrong with me. Getting involved in support groups/classes and reading books on domestic violence was huge

One woman said that she was too defensive to accept the word "abuse," so her counselor gently brought up the subject by talking about "control" instead. She would have shut him down if he had told her she was abused—

My counselor changed my life and made a big impact on me.
He didn't use the word "abuse" but addressed behaviors instead. Everything he said was soft and gentle and kind. "Are you being controlled?"
He knew he couldn't use the word abuse. He would address behaviors. "It's not okay for your husband to expect you to clean up, and cook,
when you come home from a long drive."
I needed to hear it from a man. I told him I can only live 50 more years, I'll just have to get through it. He told me that was a sad way to live. He said, "I've been a counselor a long time. The longest I've ever seen a marriage this bad survive is 11 years."

Looking back, it's plain as day, but at the time, I didn't know it was abuse.
I didn't know I was experiencing emotional abuse.
All of these "marriage" books, such as The Excellent Wife, need abuse disclaimers [telling people these techniques are harmful if used with an abusive husband]. However, that isn't the only answer because being abused was so familiar to most of us that we didn't recognize it as abuse until we got out. Hindsight is 20/20. Gaslighting blinded me to my own situation.
I thought I was suffering for Christ.
I have such a heart for victims of abuse now. I'm almost glad I've experienced it.

All those people in my church said, "Oh, that could not have happened to her. She'd have never stayed married to him and had

all those children. It must be a lie." We'd been married almost 30 years.

I heard the song by Casting Crowns, "Thrive," and the words, "We were made to more than just survive." And I knelt down in my kitchen and just said, "Lord, something is so wrong, and I do not know what it is. I need you to rescue me." I was just a shell of a person at that point.

I couldn't even trust my own perceptions, couldn't figure out why I was depressed. I just felt like a horrible wife, and he was telling me I was a horrible wife. For him, everything was a competition. He had to be better at everything. And he would correct everything. I was cutting carrots for a salad one night, and he said, "Well, you need to do this. It's more efficient." I said, "I'm not trying to be efficient. I'm just making a salad."

How could I have missed it? But I was the good wife. I was not going to talk badly about this man. I was going to encourage him. I was going to respect him. You know: Love and Respect. That's why I checked my brain at the door. I told myself, "It doesn't matter how the man's acting. You will treat him as if he's awesome sauce, even if he's evil." That's the level of denial I will never live in again.

I can't explain to you unless you've heard enough about emotional abuse, how he would draw me in and then reject me, make me want him emotionally and in every other way, and then reject me.

These kinds of contradictory situations are common in abusive marriages. Many people call it "mind-games" or "crazy-making." For example, a husband demanding the wife initiate sex and do what "turns him on," but when she does exactly that, he rejects her and ridicules her as not being attractive enough.

Or a husband telling the wife and kids to stand up for themselves if they want to be respected, but lashing out in anger and threatening to throw them out when they do.

Or a wife of thirty years asking for sex, but telling her husband he doesn't deserve to have sex with her because he had sex with someone else when he was a teen.

Or a husband who says his wife is trying to vilify him, when in reality she is trying to cover for him because he backed out of yet another family birthday party at the last moment.

We tend to equate abuse with angry outbursts, threats, or name-calling. That isn't the full story. These incidents come down to one key message: "You are required to fulfill all my needs. But sadly, you are not good enough and will never be good enough. Keep trying… and perhaps someday you will please me."

6. *Someone I Respected Told Me I was Free to Go—If I Wanted To*

Although each person has the responsibility to protect themselves and their children, many people they feel better if they have the support or permission of a respected figure: perhaps a doctor, parent, or religious leader.

Sometimes people find themselves in the hospital for stress, anxiety, panic attacks, or depression—or for physical injuries due to abuse—and their doctor or nurse or advocate discusses warning signs with them.

Other times, the hospital requires patients to be released from medical care into a *safe* situation. This gives the abused spouse permission—and if necessary, an excuse—to avoid going back to the abuser.

Many people of faith believe that in some way a pastor speaks for God on matters of morality. If the pastor or Christian counselor says they are free to go, they believe they have God's blessing to leave.[88]

One of our pastors at church was an expert on abuse,
having been raised by a violent father in a Christian
minister's family.
He gave a talk to our domestic violence survivors group.
He explained the abuse cycle and said, "God is all powerful.
But he'll never change a person against their will.
Sometimes it is time to cut the anchor chain and let the boat drift away."

88 Part of healing from abuse is making important choices on your own, whether anyone approves or not. You can listen to your instincts and get to safety without consulting others. Also, certain churches are more understanding of divorce than others: For example, "Lutheran (70 percent), Methodist (63 percent) and Presbyterian/Reformed pastors (62 percent) are most likely to believe domestic violence took place if a church member files for divorce and cites domestic violence as a cause. Baptist (49 percent) and Pentecostal (40 percent) pastors are less likely," according to a 2017 survey done by LifeWay Research (a research organization connected with the Southern Baptist Convention). Retrieved 12/31/19, **http://www.bpnews.net/48369/church-response-to-domestic-violence-focus-of-study**.

By the way, it's important to know that the church has changed over the past thirty years. In the 1990s, it was common for many churches to give only two reasons for divorce (adultery and abandonment), but now physical abuse is recognized by three out of four Protestant pastors as an acceptable reason. In fact, now it is the most accepted reason!

I believe that much of this is due to mandated reporting laws that hold pastors legally responsible for calling law enforcement when someone's life is in danger. If your state doesn't require pastors to be mandated reporters, consider using your vote and voice to change that.

In a survey of a thousand Protestant pastors and a thousand American churchgoers on five reasons people get divorced, researchers found the majority of pastors are very understanding when adultery, abuse, or abandonment occurs. In fact, pastors are more understanding than the churchgoers themselves! If you must get out, they do not see it as a sin.

> *Overall, Protestant pastors are more likely to condone divorce in cases of domestic violence than for other commonly cited reasons for ending a marriage. Nearly 3 in 4 pastors say it's not a sin to divorce for abuse.*[89]

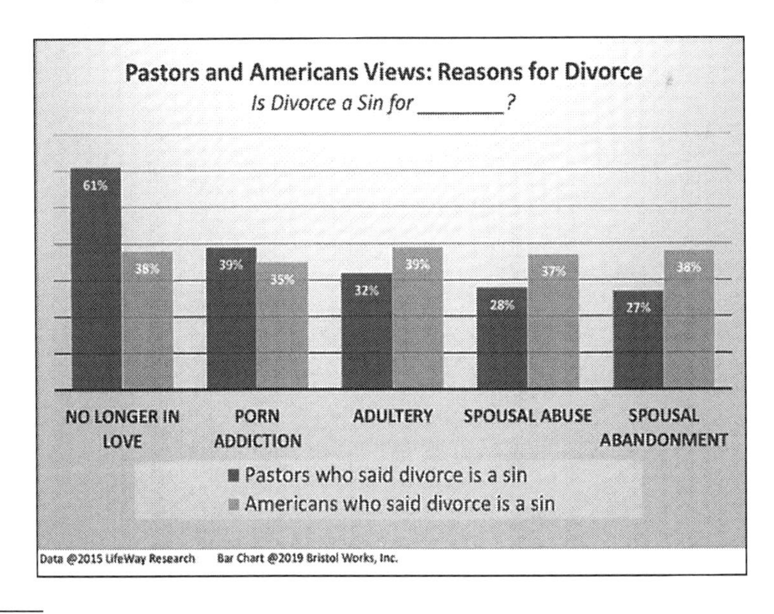

89 Timothy C. Morgan, "One in Three Americans Say Divorce Is Still a Sin in Cases of Abuse: Pastors Are More Understanding When Adultery, Spousal Abuse, or Abandonment Occurs," ***Christianity Today*** (8/18/15), accessed 1/26/19, https://www.christianitytoday.com/news/2015/august/one-in-three-americans-say-divorce-is-still-sin-in-cases-of.html.

7. An Old Friend Told Me I Was Worthy of Love, Not Disrespect

Sometimes the motivation comes from an old friend who says something like, "You were one of my favorite people in high school. You were fun and full of energy. I still see that fantastic person deep inside you. I don't see you as over-the-hill. To me, you're still wonderful. You don't deserve this."

This affirmation says you are valuable, just as Jesus says.

Somehow, one heartfelt comment can change everything! This simple statement unlocks the door. It can be powerful. It can break the chains and help a person see their worth to others and to God.

It was about this time that God brought an old dear church friend and fellow singer back into my life for our 35th church reunion—our choir reunion. Someone who knew me back in the day. The innocent me… The me I wanted to be again, [though I] was only the shell of that person.

This friend saw the [older me who felt unattractive], and we talked on the phone afterward. I spilled everything. And I was told I was beautiful on the inside and outside, just like I was 35 years ago, and to just believe in myself. That God doesn't want me to suffer like this.

Well, I hung up and thought if this person can see the real me through all this yuck, then that's how God sees me, too.

One or two conversations was all it took for her to realize God saw her as valuable, too! That helped her along her long, slow path to get away from a violently abusive husband.

An ex-wife of a Southern Baptist pastor who'd had three long-term affairs, plus numerous other sexual liaisons, said—

> *I think you have to get to the point where you realize your own worth. And your worth is in Christ. Your spouse has likely spent years ripping you apart, and tearing you down, and making you doubt yourself.*
>
> *You have to get to the point where you start to realize that*

you're a cherished child of the King, and he does not want you to live like that. You are not honoring him by allowing someone to tear you down over and over and over again.

And you know, you're not honoring him by putting your children through that. You're not honoring him by being this long-suffering martyr of a spouse... That is not what he wants for us...

I don't believe [in] divorce for irreconcilable differences, just because you can't get along, [but] that is not what we're talking about. We're talking about a totally different situation, where you've got somebody in the marriage who is seriously disturbed, who is seriously abusing—either physically, spiritually and/or emotionally—one person in the marriage.

8. A Friend Walked with Me and Gave Me Courage

Two women friends started talking at a high school playoff softball game. They had been friends for years. Their kids had played on the same sports teams since childhood, and neither woman had known the other was being abused.

That one conversation, where they both admitted being abused by their husbands, turned the tide. They came to my support group at church and told their heartbreaking stories.

Over the next few months, they became champions for each other as they set boundaries for their husbands, hoping to keep the marriage together. They navigated the ups and downs of holding them responsible for the disrespect and meanness. One said—

People think domestic violence is a daily occurrence. It's not.
It's walking on eggshells all the time. It's wondering what might set him off.
It's the belief that if I can control everything
there is no chance he'll explode at me.

Sadly, neither husband chose to change, even with pastoral involvement. Both women divorced to protect themselves and their children, and they moved on with their lives. They supported each other, ran errands for each other, and stood by each other's side.

Today they are both safe and free from constant anxiety.

9. Prayer: God Told Me I Could Go

Some people of faith have told me that God finally released them from their marriage, telling them it was okay to go. God gave them a Bible verse, a sign, or a dream.

This happens to many devout people: Even though they have biblical grounds for divorce for many years, they cannot leave. They are obsessed with staying (some therapists call this a trauma-bond), even if it means more betrayal and abuse.

I had a dream. I was a bird in a birdcage, and the cage door was open.
The message was, "You can fly free if you wish, but the door may not be open again."
I flew out. I knew that my courage would fail me if I didn't go then.

For other people, it is a Bible passage that speaks to the issue.

I will instruct you and teach you in the way you should go.
I will counsel you with my eye on you.
—Psalm 32:8 (NIV)

Many great people in the Bible prayed and asked for help. God gave them wisdom, sometimes even in the form of signs and dreams. James 1:5 (NIV) says, "If any of you lacks wisdom, you should ask God, who gives generously to all without finding fault, and it will be given to you."

One woman whose pastor prohibited all divorce, even from her physically abusive husband, explained how she heard from God—

It took years. Counseling. Praying. Trying to gather my courage. I was so afraid. I finally set a date for myself, a goal for getting out.

That month passed. I was praying the Lord would give me two days when my husband wasn't home. [That was] almost impossible, as he was forever unemployed. He got a job; he hadn't been there long when he came home to tell me they were sending him away for a week's training out of state.

It took me a few minutes to realize this was an answer to my prayer. I had two weeks to make plans, tell my family and close friends, and figure out where we would go. I scheduled time off work and told my supervisors. The week I moved out was exactly a year to the month and day I originally set the goal for myself a year prior.

One woman tells the story of her grandmother praying to God for a sign to leave her husband.

Elizabeth Blakeley
@abirdcalledhope

Replying to @GGBaskerville

My grandma told God that if her husband came home and said a certain phrase, then that would be her sign to leave. He came home and said it. As much as she disliked divorce, she left. Her counselor said he had the potential to be very dangerous.

7:11 PM · Jun 20, 2019 · Twitter for Android

3 Likes

Gretchen Baskerville @GGBaskerville · Jun 20, 2019
Replying to @abirdcalledhope
Great story. She wanted to be sure. She was willing to leave, but she needed the sign it was the right thing. I hope others are watching for Lord to let them know: "It's time to go."

4

10. My Spouse Divorced or Abandoned Me

We haven't talked much about your spouse leaving *you*. But when this happens, it is incredibly painful, especially if you were trying to hold the relationship together and were a faithful, caring spouse.

It is not only a heartbreaking betrayal of the marriage; it is also personal rejection. You feel discarded, worthless, and kicked to the curb.

You need time to repair your sense of self-respect and worthiness as a human being.

The benefit to being the rejected spouse is that you often get more sympathy from the church.

One day, a woman's husband disappeared while their family of seven was living and serving as missionaries overseas. She checked the hospitals and couldn't find him. She tracked his credit card use in an attempt to locate him. Finally, she looked at their bank balance and realized he had drained their life savings. He had bought an airline ticket and fled back to the United States. She didn't find him for years.

She received a lot of emotional support from her pastor and church. When asked about her anger toward her ex-husband, who had also been a pastor, she said—

> *He took all of our savings and left me and our five minor kids in a third-world country with $700 to our name. [I had to stay alone in that country for two more years waiting for our adopted kids to get visas to enter to the U.S.]*
>
> *I have stared into the abyss. My nine-year-old son had died. My husband of more than twenty-five years walked away from our marriage, from God, and our kids... My kids were devastated when their dad left. They did not know the bad things about him.*
>
> *All of our lives, his words and actions never matched. He told me he loved me fifty times a day... that all he lived for was me and the kids. It was enough to keep me in the marriage. The day he walked out and left me with no money—even though I was upset and cried—it all fell into place. Finally, his words and actions matched.*
>
> *He refused to pay child support, and I had to have him arrested. I should have left him, but I am just glad it is over!*

It took six years for law enforcement to find her ex-husband. He was arrested and delivered a few thousand dollars in unpaid child support, then stopped paying again.

> *I forgive him. I teased my therapist I would write him a thank-you note for leaving me. I am so glad it is over. I'd rather have no-one than to spend another day with him. He has not changed at all, from what I hear. It's really sad.*

And how is she now?

> *Joy is my target. I can get to joy. Joy is soul-nourishing. Happiness is a moving target. Some of the richest most famous people in the world are the most miserable. Joy comes from pouring your life out in service to others. Doing unto others. Living for Him. I am [in my 50s]. I am planning to leave the U.S. and spend the next 10 years in [the same Asian country where my husband abandoned me] serving the people there. I will work with a group that provides schooling and therapy for kids with brain injury. I'll be mentoring young people and sharing the gospel. I speak the language and love the people and the culture!*

One of the leading researchers on divorce, Dr. Mavis Hetherington, wrote, "In the early period, the 'left' spouses were the most unhappy and resentful, but by the end of the second year, there were few differences between those left and the 'leavers'... [In] the second year there was an upsurge in emotional wellbeing as people began to adapt to their new life situation."[90] So if you got left, you may feel worse than the "leavers" for the first two years, but you too will find your stride.

If You Decide to Leave

If you decide to leave (and that is 100% your decision), here are some tips to make the divorce process better (meaning lower conflict, fairer, a faster process, and fewer attorney and court fees). You don't need to do all of them—or any of them—but doing a few might make your life a little easier.

I interviewed a Christian divorce attorney, and he said one of the biggest mistakes his clients make is waiting until they have *all* the of financial documents *before* they file for divorce. (Your attorney is able to get bank balances, retirement vesting, and other financial documents. That's their job. So if you're in a dangerous situation, get out now, and don't wait to finish this list.)

Do not tell your spouse you are divorcing until you are ready to go.

When you tell your spouse you are leaving, separating, or divorcing, some may take it in stride, but brace yourself for the possibility of a

---

90 Hetherington and Kelly, *For Better*, 50-51.

complete personality change. Some abusers become aggressive and physically violent when they realize the stability of their life, their finances, and their public image are at risk. Some will immediately become obsessed with money and clean out the bank accounts. Some may threaten you with weapons, even if they never had before.

The Escape Plan for Those Considering Separation or Divorce

This plan includes some items to collect and factors to consider. It also includes tips for protecting yourself and your children. The lists below are in no particular order. **An important note: These are basic lists for people who are in difficult relationships but *not* in physical danger right now.**

What if You're in Danger Right Now?
Call 911. If you can safely get out, grab the kids and leave. If you cannot get out safely, you may need to agree to any demand to keep the peace until you can escape. Do what you must to stay alive.

What If You Live with a Violent Person?
Educate yourself on what to say and do when in dangerous situations. Go to these websites from a safe computer (work, library, friend's house) and follow their recommendations.

1. National Domestic Violence Hotline: wwwthehotline.org
2. Focus Ministries: https://www.focusministries1.org/SafetyPlan.pdf (don't forget the "1" in the URL)

For those in troubled marriages but not in immediate physical danger, the lists below can be useful in making your plan to leave. To get ready, I would recommend you go through them point by point. It might take some time to gather the information. Every state is different. I am not an attorney, so please get legal advice that pertains to your state and situation.

And again: Call 911 if this is an emergency.

THE FINANCIAL LIST

Gather these items, if possible. If not, your attorney can do this.

1. Cash and bank accounts: Make copies of statements for checking, savings, and money market accounts. Get the login/passwords, and have an ATM card.
2. Investment accounts: Fidelity, Betterment, WealthFront, Vanguard, etc. Make copies of statements or take screenshots of the totals for these investment and brokerage accounts.
3. Tax Returns: Photocopy or photograph the past three years of tax returns, including every page. Include any letters from the IRS or your state claiming that you owe money.
4. Retirement accounts: Photocopy or photograph statements from IRAs, 401(k)s, State Teachers Retirement (STRS), federal retirement plans, pension plans, stocks, bonds, or mutual funds. It's important to have these divided in the divorce decree.
5. Social Security and Medicare numbers: Photocopy or photograph the cards and documents for those in your household. Be aware that if you were married more than ten years to your spouse before you divorced, you may be entitled to Social Security benefits on your ex-spouse's record (even if they have remarried). To learn more about this, go to https://www.ssa.gov/planners/retire/divspouse.html
6. Document income: Make copies of the last paystub for both of you. Plus, monthly disability, social security, trust income, bonuses, retirement, support, or other income.
7. Credit cards: Make copies of the last credit card statements. Make a list of all credit card numbers, expiration dates, and CCVs.
8. Know your expenses: Make copies of the last bills for gas, electricity, trash, water, mobile phone, internet, gardening/pool, cable TV or subscriptions, cleaning, snow removal, groceries, meals out, coffee, takeout food, and maintenance, etc. Note your monthly rent or mortgage, homeowners/renter insurance,

car payment, gasoline, car insurance, parking, property taxes, homeowners association dues and special assessments. Doctors, presciptions, vision, dental, and therapy. Download free form at www.lifesavingdivorce.com/forms

9. School records and school ID cards: Photocopy or photograph.
10. Check your bank safety deposit box: Consider moving any of your own personal valuables, heirlooms, and jewelry, to a family member or friend's house. Photocopy or scan all important documents (deeds, bonds, stock certificates).
11. Find out about government assistance, if necessary. If you have a job, you are one step ahead. But if you are worried about finances, make a call to your state's welfare office or "temporary assistance" office and ask about their requirements.
12. Photocopy or scan lists of addresses: Church directories, company address lists, neighborhood lists, school/college address lists.

THE ASSETS LIST

Again, if you can't collect all the documents on this list quickly and easily, your attorney can do much of it.

1. Automobile: Photograph or photocopy the pink slip (proof of ownership), the loan statements, license plate number, VIN number (in the front window), repair history, and most recent registration.
2. Real Estate: Monthly mortgage bill (or name and address of landlord), property tax statements, title or deed to real estate, homeowner's insurance, HOA (homeowner's association fees).
3. Bills/Debts: Monthly statements for student debt, credit cards, furniture, or any other debt.
4. Businesses: Three years of tax returns for any companies in which or your spouse hold 25% or more of the company.
5. Any gifts given to you, especially if it came with a card or note showing it's a gift for you. Gifts belong to you. The giver usually cannot take it back in a divorce. If the giver is your spouse or

someone from your spouse's family, they may try to claim it was a loan, not a gift. Once you are married, your engagement ring and wedding ring are usually considered gifts that belong to you, even after the divorce, but check with your attorney

6. Ask your attorney about locking your credit by contacting Experian, TransUnion, or Equifax so that your ex-spouse cannot take out new credit cards in your name.
7. Make a video record of your house and your belongings. Using your smartphone (or a friend's), walk through the house, attic, basement, garage, and any storage sheds. Point out verbally the important furnishings or belongings, anything worth over $100. Make comments about anything important to you. You might also show the condition of the house, so that if your spouse damages the house, you have proof of how it looked on that date. You can usually upload this video directly to Dropbox or Google Drive just in case your phone is lost or stolen.

THE LEGAL LIST

Photograph or photocopy the following. Your attorney may be able to do much of this if you cannot find this information quickly and easily.

1. Marriage certificate, prenuptial agreement, postnuptial agreement. Even if you voluntarily signed a prenuptial agreement at your spouse's request, and later you discovered the depth of your spouse's problems, you may be entitled to a fair split of the assets, child support, and spousal support anyway. Many states will not let the higher-income spouse shirk their statutory duty to support the lower-income spouse and children.
2. Government ID such as driver's licenses, passports, birth certificates, social security cards, Medicare card.
3. Legal documents such as living trusts, life insurance trusts, other trusts.
4. Restraining orders.
5. Professional licenses, work permits, visas (H-1B), and green cards.
6. Employment and employment agreements: If your spouse is

an executive or a salesperson who gets commissions and/or bonuses, there may be an employment contract that promises commissions, bonuses, or benefits such as stock or stock options, company car, company phone, or deferred compensation.

7. Letters, emails, texts, or notes that may indicate that your spouse had pressured you to give up your right to the family assets (for example, quitclaiming real estate).
8. If your spouse has a pension or retirement plan, your attorney may want you to hire a QDRO expert to make sure you get your fair share, divided and included in the divorce judgment. Look at it this way: Why wouldn't you want to pay an attorney $2,000 to get $200,000?
9. Medical/dental insurance cards, prescription medication lists, immunization lists, lists of doctors/hospitals, medical history, medical conditions, surgeries, etc. Psychological history (dates and counselors seen).

THE SAFETY AND SECURITY LIST

1. Mail delivery. Consider opening a private mailbox to keep your spouse from looking at your personal mail. Also, you may want to ask your attorney about enrolling in the Address Confidentiality Program if you are in a domestic violence situation. You might want to go to the Wikipedia page that has links to each state's program and phone number. https://en.wikipedia.org/wiki/Address_confidentiality_program
2. Mobile phone. The 911 Cell Phone Bank is a U.S. program that gives away free emergency phones that only connect you with 911. Or you may want to get a "burner phone," an inexpensive phone using prepaid phone cards, if your own phone is being tracked or used to listen in to your conversations. Consider opening a new bank account, PO box, new Google account, new email address, remove tracking apps off your phone, send a copy of all documents to a friend/family/Google drive, use Whatsapp encrypted phone calls, etc.

3. Phone numbers in your wallet. Keep a paper list of important phone numbers in your wallet and in an emergency bag, just in case your phone is lost or stolen.
4. Child porn. If you run across child porn images (real or not), report it immediately to law enforcement. Do not print it or send it or show it to anyone. Contact the National Center for Missing or Endangered Children and follow their instructions: http://www.missingkids.com/gethelpnow/cybertipline or by phone (1-800-843-5678). Do not transfer, email, or print any child pornography. That is illegal, and it is also unnecessary. If you wish, you can turn over the pedophile's computer/laptop to the police. But a good first step is to report child pornography online to the National Center for Missing and Endangered Children: https://report.cybertip.org/
5. Document your spouse's behavior in a diary, journal, or calendar. Keep track of any behavior you observe: conversations, threats, accusations, confessions, excuses, strange credit card charges, phone charges, online video viewing logs and charges, websites visited, obvious or subtle threats, arrests, police calls, criminal activity, witnesses, observations, damage or disappearance of property, or vandalism. Give copies, photos, or scans to trusted friends.
6. Save and print important emails and text messages (including the date). Save voice messages. On some phones, you can save voice messages long-term, move them to a flash drive, upload them to a cloud service, such as iCloud, Google Drive, Dropbox, or email the audio file to someone else as proof.
7. Make duplicate keys for your house, car, shed, file cabinet(s), closets, or storage units. Get the combinations for locks or safes. Store these at a trusted friend/family's home.

THE "BEING SMART" LIST

1. Store up cash over the next 90 days. Your grandmother may have kept "mad money" stuffed in a jar in the cupboard (an old phrase meaning, "enough money in your purse so you can call

a cab to leave a date who made you mad": you don't have to put up with bad behavior; you can stand up for yourself and get away from the person). You can, too.

2. Start telling trusted people the truth about your marital problems. Find a friend or two who will help you. If they don't believe you, just move on and find those who do. If you are in physical danger, tell trusted neighbors, friends, and clergy. Give them a copy of any restraining orders you have and a large, clear photo of your abuser. Tell them what to watch for and when to call the police.

3. Optional: Track yourself. If you wish to be tracked by trusted friends/family members, set up a free tracking app on your smartphone, such as Life360. This allows your friends to know where you are, even if you don't answer the phone. Find out how to turn off any tracking app that you share with your ex, or other tracking software your ex-spouse may have installed on your electronic devices. (Sometimes it's nearly impossible to remove spyware, and in these cases, it is best to get another phone.)

4. Clear your Internet history, but be aware that it may not be possible to completely clear all searches. Do an internet search for how to clear the history on your particular browser. Type in the search bar: "How to clear my internet history for [Chrome, Safari, Internet Explorer, Firefox, etc.]." Use DuckDuckGo.com browser for secure searches. It may be best to use a safe computer at work, library, friend's house, or a hotel's business center.

5. If you are likely to be in physical danger, figure out an escape plan now so you can take the children with you. Keep an emergency bag (a "flight bag") packed and ready at all times. It should contain clothing, cash, spare medicine, photocopies of documents, etc. Don't forget to take or scan your favorite family photos, including a good photo of the abuser. Angry spouses may delete, damage, or burn photo albums.

6. Make a call to a domestic violence shelter and find out what services they offer. Call friends in advance to see if they can help you—or if they know of someone who can let you stay with them. If you are nervous about making a call like this, you can

call anonymously from a friend's phone. For more detailed lists on protecting yourself from an abuser, go to Focus Ministries' nine-page safety plan: https://www.focusministries1.org/SafetyPlan.pdf or TheHotLine.org.

7. Pick a "safe word" that only you and your children know—not the abusive spouse or any of their relatives or friends. Teach your children to either call you, call 911, or get away if they hear the safe word. For example, my friend Jennifer handled it this way—

    i. *My kids knew if I said our safe word, it was time to go. "Spooky" was our word (that was our cat's name). "I think Spooky needs you." My daughter would grab her younger brothers and the car key and head for the car. She would buckle them in. Our "flight bag" of emergency clothes and documents was already in the car. The kid would wait, and I'd be out the door running for the car. I explained it to the kids this way: "Sometimes if we are frightened or nervous, we need to get Mom and you to safety. We need to give Daddy a 'time out' by himself for a while."*

    ii. *I hid my car key behind one of the screens that covered the vents under the house. It was loose, and the key had a string on it. (Also, we had a safe word in case someone came to get them from school or the babysitter's or daycare. If the person doesn't know it, then the kids should not be released. And this is a word only Mommy and the kids know. Not Daddy or his girlfriends or relatives.)*

8. Once you file for divorce, consider communicating with your spouse in writing only, and keep detailed documentation. Look at the OurFamilyWizard application, or other co-parenting apps, and become familiar with how it works. Those apps are lifesavers; they are admissible in court, and they make it very difficult for people to change dates, wording, and pretend they didn't receive an email. The court may require that the couple share the expense. It is about $6 per month.

9. You might want to change all personal financial passwords immediately, so your partner cannot get into accounts where they don't have authorization.

10. Set up two-step verification on your personal bank accounts, social media, photos, shopping, and other online accounts. When someone logs into these accounts from their computer, a verification code is sent to your phone. The code must be entered within a few minutes to allow access to the account.

11. To safeguard your technology, visit www.techsafetyapp.org or https://hackblossom.org/domestic-violence/index.html#safety for tips.

12. If possible, buy a new mobile phone and laptop and install the software from the manufacturer; don't just transfer software from your old computer. Some abusers put spyware (keystroke recording or tracking software) on your computer or phone. It is nearly impossible to de-install, and the software company often won't help you do it. If you think your ex-spouse is capable of this, consider either getting new devices, or see a specialist who knows how to wipe clean and reinstall software without accidentally reinstalling the spyware from your current backup.

13. Do some research on divorce in your state. Every state is different, and they change their policies periodically. There is no federal U.S. divorce law. Find out how to file for divorce at your local courthouse. Some states have a longer waiting period; some have reduced fees for disabled persons; and some have no waiting period in cases of domestic violence. Some states have online calculators to determine how much child support and spousal support you will likely receive (or pay).

Almost all U.S. states have no-fault unilateral divorce now, so it is not required to prove your spouse's guilt. This will likely save you time and thousands of dollars. (Many Christians choose to go with a no-fault divorce even if their spouse is an abuser or unfaithful or has other serious problems, just so the process is faster and less expensive. Ask your attorney about your options.) Also, if your spouse is missing, each state has a different law for getting divorced. Having a little education will make you feel more prepared.

Courthouses usually have instructions online, or you can see the Court Clerk. Be sure to talk with a legal professional (an attorney or paralegal) to discuss your particular situation. (This book is not legal advice.)

Remember, in most states you are entitled to a "fair and equitable" division of assets: in other words, roughly half of the money, cars, possessions, retirement accounts, savings accounts, stock, property, and even the business growth that occurred during your marriage (starting the day you married), even if you didn't work professionally during the marriage.

14. Ask your attorney about removing weapons such as knives, guns, and martial arts weapons from the house, or hide them. In some states, it is legal to remove ammunition from weapons and lock it up, and to take weapons to someone else's house for safe keeping. If you are in a state where the laws prohibit this, get yourself away to safety.

But I'm Not Ready! This Is Too Much for Me!

For some people, this list is empowering. It gives them hope and something positive to focus on.

But if this list looks intimidating to you, I get it.

If your head is spinning because your ex-spouse handled all the finances, that's okay. You may be saying to yourself, "That's an overwhelming list. I could never do it." That's okay, too. Leave it for your attorney to do. They do it all the time.

If you are in danger right now, ***get out***. Don't even bother working on the list. Just get yourself to safety.

For others, perhaps you aren't ready to get divorced, but you just want to get safer than you are right now. You want to learn to protect yourself and your kids better. You want a plan just in case something goes wrong. For you, just pick a few items on the list, and get started!

One abused woman in my group had been physically disabled due to a work injury for many years. She had minor children and her elderly, wheelchair-bound mother living with her. She'd been married for over 25 years and had been traumatized by every type of abuse: emotional, physical, sexual, and financial.

At first, it seemed impossible to get away from her abusive husband. It looked like she was trapped forever. She was even too frightened to take a printed copy of this escape plan, for fear her husband might find it. But she hid a PDF copy of the "Escape Plan" on her phone, and she started working on it. Here's what she said:

I was told often by my abusive husband that no one else would want me. And if I left and divorced him, I would be homeless and he would get the kids. We had already lost everything: my childhood home, filed for bankruptcy, failed marriage... Abusers rationalize everything: They tell you, "It wasn't that bad. You're exaggerating."

Within four months, she told me she was ready to go. (I couldn't believe it!) She was terrified, but she felt she wanted to set an example to her teenagers so they wouldn't marry abusers.

She told the people in our group, her pastor, and her neighbors (who were police officers), and she kept them informed. She filed for divorce and had her husband served while she was in a safe place.

Although her husband reacted strongly, she had prepared herself for the onslaught of accusations and threats and kept her distance.

As she got stronger, she learned to stand firm. For a while she got pulled back into his manipulations. But after she learned some techniques to minimize contact, it got better.

He still calls, texts, and emails her, but she doesn't fall into his emotional games as much as she used to. And though money is very tight, she and her family finally have peace and feel safe.

After years of watching their father humiliate and brutalize their mother,
the children are all grateful Mom finally divorced their dad.

Bible Promises When You Need Courage to Leave

If you are a person of faith, I would recommend that you pray for strength and pray about timing. Some people are able to get to safety the moment the scales fall off their eyes and they recognize what is happening.

For others, they need a crisis or a confirmation from God. This gives them the strength to leave a destructive marriage. Something that may have seemed impossible a month ago, becomes possible through prayer.

Abuse makes you feel helpless. And abusive spouses *want* you to feel helpless. But God will help you. God loves you. He will not leave you.

He will help you as you take the first steps.

***"Though the mountains be shaken and the hills be removed,
yet my unfailing love for you will not be shaken nor my
covenant of peace be removed,"
says the LORD, who has compassion on you.
— Isaiah 54:10 (NIV)***

***"Is not this the kind of fasting I have chosen:
to loose the chains of injustice and untie the cords of the yoke,
to set the oppressed free and break every yoke?"
—Isaiah 58:6 (NIV)***

***The Spirit of the Sovereign LORD is on me,
because the LORD has anointed me to proclaim good news
to the poor.
He has sent me to bind up the brokenhearted,
to proclaim freedom for the captives
and release from darkness for the prisoners...
—Isaiah 61:1 (NIV)***

WHAT DOES THE BIBLE SAY?

Over the years of leading divorce recovery groups at my church, I've met many people who do not know what the Bible says about divorce. Many people are under the impression that God prohibits all divorce. But that is not true.[91]

They need to know God's protection of the vulnerable, and how he set up laws to release spouses from a hardhearted or unfaithful spouse.

THE BIBLICAL REASONS FOR DIVORCE

I believe in the sanctity of marriage: that God intended marriage to be lifelong, faithful, and loving.

But Scripture shows...

God allowed divorce to protect an innocent spouse from a hardhearted spouse.

In the Bible, the concept of "hardheartedness" applies to the person who is unrepentant—and we can infer from this that they broke at least one of their vows repeatedly.

The term "hardhearted" doesn't apply to the victims of the hardhearted behavior. It does not refer to a person who has decided to leave because they can no longer trust a chronically abusive or unfaithful spouse.

This chapter is about the *acceptable* biblical reasons for divorce, which

---

91 | Many of the insights in this chapter are based on the work of Christian theologians/pastors David Instone-Brewer, Craig Keener, Herb Van der Lugt, and scholar of Jewish history Rachel Biale.

are based on the Bible and the biblical marriage contract laid out in the Old Testament. These acceptable biblical reasons for divorce include:

a. **Adultery/sexual immorality**, meaning infidelity, as well as other sexual sins and sexual deviations.
b. **Physical neglect or abuse** (depriving a spouse of appropriate food, clothing, the basics of life).
c. **Emotional neglect or abuse** (withholding mutual loyalty, love).
d. **Abandonment**, ongoing hardheartedness leading to the neglect of (b) and (c) above, whether willful or unintentional.

THREE CHRISTIAN VIEWS OF DIVORCE

Christian view	Number of acceptable reasons to divorce	Verses used to support this view
Biblical View	**4 reasons** 1. Adultery/sexual immorality 2. Physical neglect/abuse 3. Emotional neglect/abuse 4. Abandonment by unbeliever	Ex. 21:10-11, Deut. 21:11-14, Gen. 2:24, Mal. 2:13-16, Matt. 5:31-32, Matt. 19:8, 1 Cor. 7:15. Plus verses telling us not to associate with people with serious sins, including all types of abuse and sexual immorality: 1 Cor. 5:11-12, Eph. 5:3-7, 2 Tim. 3:1-5. Those who don't care for their family are worse than unbelievers: 1 Tim. 5:8
New Testament Only View	**1 or 2 reasons** 1. Adultery/sexual immorality 2. Abandonment by unbeliever	Gen. 2:24, Mal. 2:13-16, Mark 10, Matt. 5:31-32, 1 Cor. 7:15
Permanence View	**0** (no acceptable reasons for divorce)	Gen. 2:24; Mal. 2:13-16, Mark 10

Biblical View—4 Reasons

This view was common among the Puritans and the English Reformers, and it is held by many in Protestant churches today. A LifeWay Research study showed that 7 in 10 pastors consider physical abuse as an acceptable reason for divorce, not a sin. Acceptance of chronic emotional abuse is growing as well.

Viewpoint: Those holding this view argue that we need to understand the scriptural text, the society, and the history of the biblical world in order to fully understand God's desire for marriages. The Law of Moses allowed for divorce, and Jesus referred to sexual immorality as well as the concept of "hardheartedness," which applied to the person who is unfaithful or abusive or who willfully withholds basic emotional and physical needs. Paul, too, reminded people of the Jewish law regarding marriage vows and abandonment. From a biblical perspective, therefore, there are multiple acceptable reasons for divorce.

New Testament Only View—2 Reasons

Without looking at the Old Testament or the Jewish roots of Christianity, some churches look only at the two New Testament passages that address the issue of divorce.

Jesus said in Matthew 5:31-32 and Matthew 19:8-9 that sexual immorality (*pornea*) was an acceptable reason for divorce. And that word *pornea* means any kind of sexual immorality from cheating, to pedophilia, to porn addictions, to name a few.

The Apostle Paul in 1 Corinthians 7:15 said if an unbelieving spouse abandons the marriage, this too was an acceptable reason for divorce. He says he allows this because God has called us to live in peace.

Viewpoint: Christians who focus only on the New Testament and discard guidance or wisdom from the Old Testament, and any insights from the culture at the time of Christ, still accept the "plain meaning" of these Bible verses, allowing two reasons for divorce.

Permanence View—No Reasons *(Note: Very few churches hold this view, together with perhaps 1 in 5 pastors)*

Some church leaders do not accept *any* reasons for divorce. This is not a common view, since Jesus (Matthew 5:31-32; Matthew 19:8-9) and the Apostle Paul (1 Corinthians 7:15) clearly give acceptable reasons for divorce: sexual immorality and abandonment. However, some Protestants do hold this view. They base it on Genesis 2:24 ("the two shall become one flesh") and Malachi 2:13-16 ("I hate divorce…") and argue that you cannot separate "one flesh" without destroying it.

Viewpoint: People who hold this view believe, based on Genesis 2:24 and Malachi 2:16, divorce is never allowed, not even for adultery, abuse, or abandonment.

DIVORCE: STARTING AT THE BEGINNING—GENESIS

Earliest Biblical Law and the People of Israel

Since Genesis speaks of the beginning of the world and is the first book in our Bible, Christians often start here.

Genesis 2:18-24 NASB	*Then the Lord God said, "It is not good for the man to be alone; I will make him a helper suitable for him." Out of the ground the Lord God formed every beast of the field and every bird of the sky, and brought them to the man to see what he would call them; and whatever the man called a living creature, that was its name.* *The man gave names to all the cattle, and to the birds of the sky, and to every beast of the field, but for Adam there was not found a helper suitable for him. So the Lord God caused a deep sleep to fall upon the man, and he slept; then He took one of his ribs and closed up the flesh at that place. The Lord God fashioned into a woman the rib which He had taken from the man, and brought her to the man.* *The man said,* *"This is now bone of my bones,* *And flesh of my flesh;* *She shall be called Woman,* *Because she was taken out of Man."* *For this reason a man shall leave his father and his mother, and be joined to his wife; and they shall become one flesh.*

In Genesis 1, we see both were made in God's image. Both are called, "Very good." The man and woman's job was to "Be fruitful and multiply, and fill the earth, and subdue it; and rule…" This is not just Adam's job. This is Eve's job, too.

According to the Bible, God's plan for people who choose to marry one another is for them to leave their parents' households to start their own household and to rule creation together. (Of course, we see in other places in Scripture that marriage and family are not God's *only* plan for his people—for example, the Apostle Paul and Jesus himself both model godly singlehood.)

Israel was different from other ancient civilizations of its day in that the law told the man and woman to leave their parents and initiate a new home. In comparing laws about marriage and divorce from other nations in the ancient world, we discover this command to leave one's parents and start a new home together was radical. In most cultures, the woman came to the man's home and served his family (most directly, his mother—which could be oppressive).

Jesus talked about this verse, and we will look at that later. For now, let's start with the Bible prior to Jesus, then move to the time of Jesus.

Early Israelite Marriage Contracts and Wedding Vows

When discussing divorce, it is best to start with marriage. In the Bible, we see laws from a time much earlier than ours, when women were not usually recognized as having rights equal to those of men, and most laws treated them as second-class rather than as people with full rights (in some cultures, they were treated as the mere property of men).

This is not God's way, ultimately, but as we read Scripture, we can see God's attempt to ensure justice and protection for women and the vulnerable, even in the midst of societies that were built for the benefit of men more than women.

We find the first three marriage requirements in the Book of Exodus, in the Law of Moses. The husband is required to give her—

- her food
- her clothing
- her marital rights

We get these vows from Exodus 21:8-11, which says if a man has a slave wife, and then takes a second wife, the first wife must be cared for at the same level and expense. In other words, she had to be treated at *wife* level, not demoted to *servant* level. If the husband refused to provide for her, he must set her free.

Exodus 21:10-11 (NASB)	*If he takes another wife to himself, he shall not diminish* ♦ ***her food,*** ♦ ***her clothing, or*** ♦ ***her conjugal rights*** *(some translations: marital rights, meaning love)* *And if he does not do these three things for her, she shall go out for nothing, without payment of money.*

The Law of Moses was clear about the promises a man must keep. The Israelites included this wording in their marriage contracts. Their marriage vows included the promise of food and clothing and marital rights.

Archaeologists digging in Israel have found actual marriage contracts. The Hebrew word for these marriage contracts, or marriage covenants, is *ketubah* (or *ketubot*, plural). The vows in an early *ketubah* were different from today's vows.

In biblical times, the man promised the same three obligations to his wife before the witnesses of community and family. These three obligations, as well as the bride price or dowry, were part of the agreement. First, we will look at the husband's obligations to his wife.

Three Obligations of the Groom in the Marriage Contract

The Bible verses from Exodus 21:10-11 show us Jewish marriage contracts required a man to carry out certain obligations to his wife. It was a one-sided covenant, from the man to the woman. Only a man could enact a divorce, so this covenant was the only protection a woman had. The husband promised to take care of his wife in three ways:

1. Food	Food was to be above the quality of slave or servant's food. (It was the amount of money a man would have to pay his neighbor to provide food to his wife in case the husband went on a long trip.)
2. Clothing	Clothing was to be suitable for her age and for the season of the year.
3. Marital rights (also known as "Conjugal rights")	Marital rights meant conjugal love and physical affection.

Jewish law was precise about the minimum food and clothing to be provided to the wife, down to the type and weight and value of the food to be provided. This *ketubah* was a covenant, and everything was spelled out clearly, so the court would be able to determine if the agreement had been broken. This attention to detail even included sex. The rabbis made sure the husband gave his wife appropriate levels of intimate contact and sex.

If a husband did not take care of the basic needs of his wife, she could demand a certificate of divorce and leave him. As we see in this verse, she would leave the marriage without owing her husband anything, and she was free to remarry.

Exodus 21:11 (NASB)	*And if he does not do these three things for her, she shall go out for nothing, without payment of money.*

As wives were not allowed to enact divorce at that time, she, the community, the witnesses, and/or her family might approach the court if her husband refused to meet his obligations. They could compel him to give her a certificate of divorce.

Safety Net for the Wife in the Marriage Contract

In addition to the three obligations of a husband to his wife (above), the Hebrew marriage contract also discussed a financial safety net for the wife. Usually valuables were held in trust by the husband and set aside to protect the wife in case of death or unjust divorce. It was made up of:

- **Bride price**—paid by the groom and promised to the bride. It was a promise of payment for the bride in the event of his death or divorce caused by his fault.
- **Dowry**—paid by the bride's father (often money or durable valuable household goods).
- **Additional valuables**—in some cases, part of the husband's property or funds when he passed away.

The groom held the money in trust and gave it to his wife if he divorced her or if he died. This was not the husband's money to spend. He could invest it and make a profit from it, but the bride price, dowry, and additional valuables were hers in case of death or divorce.

We know from the writings of the prophets that divorce was common in Old Testament times, and this type of trust fund was important for women, who were completely vulnerable.

We see the bride price and dowry mentioned in many biblical passages.

Bride Price

- Genesis 24:53 — Abraham's servant paid a bride price for his son's wife, Rebekah.
- Genesis 29 — Jacob gives 7 years of labor in exchange for each of Laban's daughters, Rachel and Leah.
- Genesis 34:12 — A bride price is offered for Jacob's daughter.
- Exodus 22:16-17 — The Law of Moses requires a bride price to be paid.
- 1 Samuel 18:25 — King Saul told David to pay him a bride price to marry his daughter.

Dowry

- Joshua 15:17-19, Judges 1:15 — Caleb gives his daughter land and springs when she marries.
- 1 Kings 9:16 — The father of one of King Solomon's wives gave the city of Gezer as her dowry.
- Micah 1:13-16 — "Using divorce imagery, the Lord condemns sinful Lachish and instructs that the faithful city of Moresheth Gath be given its dowry as it goes into exile."[92]

Is Marriage an Unconditional Covenant?

In the Bible, there are two types of covenants: *Conditional* and *Unconditional.*

Conditional covenants are like today's business agreements: Each party agrees to do or provide something valuable. If they fail to do it, the contract is broken, the other party no longer has to perform their end of the bargain, and there are penalties. (Think of an apartment rental agreement.)

Unconditional covenants are agreements that are one-sided and cannot be broken. Only God can enter an unconditional agreement, because

---

92 Charles S. Shaw, ***The Speeches of Micah: A Rhetorical-Historical Analysis,*** (Sheffield: Sheffield Academic Press, 1993), 42-43, 52. Also see note about Micah 1:14 from ***Ellicott's Commentary for English Readers*** (https://biblehub.com/commentaries/ellicott/micah/1.htm) describing this as a dowry.

only God is capable of making such an unbreakable agreement, as he cannot fail and cannot sin. (Examples of these unconditional covenants can be found in Genesis 9 and 15; in Numbers 25; in 2 Samuel 7; and in Jeremiah 31.)

God's Two Conditional Covenants

- Covenant with Abram (Abraham) in Genesis 17 — God made a commitment of land to Abram; Abram agreed to keep the sign of the covenant.
- Covenant with Israel at Sinai in Exodus 19-24 — God promised to make Israel his people; the people were required to obey fully and keep the covenant. (We see in Jeremiah 3:8 that God divorced Israel for not keeping its side of the covenant.)

Marriage is a ***conditional covenant***. It requires promises in the form of vows that are based on Exodus 21:10 (food, clothing, love) and reiterated in Ephesians 5:28-29 (nourish, care, and love).

The concept of faithfulness, "forsaking all others" was added by Jesus' words.[93] (It's important to note that the vow for the woman to "obey" the husband is not a New Testament or Jewish vow. It is a Roman addition and is not often used anymore.)[94]

The marriage covenant can be ended if the vows are broken.

The other party can choose to keep trying, but they are permitted to declare that the covenant is ended. And of course, in most countries, marriage and divorce are handled in civil court, not in religious court.

Even Jewish marriage contracts were legal documents.

Babatha's Marriage Contract

God wanted women to be protected, as we've seen in Exodus 21. The Jewish marriage contracts were written to protect women. It was a prenuptial agreement that protected a woman in case of death or divorce.

This is a marriage contract found in a cave near the Dead Sea, regarding a 21-year-old woman named Babatha, second wife of Judah.

---

93 David Instone-Brewer, ***Divorce and Remarriage in the Bible*** (Downers Grove: InterVarsityPress, 2003), 229.

94 Ibid., 232-233.

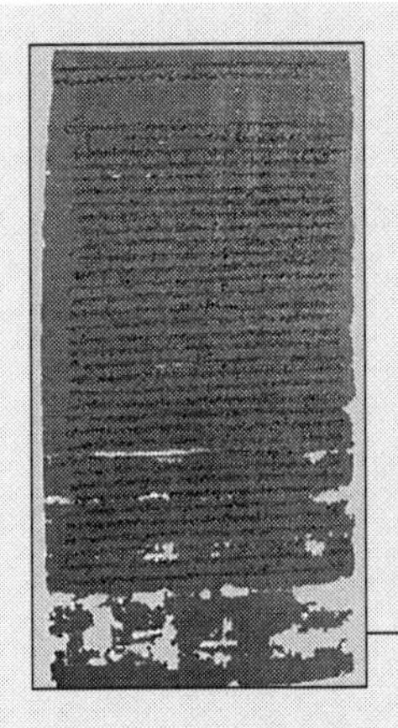

Her husband Judah promised in the contract: "I will [feed you] and [clothe] you and I will bring you (into my house)," and he promises to give her "the due amount of your food, and your bed, and your clothes..."

Her ketubah was: 400 denarii, worth about 2 years' wages, which would be paid to her if he divorced her, or if his heirs (after his death) sent her away.[95]

Babatha's Ketubah *(Marriage contract)*

Reasons for Divorce in the Bible

From the Law of Moses until the fall of Jerusalem to the Romans in AD 70 and beyond, Jewish law allowed divorce in these circumstances:

1. Breaking of Marriage Contract, the *Ketubah*. Exodus 21:11 (See: The 3 Obligations of the Marriage Contract, above.)

2. Indecency or a "matter of indecency" in a woman. Deuteronomy 24:1-2.

Deut. 24:1-2 (emphasis mine; 'evrat daver, is translated here as "matter of indecency.")	"When a man takes a wife and marries her, and it happens that she finds no favor in his eyes because he has **found a <u>matter of</u> <u>indecency</u> in her**, and **he writes her a certificate of divorce** and puts it in her hand and sends her out from his house, and she leaves his house and goes and becomes another man's wife..."

95 The story of the Babatha Ketuba (Babatha's marriage contract) was brought to my attention by David Instone-Brewer (https://alchetron.com/Babatha). Further information was gathered from the Nova special "Ancient Refuge in the Holy Land," https://www.pbs.org/wgbh/nova/video/ancient-refuge-in-the-holy-land. (Video not available, but the transcript is.) See also the entertaining video lecture by Dr. Henry Abramson (11/13/14) "Who Was Babatha?" https://jewishhistorylectures.org/2014/11/13/who-was-babatha-jewish-biography-as-history-dr-henry-abramson/. The English language translation line by line: http://cojs.org/babatha-s_ketubah-_an_early_marriage_contract/.

The Meaning of "A Matter of Indecency"

So, what does *a matter of indecency* mean in Deuteronomy 24? At the time of Jesus, it was a topic of intense debate. Two important and influential Jewish schools of Torah (the Scriptures) had opposite interpretations of the verse. Specifically, they did not agree on the meaning of "a matter of indecency" (*'evrat daver,* in Hebrew). In most English translations, we simply use "indecency," but literally it reads "indecency of a matter," which rabbis of Jesus' day framed as "a matter of indecency."

One group of Jewish teachers (those who followed the biblical interpretations of the scholar Shammai) interpreted "a matter of indecency" as meaning something extremely serious and sexual, such as adultery.

The other group of rabbis (who followed the teaching of the scholar Hillel) split the phrase and turned it into a legal loophole that allowed for easy divorce: "A matter" or "indecency."[96] They argued you could divorce for "adultery" *or* "a matter."

Interpreting it this way, "a matter" meant *anything* the husband found objectionable—for example, if a wife ruined his meal.

These two scholars lived about the time of Jesus, so this was the backdrop of the Pharisees' question to Jesus. They were really asking Jesus, "Is Hillel's view right? Can you divorce for 'any matter'?"

The Pharisees weren't asking Jesus to explain his full view on divorce and to give every acceptable reason for divorce. They were asking whether he sided with Shammai or Hillel on this one particular point: What does "a matter of indecency" mean? "Any cause," or just sexual immorality?

Jesus answered their question: sexual immorality (Matthew 19:3). He was not giving his complete analysis on every acceptable reason for divorce.

Why haven't we been taught this? Because even though Jewish scholars have studied this debate for centuries (the debate lasted about a century, starting before the time of Christ, then died out), early Christians—in the wake of the destruction of Jerusalem, Roman persecution, and trying to survive—did not.

Christian scholars rediscovered it in the 1800s and remarked on it; for example, in the 1841 book *The Works of Flavius Josephus,* the commentator says, "The words of Josephus are very like the words of the Pharisees to our Saviour upon this very subject [Matthew 19:3] "Is it lawful for a man to put away his wife for every cause?"

---

96 Instone-Brewer, ***Divorce and Remarriage in the Bible***, 111.

Then, after the Dead Sea Scrolls were examined in 1947, the topic got more attention. In 1949, one New Testament scholar, Henry Alford, wrote that Josephus had gotten an "any cause" divorce and that Jesus had been asked to take sides in the Shammai-Hillel debate on divorce.[97]

	Rabbi Shammai or *House of Shammai (Shammaites)*	**Rabbi Hillel** or *House of Hillel (Hillelites)*
Lived	50 BC – AD 30	110 BC – AD 10
Followers	Only worthy students could study the Bible	Everyone can study the Bible
Viewpoint	Usually a strict interpretation of the Bible	Usually a less strict interpretation of the Bible
Interpretation of Deut. 21:1-4 phrase "matter of indecency"	A prohibited sexual relation	An unseemly matter
Meaning	Adultery	Adultery or "any cause" (including the wife ruining a meal or a man finding another woman more attractive)
Other reasons for a valid divorce	Breaking the marriage contract, the *ketubah:* food, clothing, marital rights	Breaking the marriage contract, the *ketubah:* food, clothing, marital rights
Comments	In Matthew 19:3, we see Jesus sides with Shammai in his reply to the Pharisees. (See full explanation below.)	Hillel's grandson is mentioned in Acts 5:33-40 as an honored Pharisee and teacher of the law. He saved the lives of Peter and the other disciples.
History	Shammai's school declined when Jerusalem was destroyed by the Romans in AD 70.[98]	Hillel's views became the majority view. His followers persuaded the Romans to allow them to establish a community at Jamnia.

97 Instone-Brewer, ***Divorce and Remarriage in the Bible***, 158.
98 Instone-Brewer, ***Divorce and Remarriage in the Bible***, 142.

Certificate of Divorce = The Wife "Goes Out" and Is Free to Remarry

As Deuteronomy 24:1-4 shows (above), a husband who finds something indecent in his wife may choose to write *"a certificate of divorce,"* hand it to her, and send her out of the house. With the certificate in hand, she had proof she was free to remarry. This teaching is from the Law of Moses.

In the first five books of the Bible, the Law of Moses, divorce is mentioned many times. It was a necessity in cases of hardheartedness, and it was simply a fact of life.

Based on Jewish writings we have from around the time of Christ, there was a fair amount of divorce.

There were two phrases that went together: "Hand the wife a certificate of divorce," and "send her out." Let's take an example from the Book of Deuteronomy. Here Moses gave a law to protect a low-status wife. In this case, an enemy woman who was captured, perhaps in battle.

Remarkably, even this foreign wife who had originally been taken as a prisoner of war could expect the same food, clothing, and marital rights from her husband as Israelite wives, except she had no bride price or dowry.

If her husband no longer wished to treat her as a wife, he could not dishonor her by selling her, reducing her to slavery, or forcing her to serve him, his brothers, his children, etc. He had to "let her go wherever she wishes," which meant giving her a certificate of divorce and giving her the ability to remarry.

Deut. 21:11-14 (NIV, emphasis mine)	"...if you notice among the captives a beautiful woman and are attracted to her, you may take her as your wife... After she has lived in your house and mourned her father and mother for a full month, then you may go to her and be her husband and she shall be your wife. `If you are not pleased with her, let her go wherever she wishes. You must not sell her or treat her as a slave, since you have dishonored her."

This wife had little choice about the divorce, just as she had had little say in the marriage. There were very few ways for her to say no, or to veto it. She was sent away. But she was free to go wherever she wished. She might remarry and stay in Israel or go back to her home country.

God Gives a "Certificate of Divorce" to Israel

In several places in the Bible, God himself is so fed up with the sins of Israel in worshipping foreign gods, he—

a. Gives her a certificate of divorce and
b. Sends her away.

Isaiah 50:1 (NASB, emphasis mine)	Thus says the LORD, "Where is the **certificate of divorce** by which I have sent your mother away? Or to whom of My creditors did I sell you? Behold, you were sold for your iniquities, and for your transgressions your mother was sent away."
Jeremiah 3:8 (NIV, emphasis mine)	"I [God] gave faithless Israel her **certificate of divorce** and sent her away because of all her adulteries. Yet I saw that her unfaithful sister Judah had no fear; she also went out and committed adultery."

These passages show the prophets describing God as one who followed Jewish law on how to divorce a wife. In this case, "adultery" did not mean literal physical sex; it meant worshipping other gods, the deities of the surrounding peoples. It is spiritual adultery, using the word *adultery* as God's metaphor for emotional betrayal.

God: "I Hate Divorce"? No! Bad Translation

The Hebrew text of the Bible doesn't say, "I hate divorce."[99] The interpretation of this verse, Malachi 2:16, in some versions of the Bible is incorrect.

---

99 "Interlinear: Malachi 2:16," ***Biblehub.com,*** accessed 12/13/19, https://biblehub.com/interlinear/malachi/2-16.htm. Compare 21 major Bible translations: www.lifesavingdivorce.com/malachi

Rather, it should be translated this way:

> ***So be on your guard, and do not be unfaithful to the wife of your youth. "The man who hates and divorces his wife," says the Lord, the God of Israel, "does violence to the one he should protect," says the Lord Almighty. So be on your guard, and do not be unfaithful.***
>
> ***—Malachi 2:15b-16 (NIV, 2011 update, emphasis mine)***

The same verses in the English Standard Version (ESV, emphasis mine) read like this:

> ***...let none of you be faithless to the wife of your youth.*** "For the ***man who does not love his wife but divorces her,"*** says the ***LORD, the God of Israel, "covers his garment with violence," says the LORD*** of hosts. ***So guard yourselves in your spirit, and do not be faithless.***

The book of Malachi was written about 500 years before Christ. For the first 2,100 years it was interpreted as an anti-abuse verse, not an anti-divorce verse. That's how the great Bible translators Jerome, John Wycliffe, Martin Luther, and John Calvin viewed it. But then King James's translators changed it into an anti-divorce verse in 1611, and that continued the next 385 years.

That ended in 1996 after the Dead Sea scroll fragment of Malachi 2:16 was published, and many scholars interpreted it again as an anti-abuse verse. The New International Version (NIV, 2011 update), English Standard Version (ESV) and Christian Standard Bible (CSB) have this anti-abuse interpretation, not the "God hates divorce" wording.

In the book of Malachi, God says he is fed up with his people's disrespect toward him. God threatens to cut off the covenant with Judah.

God rebukes and warns them due to their many betrayals, including the following:

- Judah disrespects God by violating the covenant. The priests cheat God by not offering the appropriate sacrifices (1:6-8).
- Judah profanes God by marrying foreign women who serve foreign gods, leading to spiritual adultery (2:11).
- Judah has been unfaithful by dealing treacherously with the wife

> of his youth, even though she has been his companion all these years (2:14).

This entire book is about breaking promises. And God's hatred toward divorce is focused on those who break the marital contract by doing wrong and acting treacherously.

First, we see the Lord is angry with the people and no longer accepts their offerings with favor.

Malachi 2:13 (NASB)	"This is another thing you do: you cover the altar of the LORD with tears, with weeping and with groaning, because He no longer regards the offering or accepts it with favor from your hand."

Why won't God accept their offerings? Because of treachery and marrying the daughter of a foreign god (meaning marrying a heathen woman, or worshiping a heathen goddess).

Malachi 2:11 (NASB, emphasis mine)	"Judah has dealt treacherously, and an abomination has been committed in Israel and in Jerusalem; for Judah has profaned the sanctuary of the LORD which He loves and has married the daughter of a foreign god."

What kind of treachery does God condemn? Betraying the wife of your youth, who has been your companion and is legally your wife by the marriage covenant.

Malachi 2:14 (NASB)	"Yet you say, 'For what reason?' Because the Lord has been a witness between you and the wife of your youth, against whom you have dealt treacherously, though she is your companion and your wife by covenant."

The treachery behind this makes God angry. He hates divorce *by those who get rid of their wives wrongly*.

Malachi 2:16 (ESV, emphasis mine)	"For the **man who does not love his wife but divorces her,"** says the LORD, the God of Israel, **"covers his garment with violence,"** says the LORD of hosts. So guard yourselves in your spirit, and **do not be faithless.**

Notice God's summary statement: "So guard yourselves in your spirit, and **do not be faithless.**" God is not saying, "Don't divorce for any reason." In fact, we see Israelites returning from exile taking vows before God to divorce their foreign wives (Ezra 9-10).

It is treachery that God hates.
God permits justified divorce.

Only Men Could Give a Certificate of Divorce

Prior to the time of Jesus, only men could enact a divorce.[100] Women had no veto power and could be divorced without their consent until about 100 years before Jesus. However, a woman's marriage covenant, her *ketubah,* protected her rights and would financially support her in case of a divorce (unless she was an adulteress).

If a man was hard-hearted and treated his wife like a slave—for example, refusing her appropriate food, clothing, and love, yet wanting to keep her to himself—she could ask Israel's courts to get involved and force him to give her a certificate of divorce. The court would fine him, or even beat him with sticks, until he "volunteered" to write the certificate.[101]

It's fascinating, as well, to read the Mishneh Torah (Gerushin 2:20) on the topic of the courts forcing a man to divorce his wife and set her free to remarry.

He wasn't allowed to appear to be a good member of society when he was acting in an evil way by refusing to grant a required divorce.

---

100 Instone-Brewer, ***Divorce and Remarriage in the Church,*** 152. Women at Jesus' time could ask for a divorce due to neglect. One woman-initiated an "any cause" Jewish divorce in the early second century. This record was part of the Dead Sea Scrolls, according to Dr. David Instone-Brewer.
101 Rachel Biale, ***Women and Jewish Law*** (New York: Schocken Books, 1984), 98. See also Instone-Brewer, ***Divorce and Remarriage in the Bible***, 86.

No doubt many parents, relatives, and concerned community members wanted to protect their daughter or neighbor from poor treatment and make sure her dowry as the innocent spouse was secured.

Alimony and Child Support in Ancient Judaism

We don't know how common divorce was in biblical times, but because a husband could divorce his wife without her permission or consent, society at that time had a way of giving the wife a safety net.

Israelite law was better than that of some neighboring countries. It protected women from financial disaster in various ways by insisting on a marriage contract.

- The marriage contract, the *ketubah,* included a list of the husband's obligations to his wife in terms of food, clothing, and love, plus an amount of money or goods set aside (as agreed to by the husband and the woman's father) to care for her and her children in case of divorce or his death.
- The husband's obligations were laid out in the Bible in Exodus 21:10: food, clothing, and marital rights (sex and physical affection). However, "[the] man could not force his wife to have sex, or vice versa, and the illegality of marital rape became well established in Judaism at a relatively early stage."[102] This gave her security.
- The Jewish laws in the Mishnah were very precise and specified the minimum food, clothing/wool, and physical affection/sex she was to receive, along with the minimum amount of money/goods she would receive if he sent her away. These aren't laws in the Bible but were written by rabbis who wanted to give guidelines for their time and culture.
- It required the husband to give the wife a certificate of divorce and *then* send her away. Only after he gave her the certificate would she leave the house and find another husband to provide for her. Until then, he was obligated to care for her. The courts also required him to act quickly, rather than planning a divorce long before he enacted it.

---

102 Instone-Brewer, ***Divorce and Remarriage in the Bible***, 107. "The man could not force his wife to have sex, or vice versa, and the illegality of marital rape became we established in Judaism at a relatively early stage." b. 'Erub. 100b, says a wife cannot be compelled to have sex.

- Marriage was the norm in Jewish culture, and everyone would expect a woman of childbearing age to remarry.[103] With a certificate of divorce, a woman might find a new husband and remarry right away. There was a moral obligation for men to remarry if they didn't have children, to make sure they multiplied. Even Babatha (the Jewish woman whose *ketubah* we saw in the sidebar earlier), who had her own income, chose to remarry (as a second wife).
- If the wife was the innocent spouse and was sent away without good reason, she took her marital covenant (the trust fund of money or goods set aside) with her.

The size of the *ketubah* fund depended on the wealth of the father and the amount the husband put in (there was a minimum amount, but he could add more). The laws in Judaism changed over the centuries, but basically, the man would pay an amount (a *mohar*, equivalent to about one year of support)[104] into this fund.

If he could not afford it before the wedding, it could be paid at a later time (when he divorced his wife), but the amount was fixed by the marriage contract.

In his book on ancient Jewish traditions regarding divorce, David Instone-Brewer said that husbands who cared deeply for their wives would write a *conditional* certificate of divorce just before leaving for a long trip.[105] If the husband was killed by bandits or lost at sea, his wife did not have to spend time and money proving his death (proof required one witness). She could simply divorce and remarry, thus protecting herself and the children from financial ruin.

The Innocent Spouse Is Protected

Jewish law protected the innocent spouse. If the husband divorced an innocent wife, she was able to keep the entire amount of her marriage contract (the *mohar* and dowry and any additional amounts).

---

103 Ibid., 110. The same expectation existed for widowed or divorced men, who were expected to remarry if they did not already have a minimum of two children. In the Old Testament, the responsibility for having children was the man's, not the woman's. So men of advanced age without children were expected to remarry and produce offspring.

104 Chaim Benish, ***Medot Usheurai Torah***, 398-405. He would pay a ***mohar*** whether this was the woman's first marriage or if she was divorced or widowed.

105 Instone-Brewer, ***Divorce and Remarriage in the Bible,*** 122.

On the other hand, if the wife committed adultery, and her husband sent her away, she lost all or part of the money that was part of her marriage contract. Her husband kept the *ketubah*.

A cold-hearted man might want to punish his wife by withholding food. A miser might want to save money by refusing his wife appropriate clothing. But these hard-hearted husbands thought twice before giving her a certificate of divorce and sending her away with her *ketubah*, which was held in trust for her.

In fact, men who hated their wives but refused to divorce them were a serious problem in Judaism, just as they are today. Thankfully, today wives can file and get away from a hate-filled husband.

DIVORCE IN THE NEW TESTAMENT

Jesus and the Divorce Debate

Jesus was asked a question by the religious leaders. The Pharisees were jealous of his popularity and wanted to trip him up. We find two versions of the question:

- **Question in Mark:** (Mark 10:2) The Pharisees came to Jesus and wanted to test him by asking: "Is it lawful for a man to divorce his wife?"
- **Question in Matthew:** (Matthew 19:3) The Pharisees came to Jesus and tested him by asking, "Is it lawful for a person to divorce his wife for *any* matter?" (emphasis mine)

If you have read this entire chapter, you realize the version in Mark, as it stands, doesn't make sense. We already know the Law of Moses in the Bible allowed divorce, and that even God divorced Israel. And we know the Mishnah (the detailed Jewish law) specified the conditions for divorce.

Anyone in Jesus' time knew that divorce was permitted and knew what a valid divorce was.

This is why scholars believe the question in Mark is not about whether the Bible allows divorce. Instead, as we covered earlier, it is shorthand for the debate between the two rabbis, Hillel and Shammai, that started some thirty years before. The debate was: "Is it lawful for a man to divorcc his wife *for any matter* (any cause or any reason)?"

The Pharisees were trying to force Jesus to take sides between Shammai and Hillel. And it mattered to them, because Jewish people could take their marriage contract to either the Shammaite Court (toughest standards) or the Hillelite Court (any reason for divorce is okay) to determine which spouse got the marriage contract money.

Jewish School of Shammai[106]	**Jewish School of Hillel**
Toughest rules about divorce	Most lax rules about divorce
They believed Deut. 24:1 meant: A man should not divorce his wife, except if he found ***a matter of indecency*** in her.	They believed Deut. 24:1 meant: A man may divorce his wife for ***any matter***, for example, anything objectionable. They called this "any cause."
This verse is about **adultery.**	This verse opens the door to divorce for ***any reason.*** (Similar to "no-fault" or "irreconcilable differences" divorce today.)
Breaking the marital contract was grounds for a valid divorce.	Breaking the marital contract was grounds for a valid divorce.
Protects women from unjust divorce.	Makes women vulnerable to unjust divorce.

Jesus reminds them to go back and think about God's original purpose in marriage.

Genesis 2:24 (NASB)	"For this reason a man shall leave his father and his mother, and be joined to his wife; and they shall become one flesh."

106 Instone-Brewer, ***Divorce and Remarriage in the Church***, 141-60. During the Fall of Jerusalem, AD 70, the Shammaite school "virtually disappeared" along with several other groups, such as the Sadducees, according to Instone-Brewer, which is why the significance of this conflict was not discussed in the context of divorce until the Dead Sea Scrolls were discovered.

And Jesus adds:

Mark 10:8b-9 (NASB)	"So they are no longer two, but one flesh. What therefore God has joined together, let no man separate."

Jesus says, from the beginning, God intended marriage to be—

- lifelong
- monogamous
- binding in God's sight

Jesus teaches here that divorce is not God's ideal, but he agrees with the law of Moses that sometimes it is necessary. He is clear why marriage is supposed to be a life commitment neither spouse should break. It was not a merely temporary agreement. Its purpose was for two people to grow together in love and commitment so as to become one flesh.

But again, at the same time, Jesus agrees with the Law of Moses *allowing* for divorce.

Then the Pharisees followed up with another question. They want to catch Jesus in a trap. Jesus had just said that marriage was meant to be lifelong; yet the common belief was that a man was *required* to divorce a wife even *suspected* of adultery (even though that does not appear in the Bible).

Matthew 19:7-9 (NIV)	"'Why then,' [the Pharisees] asked, 'did Moses command that a man give his wife a certificate of divorce and send her away?' "Jesus replied, 'Moses permitted you to divorce your wives because your hearts were hard. But it was not this way from the beginning. I tell you that anyone who divorces his wife, except for sexual immorality, and marries another woman commits adultery.'"

In saying this, Jesus establishes these claims:

1. Moses permitted divorce. The Law of Moses is a concession because people are hard-hearted and refused to give their spouse the care the law required.
2. Jesus says the school of Shammai's interpretation of Deuteronomy 24:1-4 is correct: *Indecency* refers to sexual immorality,

not just anything that annoys a husband. Remarriage is okay for the innocent spouse. (His disciples obviously didn't expect this. They sided with Hillel, as Jesus did on some occasions.)

3. Jesus is arguing that divorces for Hillel's "any matter" were invalid; therefore, the certificate of divorce for a frivolous divorce is invalid, and any consequent remarriage is invalid. This is why Jesus' disciples were so shocked. They were used to easy divorce and easy remarriage.

   Jesus' statement was revolutionary in protecting innocent women far more than Hillel's followers required and penalizing those who get frivolous divorces.

   Some scholars today say Jesus abolished Moses' law about acceptable divorce in Exodus 21, but this does not seem likely. Jesus never says he disagrees with the allowance for divorce in the Law of Moses. If Jesus was overthrowing the Law of Moses in this regard, he would have said something when the Pharisees brought up the topic of certificates of divorce. And Jesus said nothing forbidding remarriage after a *valid* divorce. He only condemned remarriage after an invalid "any matter" divorce.

4. Jesus also explains divorce is *permitted* in the case of adultery but is not *required.*

What Is Sexual Immorality? Adultery and Other Sins

In the Matthew 19:9 response, Jesus uses the word *pornea,* which is used for sexual immorality. In Matthew 5:32, a similar passage from the Sermon on the Mount, Jesus uses nearly the same phrase and mentions men who divorce their wives for anything but sexual immorality (*logou porneia).*

This word *pornea* means more than adultery. (Although *pornea* has a wide meaning, we have to be careful about arguing from the exact meaning of a Greek word. Jesus was almost certainly speaking Aramaic.)

The writer of the Book of Hebrews uses two words for sexual immorality. If they meant the same thing, two words would not be needed.

Hebrews 13:4 (NIV, emphasis mine)	"Marriage should be honored by all, and the marriage bed kept pure, for God will judge **the adulterer** and all **the sexually immoral.**"

By judging both adulterers *and* the sexually immoral, we see God prohibits immoral sexual behavior in addition to adultery. Any sexually immoral conduct that disrupts the marriage is a problem to God.

The Apostle Paul on Divorce and Remarriage

Paul spent most of his ministry in Rome, Ephesus, and Corinth, at the hub of the Roman Empire, more than a thousand miles from Jerusalem. He was a Pharisee by training, but he was born far from Jerusalem, in a world dominated by Greco-Roman thinking. Rome was the center of commerce, life, and art.

Unlike Jewish divorce requiring a document, Romans divorced by simply walking out the door (or being asked to leave). Abandonment was a simple method of divorce.[107] And both women and men could initiate a divorce.

This caused confusion for the Corinthian Christians who were brought up with the Jewish law, so they wrote a letter to Paul asking what to do. If they were married to an unbeliever, and their spouse left without giving them a certificate of divorce, were they still married? Was it a valid divorce?

If they weren't handed a certificate of divorce, could they remarry? Were they now an "*agunah*,"[108] bound in a marriage that didn't really exist, but unable to remarry?

Paul answered the Corinthians' question by reminding them that breaches of marital duty were serious. In the famous New Testament chapter about marriage and divorce (1 Corinthians 7), Paul follows the same pattern as Exodus 21. He alludes to the example of the slave wife who is given the same food, clothing, and marital rights as a native-born Israelite woman, as explained below.

---

107 Instone-Brewer, ***Divorce and Remarriage in the Bible***, 190.

108 Biale, ***Women***, 102. An *agunah* is an "anchored" or "chained" woman and refers to situations where the marriage is over but the woman is legally still married and cannot remarry.

1 Corinthians 7:3 (NIV)	"The husband should fulfill his marital duty to his wife, and likewise the wife to her husband."
1 Corinthians 7:33 (NASB, addition mine)	"...but one who is married is concerned about the things of the world, how he may please his wife... [a reference to material provision, such as food and clothing, as well as love]"

Paul, following this concept, says abandonment is automatic grounds for a valid divorce (on the basis of neglect of marital duty, e.g. food, clothing, and marital rights), even if the spouse does not receive a certificate of divorce (Instone-Brewer, p. 275, *Divorce and Remarriage in the Bible*).

He says the Christian is free.

We can infer this means free to remarry, since that was how it worked in the Jewish law Paul is using as his template here. Some scholars disagree, but Paul sees this as a pragmatic issue and says in verse 15, "God has called us to live in peace."

He does not encourage the Christian to beg the spouse to return. He teaches the Christian to let him or her go and build a new, peaceful life for themselves.

Paul uses his discernment. He realizes the culture is completely different in Rome than it was in Jerusalem, so he makes a judgment call. In 1 Corinthians 7:15, he comforts the panicked Jewish believers in Corinth by saying that abandonment constitutes a valid divorce and they can remarry (they are "not under bondage," or in other words, not bound to that marriage).

And, setting a good example for all of us in the church who are tempted to tell others what God requires them to do, Paul humbly says six times in this chapter that he's giving his opinion or deferring to the conscience or judgment of those who are in the situation, not speaking for God.[109]

Again, the principle he is following is that "God has called us to live in peace." In other words, Paul uses his biblical training and inspiration. He uses his wisdom and adapts to the reality of the situation, while making room for other believers to follow what seems best to them.

---

109 I cannot think of any other chapter in the Bible where Paul admits six times he is not giving a command from the Lord, but giving his opinion and/or deferring to the conscience and judgment of those actually in the situation (1 Cor 7:6-7, 9, 12, 25, 37-38, 40).

Today, many pastors and scholars believe that a similar teaching applies to Christians who violate their marriage vows and refuse to change their behavior. They should be considered as unbelievers. Of course, if there is a change of behavior, reconciliation is possible. But if the other party cannot or will not reconcile or has already remarried, it is necessary to move on with life.

Paul, being a well-trained Pharisee, accepted the Law of Moses as well as Jewish law on the topic of marriage contracts: If one spouse is hardhearted and refuses to take care of their spouse according to the marriage covenant, this constitutes grounds for a valid divorce. By bringing up sex and material care between spouses in 1 Corinthians 7, we see Paul applied the three Jewish marriage contract requirements to Christian marriages.

Christians who stubbornly ignored their church's call to honor their marriage vows could be treated as unbelievers, according to Jesus in Matthew 18:17. A spouse who is abusive—physically or emotionally—is sinning. And if they continue in sin, they can be treated as an unbeliever.

Matthew 18:17 (NIV)	"If they still refuse to listen, tell it to the church; and if they refuse to listen even to the church, treat them as you would a pagan or a tax collector."

Women, You Must Remarry—Fast!

In the first century AD, women of childbearing age were expected to remarry, both in the Jewish world of Jesus and in the Roman world of Paul. In fact, in early Roman law, a divorced woman of childbearing age was required to remarry within six months.

Later it was extended to 18 months, and anything beyond that had penalties. "Remarriage after divorce was considered a fundamental right in the first century world." It was also an obligation.[110]

110 Instone-Brewer, *Divorce and Remarriage in the Bible,* 299.

CHRISTIAN LEADERS AND DIVORCE

Christians have interpreted the words of Christ and Paul and the Law of Moses in many ways.

Don't let anyone tell you there's only been one interpretation (theirs).

Some churches, such as the Roman Catholic Church, have even been *stricter* than Jesus, suggesting there is no acceptable reason for divorce and subsequent remarriage.

But even the Catholics have, over time, adapted their teachings to address the problems in society by allowing more than a dozen reasons for annulment.[111] Destructive marriages wreck individuals, tear at the church, erode the family's wellbeing, disrupt neighborhoods, and destroy the peace and harmony of the Christian community.

Over the centuries, common sense and decency have caused churches to accept divorce where there are serious reasons.

The Reformers

Erasmus "concluded that Paul allowed divorce with remarriage after desertion by an unbeliever, and that Jesus' exception allowed remarriage after divorce for adultery."[112]

Martin Luther considered the adulterer to be already spiritually dead,[113] so the other spouse could remarry. He also considered marriage and divorce to be a civil, not religious, matter. In fact, Martin Luther, in his writings "Commentary on the Sermon on the Mount," says that in some cases it is unreasonable to hope that the guilty spouse can change. Because of this, he argued, we shouldn't allow a guilty spouse to be forgiven over and over again; that's simply an abuse of the innocent spouse's kindness. Luther doesn't think mercy should be shown repeatedly in these cases because it is not right to force a spouse to take back their misbehaving spouse:

---

111 "Grounds of Marriage Nullity," ***The Roman Catholic Archdiocese of Atlanta*** (2019), accessed 8/17/19, https://archatl.com/offices/metropolitan-tribunal/grounds-of-marriage-nullity/.

112 Instone-Brewer, ***Divorce and Remarriage in the Bible,*** 259-260. For those wanting a detailed analysis of various Christian views on remarriage over the centuries, see Instone-Brewer's summary on page 288.

113 Ibid.

> "Yet, our advice would be to such as claim to be Christians, that it would be much better to exhort and urge both parties to remain together, and that the innocent party should become reconciled to the guilty (if humbled and reformed) and exercise forgiveness in Christian love; unless no improvement could be hoped for, or the guilty person who had been pardoned and restored to favor persisted in abusing this kindness, and still continued in leading a public, loose life, and took it for granted that one must continue to spare and forgive him. In such case I would not advise or order that mercy should be shown, but would rather help to have such a person scourged or imprisoned. **For to make a misstep once is still to be forgiven, but to sin presuming upon mercy and forgiveness is not to be endured.** For, as before said, we know already that it is not right to compel one to take back again a public whore or adulterer, if he is unwilling to do it, or out of disgust cannot do it."[114]

Zwingli allowed additional reasons for divorce.[115] John Calvin and Martin Luther wanted the death penalty for adulterers, but both allowed *both* spouses to remarry.[116]

Calvin allowed remarriage after the abandonment of an unbelieving spouse, and he went further: in "Ecclesiastical Ordinances," he allowed divorce for "impotence, extreme religious incompatibility, and abandonment."[117] Luther and Calvin interpreted Malachi 2:16 as an anti-abuse verse.

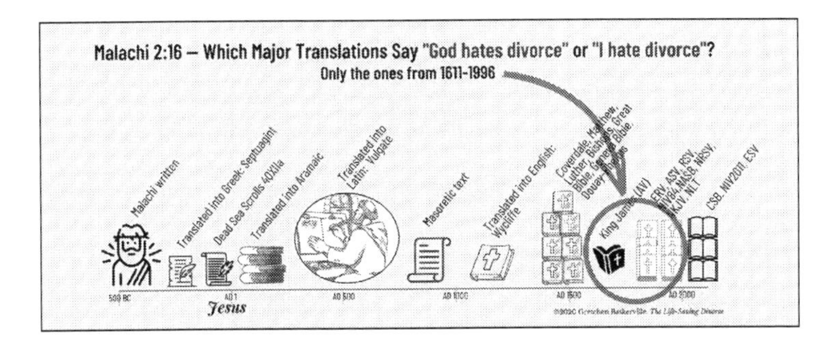

---

114 Martin Luther, "Commentary on the Sermon on the Mount," trans. Charles A. Hay (Philadelphia: Lutheran Publication Society, 1892), 88-89. Emphasis mine.

115 Instone-Brewer, ***Divorce and Remarriage in the Bible***, 262.

116 Nelson Blake, ***The Road to Reno,*** (New York: The Macmillan Company, 1962), 24.

117 Instone-Brewer, ***Divorce and Remarriage in the Bible***, 262-263. Also see www.lifesavingdivorce.com/calvin.

The English Reformers on Divorce and Remarriage

The early English Reformers convened a committee on divorce and remarriage in 1547 and brought a report in 1552. Their recommended grounds for divorce were—

- adultery
- desertion
- cruelty
- several years' absence with presumption of death
- mortal hatred ("Such violent hatred as rendered it in the highest degree improbable that the husband and wife would survive their animosities and again love one another"[118])

These were the leaders of the English Reformation nearly 500 years ago. They allowed remarriage for the innocent party.

The Puritans

We have divorce records from the Puritans living in Massachusetts. They allowed divorce for many more reasons:

- female adultery
- male cruelty
- bigamy
- desertion
- failure to provide
- impotence[119]

The Puritans rejected the Roman Catholic and Anglican view of marriage as a sacrament and therefore unbreakable. They considered Roman Catholic views to be a "popish invention, with no basis in the Gospels."[120] They saw marriage as a civil matter, not a religious one.

According to the New England Historical Society, "In 1620, [Plymouth Plantation] leaders decided marriage belonged to the courts, not to the church. Therefore, they concluded, the courts could grant a Puritan divorce."[121] They often granted alimony to the wife if she was the innocent party.

---

118 Blake, ***Road***, 26. The English Reformers' report was called ***Reformatio legum ecclesiasticarum.***

119 Glenda Riley, ***Divorce: An American Tradition*** (Oxford: Oxford Press, 1991), 13. Male adultery wasn't accepted as grounds for divorce in Massachusetts until the late 1700s. In a farming society, female adultery was considered much worse because a child could make a claim to inherit the land. Regarding impotence, in virtually all ancient agrarian societies, even in Jewish society prior to Christ, the inability to bear children was a serious problem. Men were responsible for having at least two children.

120 "The Puritan Divorce Allows Escape From the Chain of Matrimony," ***New England Historical Society*** (2019), accessed 8/17/19, http://www.newenglandhistoricalsociety.com/puritan-divorce-allows-escape-from-the-chain-of-matrimony/.

121 Ibid.

Puritan Divorces in Massachusetts 1639-1690

TABLE I

CASES OF DIVORCE AND ANNULMENT OF MARRIAGE IN MASSACHUSETTS, 1639-92

No.	Where Found[1]	Date	Case	Cause	Court	Decree
1	C. R., I, 283	Dec. 3, 1639	Second wife *v.* Jas. Luxford	Another wife	Assistants	Marriage void
2	W., 42	Mar. 5, 1643/4	Anne *v.* Dennis Clarke	Desertion, adultery	Assistants	Mar. dissolved
3	W., 42; C. R., II, 86	Nov. 13, 1644	Eliz. Frier *v.* J. Richardson	Another wife	Assistants	Marriage void
4	C. R., IV, i, 32	Oct. 16, 1650	Wm. *v.* Eleanor Palmer	Deser., remarriage	General court	Mar. dissolved
5	C. R., III, 277, IV, i, 89	May 26, 27, 1652	Dorothy *v.* Wm. Pester	Long absence	General court	Leave to marry
6	C. R., III, 350, IV, i, 190	May 14, 1654	Dorcas *v.* Jno. Hall	Desertion, adultery?	General court	Mar. dissolved
7	Suff. Files, 257	Before 1656	Sam. and Apphia Freeman	None given	Assistants	See text
8	Suff. Files, 257; C. R., IV, i, 272, 380, 401	1655-59	Joan *v.* Geo. Halsall	Adultery	Assists. to general ct.	Mar. dissolved; reversed on ap.
9	C. R., I, 85, IV, i, 259, 269	June 9, 1656	Petition of Wm. Clements	None given	Co. ct. on ref. of g. ct.	Denied
10	C. R., IV, i, 282	Oct. 14, 1656	Petition of Mary Batchiler	Deser., remarriage	Co. ct. on ref. of g. ct.	None appears
11	C. R., IV, ii, 8	May 22, 1661	Rachel *v.* Jos. Langton	None given	General court	Mar. dissolved
12	C. R., IV, ii, 91	Oct. 21, 1663	Mary *v.* E. White	"Deficiency"	General court	Denied
13	Suff. Files, 651	Sept. 9, 1664	Petition of Sarah Helwis	Deser., remarriage	Assistants	Mar. dissolved
14	Suff. Files, 913	Jan. 28, 1668/9	Christ. and Eliz. Lawson	Adult., cruelty of h.; bad cond. of wife	Assists. from co. ct.	None appears
15	Plym. Rec., v, 33	Aug. 3, 1670	James *v.* Eliz. Skiffe	Desertion, adultery	General court	Mar. dissolved
16	C. R., IV, ii, 465	Oct., 1670	Eliz. *v.* Henry Stevens	Desertion, adultery?	General court	Mar. dissolved
17	Suff. Files, 1148; N., 32	Oct., 1672	Kath. *v.* Ed. Nailer	Adultery, cruelty	Assistants	Mar. dissolved
18	Suff. Files, 1360; N., 30	Mch. 4, 1674/5	Mary *v.* Wm. Sanders	Deser., remarriage	Assistants	Mar. dissolved
19	Suff. Files, 1644; N., 91	1673-77	Hugh and Mary Drury	Disease and imp. of h.	Assistants	Sep. b. b.?
20	Rec. Suff. co. ct., 506	Before 1678	Philip and Mary Wharton	See text	See text	Mar. dissolved
21	Suff. Files, 1741; C. R., V, 203; N., 127.	Sept. 9, 1678	Hugh *v.* Dorcas March	Another husband	Assists.; app. to g. ct.	Denied on app.
22	C. R., V, 188	May 9, 1678	Mary *v.* Henry Maddox	Long absence	General court	Leave to marry
23	N., 127	1678	Hope *v.* Sam. Ambrose	Desertion, adultery, failure to provide	Assistants	Mar. dissolved
24	N., 138	1678	Rebeckah *v.* Rich. Cooly	None given	Assistants	Mar. dissolved
25	Suff. Files, 1807; C. R., V, 248, 249	Oct. 15, 1679	Mary *v.* Aug. Lyndon	None given	General court	Mar. dissolved
26	N., 144	1679	Mary *v.* Job Bishop	Deser., remarriage	Assistants	Mar. dissolved
27	N., 147	1679	Mary *v.* Jos. White		Assistants	
28	N., 163	1680	Sus. *v.* Ed. Goodwin	Deser., fail. to prov.	Assistants	Mar. dissolved
29	N., 197	1681	Sam. *v.* Mary Holton	Adultery, desertion	Assistants	Mar. dissolved
30	N., 200	1681	Dorcas *v.* Christ. Smith	Deser., fail. to prov.	Assistants	Mar. dissolved
31	N., 208	1681	Rachel *v.* Lawrence Clenton		Assistants	Mar. dissolved
32	N., 227	1682	Eliz. *v.* Robt. Street	Bigamy	Assistants	Mar. dissolved
33	N., 229	1683	Petition of Ann Perry		Assistants	Denied
34	N., 240	1683	Eliz. *v.* Nich. Maning	Incest, desertion	Assistants	Mar. dissolved
35	N., 256, 258	1684	Sarah *v.* Thos. Cooper		Assistants	Mar. dissolved
36	Suff. Files, 2347	Sept. 17, 1685	Petition of Thos. Winsor	Adultery	Assistants	Mar. dissolved
37	N., 326	1690	Phillip *v.* Hannah Goss	Deser., remarriage	Assistants	Mar. dissolved
38	N., 242	1690-91	Mary *v.* Sam. Stebbins	Adultery, desertion	Assistants	
39	N., 331	1691	Hannah and Josiah Owen	Affinity (bro's wife)	Assistants	Marriage void
40	N., 342	1690	Sam. and Reb. Newton	Affinity (uncle's wid.)	Assistants	Marriage void

[1] N. = NOBLE'S *Records of the Court of Assistants*, I; W. = *Record of the Court of Assistants*, in WHITMORE'S *Bibliog. Sketch.*

The first known divorce in America was on December 3, 1639, when Elizabeth Luxford discovered her husband James Luxford already had another wife and went to the court for justice.

The magistrates were not pleased with James. They granted Elizabeth the divorce, took James's property, gave it to Elizabeth, and—

> "Next, the court turned its wrath on the deceitful Luxford. Not content with levying a fine of £100 on the bigamist, it sentenced him to 'be set in the stocks an hour upon the market day after the lecture,' and to be banished to England 'by the first opportunity.'"[122]

Conclusion: What Is the Bottom Line?

1. Malachi 2:16 should be interpreted as an anti-abuse verse, not an anti-divorce verse. It condemns treacherous husbands who divorce their wives without cause. The book of Malachi was written nearly 500 years before Christ. In the 2,400 years since then, it has been interpreted as "God hates divorce" for only 385 years (1611-1996). No new major translation since 1996 (NIV 2011 update, CSB, or ESV) has interpreted it that way.
2. As shown above, there are four reasons for an acceptable biblical divorce. Jesus did not require divorce in these situations, but he did allow it. Remarriage was normal and expected in the case of valid divorces.
    a. **Adultery/sexual immorality**, meaning infidelity, as well as sexual sins and sexual deviations.
    b. **Physical neglect or abuse** (depriving a spouse of appropriate food, clothing, the basics of life).
    c. **Emotional neglect or abuse** (withholding mutual loyalty, love).
    d. **Abandonment,** ongoing hardheartedness leading to the neglect of (b) and (c) above, whether willful or unintentional.

---

122 Riley, ***Divorce,*** 12. The accompanying table is from George Howard, ***A History of Matrimonial Institutions, Vol 2.*** (Chicago: University of Chicago Press, 1904), 333.

3. Great Christians leaders of the past, theologians, and church councils have debated these issues for 2,000 years. There are no "good old days" when all Christians agreed on this topic. They have all held different views and based their interpretation on the situations facing them.
4. If you are in a destructive marriage, you do not need a religious leader to give you permission. It's your job to protect yourself and your children. Although it is nice to have your pastor's support and blessing, legally, a pastor has no say in your divorce. You, not they, deal with the aftermath of the divorce. You, not they, are the one dealing with the trauma and destruction of a dangerous marriage. Only you know what is happening behind closed doors. Only you can determine when "Enough is enough."[123]

"We cannot leave it up to a minister or a church leadership team to decide when a marriage ends; it is up to the individual victim, in prayer before the Lord. Only they and the Lord know what their life is really like."[124]
—David Instone-Brewer

123 Instone-Brewer, ***Divorce and Remarriage in the Church***, 104.
124 Ibid., 105.

RAISING KIDS AFTER DIVORCE

Divorce is an agonizing and difficult decision for a loving parent to make—probably the most difficult decision in their life. The top fear for most parents is that divorce will cause lifelong damage to their children. Even if there is physical or emotional abuse, infidelity, child molesting, or drug and alcohol addictions, parents hesitate to get away because of messages they've gotten (from both church and secular society) that divorce will doom their children:

- "You will destroy your kids if you divorce."
- "Your children will have life-long damage, will be unhappy, and will fail in life."
- "Your children will abuse drugs, be sexually promiscuous, marry too early, and divorce when they grow up!"

People give us messages saying we are selfish; that we are divorcing because we just couldn't manage to stay married like everyone else; or that we are sacrificing our children's future because we are self-focused.

Messages from Christian websites, marriage books, and pastors often imply that divorce is among the worst things that can possibly happen to a child, that it's a major disaster, and that the results will significantly hurt the child's wellbeing for the rest of their lives. They claim that any parent who drags their child through a divorce is self-centered, impulsive, and was looking for a quick way out.

But they are wrong.

The good news is: Most children turn out fine after a life-saving divorce.

You hear these doom-and-gloom claims on the news, at church, in Christian marriage books, from marriage-at-any-cost think tanks, and from organizations like Focus on the Family. We've heard these warnings for years. And unfortunately, we believed them. It is an echo chamber. We heard them so many times, we thought they must be true.

But they aren't.

A conservative radio talk show host did a program on divorce.[125] He interviewed a rabbi, a priest, and a pastor, asking them if people divorced too easily. "Yes," they all said.

Then the host asked if they knew someone close to them who'd gotten divorced. "Yes, my parents got divorced," said the rabbi.

"Do you believe they divorced too easily?" the host asked.

The rabbi said, "No, no, no, I can only tell you my mother had to get out of that marriage."

The priest said, "My parents divorced, and I think it saved my mother's life."

The pastor said, "My brother is going through a divorce right now."

"Do you believe he's divorcing too easily?" asked the host.

"No, no. I know how much they've struggled," said the pastor.

The radio host concluded, "Each of you have said that people divorce too easily. But the people you know best who divorced, you don't think they divorced too easily at all!"

Maybe you can relate. Maybe someone close to you got divorced due to abuse or infidelity or severe addictions. How did their kids turn out?

Maybe one of those kids is you. Most children of divorce are responsible, hard-working, decent human beings. They are good friends, good coworkers, and good spouses.

So What's the Truth?

This chapter will help answer this question. Before we begin, however, I want to make it clear that I am not a child psychologist. I'm just a lay divorce recovery leader. What I share with you in this book, and this chapter specifically, comes out of my personal experience with life-saving divorce, more than twenty years of work with other people who have gotten life-saving divorces, and hours of interviews.

---

125 See Dennis Prager's show on 9/5/19, in which he reminisces about past radio shows.

In addition to that, I've read scientific research that most people never have seen and don't know about because it rarely or never makes front page headlines. I've bought the journal articles that are behind paywalls. I've tracked down the major, groundbreaking studies you've never heard of.

But that doesn't mean I know your specific situation.

For parents with concerns about their children's wellbeing and adjustment to divorce, I highly recommend seeking professional support and feedback into your circumstances. If you can access therapy for you and your children, by all means do so! Also, included in this chapter are further resources on how divorce affects children and what can be done to support their flourishing and healthy adjustment.

In this chapter, we will cover the two types of divorce; we will look at research studies that indicate that most kids in life-saving divorces come out fine; and we will examine surveys that show most children of divorce bounce back after those first two rough years.

We will also see studies that show most children of divorce don't do drugs, or have any serious emotional, psychological, or social problems.

Finally, we'll discuss tips on how to be the best parent you can be—both during the divorce itself, and as you are rebuilding your life after it's official.

Family Researchers Know that Life-Saving Divorces Are Good for Kids

Real family scholars and researchers know the truth: about 8 in 10 kids turn out okay after divorce. They also know one other fact:

Divorce is often the best option for children trapped in high-distress homes.

If your marriage has serious problems that cause agitation, fear, and stress in your home, your children are being affected. Sometimes you cannot put your finger on it; you are scared, but you can't explain why you are, especially if you've never been hit. Even if there is no fighting, screaming, or overt conflict, the anxiety and agitation are palpable.

For other people, there may be obvious betrayals such as adultery, abandonment, severe addictions, or physical abuse that are easier to identify. But tension, worry, or fear are signs that this situation is hard on you and on the wellbeing of your children. And researchers know that kids are probably better off if there's a life-saving divorce.

In fact, on average, children are happier *after* a life-saving divorce than they were during the marriage. Watching Mom or Dad being betrayed, abused, or manipulated is bad for kids. It's as bad as being abused or molested themselves—maybe even worse. A safe, loving, single parent home is better than a tension-filled, high-distress two-parent home.

Children are usually relieved to be away from walking on eggshells and living with worry and mind-games, even if they are in a poorer, single-parent home. They tend to find peace and calm after divorce, as long as they have one decent parent who loves them and has a warm, close relationship with them.

But the opposite is also true: Divorces where there is low- or medium-distress, and the couple feels unfulfilled, disappointed, or dissatisfied with the marriage, have poorer outcomes for kids. In *these* divorces, kids still do fine generally, but they are less happy than they were when the couple was married.

Makes sense, right? The kids thought the marriage was happy. They liked their parents. There wasn't much tension. They weren't subjected to horror. Now their life has gone through upheaval for apparently no reason that they can see.

Family scholars and researchers know that the outcome after divorce is different for these two types:

- **High-distress**: Desperate, scared, tense, controlling, dominating, anxious families, even if the problems are hidden or covert and there's no obvious conflict or infidelity
- **Low-distress**: Unfulfilled, disconnected, disappointed, dissatisfied low-conflict families

The Two Types of Marriages: Desperate, or Dissatisfied?

Organizations that are truly research-based know there are two types of marriages. One type of marriage can be improved by learning problem-solving methods, conflict-resolution skills, and other cooperative therapeutic interventions.

The other type of marriage has such long-standing patterns of control by one of the spouses that the outlook is grim. A spouse who uses fear and intimidation on a regular basis has serious character issues that are very dangerous and nearly impossible to change—issues that therapists often consider treatment failures.

The Gottman Institute, a pro-marriage organization which does training for therapists, says that dominance, fear, and intimidation are such serious problems that it may be irresponsible or even illegal for counselors to do couples therapy with spouses in this situation:

> **"Research suggests that 50% of couples seeking therapy have experienced violence in their relationship, whether they are telling you or not**... Battery is evidence of what Dr. Gottman calls Characterological Violence, where one partner clearly demonstrates controlling and dominating behavior. In this case, refer to a treatment center, hotline, shelter, specialist, or the police. If you suspect battery is present but one or both partners are denying it, refer. If you're not sure, refer. It's irresponsible, unethical, and likely even illegal for you to begin couples therapy when Characterological Violence is present."[126]
> —Zach Brittle, LMHC (emphasis mine)

Institute for Family Studies, a conservative, pro-family, pro-marriage organization, says divorce may be the best option in difficult or dangerous marriages in an article they published in 2017 that discouraged divorce.

> "In some cases, divorce may be the best option for husbands and wives in a difficult or dangerous marriage. Domestic violence, drug and alcohol abuse, and infidelity—among other things—are certainly legitimate grounds..."[127]

The director of the National Marriage Project, a pro-marriage organization that exists to strengthen marriages and encourage pro-family legislation, wrote this:

> "...In cases where children are exposed to high levels of conflict—like domestic violence or screaming matches between parents—they do seem to do better if their parents part."
> —W. Bradford Wilcox[128]

---

126 Zach Brittle, "V is for Violence," ***The Gottman Institute*** (10/28/14), accessed 9/12/19, https://www.gottman.com/blog/v-is-for-violence/.

127 Wilcox, "Three Reasons."

128 Wilcox, "The Evolution of Divorce."

One of the top researchers in the area of marriage and family, Dr. Paul Amato, says that in *low*-marital discord families, children indeed do *worse* if the parents divorce. But in families that involve **high-marital discord**, children may be *better off* if their parents divorce. And he mentions that researchers and studies have found this over and over.

"Studies show that when parents exhibit chronic, high levels of conflict and hostility, children benefit by escaping from adverse home environments."[129]

"...children [in high-distress families] are no worse off, and perhaps better off, if their parents split up."[130]

As a Christian and a former long-time supporter, I hate to say it, but Focus on the Family uses Paul Amato's name and research in articles that promote the message that divorce is always bad for children.

Messaging from Focus on the Family, unfortunately, has not been safe for abuse victims and children in dangerous marriages.

In their zeal to keep as many marriages together as possible, this organization has kept dangerously silent on the real problem of domestic violence and emotional abuse and the important of divorce in these cases. It has instead promoted a "God wants you to stay married at all costs" message that has contributed to the victimization of devoted Christians who want to obey God but are being abused by their spouses.

Usually, they promote this message through scare tactics and judgment, implying or outright stating that divorce will permanently damage children, and accusing parents who divorce of being flippant and selfish, or of being quitters who are looking for an "easy out," people who are not serious about the marriage commitment or about God's will.

They also use the work of researchers to support this message when, in fact, those researchers do not support it. As you can see from his own words, for example, Dr. Paul Amato has disagreed for years with Focus on the Family's message that divorce is universally detrimental to children.

---

129 P. R. Amato, and B. Hohmann-Marriott, "A Comparison of High- and Low-Distress Marriages that End in Divorce," *Journal of Marriage and Family* 69, no. 3 (2007): 621-638.

130 Paul Amato, "Reconciling Divergent Perspectives: Judith Wallerstein, Quantitative Family Research, and Children of Divorce," *Family Relations* 52, no. 4 (Oct. 2003): 337.

Another psychologist and author, Dr. Judith Wallerstein, is often quoted by pro-family organizations that seek to show negative life-long consequences of divorce.

But in reality, Dr. Wallerstein stridently says she too is not against divorce.

Wallerstein also says that growing up in a high-distress two-parent family has "tragic" consequences for children in their adult years.

> "Children raised in extremely unhappy or violent intact homes face misery in childhood and tragic challenges in adulthood."[131]

> "**I am not against divorce. How could I be?**
> I've seen more examples of wretched, demeaning,
> and abusive marriage than most of my colleagues.
> I'm keenly aware of the suffering…
> I'm also aware that for many parents the decision to divorce
> is the most difficult decision in their lives;
> they cry many a night before taking such a drastic step.
>
> "And I am, of course, aware of the many voices on the radio, on television, and in certain… religious circles that say divorce is sinful… **But I don't know of any research, mine included, that says divorce is universally detrimental to children.**"[132]

Wallerstein wrote this in 2000 (emphasis mine), more than twenty years ago. I am perplexed as to why pastors and Christian family organizations posted articles in 2007 and beyond, quoting her in order to send a false message that all divorce is harmful for kids.

In fact, in 2003, Wallerstein authored a book on kids and divorce. When asked when is the "best" time to divorce, she wrote (emphasis mine):

> "The trouble is, there's no simple answer… **If there's chronic violence at home, the answer is 'the sooner the better,' unrelated to the age of your child.**

---

131 Judith S. Wallerstein, Julia M. Lewis, and Sandra Blakeslee, ***The Unexpected Legacy of Divorce*** (New York: Hyperion, 2000), 300. Wallerstein recommended divorce where there was abuse or conflict. See www.lifesavingdivorce.com/wallerstein

132 Ibid., xxxix (emphasis mine). Other family scholars criticized Wallerstein's research methods and conclusions (she studied only 60 families), as their own evidence showed that the effects of divorce on children is not as negative as Wallerstein claimed. See footnote 130. She reported 7 in 10 children of divorce turned out "average," "very well," or "outstanding."

By violence I mean physical attack—hitting, kicking, throwing objects—or chronic threats of physical violence. Exposure to violence has serious consequences for a child's development that may last well into adulthood. They fear for your safety. They fear for themselves and their siblings. **If there's repeated high conflict in your marriage, accompanied by yelling, screaming, and pounding the table, then I'd also say the sooner the better...** In some high-conflict homes, serious differences between the partners are a recurrent theme in everyday life."[133]

Those who study data on high-distress marriages, kids, and divorce, have known the truth for a long time (there were important studies on this subject in the 1980s, 1990s, and 2000s).

If you're in a high-distress home, whether the conflict is overt or not, your children likely will be better off if you divorce.

Family researchers know it's often better for kids if parents divorce to escape a marriage that is filled with worry and turmoil, often due to "hard" reasons for divorce—domestic violence, sexual immorality, or drug/alcohol addictions—rather than "soft" reasons, such as childcare issues, household chores, growing apart, or in-law problems.[134]

A 1985 study done by another leading researcher in the area of family and marriage, Dr. Mavis Hetherington (and some associates), also reported that some children who are exposed to high levels of marital discord prior to divorce *adjust better* than children who experience low levels.[135]

Am I in a High-Distress Marriage?

You are in that high-distress category if your spouse's behavior or attitude is so troubling that you are concerned for your health or mental wellbeing, or that of your children.

---

133 Judith Wallerstein and Sandra Blakeslee, ***What About the Kids?*** (New York: Hachette Books, 2010), 127-128.

134 Alan J. Hawkins and Brian J. Willoughby, "Reasons for Divorce and Openness to Marital Reconciliation," ***Journal of Divorce & Remarriage*** (Aug. 2012): 461.

135 Hal Arkowitz and Scott O. Lilienfeld, "Is Divorce Bad for Children?" ***Scientific American*** (3/1/13), accessed 9/10/19, https://www.scientificamerican.com/article/is-divorce-bad-for-children/.

If you look at Chapter 4, you can evaluate your situation yourself. For many people, a life-saving divorce was God's gift to them.

When no-fault divorce laws started passing one state at a time, starting with Governor Ronald Reagan in California in 1969, researchers wanted to see the effect. Over the years, they saw the suicide rate for wives drop about 8-16%. And the domestic violence rate by and against both men and women dropped 30%. The homicide rate of women murdered by an intimate dropped 10%.[136] (You can read more about this in Chapter 2).

Pastors, Christian marriage authors, and Christian pro-family organizations need to be honest in their sermons, books, blogs, and radio programs; otherwise, they are pressuring innocent spouses and children to stay in abusive and destructive marriages.

And pastors and church leaders must stop pushing or threatening parents to stay in nightmarish unions. This is a major problem in Christianity, and no doubt in other religions as well.

Levels of Distress for the Children

This graph shows five types of marriages that may end in divorce.[137]

- **Very low distress** — The couple is able to resolve marital problems. The children feel safe and accepted. They observe genuine apologies, their parents making up, and behavior leading to a better relationship. There's usually peace and calm in these homes.
- **Low distress** — Couple resolves most of their problems.
- **Medium distress** — Couple has some ongoing problems that aren't resolved.
- **High distress** — Couple has serious and ongoing problems that don't get resolved.
- **Very high distress** — Couple has serious problems that do not get resolved. Family members may feel tense and anxious. Sometimes the problems are hidden and covert, with no fighting, screaming,

---

136 Betsey Stevenson and Justin Wolfers, "Bargaining in the Shadow of the Law: Divorce Laws and Family Distress," *The Quarterly Journal of Economics* (Feb. 2006): 267, 286.

137 The graph is adapted from the Parents' Marital Discord chart in Paul Amato, "Reconciling Divergent Perspectives." For those wishing to learn more, this is one of the most interesting and highly detailed comparisons of "staying" versus "leaving" and the effect on children.

or violence. One type of destructive behavior may be replaced with another type. Family members walk on eggshells. Peace, calm, and safety are rare. The spouse who is most invested in the relationship may keep trying harder or blaming themselves. They may feel despair and confusion, but the tension doesn't get resolved.

OUTCOMES FOR CHILDREN AFTER DIVORCE
By Level of Distress in Marriage

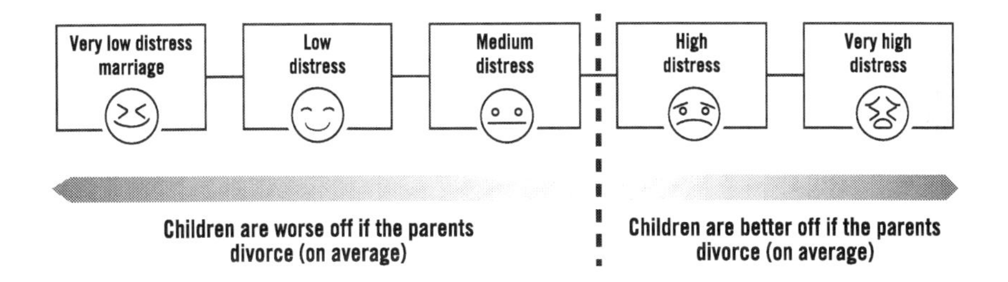

Research has found that divorce is bad for kids in cases of "very low-," "low-," and "medium-distress" marriages.

And that makes sense. Normal marriages have problems, and it's good for children to see their parents working through them, discussing them, and "kissing and making up." In these homes, divorce is truly tough on kids because the spouses are decent people, but one or both have a weak commitment to marriage in general or to this marriage in particular.[138]

But in "high-" and "very high-" distress marriages, tension is palpable even if there is no violence, yelling, or visible conflict.

Research has found that it is likely better for children if their parents divorce than to stay in these anxiety-filled or agitated situations.[139]

"When parents reported high levels of discord, ... offspring with divorced parents were better off than offspring with continuously married parents."[140]
—Dr. Paul Amato

138 Amato, "Reconciling Divergent Perspectives," 332.
139 Ibid., 337.
140 Ibid.

What Is More Damaging—A Toxic Marriage or a Divorce?

As we saw in the chart above, a very high-distress marriage is often so harmful that the problems caused by the divorce process are minimal in comparison: in fact, ten times less. People going through life-saving divorces aren't looking for a "grass is greener situation." They are looking for *relief*.

Finding a new spouse is the last thing on their mind. They just want escape from the nightmare. For them, the answer is clear: *Staying in this marriage is endangering my health and wellbeing, and that of my children. I have to go.*

Those who promote marriage at any cost often compare the health of married people with divorced individuals, and then they criticize those who divorce. This doesn't seem like a fair comparison, because it is not making an accurate comparison.

It's better to compare real-life choices. They should compare the divorcees who left high-distress marriages with the individuals who *stayed* in high-distress marriages.

The longer people stay in these high-distress marriages, the more damage they and their kids sustain. (I don't say this to shame anyone. Most people weren't told the truth, and they genuinely thought what they were doing was best morally, spiritually, and emotionally for their children based on the messages they got from society and religious authors or leaders.)

Damage to Child's Well-being in High-Distress Marriages

These two charts show only the "very high-discord" and "high-discord" marriages. These are the homes that are very hard on children and do considerable damage.

Damage to Child's Well-being in ***Very*** ***High-Discord Marriages***

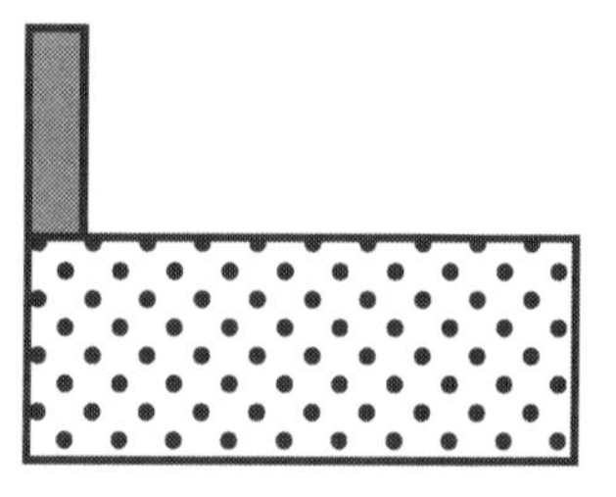

In these very high discord marriages, the damage to the kids is ten times higher if the parents stay together than if they divorce.

Damage to Child's Well-being in ***High-Discord Marriages***

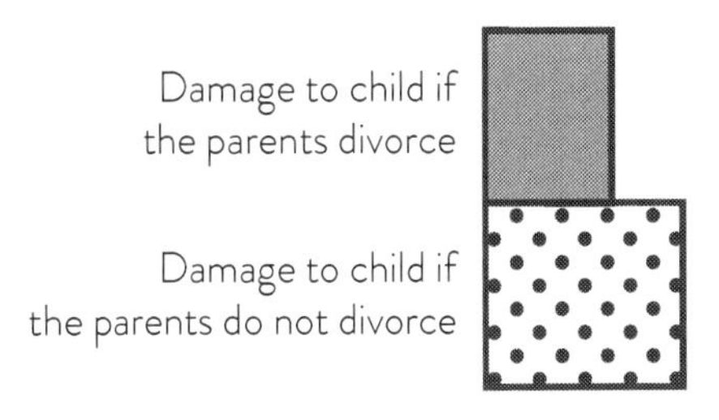

In these high-discord marriages, the damage to the kids is one-and-a-half times higher if the parents stay together than if they divorce.

(These charts were simplified from charts presented in the 2003 "Reconciling Divergent Perspectives" study.)

Looking at the next chart, we see that traumatic injuries (physical or emotional) can happen any time in life, including long before the marriage. When you see a divorced person with issues, or a child acting out, don't automatically blame it on the divorce.

LIFETIME TRAUMA AND STRESS

Birth → Marriage → Divorce begins → Divorce ends

A	B	C	D
Childhood, adolescent, adulthood trauma or stress	Trauma or stress during the marriage, whether from the relationship with spouse or other factors	Trauma or stress during the divorce process	Trauma or stress after divorce, moving on with life

Trauma may occur at any point in a person's life:

A. Before the marriage (childhood / adolescence / adulthood) due to death, illness, physical/sexual/emotional abuse, neglect, abandonment, substance abuse, observing violence, etc.

B. During the marriage (covert, hidden abuse, domestic violence, betrayal, squandering family resources, infidelity, neglect, etc.)

C. During the one-to-four-year divorce process. Stress is caused by big changes happening all at once (moving to another home, changing schools/job, change in income, legal anxieties/costs, court disputes, change in social status and friendships, plus, in some cases, stalking, restraining orders, and threats.)

D. Postdivorce, there may still be a high-conflict ex-spouse, trauma, parenting challenges, or adjustments to a new job or income level.

Some people come through divorce better than others. About 7 in 10 adults are at the same level or better than they were before the divorce. But sadly, 3 in 10 report being worse off.

Why are 3 in 10 worse off? That may be because they have difficulty earning a living after an unwanted divorce. Or perhaps a vengeful spouse attacked them with drawn-out legal action and court expenses during the divorce process.

Some individuals may be worse off due to the accumulation of a lifetime of trauma or the existence of health issues (some starting long before the marriage). They may struggle with major depression.

Some have sustained trauma at the hands of their spouse, who undermined their confidence or health and made them unable to defend themselves. Or they may be worse off due to things completely unconnected to the marriage, such as a car accident, natural disaster, or a job loss due to a business closure.

For pastors and others, it's important to be compassionate and patient with those who are struggling. Most people will improve dramatically three years into the divorce and will get back on their feet. Others (those 3 in 10) will grapple with difficulties perhaps for the rest of their lives. It's not their fault. Offering friendship, support, and encouragement will mean a lot to them.

So here's the big question:

Why do some people automatically tell us that divorce is going to hurt us (and our kids) more than a toxic marriage?

I suggest this advice may be well-meaning, but often the advice-giver is ill-informed. Only you know how much chaos is occurring in your marriage. Only you know how much you can take. It's your call. Only you can decide when you can no longer accept it or deal with it.

Why All the Bad Advice?

But why, you may be asking, do religious leaders and organizations put this kind of pressure on people who are in such dangerous situations?

Sadly, I fear it is because life-saving divorce doesn't fit our religious narrative. Many Christian marriage authors imply that problems in any nuclear family—mother, father, and kids—can all be solved if the godly spouse tries harder.

This just simply isn't true. There are no guarantees, and *no one should sacrifice their or their child's wellbeing for this false message.*

This delusion causes people in desperate situations to cling to hope and stay in harm's way when it would be better if they got to safety. People of faith need to understand that more than 40% of divorces are life-saving divorces.

God cares about children, and he cares about adults. We must stand beside those who choose safety—offering support, not judgment.

"Because of the violence done to the oppressed, because of the painful cries of the needy, I will spring into action," says the LORD. "I will provide the safety they so desperately desire."
—Psalm 12:5 (NET)

We need to accept that some marriages are destructive to vulnerable individuals. In those situations, it is dangerous for pastors to pressure or threaten parents to stay together, compelling children and adults alike to live in fear, terror, anxiety, and stress.

We dare not leave our children in this situation to watch as one parent lies, threatens, manipulates, dismisses, neglects, or terrorizes the other.

Even if the toxic culture in the family is not visible on the surface—

for example, if there is infidelity or sexual immorality the children never witness—it causes conflict between the parents in the form of desperation, rage, excuses, disrespect, tension, and deep unhappiness that is sensed by the children.

"Witnessing a parent being victimized
is often more psychologically damaging to children
than injuries from direct child abuse."[141]
—Dr. Steven Stosny

Someone might say, "Just don't fight in front of the children." But hurt, worry, and outrage over repeated betrayal cannot be hidden. Children perceive conflict, tension, and fear even without their parents yelling at one another. Once they are adolescents, many hope their abused parent gets out.

You are not honoring God by allowing someone
to tear you down over and over and over again.
You're not honoring him by putting your children through that.
You're not honoring him by being this long-suffering martyr.

Sometimes kids see the need for divorce more clearly than parents. In one interview, a mother told me about the day her divorce was final:

My daughter sent me a text: "How are you doing?"
I said, "I'm doing okay, except when I think of you precious kids."
She said, "This just feels like the legalizing of something that's been true a long time."

141 Stosny, "Emotional Abuse."

DIVORCE MAY BE THE BEST WAY TO PROTECT YOUR CHILD

My Story

Like most good parents in a terrible marriage, I was fearful about what divorce might do to my children. I had two little ones around preschool age, and I worried about them.

As a committed Christian, I wasn't a quitter. I always wanted to be a wife and mother. I had really loved my husband, and I was prepared for the normal ups and downs of marriage. I didn't expect constant wedded bliss, flowers, and champagne.

But over time, I saw abnormal behaviors and ignored them, pretending I didn't really see them. Then I put up with worse and worse incidents. I doubled down; we went to counseling, and I told myself, "We're going to solve this."

I wanted my marriage to work. We were active at our church. I'd heard pastors say that 95% of divorce was for falling out of love. I was not going to be one of *those* people.

For years, I'd heard on Christian radio and read in Christian books that divorce caused most girls to get into drugs, get pregnant as teenagers, and run away from home. I got the message that most boys from divorced families dropped out of school, were alcoholics, and wouldn't thrive because they had no male role model.

And forget putting kids into daycare! I was told *that* would destroy their lives forever.

What was I going to do? Years of lies, secrecy, mistrust, and sexual immorality were never resolved. I had no confidence or evidence of improvement, just a vague hope that things were better. And even though I said nothing in front of the kids, my little children sensed it and showed signs of anxiety, tension, and agitation.

I waffled back and forth, wondering "Maybe it won't happen again. Perhaps I should give it more time?" Finally: the last straw came. I was shocked and numb. I wasn't thinking; I reacted viscerally. We had to get out.

We needed a life-saving divorce.

Those first two years were tough. We had very little money for the first five years. I needed car repairs. I was scared, crying, lonely, and overwhelmed. The kids cried because they missed their dad (even though they saw him frequently). They wanted us to get back together. They didn't know the whole truth about the marriage problems, because I didn't want to burden them with information they were too young to handle.

We had stress during those two transition years, and adjustments when I worked full-time, but we also had peace—and I had a sigh of relief that my husband was out of the home.

We had the usual ups and downs in middle school: a few bad grades along the way, a few challenges here and there, lost homework papers, missing assignments, or too many hours video gaming. (And way too much junk food!) But the kids never had problems with drugs, alcohol, teen pregnancy, dropping out of school, or any of the other things I worried about.

Now, nearly 25 years later, I would say divorce was the toughest and one of the most important decisions I ever made.

It was the right thing to do.

My children turned out well. They have both finished their educations, have good jobs, and are doing well in life. They are happy and well adjusted. They are good citizens, good employees, and good friends and neighbors. They are both close to me, and they chose to have a warm relationship with their dad.

What more could a parent want?

And because my church stood by me (and later encouraged me to co-lead a small group for other mothers), my children viewed that church in a positive light. We saw ourselves as a strong, loving family, not a broken family.

I hear this from a lot of life-saving divorce families.

Many children from high-distress families
say they are grateful their parents divorced.

A quote from my adult daughter:

> "I tell friends I feel fortunate my mother filed for divorce when I was in grade school. I would rather be brought up in a loving home with one healthy parent than an unhappy, stressed-out home with two parents."

I have zero regrets. From my standpoint, my children were much happier and peaceful than they had been when I was married. My adult children agree.

This scenario isn't unusual. This is what the leading researchers find, too:

> "For most youths, the legacy of divorce is largely overcome. Twenty years after divorce, most men and women who had grown up in divorced families and stepfamilies are functioning reasonably well. Only a minority still exhibited emotional and social problems."[142]
>
> —Dr. E. Mavis Hetherington, John Kelly

Bradford Wilcox, the senior fellow for the Institute for Family Studies, wrote that two years after the divorce, 50% of parents turn out fine, too, and 20% turn out much happier after a divorce.[143] He was quoting Dr. Mavis Hetherington, who also says that in some cases, the parent's health may improve, especially if the divorce was due to a high-conflict home with a spouse who had been "distant or hostile."[144]

I want to be honest. Not all people will bounce back after a divorce, even though the majority do. The conclusion is that the vast majority of parents and kids turn out fine two years after divorce, but some, of course, do not. Divorce isn't a magic cure to wipe away everything you and the children have been through. Some parents and children do have life-long struggles.

Naturally, a lot depends on the kind of abuse you and the children have witnessed and endured, your personalities, and the mental health

---

142 Hetherington and Kelly, ***For Better***, 253.

143 Wilcox, "The Evolution." He is quoting leading family and marriage researcher Dr. Mavis Hetherington.

144 Hetherington and Kelly, ***For Better,*** 59. Hetherington has been a leading researcher in the area of marriage, families, and divorce for more than forty years.

of the parents and the children before the divorce. A lot depends, too, on the support (therapy, trusted friends and family, church community) that you and your children have access to, as you navigate life during and after the divorce.

Likelihood of Health Problems for Children Who Suffer or Witness Abuse

Doctors and researchers have known since 1998, thanks to the ACE Study through Kaiser Permanente,[145] that children who have been abused or exposed to abuse are at a higher risk when they become adults for major diseases such as ischemic heart disease, cancer, chronic lung disease, skeletal fractures, and liver disease.

If children had been exposed to **four or more** of following seven categories, their health as adults was likely to be affected. The more categories they'd been exposed to, the higher the risk was, including increased health risks for alcoholism, drug abuse, depression, and suicide attempts.

The Seven Adverse Childhood Events (ACEs in 1998):

- psychological abuse, physical abuse, sexual abuse
- violence against mother
- living with household members who were substance abusers, mentally ill or suicidal, or ever imprisoned

Medical professionals have known for more than 20 years that it's best to get children out of these situations.

In 2019, a much larger and more sophisticated ACE Study was done. They added emotional abuse to the list of adverse childhood experiences (ACEs). Instead of "violence against mother," they changed it to "intimate partner violence." They added parental divorce and removed the mention of suicide.[146]

They found that people who had four or more of these ACEs made up 16% of the study, and those people on average had "poorer health and

---

145 V.J. Felitti, R.F. Anda, D. Nordenberg, et al. Relationship of childhood abuse and household dysfunction to many of the leading causes of death in adults. Am J Prev Med 1998;14:245–58

146 M.T. Merrick, D. C. Ford, and K. A. Ports, et al., "Vital Signs: Estimated Proportion of Adult Health Problems Attributable to Adverse Childhood Experiences and Implications for Prevention—25 States, 2015–2017," ***Centers for Disease Control and Prevention Morbidity and Mortality Weekly Report*** 68 (2019): 999-1005..

life outcomes," including dying earlier.

The Eight Adverse Childhood Events (ACEs in 2019):

- physical abuse
- emotional abuse
- sexual abuse
- household member substance misuse, incarceration, mental illness, parental divorce, or witnessing intimate partner violence

"There's a lot of evidence connecting these things," the study found, and it has become clear that the more harmful incidents a child suffers, the more likely their health suffers later. "Trauma really is a public health crisis that everybody needs to start addressing…"[147]

What does all this mean?
Abuse is bad for kids, whether they are seeing it or experiencing it.

Will the children start to do better when you leave and get to safety? Yes, in most cases! A lot depends on the degree of warmth and caring in the relationship they have with their parents or adult family members, as well as their own emotional makeup, as we will see later in this chapter.

Nevertheless, the majority of kids are resilient; and, as we've seen, *staying* in a high-conflict marriage also causes life-long struggles for parents and kids.

Simply having two parents does not protect kids
from suffering the damage that ongoing exposure to abuse inflicts on them.

We see instead the overall resilience of children whose families went through a life-saving divorce.

In an informal survey of parents in my online group, 8 in 10 survey respondents reported that one or more of their children felt that the divorce was the best solution in a terrible situation. Fewer than 1 in 10 said all of their children opposed the divorce.

---

147 Mike Stobbe, "US Health Officials Link Childhood Trauma to Adult Illness," ***AP News*** (11/5/19), accessed 11/8/19, https://apnews.com/bf647b36c0a64e4b935b96426d5baf86. The source is Jim Mercy, who oversees the CDC's violence prevention programs, and Dr. Dayna Long, a researcher at the UCSF Benioff Children's Hospital Oakland, commenting on the 2019 ACE Study, as quoted by Mike Stobbe.

FOUR STUDIES THAT SAY KIDS WILL MOST LIKELY BE FINE AFTER DIVORCE

1. If I Divorce, Will My Children Have Long-Lasting Damage?

Your child is not likely to have long-lasting damage from a divorce. Most children do not have any serious problems psychologically, socially, or emotionally. In fact, three in every four children from divorced homes have no serious problems at all.

While experts acknowledge that the first two years of the divorce are stressful, it doesn't have long-lasting effects on most kids. Moving, going to a new school, observing conflict between parents, and going back and forth between homes does cause real pain for children during the transition, but in the long run, the kids turn out a lot like their friends from two-parent homes.

The chart below shows that in non-divorced homes, 10% of children are likely to have serious problems. In divorced homes, about 20% of children are likely to have serious problems. As you can see from the graph, the vast majority of youths—whether their parents are divorced or not—go through life without any serious problems at all.

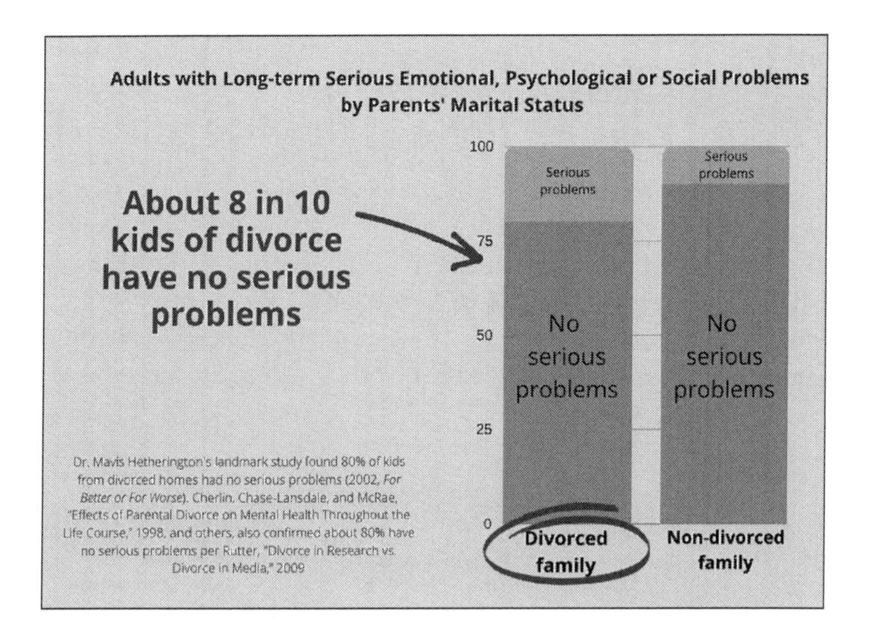
Adults with Long-term Serious Emotional, Psychological or Social Problems by Parents' Marital Status
100
75
50
25
0
Serious problems
Serious problems
About 8 in 10 kids of divorce have no serious problems
No serious problems
No serious problems
Divorced family
Non-divorced family
Dr. Mavis Hetherington's landmark study found 80% of kids from divorced homes had no serious problems (2002, *For Better or For Worse*). Cherlin, Chase-Lansdale, and McRae, "Effects of Parental Divorce on Mental Health Throughout the Life Course," 1998, and others, also confirmed about 80% have no serious problems per Rutter, "Divorce in Research vs. Divorce in Media," 2009

Dr. Mavis Hetherington wrote:

> "In the short run, divorce is brutally painful to a child. But its negative long-term effects have been exaggerated...
> "Twenty-five percent of youths from divorced families in comparison to 10 percent from non-divorced families did have serious social, emotional, or psychological problems. But most of the young men and women from [the study] looked a lot like their contemporaries from non-divorced homes. Although they looked back on their parents' breakup as a painful experience, most were successfully going about the chief tasks of young adulthood: establishing careers, creating intimate relationships, building meaningful lives for themselves."[148]

Demographer Andrew Cherlin confirmed Hetherington's findings but added: (1) the mental health risk for children ranges between 20% to 25%,[149] and (2) part of the children's behavior problems existed before the divorce, due to *marital conflict, substance abuse, or violence,* rather than being caused by the divorce itself.[150] This gives hope to parents who wish to rescue their kids by reducing the exposure to harm.

Although there *are* studies that show children do not adjust well after high-conflict divorce, there are many that say they are resilient and do adjust well.

So what's the truth?

A team of researchers from the Netherlands worked to reconcile the disagreement between a number of studies. Their main finding in 2018 was that kids who had a lot of trauma while their parents were married recovered very well after the divorce. We'll talk later in this chapter about high-conflict legal battles, and how to reduce the tension in the home.

But they also found that children whose parents had intense, bitter, high-conflict legal battles during the divorce experienced slightly lower

---

148 Hetherington and Kelly, ***For Better,*** 7. "Ten percent of youths from non-divorced families, compared to 20 percent in divorce and remarried families were troubled," p. 228

149 Virginia Rutter, "Divorce in Research vs. Divorce in Media," ***Sociology Compass*** 3, no. 4 (2009): 707-720.

150 A. J. Cherlin, P. L. Chase-Lansdale, and C. McRae, "Effects of Parental Divorce on Mental Health Throughout the Life Course," ***American Sociological Review*** 63, no. 2 (1998): 239-249.

levels of adjustment, due to depression.[151]

To summarize, children are resilient. Those whose parents escaped a traumatic marriage adjusted well after divorce, on average.

Those first two years are tough because of all the changes. For example: moving to a new home, legal conflict between parents, switching schools, and possibly losing friendships. During those early years, kids may blame the divorce on themselves, unless the parents help them see they did nothing to cause it. Some children do better than others because they have high self-esteem and feel comfortable in new situations. And of course, each parent's personality and resilience and capacity for change matters too.

In other words, if your child was fine before the divorce, they will have some additional stress, fear, and anxiety about all the changes; but on average, within two years, they are likely to go back to normal. An empathetic, nurturing parent can bring a lot of comfort during this time. In this chapter, we'll discuss ways to help your children cope through those first tough years, and what to do if your ex-spouse increases the conflict during and after the divorce.

2. If I Divorce, Will My Kids Have Drug and Alcohol Problems?

Your kids are not likely to have alcohol or drug problems. The vast majority of kids in single-parent and stepparent families do not have *any* substance abuse problems. In fact, the majority of *all* adolescents don't have any drug or alcohol abuse problems, no matter what their parents' marriage was like.

- Only **6 in 100 adolescents in single-mother** families had substance abuse problems. 94 in 100 have no substance abuse problems.
- Only **5 in 100 adolescents in two-parent families** had substance abuse problems. 95 in 100 have no substance abuse problems.

---

151 Reine van der Wal, Catrin Finkenauer, and Margreet Visser, "Reconciling Mixed Findings on Children's Adjustment Following High Conflict Divorce," ***Journal of Child and Family Studies*** (11/6/18).

Substance Abuse Problems Among Twelve- to Seventeen-Year-Olds[152]	
Number of kids with abuse problems	**Family Type**
3.4 in 100	Mother + father + other relative (Example: grandmother, aunt, etc.)
4.5 in 100	Mother + father
5.3 in 100	Mother + stepfather
5.7 in 100	Mother only
6.0 in 100	Mother + other relative
7.2 in 100	Other relative only
8.1 in 100	Other family type
11 in 100	Father only
11.8 in 100	Father + stepmother

3. If I Divorce, Will My Kid's Marriage End in Divorce, Too?

Most adults whose parents divorced *do not* divorce. The majority of people whose parents divorced have lifelong marriages. However, children from divorced homes are a bit more likely to get divorced than children of married parents.

According to 2018 figures[153]—

- Most people who marry *never* divorce.
- Those people whose parents *did* divorce have a 47% divorce rate.
- Those people whose parents did *not* divorce have a 40% divorce rate.
- In other words: There's very little difference between these two groups, only 7%. The gap has narrowed in the past 25 years.

---

152 Chart and description by Dr. Bella DePaulo, using data in the Hoffman and Johnson "Adolescent Drug Use" study, which draws information from the principle source of data about drug use in the United States. Bella DePaulo, ***Singled Out*** (New York: St. Martin's Griffin, 2006), 176-177.

153 Nicholas H. Wolfinger, "Trends in the Intergenerational Transmission of Divorce," ***Demography*** (Sept. 1999): 415-420. Updated with 2018 data via personal correspondence April 2020.

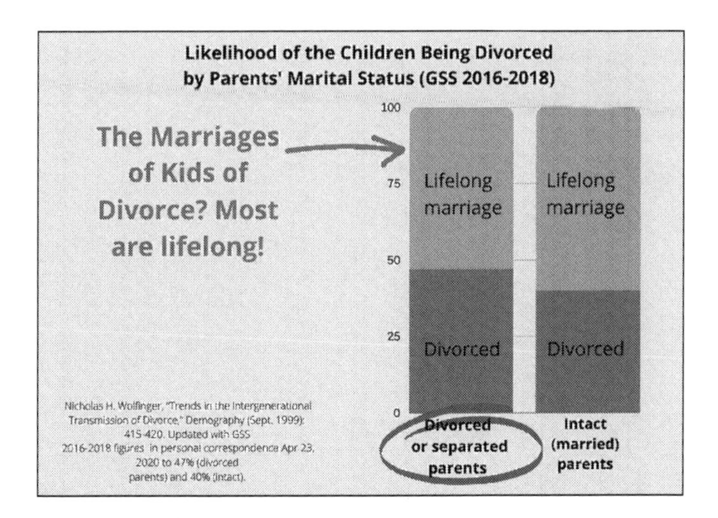

4. If I Divorce, Will My Kids Drop Out of High School or Get Pregnant?

Your teens aren't likely to drop out of high school or get pregnant—no matter what type of home they're in. Single parents and remarried parents do as well, or nearly as well, as two-parent families.[154] In fact, single-parent households have less money for drugs and alcohol, so children are less likely to abuse them.

High School Dropouts	Unwed Teen Pregnancy
1 in 100 teens from mother+father homes	4 in 100 teens from mother+father homes
5 in 100 teens from mother-only homes (only 3 in 100 if the mother was remarried)	9 in 100 teens from mother-only homes (only 6 in 100 if the mother was remarried)
11 in 100 teens from father-only homes (only 5 in 100 if the father was remarried)	13 in 100 teens from father-only homes (only 6 in 100 if the father was remarried)

For every 8 single mother families, there was 1 single dad family. Why do they fair worse? Perhaps the mother has substance abuse or mental health problems, is incarcerated, or not involved, making supervision more difficult. Or perhaps parental alienation or court rulings have decreased her involvement.

154 Dr. Michael Kozloski using data from Wave 2 (1996) of Add Health, weighted to be nationally representative.

5. Are Two Parents Always Better Than One?

A peaceful, single-parent home or stepparent home is a good choice over a high-conflict two-parent home. But if your marriage doesn't have much conflict—let's say your marriage is low conflict or medium conflict—it's likely best for your child if you stay married.

A study from 2009 shows that kids in a single-parent household do no worse than they would in a two-parent home that has a lot of conflict.[155] In fact, one study found when fathers engaged in high levels of antisocial behavior, the more time they lived with their children, the more conduct problems their children had.[156]

After a divorce, the children on average perform at about the same level in school as they did before the divorce. In fact, children in **high-conflict married** homes are more likely to have the following problems than kids in single-parent homes:[157]

- binge drinking
- using marijuana
- marrying too early
- divorcing

And it makes sense: If a marriage is full of chaos and problems don't get resolved, the children find ways to escape the misery somehow. They may numb themselves with alcohol or drugs or run off to marry the first person who will get them away. If the victimized parent stays in the nightmare, instead of setting boundaries and saying "no" to the abuse, the children may even develop serious problems such as personality disorders themselves. Kids need to have at least one safe parent who can model good boundaries.

6. Will Sending My Kids to Daycare Damage Them?

The answer depends on three issues:

- your child's age
- the time spent in daycare
- the quality of the daycare

---

155 Musick and Meier, *"Are Both Parents,"* 826.

156 Jaffee, et. al., "Life with (Or without) Father," *Child Development,* Vol. 74, (2003), 109.

157 Musick and Meier, *"Are Both Parents,"* 826.

Childcare isn't the ideal option for infants and toddlers ages 0-2; but if your child is age 3 or older, and the caregivers and program are good, childcare can be a benefit to your children.[158] It's also best not to have kids in daycare all day, every day; however, this is the *ideal*, and it must be said that people escaping a destructive marriage who don't have much income do not always have the luxury of reducing their children's time in daycare. Single parents who have to work long hours or multiple jobs just to make ends meet are doing a wonderful job of taking care of their family in a hard (sometimes a seemingly impossible) situation, and they deserve our respect and support.

What is "good quality childcare"? You should look for childcare with—

- a good ratio of staff to children
- trained caregivers
- stability, not a lot of changes in location or staff

Of course, some of the success of childcare also depends on the wellbeing and personality of your children, and the quality of the activities you do with them when you're at home with them. Getting out, taking a walk, having fun, going to the library, visiting the pet store, or getting a snack are all ways of sustaining a warm and caring bond.

Divorce Is *Not* as Harmful as It Used to Be

Divorce used to be seen as very harmful to children. Research done decades ago showed evidence of substantial harm.

But more recent studies show a different story. Now, on average, children of divorced homes have almost the same outcomes for school success and behavior issues as children from two-parent intact homes.

> "...many children experience short-term negative effects from divorce, especially anxiety, anger, shock and disbelief.
> These reactions typically diminish or disappear by the end of the second year. Only a minority of kids suffer longer."[159]

---

158 Christine Felfe and Rafael Lalive, "Early Child Care and Child Development: For Whom It Works and Why," ***IZA DP*** No. 7100 (Dec. 2012): 33.

159 Arkowitz and Lilienfeld, ***"Is Divorce Bad."*** The article is quoting findings by psychologist E. Mavis Hetherington of the University of Virginia and her then graduate student Anne Mitchell Elmore.

There are several reasons divorce is less damaging than before —

1. **Social acceptance.** Divorce is now common in society. About 4 in 10 people who have *ever* married have gotten a divorce.[160] In general society, divorce is now seen as unfortunate, but not rare or disgraceful. Children and their parents are not treated as second-class citizens as often as before, although it is still a stigma in many churches and religious communities.
2. **Legal changes.** Divorce no longer requires the innocent spouse to prove publicly that the other spouse is a horrid person. Prior to 1969, when California (under Governor Ronald Reagan) was the first state to pass no-fault divorce,[161] one spouse had to *prove* publicly in court that the other was unfaithful, drunk, abusive, addicted, a child molester, or a felon. This might require witnesses, investigators, photographs, testimonies, and a court trial, as well as a lot of hostility, time, and money. Even after all that, a judge could say no to the divorce. Today, a divorcing couple can choose a no-fault or irreconcilable differences divorce to keep the conflict lower, move quickly through the court system, divide the assets, protect their children and neighbors from knowing the ugly details, and move on.
3. **Religious acceptance.** Many (but not all) Christian denominations have relaxed their harsh stances against divorced people. In the 1920s, marrying a divorced person was somewhat scandalous. Today, about 1 in 4 evangelical Christians have gone through a divorce.[162] About 3 in 4 pastors condone divorce in cases of infidelity, abandonment, or physical abuse. Children from homes where the marriage is later annulled are considered legitimate children legally.[163]

---

160 Dan Hurley, "Divorce Rate: It's Not as High as You Think," ***New York Times*** (4/19/05), accessed 6/17/18, https://www.nytimes.com/2005/04/19/health/divorce-rate-its-not-as-high-as-you-think.html.
161 Before all 50 states passed laws allowing a person to divorce without proof of wrongdoing, divorces were a battlefield. (It took about 30 years for **most** of the U.S. states to pass "no-fault" divorce. California was the first to pass it in 1969. New York was the final one in 2010.)
162 "New Marriage and Divorce Statistics Released," ***The Barna Group*** (3/31/08), accessed 9/11/19, https://www.barna.com/research/new-marriage-and-divorce-statistics-released/.
163 Children from annulled marriages are considered legitimate. Roman Catholics who divorce can still take communion.

How Do I Become the Best Parent I Can Be?

How do you parent a child during and after divorce, when you may still be reeling from stress and anxiety yourself?

Frankly, it is tough for every good parent, and the transition of divorce can seem to take forever. We may be exhausted, worn out, and apprehensive about the legal process. We may be trying to figure out how to pay the bills. We may be worried about our kids.

Research shows that parents do best when they:

- have a warm, close, and affectionate relationship with their kids
- do fun things outside the home with the kids (walks, hikes, beach, museums, sports, volunteering, visiting the library or pet store, or parks)
- do projects inside the home with the kids (maybe reading together, planting a garden, singing, cooking, drawing or painting, hanging photos, or repairing something)
- don't punish when they are angry, upset, and irritable

Common Mistakes of Single Mothers and Fathers

As we look at this list, I want everyone to keep in mind that these mistakes are completely understandable for single parents to make. After all, they're doing the work of two parents, and they're usually doing it while under an immense amount of stress, themselves!

If you are a single parent and worried about making mistakes, make sure to give yourself some credit for all you are doing. God sees your efforts and showers you with grace and compassion.

The struggle may be intense right now, but it will not always feel this way, and you can count on God's presence and strength—together with the support of those you love—to help you get through the intense times and into the peace that comes after.

Single Parent Mistake 1: Being Less Supportive to Their Kids

Be warm and affectionate. When your kids are nervous, worried, or frightened, talk with them and help them calm down. Typically they are worried about changes in their life due to the divorce.

Kids may need you to bring it up.
Ask them about their feelings and give them comfort.

Tell them that there are still more changes in the future, but eventually life will become a bit happier and more peaceful. Tell them there will be ups and downs and struggles, and you'll just walk though one challenge after the next, but eventually there will be a better future.

Tell them the Lord is watching over you all. Simply talking about their worries to a loving and positive parent makes them feel better, not worse.

Many people avoid the topic of divorce with their kids, falsely thinking it will make their kids have more pain if they discuss it directly. (This was my mistake for the first few years. I should have talked with my kids right away, rather than shying away from the topic, in hopes that I wouldn't cause them pain.) In reality, addressing the topic allows kids to release their pain and accept a warm hug, encouraging words, and positive comments about the future.

"I know it's difficult right now, and I think it will continue to be tough for a while longer,
but I believe God will help us through."
"No matter what happens, I am here for you. I am going to take care of you."

Kids Need Basic Explanations. Kids want to make sense of what is happening. They want answers that explain their observations, and they want the feeling of safety and security.

Kids also need help interpreting. They see the actions and the words, but they don't always conclude the right thing. As the saying goes—

"Children are keen observers and poor interpreters."
—Rudolf Dreikurs, Austrian psychiatrist[164]

Your children might be watching the relationship fall apart and coming to their own conclusions about what's happening. They need help from an adult who sees the bigger picture.

For young children under 12, you might say something like this, in your own words:

---

164 Amanda Smyth, "Children Are Keen Observers but Poor Interpreters," ***A Cooker and a Looker*** (4/29/15), accessed 12/28/19, https://cookerandalooker.com/children-are-keen-observers-but-poor-interpreters/.

"Mommy and Daddy have some serious problems. Daddy (or Mommy) has done some very harmful things, and even though I have forgiven him/her over and over, it has continued. At some point, it's better to end the marriage than to have this bad behavior in our home."

If appropriate and there was no direct child abuse, you can add: "I know you love Daddy (or Mommy), and you want to spend time with him/her, so I want you to know that you will see him/her [every Wednesday night and every other weekend, or whatever the schedule is]. Let's pack a bag with the clothes, shoes, toys, and games you want to take with you."

Kids want to love both parents, and being calm helps them adjust. Later in this chapter, we'll talk about bitter divorces that involve severe conflict and how to deal with them.

Kids Blame Themselves for the Divorce. A common mistake kids make is believing that they personally are to blame for Mommy and Daddy splitting up. Children often blame themselves in this way, due to their child-like concrete concepts of cause-and-effect. They are good at sensing tension, but they may not perceive the real reason behind the conflict, so they assume they caused it.

Many small children think their mistakes or wrong actions (spilled milk, hitting a sibling, or disobedience) *caused* their parents to divorce. Sometimes this is a conclusion they came up with themselves. This is just how they interpreted the situation. So it is important to find out what children believe, especially those under twelve years old. They might be carrying a load of guilt that isn't based on truth.

You might say something like, "You aren't to blame for the divorce. You didn't cause it. This is between Mommy and Daddy. Kids don't cause divorce."

You may have to tell them this from time to time, whenever they seem to think the burden for the marriage falls on them.

Kids Think They Can Get You Back Together. This is the other side of the coin: kids think they can fix the marriage. Old movies such as "The Parent Trap" depict the fantasy of kids magically fixing their family if they can just help Mom and Dad spend romantic time together.

If your kids do this, you might say something like, "Sweetheart, I know you care, but this is between Mommy and Daddy. This isn't something kids can fix."

Advice from researcher Dr. Judith Wallerstein (emphasis mine)—

"You may not be comfortable with my final piece of advice on raising children after divorce. What I'm about to describe is not advice you've heard before, and frankly it may be difficult for you to do. It draws on what I learned from talking to young adults whose parents divorced twenty-five years ago and who have been describing their thoughts, feelings, and experiences to me at regular intervals through all these years.

"Based on what they have told me, **I am recommending that as your children go through adolescence and enter young adulthood, you need to carry on an open-ended conversation about what caused your divorce and what you have learned about how to avoid the mistakes you made.** Your goal in these conversations is to convey your hopes for their happier future and your confidence in their ability to succeed in love and in creating a committed relationship.

"Why do this? Why not simply bury the past and get on with life? Won't dredging up past hurts just make things worse? My answer is an emphatic no. Your children need to know what went wrong in your marriage so they'll have a better chance of creating a lasting, happy marriage of their own. Moreover, they need your loving encouragement to feel hopeful that they will [be able to form stable partnerships of their own]."[165]

Single Parent Mistake 2: Being Too Harsh When They Discipline

Parents with extremely harsh child discipline are critical and angry much of the time. They pride themselves on being good disciplinarians, but their kids walk on eggshells, always nervous about setting Mom or Dad off. These parents:

- change their rules unpredictably
- discipline in an inconsistent manner (consequences are much harsher than warranted or are not always enforced for the favorite child)

165 Wallerstein and Blakeslee, ***What About,*** 341-342.

- don't keep their promises (look for excuses to deny the child a promised treat, for a birthday, for example)
- punish kids *before* they do anything wrong
- over-punish a child who spills something accidentally or makes a mistake

Obviously, this harsh approach drives the children away and makes them mistrust authorities. This is the parenting style that correlates with juvenile delinquency.

Instead, encourage your children verbally. Many parents think praising their children will make them spoiled, lazy, and unmotivated, but children who are praised and encouraged are happier. And happier people do better in life. Instead of praising kids for their brains or athletic skill, praise them for their patience and persistence.[166]

The problem is not harsh vs. permissive parenting. Instead, it's about finding a way that avoids the two extremes—

1. Have clear, consistent rules that you develop with your kids. Post them somewhere.
2. Give kind and firm consequences for breaking the rules.
3. Patiently explaining the reasons behind the rules.
4. Don't discipline out of anger. Wait until you calm down.

For more reading on how to parent kids with respect, care, and healthy boundaries, you may want to try the book *How to Talk so Kids Will Listen and Listen so Kids Will Talk*, by Adele Faber and Elaine Mazlish. It's a very readable book and has lots of resources, exercises, examples, and scripts to show parents the kind of communication with their children that is most likely to cultivate a healthy relationship.

"I was a child of harsh and strict parenting,
and I have struggled as a mother to not parent the same way.
Most of us who rebel against harsh parents
are not necessarily rebelling against the strict rules.
The cure for harsh parenting, therefore, isn't permissiveness,

---

166 I like the insights from Carol Dweck on how to praise children for persistence and trying rather than traits like physical beauty or athletic skill. See her TED talk "The Power of Believing You Can Improve," which helps set children up for a growth mindset: https://www.ted.com/talks/carol_dweck_the_power_of_believing_that_you_can_improve?language=en.

which is what I discovered as I matured and eventually
became a mother.
We who rebel, rebel against unkindness.
When I was a child, I wanted to be loved, respected, and
valued, like everyone else."[167]

Single Parent Mistake 3: Being Less Positive and Encouraging

One of the toughest challenges is separating love from approval. It's natural to combine them so that we love only those we approve of. But a loving parent wants to show affection to their children even when they aren't perfect. We can do this by separating *who our children are* from *what our children do*.

Love is the unconditional care and affection a good parent has for their children simply because they are theirs. A good parent will do nice things for their children because they are their children—for example, serving their favorite food once a week—even when they have done something wrong or irresponsible.

A good parent says kind words and gives encouragement to the children regularly, not just when they win an award or make the parent look good. In other words, love is doing something the child sees as loving without requiring anything in return.

Approval is different, and it is directed at the behavior, not at the child themselves. Good behavior earns approval, while bad behavior receives disapproval.

Good parents disapprove of their children's actions when they are lying, stealing, harming others, being lazy, etc. Good parents give children reasonable consequences: for example, asking them to pay for damage they caused deliberately (not accidentally); inviting them to apologize; allowing them to feel the pain of bad grades and other bad conduct.

As a newly divorced parent, at first I wanted to make up for the hurts my children had experienced. I wanted to protect them from all pain.

But over I time, I realized my real job in life was to raise my children to be good citizens, good neighbors, good employees, good friends, good bosses, and good coworkers. My parenting decisions became clearer when I focused on that.

---

167 Luma Simms, "The Difference Between Harsh and Austere Parenting," ***IFS Studies*** (4/27/17), accessed 7/1/17, https://ifstudies.org/blog/the-difference-between-austere-and-harsh-parenting.

Single Parent Mistake 4: Not Supervising Their Children

Make sure your kids are doing their homework where you can see them. If they are having trouble with a subject, get them some help from teachers, after-school programs, or classmates.

Have reasonable rules about finishing homework before watching TV, playing on the Internet, or talking/texting with friends. Communicate with teachers so you know what homework is missing. (Many teachers have the class assignments and your child's missing homework on a password-protected web page that you can access any time.)

Single Parent Mistake 5: Spending Less Time with Their Kids

Going to a park or an outing with Mom or Dad can be fun for kids, especially if it involves a little treat. Some families can't have pets, but they might enjoy going to the pet store and looking at the puppies and kittens and fish.

Do fun activities or interesting projects together at home. Teach kids how to cook, how to build something, or paint and draw together. Read a book aloud together. (Our family always liked clean joke books.)

Find something the kids enjoy and have them teach you. If your kids like card games or video games, learn how to play them too. Working on puzzles is good for all ages and abilities.

This is the time to make your life calmer and peaceful by reducing your activities, limiting commitments, lowering your expenses, and reducing conflict with your ex-spouse. Without another adult helping in the home, you need more time to cook, clean, shop, do laundry and repairs, and spend time with the kids.

Single parents are often brokenhearted that they don't have the money for certain sports or activities they once did, but a warm and peaceful home gives the children a safe and loving foundation for the future.

Single Parent Mistake 6: Having Conflict with Your Ex in Front of Your Kids

Telling your children the ups and downs of your court battles and the legal process of the divorce really does damage to your children's peace of mind and wellbeing (not to mention your own!). If they know too many details, such as the court dates, they may agonize and become distressed to the point of not functioning well at school that entire week. Avoid fighting with your ex-spouse, as far as you are able to do so without getting taken advantage of.

Obviously, you can only control your own behavior; a spouse who has been abusive will very likely continue escalating and trying to force you to engage in fights with them, and you cannot control or prevent their behavior.

But you can refuse to engage, de-escalate conflicts wherever possible, and leave conversations that your ex-spouse is trying to turn into a shouting match. "Let's talk later when we can discuss this calmly," or "let's discuss this via email," and ending the phone call or leaving the room, for example, are good ways of de-escalating and refusing to join in the fight. Kids will notice that you are trying to minimize the conflict and will appreciate it.

Get educated on the techniques of dealing with abusers. There are many good books on how to divorce an abuser and not get drawn into their manipulation.

Help! My Divorce Is Bitter and Vicious — Narcissism Alert

You may be saying, "This all sounds good, but you don't know my situation. My ex is attacking me all the time. He (or she) pounces on everything I do and twists it."

I hear you! Most of the advice I give in this chapter is for the nine-in-ten "normal" divorces where there's a little conflict, but no stonewalling in court, coercion, or threats.

But one-in-ten divorces go to a different level, maybe including: intense anger and insinuations; restraining orders or defending yourself from your ex-spouse's stalking; hacking your phone or computer; false accusations; trying to get you fired from your job; financial abuse; or constant litigation.

If two or more of these factors exist in your situation, you need to take special steps to get informed on how to protect yourself. It's so much harder to divorce someone with a vengeful personality or a personality disorder. You're walking into a tornado when you're at your weakest and most vulnerable. But you are smarter and tougher than you think.

The first step is to document everything. There are entire books dedicated to protecting yourself in a bitter divorce. I would recommend Lundy Bancroft's **Why Does He Do That? Inside the Minds of Angry and Controlling Men;** Billy Eddy's book, **Splitting;** and Tina Swithin's, **The Narc Decoder.** At the end of this chapter, I'll give some specific tips.

Start by getting educated, reading these books and signing up for OurFamilyWizard, an app that documents the time and date of your communications with your ex-spouse in a way that is usually admissible in court and very difficult to falsify. It's about $5 per month. This will save you hours of time, thousands of dollars of legal fees, and constant heartbreak.

7 Common Mistakes People Make in Divorces

One Christian divorce attorney who has a lot of Christian clients shared the common mistakes he's seen his clients make:[168]

Myth: Believing that the other party doesn't deserve at all to parent the children and that the other party's presence in the children's lives has no value to them.

"You may have ended the marriage, but that other parent is still likely to be loved by the children. Even if you don't think this person can parent well, the court won't see it that way. There's no law against being a so-so parent (letting your kids watch too much TV, eat junk food, and play video games for hours, for example). However, there is a law against about being neglectful and abusive. So don't fixate on food choices and other bad behavior. Your ex-spouse can have had a thousand affairs, and it's irrelevant in the eyes of the court. There are few reasons the court will get involved, unless it's significant neglect or abuse."

Myth: Thinking that a lawyer is unnecessary, especially when there are highly contended issues such as custody/parenting time, significant asset/debt distribution, and support.

"Oftentimes, one of the parties is too trusting of the other in the divorce process. At the very least, both parties should consult with a good lawyer before proceeding with the divorce."

Myth: Believing that the court cares about the infidelity in the marriage (most states have "no fault" divorce laws) and fixating on *that* issue over all others.

"The purpose of the court is to make a decision about contended issues such as custody, parenting time, dividing marital assets and debts, child support, and possibly spousal support."

The court is not there to slap the hand of a badly behaving spouse. There won't be moral vindication in court. Don't increase your legal fees attempting to do this.

---

168 All quotes in this section are taken from a personal phone call with this divorce attorney, shared with permission under condition of anonymity.

Myth: Believing that legal separation is better than divorce. (Note: several states, like Pennsylvania, Texas, Delaware, Florida, Georgia, and Mississippi, don't have legal separation as an option. And some people stay separated because they need health insurance.)

"I highly advise all my clients to divorce rather than to legally separate. Some people think that legal separations are good because the parties can change their minds later, undo it, and reunite. However, it is far more complicated and expensive to undo a legal separation in my state than to just remarry after a divorce, which I have seen from time to time. Each state has its own laws, in fact several states do not offer legal separation, and you need to talk to an attorney to discuss the issues."

Myth: Believing you must have all your financial documents put together before your divorce.

"Due to the fact that in [most] conservative Christian marriages, the husband was the one who controlled all of the finances, the wife should definitely not delay the divorce process because she doesn't have access to all or most of the financial records. This will be disclosed in the process, which is another reason to get a lawyer."

Myth: Thinking that the person who earned more (or all) of the money during the marriage is entitled to more of the marital property upon divorce.

"This is especially the case in marriages that have operated on more complementarian, traditional lines, where the husband is the breadwinner and the wife is the homemaker."

Running a household and raising a family involve a lot of work, and the spouse who carries the lion's share of the cooking, cleaning, meal planning, shopping, clothes purchasing, laundry, errands, repair arranging, social commitments, family relationships, care for elderly parents, vacation planning, child raising, children's education and recreation, transportation, homework, and managing the family's time, resources, and efforts is contributing to the family's financial success just as much as is the spouse who is bringing home a paycheck.

Those paychecks may be made out to the husband, but her skill, timeliness, attention to detail, and dedication to maintaining the home, children, extended family, church responsibilities, and neighborhood and professional relationships yields rewards for the family. Both parties' contributions are of great value to the family as a whole, and the divorce settlement should reflect this.

Myth: Particularly with the wife, having an unrealistic financial expectations post-divorce.

"For example, the parties may have agreed when married that she would homeschool the children, and now she insists on foregoing sustainable employment so that she can continue. This is rarely realistic. The bottom line is, it costs more money to live separate lives, and the most generous spousal support award will not remedy this problem."

YOUR EX-SPOUSE: PROTECTING YOURSELF WHILE KEEPING THE TENSION DOWN

Walking the Tightrope: Be Honest, but Don't Badmouth the Kids' Other Parent

It is a challenge to talk to your children about their father or mother if feel you've been treated badly. When you're exhausted, it's easy to make a sarcastic comment or show disgust in front of the kids.

We need to remember that children usually still have love for the other parent. It's deep in their nature—and children whose parents use them as weapons against each other, or spies, or in other ways try to divide their loyalties, tend to suffer a lot of emotional distress.

Asking children to take sides usually hurts them. They love Mom *and* Dad, and they need to be allowed to go on loving both. After all, children don't often have the power to change the situation they've found themselves in. Please respect their right to have a relationship with the other parent if they wish to have one.

If that person is basically a *good* parent (or, as most of us are, a "good enough" parent!), and the children want to see them, it is important that your child have the opportunity to spend time together. That other parent is probably one of the few people on the planet who genuinely cares about your child.

Obviously, the word *good* is important. Abusive parents who simply wish to use their children sexually or for criminal behavior don't fall into this category.

Additionally, it's important for you to have a safe place (or a few safe places) where you *can* vent your feelings and receive emotional support throughout every stage of the divorce process, and as you establish any co-parenting arrangements that you and your ex-spouse put into place afterward.

Nobody can show a brave face all the time.

But all of that should not be happening in front of your child. The message here is not that you should *never* complain about your ex-spouse or vent your frustration—just that it will not be helpful for your kids to be the ones you do this with.

Your children (even when they are grown!) should not have to be parenting *you* and giving *you* reassurance and comfort. Instead, see if you can identify an adult friend (or friends), a therapist or safe pastor, or a support group, where you can safely share how you're feeling and be received without judgment, with understanding and compassion, and even with solidarity and encouragement.

God designed us to need one another, and this is even more the case when we are going through something intense and difficult like a life-saving divorce.

The Kids *Usually* Figure Out the Truth in Time

Though it often takes some time, kids tend to figure out for themselves the strengths and weaknesses of their parents. Often, they love you both and want a relationship with both parents.

In some states the court requires you to promise—as part of the divorce—that you won't trash-talk your ex-spouse. This is tough to do, especially if his or her behavior is dangerous, abusive, or irresponsible. So be cautious in what you say. Outbursts of anger won't be helpful.

But you may have to clarify things if your spouse is lying to the kids. You may want to ask your attorney how to handle this if a "non-disparagement clause" was part of your final judgment of divorce.

Here are some healthy ways of communicating:

You might want to say this... but don't	**Say this instead (and say it with sincerity in your voice)**
Your dad/mom is a selfish, evil monster.	I have agreed not to say anything bad about your dad/mom, but there were some very serious problems between us. That's why we are divorcing.
Your dad/mom didn't pick you up for visitation because he/she is a jerk.	I don't know why they didn't pick you up on the day they promised. I'm so sorry. That must hurt. *Maybe* that's something you can discuss with your dad/mom, if you choose. (Then you document it on your calendar, or OurFamilyWizard, and let your attorney know, without saying anything more to your child.)
You are stupid, just like your dad/mom.	If you had the chance to do that again, what would you do differently?
Your dad/mom is always cancelling weekend visitations at the last moment. What a jerk. They are just trying to ruin my weekend.	[Don't talk about the legal aspects of your visitation schedule. Just say:] It's just common decency and respect for a person to give 24 hours' notice before they cancel a visitation. I don't know why your dad/mom didn't tell us this time. I'm sorry your dad/mom isn't showing that kind of respect. (Then you document it on your calendar, on OurFamilyWizard, and let your attorney know, without saying anything to your child.)
[Making excuses] I'm sure your dad/mom got sick and that's why they didn't come to your birthday party.	[Show empathy. You're teaching them they have a voice, *if* they choose to use it.] I am so sorry your dad/mom didn't come to your birthday party. I have no idea why your dad/mom didn't come. I don't understand it. That's really disappointing. I'm sorry. That's got to hurt. *Maybe* that's something you can discuss with your dad/mom, if you choose.

Sure, your father/mother took you to Disneyland, but he/she is just trying to pretend to be as good of a parent as I am.	I'm glad you got to go to Disneyland. That's very exciting. What was your favorite part?
Dad/Mom might have a fancy new car, but he/she is not making child support payments or spending the money in a responsible way. What a jerk.	That sounds like fun. Did you enjoy going in the new car? (Don't discuss child support with kids. If someone is behind in child support, and you see expensive new possessions, document it and talk to your lawyer.)
Your mom/dad has cheated on me a million times. (Or any other information that is not age appropriate, such as sexual immorality or serious criminal behavior.)	I don't want to say anything bad about your dad/mom, but there were some very serious problems between us. That's why we are divorcing. I want you to have your own relationship with him/her. Someday, when it's appropriate and you want to know more, I will tell you.
Your mom/dad has a new spouse, but it's just a matter of time before they cheat again.	I hope your dad/mom has a long and happy marriage.

Optional: Praying with the Children for the Other Parent

This is truly optional. If it doesn't feel right, don't do it. You may be in the center of a big battle, and you cannot bring yourself to do it. I understand.

But for some people, it really helps them focus on God's love and move forward in life. It helps them release the anger that holds them back.

Yes, even if your ex is a difficult person, you can pray honestly in front of your kids. Here's a sample prayer you can modify to fit your situation.

Dear Lord,

Thank you for our family. Thank you for your love and care for us. We pray that you will bring each of us closer to you. Help us to do right and turn from doing wrong. We pray for [Mom or Dad] and for [names of people in the room/family/friends]. We pray that you would bless all of us and help us to love you more each day.

In Jesus' name, Amen.

What If the Children Are Angry with Me or Turn Against Me?

As a Christian divorce recovery leader for years, I've seen kids sometimes turn against a devoted parent (mother or father) with whom they've had a normal, loving relationship. It's heart-breaking to watch.

Sometimes all of the kids in the family reject that parent; sometimes only one does. The benefit of doing divorce recovery for twenty years in the same area is that I've stayed in touch with many of the families and watched them long term. A lot of these relationship tensions get resolved.

But some are heartbreaking and haven't mended.

Here's a story of adult children who rejected their mother for several years. She explained—

> *The kids were all over age 18. [All their lives I had shielded them from my suspicions about their father. None of us knew the depths of their dad's child pornography until the SWAT team broke down our front door.] At first [the kids] felt they had to take sides and pulled back from me.*
>
> *[But what could I say at that point? They had never known the truth about why Mom felt angry and had a lot of tension toward Dad. They had to figure it out themselves from the police reports and the criminal trial.] My kids wouldn't have believed me if I had told them. Just the ranting of a bitter, divorced woman.*
>
> *It took about four or five years, but they finally came around. Reestablishing [a relationship with them] took time, but every day I'm happy I'm not living with addiction. Remarriage has been wonderful and tough. My kids like [my new husband], but they are gun shy about him as a stepfather. There's always an awkward pause about how to introduce him.*

However, we have more healthy family interactions than we did. When I remarried, my oldest son said, "It's so good to have our family back." [My new husband] brought stability. It's been a journey, but I'm grateful that I'm living in truth. No more hiding, no more secrets. I have the grandchildren over now, and I am so happy they are safe.

Fortunately, you are not helpless. There are many things a parent who feels rejected can do. In 9 in 10 families who divorce, a bit of rejection or discomfort between a child and parent is not a severe, long-term problem.

Most children don't reject a parent with whom they formerly had a happy, affectionate relationship.

But in 1 in 10 divorces, it does happen. Even if you are a normal, loving parent, this can happen to you. It may have nothing to do with your character or suitability as a parent. Sometimes it happens naturally. Children just gravitate to a certain parent during stressful times.

In other cases, sometimes one parent—without justification—may turn the child against the other parent. They may even try to remove the parent from their child's life, despite having court-ordered joint custody. These children may be told that the other parent does not love them.

If severe and unwarranted, this brainwashing is a serious problem, and the child is the biggest victim. Children need every loving, trustworthy adult in their life they can get. (Notice that this type of bad behavior is not limited to one gender. It could be a mother or father who turns the child against the other parent. I've seen it both ways.)[169]

For parents, you need to prepare how to respond and what to say and do when...

- your child doesn't want to talk to you on the phone
- your child calls you by your first name instead of "Dad" or "Mom"
- your child accuses you of trying to hurt the other parent
- your child says he or she hates you
- your ex refuses to let you talk to the child

169 For a support group leader who is not a therapist, this is a tough situation. We may think we know someone well, but even pastors, counselors, and support group leaders have been fooled. It is very difficult to know a false abuse accusation from a true one without proof. Sometimes police, investigators, and court records can help.

For High-Conflict, Vengeful Divorces Only

The following twelve tips are for high-conflict divorces, where one parent is turning the kids against the other parent, and the court is being used as a war zone.

In normal situations, of course, you would parent your children in the usual way when they behave badly, but in custody battles with an ex-spouse who is vindictive, kids are pawns just trying to keep from being criticized, mocked, or hurt. They are victims, too. In these cases, parenting requires different tactics.

If you feel your child is rejecting you, and that your ex-spouse is behind it, I'm sure you're angry and very upset. Maybe it has been happening all along in your marriage, in small, subtle ways, and you've finally caught on. Maybe it's something new. You want to pick up the phone and give your ex and your kids a piece of your mind.

But don't do that. You can accidentally make it worse. Now is the time to make a game plan. Below is a list of tips put together by an expert, Dr. Kathleen Reay.

The Twelve Most Common Mistakes Alienated Parents Tend to Make with Their Children

Dr. Kathleen Reay,[170] a specialist in high-conflict divorce, provides tips for parents whose children have been alienated from them by a difficult or abusive ex-spouse. Her thoughts appear in quotations; additional clarifications are my own.

1. "When in contact with your children, don't trash, bash, berate, put down, or persecute their other parent. By doing so, you are modeling abusive behavior to your children. This will ultimately backfire on you. Your children will likely feel very uncomfortable and have less respect for you. Additionally, this kind of behavior on your part will likely push them further away from you."
2. "Don't challenge or dispute your children's loyalty to the alienating parent. Choosing to do so will only create more resistance. Remember, the greater you challenge your children's loyalty to the other parent, the more your children will resist.

170 Kathleen Reay, ***Toxic Divorce: A Workbook for Alienated Parents*** (Dr. Kathleen Reay, Inc., 2011). Thank you to Dr. Kathleen Reay for giving me permission to use her tips from her book.

Be encouraging and focus on the positive aspects of their relationship. For example, state in a warm and sincere manner, 'I'm impressed with the way you take such good care of your father.'"

3. "Don't discuss any legal information. It's important that your children do not hear any references to court actions or any other legal information. This includes not showing them any legal or court documents. Don't be surprised if your older children or teens insist that you share legal information with them to help sort out what is true and what is not. Keep in mind that legal information, including the difficult language, what court orders actually mean, and so on can be difficult for most adults to comprehend, never mind children and teens. Confusing court documents may encourage children to take sides; redirect them instead."

   Note: If you want to, you can promise to share more information with them in the future when they ask.

4. "In spite of sounding counter-intuitive, don't make demands. For example, 'What you should do is treat me with respect instead of treating me with such disrespect. I'm your parent, so don't talk to me that way.' Even though your likely intention is to attempt to control the situation with your alienated child and provide some prompt remedy, what it really says to your alienated child is this: 'You don't have the right to decide how to deal with your issues and feelings.' Remember, your child is a victim, as well. Your child has not intentionally created a pattern of rejection; your child has been drawn into it by his/her other parent."

   Note: I know people will push back on Dr. Reay's advice. So I asked a mother who is in this situation to explain why these tips work. She said: "You have to see this from the child's perspective. This is not a normal parenting situation. In the other parent's home, your child can never speak their mind and say what they really think, or they will suffer the consequences. They are in constant double-binds. They feel they can never win. It is self-defeating. In a normal parenting situation, it is good to ask for right behaviors, but from the child's point of view, they are in double-binds every way they turn. Their dad tells them everything they should or should not say. He controls and stifles them. If you demand respect, it may come back to bite you. Some parents who held a hard line look back and feel they turned their kids into narcissists themselves. And holding a hard line drives the kids toward the narcissistic parent. It's sad, but in these situations, you don't get to be a normal parent.

"My daughter would have outbursts with me. You think you ought to curb your kid's behavior. You want to come down on them. But what you're telling your child is, 'You don't have a voice.' They already feel terrified and that no one is listening. You are her only safe place. You are the only person she can rage to. The fact that she rages against you rather than dad, says you are her safe place and her safe parent. They feel that they are always in trouble always being controlled and silenced. If you get onto them, they will feel they have no safe place but drugs, alcohol, or running away."

5. "Don't interrogate. For example, 'What did your mom say to you to make you say that to me?' Although you may have good intentions (to get to the bottom of the issue and find out what was said or done to make your child react the way he/she has to you), it will backfire... make your children feel worse, and they will likely reject you more. Please note: It is perfectly okay to clarify any misconceptions that your alienated children may have about you or your situation. For example, if your child says, 'Daddy says you never loved him or us,' you can say, for instance, 'Oh, sweetie, that isn't true. The moment we met, I fell in love with your father. You and your brother were loved from the moment we knew you were going to be born. I will never stop loving you no matter what.' Whenever the need arises to clarify any misconceptions that your alienated children may have about you or your situation, remind them of specific memories you have about them or of other people, places, times, or things related to their misconceptions. This would be a great time to share any photographs or videos you may have of those times."

6. "Don't moralize. For example, 'The right thing to say to me is,' 'You really should,' 'It's wrong to...' Although the likely intention

is to show your child the proper way to deal with the issue, the meaning of the message is, 'I'll choose your values for you.' This will backfire, too.

7. "Don't pretend to act like a psychologist. For example, 'Do you know why you said that to me? You're just copying your mother. That's what she always says, you know.' Even though your likely intention is to help prevent future issues by analyzing your child's behavior and explaining his/her motives, what it really says to your child is, 'I know more about you than you know about yourself. And that makes me superior to you.' It'll backfire because your alienated child will not feel like a social equal, which will likely push him/her even further away from you."

8. "Don't yell, scream, nag, coax, lecture, or give ultimatums. All children dislike being yelled or screamed at. Nor do they like to be nagged, coaxed, lectured, or given ultimatums by their parents. They feel disrespected and tend to counter by disrespecting the parent back. The same holds true for alienated children, but generally to a greater degree. For example, 'How dare you speak to me in that tone of voice! If you do that again, then I don't want you to come around here anymore.' This kind of behavior on your part will likely induce fear in your alienated child. The child may interpret these types of messages as truth, whether you mean it or not. Your children may actually use this as a way to avoid seeing you again. It'll make it much more difficult for you and your alienated child to repair the relationship."

9. "Don't use guilt trips. For example, 'You wouldn't treat me the way you do now if I earned as much money as your father does.' Although your likely intention is to help your child see the wrong in his/her thoughts, feelings, and actions, what it really says to your child is, 'I am imposing a penance for your past mistakes because you and your other parent are at fault.'"

10. "Don't deny your children's feelings and only justify yours. For example, 'Oh, that's not true. You don't really feel upset. If anybody should feel upset, it should be me.' Alienated children need to have their feelings validated just as much as anybody else does. Although it's quite unlikely that your children will

validate your feelings, due to the pattern of rejection that is occurring, please don't let that stop you from role-modeling it to them. It will be of help in repairing your broken relationship."

11. "Don't be stubborn and child-like. Apologize for mistakes you have made now and in the past. As you're aware, alienated parents undergo a vast array of negative emotions, including anger. Although it may be very difficult to do, it's not impossible to apologize to your alienated children when you have intentionally, unintentionally, or unknowingly done something wrong now or in the past. We want to teach our children to be responsible, caring, and accountable people when they grow up. What is stopping us from role-modeling that to them? It's okay to say, for instance, 'I realize that there were many times when I had to work evenings and weekends and I wasn't able to go to your school concerts and soccer games. I apologize for not being there.'"

12. "Don't react or overreact when your children treat you with criticism, contempt, defensiveness, or stonewalling. It's very important to learn to be proactive and active rather than reactive and over-reactive with them. As difficult as it will be, it is so very important for you to do your very best and develop a hard shell like a tortoise! If you were to react or overreact, then your alienated children will likely feel no need to ever want to repair the fragmented relationship."

Sometimes an alienated parent will unleash anger on his or her children and forget that they are victims, too.

Other books and videos specifically on parental alienation:

Co-Parenting with a Toxic Ex, by Amy J. Baker. This book is practical and easy to read. It gives tips on what to watch for and give actual phrases to use when responding to your kids. It has a workbook format at the end of each chapter.

Divorce Poison, by Richard Warshak. The book is basic and practical. It covers more of the legal aspects of child custody, including situations such as kidnapping.

Toxic Divorce: A Workbook for Alienated Parents, by Kathleen M. Reay, Ph.D. This is an excellent workbook to help parents with their feelings, with strategies and tips to keep tabs on parental alienation so it doesn't progress from moderate to severe.

Video: *Welcome Back, Pluto* by Richard Warshak. This is a video for parents, containing tips for parents who wish to reconnect and reunite with their alienated children. (It is not meant to be watched *with* your children.)

Protecting Yourself

In very troubled divorces where one parent lies frequently and refuses to follow the divorce agreement, it is important to document everything, starting right away.

Some people record all conversations, if that is legal in their state. Some people never speak with the other spouse on the phone, choosing to do everything via email and text message so there is proof of what was said and agreed to.

Once you file for divorce, you may want to communicate with your spouse only in writing, if possible. Look at the co-parenting apps online and become familiar with how they work. These apps can be lifesavers, and are admissible in court in many states. Their records make it very difficult for people to change dates, wording, and pretend they did or didn't receive or respond to an email. Often the court requires the divorcing parties split the cost of these apps.

What Should You Document? When?

Start documenting immediately. Don't hit "delete" when a nasty text or threatening voicemail is left. I know you feel like you're finally free and can breathe for the first time in years, but from day one, you need to start documenting all threats, name calling, and other incidents.

The main goal of documenting is to be able to "paint a picture" for the legal authorities over the case. It needs to illuminate the pattern of behaviors that are abusive without calling it by name. It's telling the complete story, not just listing them. The more details you have, the better, because they will show the patterns (even if you can't see them at the time you're documenting them). You want to have enough details to be able to easily remember that incident from other similar incidents.

This might include: exactly what all parties said and did; how this made you feel; and what thoughts or actions you or others took because of it; what your children witnessed or reported to you, and their feelings, actions, or words in response.

Both facts and feelings are important to document! If he punched the wall beside you and you were afraid he was going to hit you, document that. If your child was upset that their parent didn't pick them up for parenting time, again, document your child's verbal, physical, and emotional response. This is a journal, with the specific purpose of keeping a record (not a bullet-point list of behaviors). As best you can, document the time and date.

Trying to survive may blind you to the fact that you must protect yourself. You're so broken down after years of mind-games, you don't realize you have to be on your toes. When your spouse realizes they can no longer control you, a lightbulb turns on, and they try a wide variety of tactics to threaten or punish you.

Document these things. They will help you later:

- *Threats against you.* "If you divorce, I'll get custody of our daughter." "You'll never get a dime from me." "I'll destroy you in court." "I'll ruin you."
- *Anger about the divorce.* Trying to stop or delay the divorce: Not responding to letters, changing addresses without telling you so they can't be served, calling your friends/family and telling them he wants to save the marriage and asking them to put pressure on you.
- *Vitriol or hate mail.* Calling you names, trying to ruin your reputation, accusing you of sleeping with everyone, accusing you of doing the very things they are doing. Saying, "if you were any kind of parent, you'd do this..." Or "you're an awful parent, your child is better off without you."
- *Stalking behavior.* Driving by your house, standing outside your workplace, calling your boss, trying to get you fired, creating a crisis so you have to leave work early, bothering your coworkers. (Get coworkers' statements in writing right away. Save their emails/texts and print them out. If you let time pass, they may not want to get involved.)
- *Not following court orders about visitation.* Coming too early, coming more than 15 minutes late, not showing up at the scheduled time

and place, picking kids up at school early and demanding the teacher let the kids out.

- *Hacking your phone or computer, which is a crime.* (This is why it may not be best to document everything on your phone.)
- *False allegations with no proof.* (Your attorney will ask them in court if they have proof.)
- *Withholding child support.* This is especially to be noted if your ex is also demanding you pay to get kids into expensive sports/lessons.
- *Financial abuse.* Emptying joint accounts, not revealing assets, refusing to pay support in a timely fashion (yet demanding you pay for the kids' sports or activities by the deadline).
- *Constant litigation.* Note this especially if it is happening over small things, such as not making a phone call at exactly 5:00 pm.
- *Disparaging comments.* These can be about your family, your sex life, accusing you of having sex partners coming in and out of your house (which, incidentally, proves they are stalking you).
- *Lies.* Claiming that something is true when it's not. Denying something that turns out to be true.

From a mother who's been through it:

> *Start documenting now. Don't just delete his hate-filled accusations, the name calling, and the threats. You'll need them as evidence later. It will not get better. It will get worse. You may be hoping it will settle down and they get involved with a new romance, but don't let your guard down. But the Lord is with you. Just keep being the best parent you can be.*

From a father who's been through it:

> *My advice is usually for the women, because they have it so much worse than I did. Think of your kids. Custody is an issue. That's why I stayed. I was afraid that I would lose my kids, and that was her first counter to me filing for divorce. She said, "You know, you're gonna lose all parental rights," and my attorney said, "No way. This guy has been a schoolteacher for 20 years. He's loved. He has a tight relationship with his kids. There's no way in hell that his kids should be totally taken away from him." And she had to bring that up once, and it was never mentioned again. Take care of your kids. Don't fear that a broken home is going to break*

your kids. Because keeping your kids in an abusive relationship will break them more.

It's normal for the divorce process and recovery to take time, and your best bet is keeping the kids out of the gory details, validating their feelings and process, getting your emotional needs met by other adults rather than expecting your kids to do that for you, and calmly and continually modelling and requesting kind, respectful treatment from each member of the family to all the others—including you!

A Final Word of Comfort

Though you may feel you're walking a lonely path, there are others who've been where you are.

Though the waters may be rough at first, there are calmer seas ahead. Get support for yourself, and maintain protective boundaries for your children as best you can; many kids, as they grow up, come to see the truth about how dangerous the marriage was.

Nearly everyone I interviewed for this book wanted readers to know that they are grateful for their divorce and are doing better. Many started this path feeling confused, discouraged, and fearful. They felt they would never survive.

But they did—with God's help.

They talked about the peace they've found and freedom from being trapped in an unworkable situation.

Even those who are in tough court battles are glad they made the decision to leave. They no longer have to live with their ex-spouse 24 hours a day, and it makes a positive difference in their children's lives.

God cares about you, and about your children, as you are going through a life-saving divorce, and you can cling to his promises of love and his presence with you every step of the way.

As a father shows compassion to his children,
so the Lord shows compassion to those who fear him.
—Psalm 103:13 (ESV)

For I know the plans I have for you, declares the Lord, plans for welfare and not for evil, to give you a future and a hope.
—Jeremiah 29:11 (ESV)

SAFE CHURCHES AND FRIENDS

In 1998, I met a woman in a Sunday school class who would change my life.

Brenda was a divorced mom, raising four children under age ten by herself on a low-paying job and almost no child support. Week after week, during prayer time, she would ask the class to pray for something: that her old car would run; that she'd find money to pay the emergency room bill for her son's broken arm; or for groceries so they could have a little birthday party.

I looked at her in awe. It was tough enough for me to raise two children on my own; I couldn't imagine anyone raising four kids alone. Yet she seemed to feel the Lord's presence all the time. I was impressed. I'm an extrovert, and I went over to talk with her. She is an introvert, and she was not quite sure if she wanted to talk much about her life.

One Sunday, our church announced they wanted to form some new small groups. The goal was to study a topic, share, and pray together. The women's director thought a single mothers' group would be great.

That launched Brenda and me into an amazing adventure that has lasted more than two decades. Together, we started a group that changed our own lives in powerful ways.

On Sundays, our little group of women would meet in the basement of the old church building across the street from our new big church. We met during Sunday school time, so we had free childcare and had time to share.

The group was small but fantastic. I've never seen so many strong, courageous women knocking it out of the ballpark every day. None of us was a professional counselor; we were all just survivors offering hope and a listening ear to each other.

Brenda and I would meet every Saturday and take a long walk, pray for each other, for our kids, and for our single mothers' group.

Over the years, all sorts of women attended: teachers, a swim coach, a small business owner, a childcare provider, a paralegal, stay-at-home moms, a caregiver, a homeschool mother, a manicurist, a disabled former airline employee, and others.

We were proud survivors.

We told our stories and shared our favorite Bible promises. We cried together and hugged each other. We were our own fellowship and community of believers. We faced loneliness, fear, exhaustion, and anxiety, but we were not alone.

Many women had trauma and depression that required professional help, and we listened. We supported each other. Every Sunday we each gave an update, discussed a topic, talked about God's provision, and explained how we had dealt with challenges that week. We prayed for each other and for our children. Sometimes we helped each other financially.

Soon we had women from other churches coming to our group. We were a family. We contributed to a fund to help with emergency needs, such as food, clothes, and shelter. Other people at church would donate business attire for job interviews, labor for car repairs, and money for counseling or dental work.

After we had done this almost every week for six years,
I realized this was the best church group I had ever been in.

There was so much closeness and caring. New women would come to our group and cry for the first three meetings, and soon they too would sense God's presence and start to feel hope and faith. They knew Jesus would never leave them nor forsake them.

In talking with hundreds of people of faith going through life-saving divorces, I've found a common thread. They feel alone—walking on a rocky path through a dark valley with fears all around them. It's them and God against the world. And a good, faith-based support group can make all the difference.

This is an example of what can happen. It really doesn't take much: just a small room and free childcare.

End of a Marriage—Loss of Identity

People of faith who divorce feel their lifelong dream of a good marriage has died a painful death. By getting divorced, they lose part of their identity as a wife or husband, and possibly even their social network. A divorce damages their good name and their reputation of being a gold-standard family. They worry about gossip and whether their children will still be invited to friends' homes.

In general, I believe that it takes good, decent people to make a good, decent society. There are many irresponsible, immoral, self-centered, or mean people who will not be made good, loving, and trustworthy by merely getting married. I'm a pro-marriage person. I love being a wife and a mother. I believe that marriages between good-hearted people are worth fighting for. For those people, learning communication skills, setting boundaries, valuing commitment, and patiently hanging in there, would stabilize them and add a great deal to our communities.

But in cases such as those I saw in the women's group, these faithful believers had found themselves in an impossible situation: stuck in a marriage so dangerous that it truly was unsafe to fight to keep it going. This reality was very, very hard for them to accept, often precisely because of their deep faith in God and their high view of marriage. In my divorce recovery group, nearly everyone was a regular churchgoer who cared deeply about God (although we welcomed people of any faith or no faith). Nearly half of us were very involved at church, participating in ministries and volunteering in kids' church.

Most of these women held onto their faith tightly, and many grew closer to God during their divorce, which is very common.[171] They may have switched churches during the divorce, but most continued to serve and donate money to church at the same level—or surprisingly, even more, which is also common.[172]

Getting out of a violent marriage makes people grateful.

---

171 "Marriage Ministry and the Cost of Divorce for Churches," ***LifeWay Research*** (2015), slide 34.

172 Ibid., slide 48. Surprisingly 61% of churchgoers who divorced say they give about the same or more than they gave to the local church in the past.

Studies have found that most churchgoers don't lose their faith during a divorce. They continue to attend religious services regularly.[173] But many feel they have failed God, despite having tried everything to fix their marriage.[174]

We as their church community can help remind them that God gives new meaning and purpose—and new identity.

For Pastors Only

You care about people who are hurting. You know that a few of your best Bible study leaders, missionaries, Sunday school teachers, and deacons and deaconesses got divorced to get out of horrible situations.

They needed a life-saving divorce.

So how can you really help?

One way to help is to stand by them and share the definition of a life-saving divorce:

Not all divorces are for falling out of love! More than 40% of divorces are for very serious reasons, such as infidelity, sexual immorality, physical abuse, chronic emotional abuse, and severe substance abuse. (Chapter 2 has the evidence for this claim.)

Just sharing this definition with other pastors, and perhaps lay leaders at the church, will be a huge help to the people you minister to. You will earn their gratitude and loyalty if you acknowledge that many people need a life-saving divorce.

The Responsibility of Pastors and Leaders

It's important to point out that local pastors and leaders, and the books and websites they promote, can inadvertently foster abuse. And this is a shame, because many abused women go to their pastor first when they feel overwhelmed by marital struggles. They don't feel comfortable going to a secular counselor. They want to keep it all in the family and not let anyone else know they have problems.

When they approach the pastor, they hope for compassion and good advice. They may even view the pastor's words as if they come from God.

173 Ibid., slide 39.
174 Ibid., slide 33.

But in some cases, they get they receive messages that give bad advice (I debunk each of these "messages" in Chapter 3):

- The pastor's wife might tell the women in the church to keep themselves in shape to keep prevent their husbands from straying, implying his cheating is her fault.
- Church groups for women might emphasize pleasing God by having a meek and quiet spirit that never expresses disapproval, suggesting that the quieter she is, the godlier he will automatically become.
- Leaders might condemn divorce as a bigger sin than infidelity.
- Christian authors might prescribe that wives be available for sex on demand, with the promise that if they comply, there will be no cheating or porn or child molesting.
- Pastors may recommend books that praise those who stay and silently suffer abuse, excusing and covering up a husband's harsh and mean outbursts as a "slip ups," and labeling a wife's anger "sinful" or "disrespectful" when she reacts to discovering her husband's betrayals, lies, or selfish behavior (or vice versa).
- Leaders may emphasize reconciliation and smoothing over problems before there is evidence of genuine change.
- Church teaching may isolate a woman by limiting her to friendships to those in the church group and discouraging her from working outside the home or church.
- Pastors may define wifely submission as doing whatever the husband wants without regard to safety or reasonableness.

All of these messages foster abuse, and it is important for us as believers to be on the lookout for these warning signs, so that we can learn to identify safe churches to join and unsafe ones to avoid.

Safe Churches Show Compassion

My husband and I were overseas missionaries. There was a counselor at our church who was a retired missionary, and so I started meeting with him and just sobbing, explaining to him what had happened. He was very compassionate, and I know God put him there at that point.

My pastor told me that one of the biblical grounds for divorce is abandonment,
and he said it included abandonment of marriage vows.
When a husband is abusive, he has abandoned his vows and is acting as an unbeliever.
He said if the unbeliever wants to leave, let him leave.
My pastor was a godsend to me.

Most people were empathetic to me—and angry at him—even his own family.
His infidelity and abandonment were inexcusable.
Those at my church were compassionate and rallied to help me.

I have been blessed by support from church.
They knew my husband was unfaithful and how hard I'd tried to save the marriage.
They respected me, and years later they hired me to be on church staff.

I needed my church family. They were such a support. They were my family.
They bought groceries for me. I moved in with a woman in her back house and rented from her. I lived there two years.
She took me in, mentored me, counseled me, and prayed with me.
People would call and ask me to come hang out with their families.
Even though it hurt me to see them so happy,
it was really good for me and my children to be with them.
They invited us for Thanksgiving and Christmas.

I'll never forget the day I told my women's Bible study at church that I had filed for divorce.
I had always hidden my marriage troubles. But finally, my marriage was over. I was devastated.

I said, "I'm going through a divorce." And I put my head in my hands and cried quietly.

One woman demanded:
"Don't you know the damage you'll do to your children if you divorce?"

Another woman in the group silently stood up and walked around the table and gave me a hug. She put her arms around me as I sobbed.
I didn't have to explain anything or defend myself.
I have never forgotten her kindness.

When I first walked into the church I was afraid I would be rejected because I was divorced.
I came the day that someone shared her divorce testimony from the front of the church.
Suddenly I didn't feel afraid.
The following Sunday I wanted to try out a Sunday school class...
I was a bit scared.
But a nice man approached me and said hello. Suddenly I didn't feel so stressed out.
I felt like running away, but I didn't.
The feeling of acceptance was overwhelming in this class, so I stayed.

In a compassionate church, devastated spouses find people who wrap them in the warmth of empathy and kindness. Caring friends and leaders bring courage, faith, and hope in God. They spend time, maybe having a cup of coffee with the divorced person and getting updates on their life.

A loving church is a gift from God to people in crisis.

Traits of Safe Churches

So what are the traits of safe churches and pastors?

One woman explained it this way—

I've worked with people in treacherous marriages who are considering divorce. They aren't jumping for joy doing this. Imagine an animal out in the forest with its foot caught in a trap. Normally an animal would never gnaw their foot off, but they are terrified, they are desperate, and they do it. These people are being cheated on, emotionally abused, physically battered, and treated with contempt. They love the Lord and honor marriage, but don't tell them to go back and put their foot back into the trap.

A safe church doesn't do that. Instead:

1. A safe church teaches that *although* marriage is meant to be lifelong, faithful, and loving, divorce is God's protection for people who are being destroyed in a marriage that is not faithful or safe or loving.
2. A safe church listens to your story without interrupting and without accusations. They pray with you. They show empathy and care. They may wish they knew more, but they don't ask unless you give them permission to do so. They feel honored that you trusted them enough to hear your divorce story, rather than trying to tear it apart and figure out where you dropped the ball.
3. A safe church knows that marriage problems aren't just spiritual; they may also be medical and psychological. So they not only give spiritual care, but they also have professional counseling referrals to specialists available—not simply "pastoral," "Christian," or "biblical" counseling, for which very little licensing, training, and professional oversight, if any, is required. A person who earned a theology degree at seminary is not equipped to provide psychological and mental health care, and churches whose pastors offer counseling in areas in which they have no training can do much more harm than good. A safe church, by contrast, can recommend professionally trained MFT or PhD licensed therapists and psychiatrists, or other mental health professionals, who are trained in the protocols to deal with abuse, sexual addictions, and trauma.

   One ex-wife of a disgraced Southern Baptist pastor and missionary pointed out the dangers of seeing someone who is not a specialist:

   My ex-husband is a classic sociopath. Very charming. All the ministers we went to for counseling over the years thought this was a conflict resolution issue. The first real psychologist he saw suspected he had a personality disorder. She saw him three or four times, not enough to diagnose him directly, but she could tell he was mentally not stable. Since he abandoned us, he has gotten a teenager pregnant and had been arrested by law enforcement multiple times.

4. A safe church cares about your children. They don't allow others to shun your kids or stop inviting them to birthday parties or treat them as "broken."
5. A safe church keeps clergy-penitent confidentiality. It doesn't share your private marriage issues with others.
6. A safe church may choose to help financially. One divorce attorney said he's seen churches pay legal fees for abuse victims.
7. A safe church considers the person who breaks the vows responsible for the failure of the marriage, not the person who files the legal paperwork.

   As the saying goes: "Divorce decrees do not cause divorce any more than death certificates cause death." A *judgement of divorce* merely reflects the truth: that the marriage is already over. The vows to love, nurture, cherish, and be faithful have been broken. And divorce puts legal and financial safeties in place for vulnerable spouses and children.

   Ironically, those pastors who focus on divorce as the problem, rather than on the sin that led to it (the infidelity, neglect, cruelty, or abandonment), show *they* don't take marriage vows seriously.

"Filing for divorce just updates the public record of the actual state of the marriage."[175]

---

175 Natalie Hoffman, "Message to a Baptist Church: You Preached Death to the Hearts of One Hundred Women Today," ***Flying Free Now.com*** (5/1/18), accessed 12/16/19, **https://flyingfreenow.com/message-baptist-church-preached-death-women/**. A good quote: "Besides, if they were to get out of their abusive relationship, they would have to initiate the end of a marriage. They would be labeled a 'covenant breaker.' A 'marriage-destroyer.' They don't realize yet that it is their abuser who has broken covenant with them. That their abuser has destroyed the marriage, but more importantly to Jesus, he has destroyed the human lives within the marriage, including his own." See also: Natalie Hoffman, "Who Burned the House Down?" ***Flying Free Now.com*** (1/21/17), accessed 12/16/19, https://flyingfreenow.com/who-burned-the-house-down/.

8. A safe church admits that God does not heal all marriages any more than God heals all cancer, all birth defects, or all car accident injuries. Having a difficult marriage does not mean you aren't a godly person.

9. A safe church describes abusive behaviors in sermons and teachings, and it gives examples (such as disdain, cruelty, put-downs, beatings, financial coercion, lying, cheating, and threats). Listing these examples gives the abused spouse support, and it puts the abuser on notice.

> "Most clergy have never preached a message
> that explicitly condemns
> wife abuse, child abuse or violence in the home."
> —Nancy Nason-Clark, author of
> *The Battered Wife: How Christians Confront Family Violence*

One grateful woman reports that her pastor gives this instruction: "If someone is pressuring you to make a decision that you are not comfortable with, always say *no*."

10. A safe church knows that abuse victims often cannot identify that they are being abused. For them, to be controlled, beaten, humiliated, or lied to is normal. They don't call it abuse. They might call it a "difficult marriage." Or they might admit their spouse has emotional outbursts. You as a church leader may recognize the signs of abuse before they do.

Especially if you are a church leader, but even if you are just a friend or family member of someone you think may be experiencing abuse, it can make all the difference in the world for you to "do your homework" first. Read up on what *actually* helps abuse victims get free, not what you assume will help. (Books like Susan Brewster's *Helping Her Get Free: A Guide for Families and Friends of Abused Women* are powerful guides here.) As one of my friends said, "Every intuition you have of ways you can help will probably in fact push her back to her abusive husband [or boyfriend], and put distance between you and her. If you want to help it takes patience and a willingness to not step in and take over. She needs you to empower her so she can trust her own voice and feelings."

Sometimes it helps if you ask if they are being "controlled" rather than abused. Or ask whether they feel as though they walk on eggshells to keep from setting their spouse off. Pastors and lay leaders may not want to become counselors themselves, but they can be trained to work with abuse victims by using the Duluth Wheel. There's training available from the Domestic Abuse Intervention Project. Their program, "Creating a Process of Change for Men Who Batter: Comprehensive Training," focuses on male abusers, but once you take the class, you start seeing the dynamics of power and control and how the training about power and control aligns with Scripture.[176]

11. A safe church views both physical and chronic emotional abuse as acceptable reasons for divorce—in addition to infidelity and abandonment. When a situation comes to their attention, they may ask the abusive spouse to go to a faith-based or secular multi-session intervention program. They don't demand the victim sacrifice more time or energy if the abuser refuses to work on the relationship.

They tell the emotional abuse victim that words matter to God—

- Cruel words are like stabbing someone with sword thrusts – Proverbs 12:18
- A lie is like a war club, sword, or arrow – Proverbs 25:18
- Life and death are in the power of the tongue – Proverbs 18:21
- Words defile a person more than physical things, such as food – Matthew 15:10-11

My husband was abusive. Despite counseling, he would not stop. I knew my church would not approve of divorce for anything but infidelity, so I had to switch churches before I filed for divorce.

12. A safe church has an emergency plan to get an abused spouse and children out of a dangerous situation immediately. Good leaders do not tell them to go back to a home where they may be abused

176 I have no connection with this organization, nor have I taken it, but I've heard multiple recommendations for it. It is a multi-day training offered in several cities during the year. https://www.theduluthmodel.org/product-category/training/

again. Wise leaders know that an abuser who feels threatened with exposure or legal papers may snap and become violent, even if they never were before. A safe church keeps the phone number for the National Domestic Violence Hotline and lets the abused spouse call from church phones to avoid detection: 1 (800) 799-7233, TTY 1 (800) 787-3224, or www.thehotline.org.

Abuse escalates over time. If you file for divorce or if he has just moved out of the house and can no longer watch and control you, he may become violent. You cannot assume—or depend on the past—to know what he will and will not do. Perhaps he has never hit you or the kids before, but this is new territory.

[My husband snapped; I sensed him seething.] I called the pastors in the morning. "I think my husband is going to kill me when he comes home. Can you come over and get his guns?" I wouldn't have expected them to come and confiscate his weapons. I was just frantic. But they didn't have the perspective to even know how to direct me how to get the proper help or even to tell me to leave the house. It was my brother who said, "Don't go back. Don't go back."

13. If a crime has been committed (assault, vandalism, theft, incest, sexual harassment or abuse, physical abuse, threats, child porn, child molesting, etc.), a safe church leader allows you to call law enforcement from their office and stays with you while you make the phone call to give you emotional support (if you want it). They encourage you to protect yourself. It is a major red flag if church leadership refuses to enlist the help and protection of law enforcement and civil authorities and instead insists on handling issues entirely in-house. This is a sign of a church that cares more about maintaining public image, avoiding scandal, and upholding the status quo than they do about stopping abuse, seeking justice, protecting and defending victims, and preventing further abuse.

I talked to our church elders and the women's pastor and our former pastor, who is somebody that's really knowledgeable about things like addiction and abuse issues. And they really actively encouraged me to get a restraining order and file for legal separation. And they told me that they would support me and come alongside my husband and hold him accountable and try to get him into treatment.

14. A safe church offers wise advice but assures you the final decision to divorce is *up to you*. They realize only you and God know exactly what is happening behind closed doors and how much you can take. Only you know whether you can ever trust your spouse in the future.

15. A safe church reaches out and offers comfort to the victim and kids first.

My husband was a high-ranking Christian professor who was caught in a child-porn sting with seven hard drives full of images. When he was convicted and went to prison, the pastor reached out to him but never reached out to me. I was treated like it was my fault.

While it's good to visit and offer support to someone incarcerated, it's best to reach out to the victims, spend time hearing their story, and ask if they need help. Not doing so makes it appear that the pastor is visiting the dangerous person because it makes for a more dramatic testimony.

Even with good intentions, churches or pastors who do this—and neglect the ordinary, non-ostentatious offering of care and support to the victim and the family—are not safe for victims. Jesus' warning about the Pharisee who prays loudly on the street corner to have their righteousness seen by men is important to remember, here (Matthew 6).

Look for churches and pastors who are quietly doing the right thing behind the scenes, not advertising their amazing efforts among the worst offenders.

16. A safe church is honest about the risks associated with marriage. They know that even if you've done everything right, you might end up in a highly destructive marriage. Simple answers don't cut it. There is no way to guarantee you'll have a good marriage. There is no way to affair-proof your marriage. There is no biblically acceptable *reason* for cheating, only *excuses*.

17. A safe church does not hold the "permanence view" or "unconditional marriage view," meaning they believe the marriage bond may not be broken or annulled for any reason. Pastors who do hold these views choose to ignore or set aside Jesus and Paul's words about acceptable reasons for divorce. One victim of serial infidelity said she listened to a pastor she greatly respected as he claimed chronic abuse and cheating were not grounds for divorce. She left the church as a result.

Only about 1 in 5 Protestant pastors hold the permanence view. But according to one LifeWay survey (a Southern Baptist-affiliated research organization) of Protestant pastors,

- About 2 in 3 pastors condone divorce for **adultery**
- About 2 in 3 pastors condone divorce for **abuse**.
- About 3 in 4 pastors condone divorce for **abandonment**.[177]

Instead of care and kindness, a few pastors may give an innocent spouse the message that divorce is the unpardonable sin, that they are going to hell for divorcing, and that it taints the image of Christ and his Church. But the Bible gives permission for people to leave treacherous marriages.

One woman visited a church and heard the pastor say, "I want to apologize to all the women that we have encouraged to stay in marriages they should have never stayed in. I want to talk to you about abuse. I want to apologize that we have made divorce seem like the unpardonable sin."

A safe church does not imply that divorce will cause you to lose your salvation.

177 Aaron Earls, "Views on Divorce Studied," ***Baptist Press*** (8/12/15), accessed 11/27/18, http://www.bpnews.net/45291/views-on-divorce-studied. About 1 in 3 (32%) said it is a sin to divorce for **adultery**. About 1 in 3 (28%) said it is a sin to divorce for **abuse**. About 1 in 4 (27%) said it is a sin to divorce for **abandonment**.

I knew I needed to find a new church when
my pastor said five times in one sermon,
"If you walk away from your marriage, you're walking away from Jesus."

In "permanence view" churches, many husbands and wives who call for justice are side-lined. Some "permanence view" churches will even excommunicate those who take legal steps to end their marriage.[178]

It is no surprise people walk away from these churches when their marriages fail. They want a loving, reasonable church with the compassion of Jesus, who healed on the Sabbath, not a legalistic, authoritarian church that locks people in misery.

18. A safe church doesn't silence victims. If your spouse is abusing you and doesn't accept your boundaries, and your church isn't listening, it's time to consider switching churches. Churches that use the "no gossip" or "no slander" or the "two-witnesses" rule to silence you are not safe churches. Safe churches don't dismiss serious concerns by casting the blame on you, calling you a "nag," "bitter," or "judgmental."

19. A safe church is open to faith-based divorce recovery groups.

Safe churches know that by ministering to divorcees and their children within the caring environment of the church, the church gains an opportunity to draw hurting people closer to God and keep children connected to church.

In 2015, fewer than 1% of divorced Christian churchgoers surveyed said their church had ministries "aimed at supporting divorced individuals." Yet 40% percent of pastors surveyed said at least one couple in their church separated or divorced in the past year.[179]

---

178 Barbara Roberts, "The PCAs Position Paper on Divorce Is Dangerous for Abuse Victims," ***A Cry for Justice*** (6/19/17), accessed 4/16/18, https://cryingoutforjustice.com/2017/06/19/the-pcas-position-paper-on-divorce-is-dangerous-for-abuse-victims/.
179 Lisa Canon Green, "Threat of Divorce Hard to Spot Among Churchgoing Couples," ***LifeWay Research*** (3/31/18), accessed 12/16/19, https://lifewayresearch.com/2015/10/29/threat-of-divorce-hard-to-spot-among-churchgoing-couples/.

20. Safe pastors communicate clearly on the topic of divorce. Look for pastors willing to admit their position directly, to save yourself a lot of time, effort, and potential harm.

A pastor in one of the largest churches in Europe is shown on video forcefully declaring: "Divorce is an abomination." Thirty seconds later, on the same video, he says divorce is okay in some situations.[180] People in marital crisis have no idea what their pastor is saying when he utters such contradictory statements. Double-speak and a lack of clarity, such as in the case of this pastor, are warning signs of an unsafe church.

One terrified missionary wife who was being abused described her pastoral counselors, who danced around the subject—

Neither of my Christian counselors wanted to say,
"You should get a divorce."
They would say, "I don't want to ever say you should have one,"
yet at the same they're telling me, "You've done everything you can,"
or "I don't see any growth here," or "You'll just kinda know."

Tips to pastors: You don't have to *command* someone to go, but you can say something like, "If my daughter or sister were in this circumstance, I would have no trouble supporting their decision to go." You can tell them you support them, and you trust their judgment. You can assure them they will not be ostracized, and you can point them to biblical reasons for divorce in Chapter 6. You can supply them with referrals for support groups inside the church or elsewhere, and assure them that whatever they decide, they will not have to go through it alone.

21. Safe pastors show humility and admit it when they got it wrong.

Ten years after my divorce, a man came to me and apologized,

---

180 Sunday Adelaja, "Is It a Sin to Divorce Your Spouse?" ***www.FaceBook.com***, accessed 12/16/19, https://www.facebook.com/Drsundayadelaja/videos/2046546089001044/. In a 2-minute interview, the pastor forcefully says, "[Divorce] is an abomination," then approves of some divorce.

saying, "I'm sorry I sided with your husband. Now I realize the truth." An apology ten years later is still appreciated.

As a person in ministry, I know it's hard to know the truth. Most pastors and lay leaders have been deceived at some point in their lives. They've discovered that a person they trusted for years turned out to be a con artist. Humble pastors know they can be wrong and can be deceived by a charming person or a friendly, generous donor. They also know the innocent spouse might not be raising the alarm because they have good reason to conceal the perpetrator's actions, especially if they are financially or physically dependent on them.

Victims don't often tell the full story. As a 20-year veteran divorce recovery group leader, I've noticed most people will not reveal the whole truth, especially if it involves felonies (for example, physical violence, theft, embezzlement, illegal drugs, DUIs, child molesting, murder, child porn, sex offending, etc.).

Abusers do damage control. When they realize their actions are likely to be exposed, they will turn their efforts to discrediting their spouse. They may tarnish their reputation, plant doubts about their motives, suggest they are mentally incapable or emotionally unbalanced, or claim that no one is on their side. The abuser will blithely claim everyone agrees with them.

My ex-husband confidently claimed everyone agreed with him that my filing for divorce was unreasonable, and I always said, "Name one." He never could. But it didn't stop him from claiming it—over and over.

Understandably, this is a difficult situation for the pastor, but after getting a lot of information, the pastor should act. I've called law enforcement when a child was involved and never regretted it. Life-saving decisions must be made, and delay in certain situations can be fatal, as high murder rates show.[181] Nearly half of women who

181 Olga Khazan, "Nearly Half of All Murdered Women Are Killed by Romantic Partners," *The Atlantic* (7/20/17), accessed 12/16/19, **https://www.theatlantic.com/health/archive/2017/07/homicides-women/534306/**.

are killed die at the hands of a current or former romantic partner.

22. Safe pastors don't tell other people details about a couple's divorce. However, if there is some legitimate reason to do so, they make an attempt to hear both sides beforehand, realizing (and admitting to others) they may never know the whole truth. They need to stay curious enough to look at evidence provided by spouses later if the spouses give it to them. Even if they still aren't sure they know the truth, at least they've heard both sides. Anyone who's been in ministry for decades knows it is easy to be fooled by people who present themselves as good and free from problems.

My pastor believed my narcissistic husband, not me, even though I offered proof.
I was shunned by the church.
It was horrible,
but we don't know if our faith is genuine until the wheels
come off in some way.

I will not forget trying to get another pastor to confront
my (now) ex-wife about her affair.
As part of my evidence, I had records of literally hundreds of messages
plus hundreds of minutes spent in conversations
between this strange man and my (then) wife.
This wasn't enough for him.[182]

23. Safe pastors encourage cooperative parenting and the fulfilling of legal, financial, and custody obligations.

[After we divorced,] my ex-husband bashed me left and right, and my son was disrespectful toward me as a result. Once my husband started going to a pastor at church, the pastor confronted him and said, "Listen, you are doing major damage here. You need to stop."
He did.

182 David Derksen, "On Hundreds of Messages Exchanged," ***Divorce Minister*** (4/14/18), accessed 8/20/19, http://www.divorceminister.com/on-hundreds-of-messages-exchanged/. His book ***Cheated On*** is valuable for those who've had an unfaithful spouse. In addition, as a licensed minister with an MDiv, he had to defend his ministerial credentials following the divorce and was successful.

Pastors can be very influential, especially in encouraging parents to avoid fighting in front of their kids, and to abide by the final custody and support agreements.

And pastors in many states are mandated reporters and who are required to contact law enforcement if a person is a danger to themselves or others, especially to children.

24. Safe pastors do not repeat and promote the myths mentioned in Chapter 3. They discourage Christian marriage books that promote these myths from being used in small groups, and church-backed marriage retreats. (See recommendations, p. 412.)

Instead, safe pastors and churches make better choices, recommending books on marriage that focus on:

- putting God first (rather than your spouse first)
- having good character, as evidenced by caring about the wellbeing of both spouses
- mutual problem-solving for meeting the needs of each spouse when they conflict
- setting boundaries when either spouse exhibits selfish or dangerous behavior
- using conflict resolution techniques and setting boundaries when a spouse is facing a marriage-endangering sin (adultery, violence, addictions, etc.)

Books and websites that tell wives they cannot disagree with their husband and frame disagreement as "disrespect" can lead to abusive relationships. A book that gives an example where a wife agreed to sex even though she had good reason to say no (illness, injury, pregnancy, exhaustion, etc.), and this resulted in a better marriage, simply encourages selfishness in husbands.

It just isn't safe to give one sinful human being complete power over another. Books and teachings that give examples that justify and excuse abuse ("you made him angry") or infidelity ("you said no to sex" or "you gained weight") set up a destructive dynamic, allowing one spouse to blame the other for their own misdeeds. Books and websites that claim "God will heal any marriage if you just pray hard enough" do a lot of damage.

As a divorce recovery lay leader, I meet a lot of women who walk into my groups defeated, due to the teachings of certain authors.

This is such a problem that Canadian marriage blogger and author Sheila Gregoire has done a research study of top Christian marriage books to determine which ones are safe for abuse victims. You can visit her website to view her ratings and detailed comments at https://tolovehonorandvacuum.com/.

How to Evaluate a Christian Marriage Book for Unsafe Messages

Does the book give anecdotes where the woman praying more or submitting more resulted in the husband changing destructive patterns, giving the impression that this is what she should do and is her only option?

Does the book state (or include an anecdote) that if a wife has more sex with her husband, he will not cheat, watch porn, be attracted to others, or display extra-marital sexual behavior?

Does the book place the burden on one spouse (usually the wife) more than the other to pray, persevere, or try harder in order for God to fix their marriage?

Does the book distinguish between normal marriage and communication problems, and problems caused by abuse?

Does the book put responsibility on one spouse to fix the other spouse's mood, actions, attitudes, or behavior?

Does the book state or imply through stories or anecdotes that wifely *submission* is the same as *obedience?*

Does it state or give anecdotes in which a wife submitting to her husband—in a situation where any reasonable person would have concerns—results in a better marriage, and gives the impression that she should do it?

Does the book imply that suffering in a difficult or abusive marriage is the same as suffering persecution for being a Christian, which glorifies Christ, and gives the impression that the suffering spouse should continue doing this?

Does the book counsel the wife to never, rarely, or cautiously show disapproval of her spouse's sinful behavior?

Does the book counsel wives to remain silent when faced with their husband's marriage-endangering sin, such as addictions, adultery, porn addiction, violence, refusal to work or support the family, chronic debt, or abuse?`

Does the book imply that if a wife is quiet and submissive enough, her spouse will naturally feel more loving toward her, giving the impression that this will automatically reduce or eliminate his destructive behavior toward her in the future?

There are two good Christian resources I recommend: The book *Boundaries in Marriage,* by Henry Cloud and John Townsend, on how learning problem-solving skills and setting boundaries in marriage; and the Christian marriage enrichment video series called, "A Lasting Promise." It is the Christian version of PREP, a marriage curriculum that has been around for thirty years. There's a book and leader guide and a fifteen-video series for small groups. It teaches oneness, forgiveness, and commitment in marriage, without adding destructive messages.[183]

Researchers of religious marriages and families observe that our own pastors, church members, and Christian marriage books sometimes send messages that the "sanctity of marriage" is so important that abused spouses believe they have no option but to stay.

A marriage book that does not discuss or identify abuse; does not admit that it happens, even in Christian homes; and does not help spouses address it effectively, gives a false message. Books that don't draw a line between normal marriage conflict and serious, marriage-endangering problems are not helpful for a person trying to figure out if their marriage is normal and then consider the options.

The result of this dangerous messaging is Christians who don't understand they are being abused or betrayed and don't have methods to address it. If they are taught that reporting abuse, expressing disagreement about a spouse's decision, and showing anger about sin is "not submissive," it creates a double bind:

> "It creates a double bind for women in Christian tradition, implying that when they are abused they have 'asked for it' and therefore do not deserve the mercy, understanding, or protection of the church, and that the church will not restrain or rebuke their abuser."[184]
>
> —Michal Gilad

---

183 The curriculum can be found here: https://www.prepinc.com/shopping/ProductList.aspx?ID=80. I have no connection with PREP.

184 Gilad, "In God's Shadow," 478.

When submission is interpreted as obedience, with the wife resigning herself to the husband's wishes, it creates a setup for abuse. The emphasis on looking to a husband to make all decisions has taught wives there is no point in trying to think through problems, consider alternatives, and evaluate them. And those who see that their husband is going the wrong way are silenced.

These messages hurt men, too. Instead of becoming a mature person and listening to his wife's viewpoint, discussing all alternatives without fighting, and trying to find a mutual solution, the husband is told that a godly man should be able to make the key decisions himself. And sometimes the wife even encourages this due to the books she has read, as this woman explains—

I was influenced by Debi Pearl… I believed so much in submission, I created a monster. I do take responsibility for doing that. I didn't express my opinion because I didn't feel I had the right to.

These teachings can hamper a husband's problem-solving ability, leaving him ill-equipped to negotiate and solve relationship difficulties with bosses, neighbors, coworkers, and family.

And it creates a wife who thinks it is wrong to do any number of basic, godly, healthy things, such as:

- standing up for herself
- putting God first
- doing what's best for the family and for her own safety
- expressing her desires
- taking initiative
- setting boundaries
- calling out bad conduct
- giving advice in areas of her expertise/responsibility
- asking straightforwardly for what she wants

In one of the most heartbreaking interviews for this book, I listened as one woman described the effect of a particular Christian marriage book, which I do not recommend, on her relationship with her husband.

We got involved in a small group that was going through the Love and Respect book [by Emerson Eggerichs]. The material in that book not only was held over my head by [my husband] but over my head by our pastor, too: "No matter what, you have to submit to him. You have to make sure your children and you give him respect." The extremeness of that looked like: A fly once landed on his food during dinner. He threw the plate of food at me, saying, "How dare you disrespect me like this in front of the kids!" He would hit me over the head with that book, and he raped me as that book sat on my nightstand.

25. Safe pastors verbally condone life-saving divorces.

Many people in life-destroying marriages crave the approval of their pastor to separate and divorce. They not only want the pastor's emotional support and empathy; they also want permission. They want to feel they are right with God, and they feel the pastor speaks for God and can give God's stamp of approval. (This is not true, as pastors are human just like the rest of us, but pastors who explicitly condone life-saving divorces can help people who believe this way get out of danger and into safety much faster than if they withhold this approval.)

Neil Schori, the pastor who testified against Drew Peterson in his murder trial, told me about his church's approach to domestic violence and divorce since the murder of one of his church members, Stacy Peterson.

"So few pastors acknowledge domestic violence happening at their church. If it is, they don't see divorce as a viable option. So they choose not to see it. But at our church, we teach the Bible verses on emotional and physical abuse. I appeal to the heart of Jesus, who sought to protect and elevate women, as well as God's heart for people. He meant us to have loving relationships. We are a church that supports divorce for these issues. People are sinful and they make bad choices, and we will never shame a victim for walking away from the behavior."[185]

185 Personal interview.

26. Safe pastors use October Domestic Violence Awareness Month to open a discussion about abuse. Some use a video of an abuse survivor telling their testimony of God's care and provision. Some pastors want divorcees to say divorce is horrible, and you should never do it because you'll be poor, struggling, and never happy again. But in reality, not all divorce is tragic. Sometimes it's life-saving, especially in the case of abuse. It is God's gracious provision to protect innocent spouses and children.

One woman told this story:

My pastor asked me to share my story in church.
I wanted people to know how God had taken us from poverty to stability and from humiliation to honor.
My life turned out fine. My kids turned out fine. I wanted to praise God's faithfulness and provision for our needs.

The woman wanted to give God credit for miraculously providing for her family. It's natural for people to want to praise God! Safe pastors are happy about God's gracious care.

27. Safe pastors don't worry that a divorce will hurt the reputation of the church.[186]

All those who minister in church want to look good to our fellow church leaders. When a high-profile divorce unexpectedly occurs in the church—especially when it's a beloved pastor, youth pastor, volunteer, trusted Bible study leader, or worship team member who steps down—it can be embarrassing to pastors who pride themselves on knowing their flock. Why couldn't this have been prevented?

Although I empathize with those 11% of pastors who worry about this, they cannot blame a couple for ruining the church's reputation.

---

186 "Marriage Ministry and the Cost of Divorce for Churches: Survey of 1,000 Churchgoers who Divorced," ***Lifeway Research*** (10/15), accessed 12/16/19, http://lifewayresearch.com/wp-content/uploads/2015/10/Churchgoers-Who-Divorced-Report.pdf. See also: "Divorce and the Church: What You Need to Know, What You Can Do," ***Focus on the Family*** (2016): 4, accessed 12/16/19, http://media.focusonthefamily.com/fotf/pdf/channels/marriage/divorce-and-the-church.pdf.

Pointedly blaming a divorcing couple for damaging the church is self-pitying. No abused spouse should say, "I am staying in this violent marriage to protect my church's reputation."

Jesus did not die for church organizations or denominations any more than he died for the institution of marriage. Jesus died for individuals. A church that cares more about its image than the wellbeing of its members is not safe. As one pastor on Twitter put it:

> *"As a young pastor I didn't realize I was trying to keep Christian couples together to protect my own narrative that we Christians (and 'good' pastors)*
> *'could forgive/redeem/reconcile' anything—even this.*
> *Or shorter: I was serving an ideology at the expense of actual women's safety."*

28. Safe churches don't force you to give up your legal rights. Some churches encourage congregants to sign a membership agreement that allows the church leaders/elders to discipline, excommunicate, and breach clergy-penitent confidentiality and share negative information about you to others, including to everyone in your all-church meetings. Some churches demand you go to them first rather than law enforcement.

If you no longer want to subject yourself to church discipline, you can resign from church membership in writing, regardless of your church's rules. (You can find an example of a resignation letter online.)[187] A church membership agreement is a legal document that can be cancelled at any time. A person can resign from membership by writing a resignation letter, dating it, and mailing it the same day via "certified, return receipt."

If the church tries to contact the former members, speak badly of them, or encourage current members to shun them, the church and the individual pastors and elders may be guilty of harassment in a court of law.

---

187 "How to Resign From a Church Whether or Not You Are Under Church Discipline," ***The Wartburg Watch,*** accessed 12/16/19, http://thewartburgwatch.com/permpage-how-to-resign-from-a-church-whether-or-not-you-are-under-church-discipline/. See also http://www.lifesavingdivorce.com/excommunication

We helped our daughter escape a marriage that was destroying her. Pastors demanded we send her back to work on her marriage. Maybe they should've spoken up with their concerns before the marriage, not afterward.

My parents had the same experience and helped me get out of my abusive marriage. Otherwise I don't know what I would have done. Afterwards the church wrote them off completely, pretending like all of their years of faithful service and their membership meant nothing.

God's word is very clear that we are to stand with the oppressed. We lost our church and so-called friends, but we have the joy of watching God's healing restoration in our girl's life. Many walk away from the church with what we went through, but our daughter's faith is strong and steady!

29. A safe pastor helps abuse victims get to safety. In my interviews and discussions with abuse victims, I have learned that some churches required abused wives to attend couples counseling for months or years, starting with lay pastoral counselors, and moving up to professional counselors—all hand-selected by the church.

After doing everything the church required, one woman said the abuse continued (and, in fact, increased). The church did not hold her husband responsible and never approved of a divorce, despite beating, bruises, and arrests by law enforcement. The woman's daughter begged her to get out so she wouldn't be killed. The woman took matters into her own hands. She divorced her husband—and divorced her toxic church.

How many Christian women and men already know their spouse has a pattern of abuse or betrayal? Yet they get messages from Christian leaders and books implying that all marriages can be fixed by the faith of just one spouse. The fact that some cheaters and abusers change should be viewed as the exception, not the rule.

The Bible already tells us how to deal with abusive people in our churches:

But now I am writing to you that you must not associate with anyone who claims to be a brother or sister but is sexually immoral or greedy, an idolater or slanderer, a drunkard or swindler. Do not even eat with such people. What business is it of mine to judge those outside the church? Are you not to judge those inside? God will judge those outside. "Expel the wicked person from among you."
—1 Corinthians 5:11-13 (NIV)

30. A safe pastor never tells an abused spouse that their suffering brings glory to Christ. They don't use Bible verses about persecution and suffering for being a Christian and make them fit your situation. Safe pastors give you verses about evil and what the Bible says we are to do in the face of it—Run and get away!

Jesus doesn't want you to be beaten for his glory.

31. A safe pastor knows that about half of divorces are for very serious reasons. So in sermons, divorcees as a group are never shamed as quitters who really didn't care about the sanctity of marriage.

A safe pastor listens for clues: Is this an unfulfilling, disappointing marriage (low-distress), or is it—behind the scenes where the pastor cannot see—controlling, hostile, or demeaning, filled with lies, double-speak, and betrayal (high-distress)?

If a pastor were to put down groups of people based on race, saying they are all lazy and stupid, we would object. But week after week, pastors put down all divorcees, making sweeping judgments like, "They were looking for an easy way out; they were immature; they were lacking in love for God."

These pastors are not paying attention. They are not listening to our stories. Pastors who pass this kind of judgment are not safe for people in dangerous marriages.

32. A safe pastor is aware that optimism makes them more liable to believe an abuser's emotional spectacle of confession and repentance, or their promise of good behavior, *without evidence of change.*

Safe pastors wisely allow some time for the victim to get to safety and separate from the abusive spouse, and they watch for consistent fruit of repentance over time. Safe pastors do *not* encourage the victim to go back to the abuser right away after tearful repentance, unless they see long-term tangible change in behavior.

The same is true of faith-based counselors. I have heard story after story of faith-based counselors sending abused spouses back to their abusers as part of "marriage intensives," because the abuser put on a convincing emotional performance. The abuse continues—even escalates. Counselors and pastors, even well-meaning ones, can jeopardize people's lives, if they are poorly trained in recognizing and dealing with abuse.

A battered wife saw an article from Focus on the Family that warned her about the horrible things that would happen to her children if she divorced. She tucked it in her Bible and read it multiple times a day, believing that she just needed to be a better wife, and praying that God would help her:

[My husband came home one day and] literally beat me and strangled me. He repeatedly banged my head against the doorframe. He stomped on my feet with his boots and broke every bone in my feet. He dragged me across the kitchen, leaving blood everywhere. He dragged me by my hair outside and kicked me. And he dragged me to the backyard, to a wooded gully, and left me for dead.

She survived and was taken to the hospital. She got a restraining order. *(Note: I requested and received documentation for these claims.)*

Her church was against divorce and told her to pray. She wondered if a marriage intensive would fix their relationship. She found a well-known $5,000 Christian marriage intensive that made a lot of claims of success for people with hopeless marriages. Perhaps these Christian therapists could make headway, where others had not. Her husband was willing to go.

Looking back now, she felt he had a strategy: the restraining order would expire by the time of the retreat, and her optimism about the retreat would keep her from seeking a new one. Plus, he was sure that the therapists' message would be "marriage is for life; you cannot divorce; and the burden is always on the wife to make things better." It was all for show.

Sure enough, at that Christian marriage intensive retreat, her husband suddenly repented. The staff considered it a "Moses Moment," a miraculous change.

But she wasn't sure. She had sent them the police report, the medical information, and the photos in advance, at their request. She asked:

"Is it safe to get back together with him?"
[The counselors] felt sure that God would protect me.
We got back together.
About a year later, he nearly beat our son to death.
I wish now I had walked out the door at that point. Getting back together with him affected my kids. He beat our son repeatedly and molested our daughter. He destroyed their lives.
I finally divorced. The process was difficult, but we have peace and safety.

A licensed Christian counselor sent me this direct message privately on Twitter and gave me permission to share it, as long as I removed name and location. (The Duluth Model mentioned is a free tool that helps abused spouses recognize abuse by giving specific examples. It can be found in Chapter 4 of this book.)

"I'm at a faith-based counseling center where marriage intensives are offered. Sometimes I think I'm the only therapist who understands DV [domestic violence] or values safety. Everyone else prioritizes 'sanctity of marriage' and works to keep the marriage together above all else. I know I'm the only one there using the Duluth Model[188] and helping these wives. Thank you for writing about this and bringing awareness to it—because I see it regularly at work."

188 See Chapter 4 for more on the Duluth Model.

33. A safe pastor doesn't encourage a wife (or husband) to have sex-on-demand for their spouse. Being married does not mean 24/7 access (when she's sleeping, when she says she doesn't feel like it, when she says it hurts; or when a husband says he's too exhausted or doesn't feel well, etc.). Each spouse's needs, limitations, and feelings are important, and sex must never be coercive.

Though men do sometimes get pressured into sex, it is far more common for women's needs and desires to be judged as less important than their husband's desire for sex at any given time. This is yet another example of times when faith-based counselors and the Christian community may ignore abuse and silence the woman (or, more rarely, the man).

> *My husband had many affairs over the 30 years we were married. My pastor and his wife wanted to see if I was "doing my part." [At the same time,] I was seeing my therapist, and she explained to me that the protocol for sex addicts is they develop a disclosure statement with their own therapist. And that disclosure statement is sent through a polygraph test, because like drug addicts need drug tests, sex addicts need polygraphs, because everything they speak is a lie. It's standard of care.*
>
> *People who are married to sex addicts need to be careful. They need to go with the currently trained professionals who recognize the partner as having trauma [from living with this so many years]. There is so much deception and gaslighting going on that licensed CSAT [certified sex addiction therapist] counselors don't put that "co-addict" or "co-dependent" label on partners anymore.*
>
> *But our pastor and his wife wanted to meet with us. The pastor told me and my husband, "That counseling is all mumbo-jumbo. The Lord can fix this. This is a spiritual battle. It has nothing to do with your brain, and there is no need for polygraph tests." My husband dropped out of seeing the CSAT counselor.*
>
> *I just felt like I was going to get put under church discipline for not obeying the pastor or continuing with our meetings, so I ended up leaving my church.*

34. A safe pastor follows their basic, God-given instinct to protect the sheep from danger. Siding with the abuser, minimizing and explaining away bad behavior, or making excuses for not acting, are traits of an unsafe pastor who is willing to sacrifice your health and wellbeing, just like the religious leaders of Jesus' day. Excusing abuse just to hold the marriage together violates Jesus' lesson on healing on the Sabbath:

Jesus taught that it is always right to save a life on the Sabbath.
Saving a life is the priority.
He got angry at religious leaders who didn't see this.

35. A safe church doesn't pressure the spouse to reconcile if the spouse has misgivings about their safety. Safe churches leave the decision to the person actually in the situation. A safe pastor realizes that without meaningful proof of behavior and attitude change, there is no safe or loving marriage possible.

And then [the pastor tried to force] me right on the spot, to make a decision: "Do you want this marriage or not?"
I said, "I can't tell you that. I don't know."
He said, "You have to know. You're either going to make this marriage work or you're not."
And I said, "But I don't know what his actions are going to be. If he's not going to repent, if he's not going to do the work… if he's just going to keep on sinning, no, I'm not. No, I'm not going to do this."
[The] pastor just ripped on me and told me if I don't continue meeting, it'll be the demise of my marriage. So clearly the whole thing was about saving my marriage. It… was about saving the marriage at all costs no matter who gets trampled on in the process.

"You don't need permission from your pastor or anyone else to divorce your abuser."
—Pastor Jeff Crippen[189]

189 Jeff Crippen, *Unholy Charade.com*, accessed 12/1/19, https://unholycharade.com/what-is-abuse/.

36. Safe pastors watch for signs of serious problems during the divorce process. Although most divorces have disagreements and friction between the spouses, the vast majority (9 in 10 divorces) settle through mediation. If you hear that a person has had to go to court more than once, this is not normal. Constant litigation is emotionally and financially draining to someone trying to parent alone, and the abused spouse may need emotional and financial support.

Other signs of a toxic divorce are allegations of stalking, abuse/restraining orders, hacking emails, false allegations without proof, not paying support, kidnapping the children, and refusing to follow the child custody arrangement.[190]

Conclusion

For those of you who are currently in a dangerous marriage, I want to encourage you: *You are allowed to consider a life-saving divorce.* No one else but you and God can see what is happening behind closed doors, and only you know when enough is enough.

Though the process of getting a life-saving divorce is hard and can feel scary, the cost of staying is usually worse. People leaving dangerous marriages need support; God did not design us to face hard things alone, and he accompanies us every step of the way.

Be strong and courageous. Do not be afraid or terrified because of them,
for the Lord your God goes with you;
he will never leave you nor forsake you.
— Deuteronomy 31:6 (NIV)

In addition to walking beside us himself, God also gives us safe friends and church communities to support and encourage us along the way. Sometimes, he does this for us in the church we're already attending—but not always.

Other times, he does this by strengthening us in wisdom to recognize

190 Aaron Thomas, "What Types of Divorce Typically Go to Trial?" ***Lawyers.com*** (2019), accessed 12/16/19, https://www.lawyers.com/legal-info/family-law/divorce/what-types-of-divorces-typically-go-to-trial.html.

that we are attending a church that *isn't* safe for victims, and by the power of his Holy Spirit, he grants us permission and courage to leave that church and find a different one, where we and our loved ones *will* be safe and supported.

The Body of Christ is made of many, many parts—many churches, many denominations, and many people—not just the one you are a part of right now. If your God-given sense of discernment is telling you that the one you're a part of now is not safe and will not support you as you get your life-saving divorce, you can listen to it!

That is the voice of God guiding you into greater safety.

You are not abandoning Jesus by changing churches, and you are not leaving God's will for your life by walking away from one particular pastor—though there are certainly unhealthy pastors who will try to convince you that you are.

Pay attention to the still, small voice of God, and he will guide you. You are beloved in the eyes of God, and your safety and wellbeing matter immensely to Jesus!

The same applies to those of you who have already gotten a life-saving divorce and are facing judgment from your church community or your pastor. If you recognize that the signs of a safe church are not present in the church you're attending, *you are allowed to leave.*

You do not need the permission, blessing, or understanding of anyone at that church: not the pastor, not your small group leader, and not your fellow churchgoers. They have no skin in the game. It's easy for them to give advice. There's no risk to them. It's not *their* safety, *their* body, *their* financial stability, *their* life or sanity, *their* children, *their* terror, or *their* reputation that's on the line.

If that church is not safe and supportive for you and your children and instead shames and judges you for getting a life-saving divorce, you can follow Jesus' teaching to "shake the dust off your feet" (Matthew 10:14, NIV) and leave, letting God guide you to a different church where you will be supported, safe, and better able to worship and serve God as a part of the body of Christ.

Bible Passages to Consider

You are free to end your association with a sexually immoral, drunk, emotionally or financially abusive person.

But actually, I wrote you not to associate with anyone who claims to be a brother or sister and is sexually immoral or greedy, an idolater or verbally abusive, a drunkard or a swindler. Do not even eat with such a person.
—1 Corinthians 5:11 (CSB, emphasis mine)

You are free to throw off a yoke of slavery.

It is for freedom that Christ has set us free. Stand firm, then, and do not let yourselves be burdened again by a yoke of slavery.
—Galatians 5:1 (NIV)

You are free to walk away from selfish, mean, out-of-control, abusive people.

But mark this: There will be terrible times in the last days. [2]People will be lovers of themselves, lovers of money, boastful, proud, abusive, disobedient to their parents, ungrateful, unholy, without love, unforgiving, slanderous, without self-control, brutal, not lovers of the good, treacherous, rash, conceited, lovers of pleasure rather than lovers of God— having a form of godliness but denying its power. Have nothing to do with such people.
—2 Timothy 3:1-5 (NIV, emphasis mine)

God doesn't like violent people.

The Lord examines the righteous,
but the wicked, those who love violence,
he hates with a passion.
—Psalm 11:5 (NIV, emphasis mine)

MALE VICTIMS OF ABUSE AND BETRAYAL

So far in this book, most of the stories and quotes are from women. And that's fair, because more women are domestic violence (DV) victims than men, and more women file for divorce, finally deciding "enough is enough."

Women have been the vanguard in bringing the topic of domestic violence to greater public awareness. And women deserve honor as the flagbearers in the outcry against abuse.

About 1 in 4 women and nearly 1 in 10 men have experienced contact sexual violence, physical violence, and/or stalking by an intimate partner during their lifetime and reported some form of impact, per the CDC. And experts believe the real number may be much higher than this, because men are less likely to report violence.

Anyone who has suffered abuse, regardless of their gender, deserves support and empathy, and they deserve to have their story heard and validated. Women face many dangers and challenges in the world and in their intimate relationships, and the truth of this cannot be overstated.

Alongside this, without denying or minimizing it, and without making suffering into a contest, it's important to listen with compassion to the stories of male victims of abuse. The one does not erase or compete with the other; they are both true. It is possible for many women to have had it bad, *and* for some men to have had it bad, too.

We can make it so that there is enough empathy to go around.

Men's stories need to be heard and understood. I don't want to ignore and erase the men's voices. Or, as Zach Brittle, a counselor at the marriage research pro-family organization, The Gottman Institute, wrote:

"... 85% of adult domestic violence victims are women. ...Maybe I should dedicate 15% of my word count to the plight of abused men."[191]

It's my goal to give proportional attention to the problems men face with abusive and/or unfaithful wives. Suffering hurts, whether you are male or female, and people who are suffering deserve support.

The first step to providing this support is for us to hear and understand the ways that abusive marriages affect male victims. Some of those ways are different than they are for female victims, and some are the same.

One significant distinction between abuse suffered by male victims and that suffered by female victims is related to physical size and degree of threat. On average, male bodies are larger than female bodies (though of course there are exceptions).

Regardless of gender, when your abuser or attacker is larger and stronger than you, the degree of danger and terror you experience is substantially worse than that experienced by a person being assaulted by someone they feel confident they could escape or overpower, if they needed to.

Both behaviors are abusive and do damage,
but the trauma inflicted at the hands of a larger, stronger abuser
often involves life-threatening terror.

This means that greater numbers of women have been traumatized by male abusers who were capable of inflicting severe, debilitating, and even *fatal* injury. Male victims experience this at a far lower rate.

Emotional abuse is another story, and for many people it may be a surprise to learn that men and women are psychologically abused by intimate partners at about the same rate, according to the Centers for Disease Control and Prevention.[192]

---

191 Brittle, "V is for Violence."

192 M. C. Black, K. C. Basile, and M. J. Breiding, et al., "The National Intimate Partner and Sexual Violence Survey (NISVS): 2010 Summary Report," ***Centers for Disease Control and Prevention*** (Atlanta, GA: National Center for Injury Prevention and Control, 2011), 2.

One of the unique ways that male victims of abuse struggle, however, is that being a victim is not seen as "manly." Men are often shamed or silenced when they have been victimized, due to some of the harmful ideas in society and the church about what it means to be a man.

We have stereotypes about men and women: that men should be tough, unaffected, and never show weakness or hurt; and that women are always the sweet, nurturing caregivers, never the "bad guy," and certainly never the abuser.

Because we believe stereotypes about men always wanting sex and women not being sexual creatures, we struggle to grasp the truth that sometimes men are coerced by women into having sex that the man didn't want (this is sexual assault and rape).

Yet the stereotypes prevent us from seeing the truth: that women are human, just as much as men are, and sometimes humans hurt and abuse others.

This concept—that women are also capable of cruelty and bad behavior—is not a new one. The idea of a cruel, evil woman is as old as human history. As the Bible says:

Now then, my sons, listen to me;
do not turn aside from what I say.
Keep to a path far from her,
do not go near the door of her house,
lest you lose your honor to others
and your dignity to one who is cruel...
—Proverbs 5:7-9 (NIV)

One way we know there are vicious, abusive wives is the many books written by the children of narcissistic mothers, who wish their fathers had taken them away and not stayed.

For the men reading this book who were victimized, I hope you know that you deserve support and care.

What was done to you was wrong—it was sin—
and you are not to blame,
nor are you any less of a man for having been abused.

There are many others like you, both men and women, who have come through a terrible time and emerged on the other side at last.

In the stories that follow, if you recognize yourself, your past, or even your current reality, I hope that you know that you are not alone. And I hope that you hear in these stories that there is hope for a better future for you, through a life-saving divorce. The men in these stories went through terrible pain, but they found a way to get to safety and rebuild their lives.

You can, too.

Married to a Self-Centered Woman—David's Story

In this first story, David was brought up in a high-achieving homeschooling family and was taught the *I Kissed Dating Goodbye* formula for courtship and marriage.

This book was wildly popular and sold more than a million copies. I don't think the 21-year-old author, Josh Harris, had any idea he would create a new set of iron-clad Christian rules about dating that would influence an entire generation, but many people took the author's recommendations as being the *only* godly way to find a mate and quoted the book as if it were the Bible.[193] As one journalist described it:

> "...the book discouraged teen relationships and proposed that courtship, in which a couple moves purposefully toward marriage with their parents' blessing and involvement, was a superior model to dating. And it argued that any kind of physical intimacy before marriage was a violation of the sacredness of married sexuality, and could lead to lifelong regret."[194]

David was a good kid, very compliant, and followed the rules. He had been taught not to date much as a teenager because he shouldn't "give a piece of his heart" to anyone but his spouse.

In many homeschool communities, a close, intimate friendship with someone of the opposite sex might be seen as a problem. And if you had sex with someone, you were permanently "one flesh" the rest of your

---

193 Sarah McCammon, "Evangelical Writer Kisses an Old Idea Goodbye," ***NPR*** (12/17/18), accessed 1/3/20, https://www.npr.org/2018/12/17/671888011/evangelical-writer-kisses-an-old-idea-goodbye. Author Joshua Harris has apologized for the damage his book has done, per this article

194 Ruth Graham, "Hello ***Goodbye***," ***Slate*** (8/23/16), accessed 9/23/19, https://slate.com/human-interest/2016/08/i-kissed-dating-goodbye-author-is-maybe-kind-of-sorry.html.

life. Breakups and broken hearts were seen as failures and tragedies, rather than the normal ups and downs of getting to know people, testing their character, and exploring their personality. They were seen as taking something away from your future spouse that you could never recover, something that would always be missing and lost, and something that, for the rest of your life, you would regret having given away.

They were seen, too, as sins—black marks on your record, tarnishing your purity in the eyes of God. The book prescribed that parents give permission at various points along the courtship pathway, teaching that this would lead to a better marriage than secular or casual dating would have. It warned against any physical intimacy, not just against having premarital sex.

Because of these strict standards, many couples who followed the teachings in this book didn't have their first kiss until their wedding day. This book, and other books in this category, implied that if you succeeded in arriving at your wedding night as a virgin, you would be rewarded by a wonderful, close marriage with great sex.

But the truth is: it does not always turn out this way, even with couples who do all the steps right.

Many of these *I Kissed Dating Goodbye* teachings were part of David's homeschool group. And the pastors at his complementarian Sovereign Grace member church told husbands to treat their wife as a queen. They said that if a man's wife, his queen, isn't happy, he has failed as a spiritual leader. He must try harder. He must lay down his life for her, sacrificing himself for her as Christ did for the Church, until she feels loved and supported.

The message was clear: If you have conflict or she's unhappy, it's the husband's fault. A husband just needs to sacrifice more. David took these teachings to heart.

To most people, this sounds wonderful. It's like music to a woman's ears. What wife wouldn't want a husband who took responsibility to make the marriage loving!

The problem with these messages is that they put the burden of the wife's behavior and marital happiness on just one person—the husband. He was seen as ultimately responsible for the spirituality and behavior of his family. The husband's godly life and righteous prayers will determine the couple's outcome for good or ill.

And if that is true—and that was the impression David had—it really doesn't matter whom he marries, as long as he marries a Christian who will submit, stay at home, and follow his lead.

As we will see in his story, a lot can go wrong and did go wrong. Those messages were a recipe for disaster.

And it's not because David wasn't a godly man. He took his faith seriously. He had looked forward to marriage. It was because the message he received was flawed—unrealistic and overly optimistic.

It set up the expectation that one person can control another adult's behavior simply by setting a good example.

This message is often given to wives in the form of the "submission and devotion" myth: that if she submits more, and performs more acts of Christian devotion (more prayer, Bible reading, church attendance, and trusting in God), her husband will change.

If you believe you can cause another person to behave well simply by being a good person yourself, you have likely heard one of these myths. (We talk about more of these myths in Chapter 3.)

In reality, each person is responsible for their own behavior before God. If they are doing wrong, they were sinning before you showed up, and they will continue long after you are gone, unless they personally put in a lot of time and effort to work on themselves and make it a priority.

This complementarian message taught David to put his wife's happiness first and set him up to expect a good marriage. It offered no instruction on setting boundaries. It didn't give advice about what to do if your spouse made unwise and unreasonable demands, or how to draw a line if their sin and destructive behavior was damaging the marriage. The message required the husband, as the spiritual head of the house, to take the larger share of the blame for his wife's choices.

In contrast, in a healthy marriage, each person seeks to grow in their relationship to God and carry their own responsibility for having a marriage that is respectful, safe, and free from sinful behavior. It is not the husband's fault if his wife chooses to sin (or vice versa). In a healthy marriage, a good spouse needs to speak up when something is sinful or unhealthy and make course corrections.

But David had been taught that a godly husband who is a good spiritual leader must make his wife, his queen, happy.

You can guess what is coming.

What happens when the wife is an abuser or a cheater—unfaithful, lying, manipulative, and selfish—and sees no reason to change? What if the husband sacrifices over and over, laying down his life for her and giving in to her unreasonable expectations, in hopes that she will become a better person?

What if she doesn't change? What if her behavior actually becomes more outrageous?

The truth is that there are a lot of people in society who are not capable of having a healthy marriage. For one reason or another—sometimes due to their childhood or a personality disorder or something else—they are self-absorbed or self-protective and are not kind, fair, respectful, responsible, or reliable. They are not "marriage material."

I'm not saying they aren't valuable or worthy of love. Many of them are fun, great conversationalists, and quite charming. And all people, regardless of their shortcomings, are valuable in the eyes of God and are made in his image.

But they aren't good marriage partners.

And nothing you can do, no example you can set, no love you can offer, will fix them. They have to do the hard work to change themselves. Sadly, many do not.

Christian marriage books and pastors rarely warn us:
Some people are just are too dangerous to be married to anyone.

Normally a person in a very difficult marriage would go to a licensed therapist and receive help, but in David's case, his church discouraged people from seeing anyone but a "biblical" or a "pastoral" counselor. (Note: A person who earned a theology degree at seminary is not given adequate training to provide psychological and mental health care, and churches whose pastors offer counseling in areas in which they have no training can do much more harm than good, as we see in David's story.)

So David was stuck with no answers for his bad marriage, until a crisis struck and he was forced to talk with people with specialized knowledge who saw the truth of the situation. It was the first time he realized it might not be all his fault.

Question: Where did you get the idea of what marriage was supposed to be?

David: It was always presented to us as the most important relationship that you would ever have, short of your relationship with God. And in some ways, it was more real than your relationship with God, because it's with a person who was there. And we were taught things like you could never actually choose the wrong person because we're all sinful beings, so it just means as long as you're both committed to each other, you don't pick the wrong person. [Your marriage might] have struggles in it, but the whole point of the covenant and the commitment was to cover over that.

I remember being arrogant when I was hearing about other people going through divorce. [I assumed] they just didn't work hard enough. Or somebody wasn't committed enough to marriage.

Honestly, now I really cringe at my heart [attitude] towards broken families. [I just thought there was nothing] the wife could do to [destroy the marriage.] That it was really, primarily the husband's fault.

I went to one of the Sovereign Grace member churches. Obviously it was a strong, complementarian upbringing. Now, it's funny, we always got this mixed message. My mom's a pretty strong personality… She went to college and she had a career, but she decided to give it up to have children and homeschool us. It was the higher calling that God calls you to do something and you lay aside your career for it. I think that set up my concept that this is the greatest calling. Where do I find a woman whose only goal is to be a mom?

We also knew you have not arrived until you've gotten married. In my mind, singleness was just the thing you had to endure until you found the person that you married. We also were very strong in the I Kissed Dating Goodbye *scene… So I never dated. I didn't date all the way through college, and my ex-wife was the first person I dated and the second person I ever kissed.*

You take a person like me, who is not very experienced with those things, and then you put someone on the opposite side who has looser physical boundaries, and it is a recipe for disaster.

I just remember when we were together, she always wanted to be physical. And I was balancing that against my morals. But then there's this very attractive lady paying me attention. And it gets really difficult. So we had premarital sex during that time. I never felt comfortable with it, and then she would say things like, "You need to comfort me, and if you don't [have sex with me right now, it] means that you don't actually care about me."

I remember we were driving down the road after she had a fight with her mom. And she said, "I want to have sex now." And I was thinking, I can't, I don't want to, this is not right. We [continued] driving down the road, and she looked at me and said, "If you don't do this, then we're over."

So we pulled over into a parking lot. It was just wrong. You can't judge yourself later after you've gone through a bunch of stuff and realize it, but you look back at the things that happened and you ask yourself, why? That was so clearly wrong.

And you know, I don't want to whitewash it. It is super appealing as a young man to want sex. So I'm not saying that I was Mr. Monk who was not interested in this. But in that situation, with pressure on it, and balancing it against what your morality is, I wanted to say, "No, I don't want to do this." But I was not being respected. There [were] so many things that now I know were red flags.

I remember one time we were going to a conference called Celebration. It was something that various churches would do. I was listening to a sermon on the tabernacle in the Old Testament. And I just remember looking at it as God trying to draw nearer to his people. I thought: we're having premarital sex right now, and I'm drawing farther away from God.

So I took Melissa aside and said, "We have to talk to somebody. We have to talk to somebody about this, because I don't feel comfortable, I don't think it's right, I think I'm dishonoring God." And she threw the book at me. She said, "If you do this we're over, we're done."

I was wrestling with that. I've [had premarital sex with her.] I feel like I need to be committed to her, I needed to go through this process [of repentance], and now she's threatening to leave me if I just bring other people into a conversation. She was strong about isolating me from other people's authority, saying, "Don't talk to them or else we're done," or, "Don't talk to them or I'm going to be really angry. Don't talk to them, or you don't really care about me, you don't really love me."

I spent my entire life working on how I could be the absolute best husband I could be. And you know, our family is very performance-oriented. There's not a slacker in the bunch of us. We are overachievers in everything we do. To be told that I am not loving? This was the one job that I actually cared the most about.

Prior to getting engaged, she went on a trip with a [wealthy] relative. And while she was on that trip, she cheated on me with some rich guy. She was like, "Oh well, I drank too much. You know, there's something I need to tell you. You should be grateful, because he asked me to run away with him and I said, no, I wanted to be with you."

It was presented as, "You should be grateful that I let this thing happen, because it just proves that I wanted to be with you more than some rich guy who wanted to whisk me away." And I remember thinking, this doesn't feel good, but yeah, that's right. I guess that is right. I guess she did choose me.

And that's so messed up. I wish I could go back and say to myself, "This is not normal. This is toxic. People who want a healthy relationship don't do this."

Often, she would start fights with random strangers. She would actually pick a fight and then expect me to get into a physical altercation with the other person. And I wouldn't do it.

I remember one time, it was over a pair of sunglasses in a store. She was the aggressor. I was standing there watching to make sure nothing bad was going to happen. And I thought, I'm giving her space to say her peace instead of swooping in and controlling her and the situation. Later on, she let me have it, and she called a meeting with the pastor at my church to talk about how I didn't physically protect her.

The pastor turned to me and said, "Yeah, you have to realize that she's the queen, so no matter what, if she feels physically attacked, you need to step in. That's your job, and you just didn't do that." And I remember thinking, how was I supposed to know that she felt physically threatened when she's the aggressor?

"I don't feel loved, I don't feel supported," she would say. And I was thinking, "That's my one job. My job is to provide a stable environment of caring and love for her, and I'm failing at this." I just constantly felt like I was failing, and she would drill that in.

For her, there always had to be an enemy in everything that she did. When she was growing up it was her [mother or other] family members—she always had to have someone else who was at fault. And she would say things like, "I could have achieved so many things if it weren't for this person."

She didn't get along with my parents really well, because she made those crazy statements, and my family doesn't take well to making false statements about things. She would get angry with my mom because my mom wouldn't drop everything at the drop of a hat to come watch the kids and babysit. And there were massive altercations between them. So we slowly isolated from my mom.

Melissa needed an enemy. She started isolating me: "Are you on your mom's side, or are you on my side?" And she would throw Scripture at me and say, "It doesn't say that I need to leave and cleave to my husband, it says you are supposed to leave your family and cleave to your wife." And growing up in a complementarian church with a strong spiritual mindset, I told myself, "Oh, this is the word of God, I have to follow this." It was things like that over many years.

For my career, I was working in technology start-up companies, and they involve some risk. I do software, so my industry makes a lot of money if I work normal jobs, but when doing start-ups, you have to go through a lean period there where you're not really making a whole lot of money. [If the company succeeds, I do very well. If it fails, money is tight.] I showed Melissa the realities of our financial situation and asked for her input. It was important we set up a solid budget with boundaries.

And she'd say, "Oh, I'm going to trust you. I agree with this, I'm going to trust you." But if anything went wrong at the start-up company, she would tell me, "You never really talked to me about this. You didn't tell me that this was going to happen… I wouldn't have agreed to that. You mismanaged our money; you're doing this because you're selfish; I can't buy the things that I want now.

You're not giving me the things that I want. I need to be able to get these things."

And everything was couched as, "I'm buying this expensive furniture for the family." Or, "Well this isn't for me, this upgraded kitchen, this is for the family." Or "I'm not getting this new van because I *want it. I'm getting it because the other van's unsafe. Do you want our children to be driving around in an unsafe van?" There was nothing wrong with our van. It just needed a brake job.*

So we were constantly blowing our budget, and that would really stress me out. And I'd come to her and say, "We agreed to this budget; these are the things that you're in charge of because you said you could be in charge of them, like groceries and household things. And if we stay within this budget, we're going to be all right."

And she'd reply, "The only reason I blew the budget is because you didn't go over with me what I was spending every day. Because if you were a good spiritual leader, you would go over this and help me." I thought to myself, maybe I really am bad at being a spiritual leader. I am so tired at the end of the day that I forgot I needed to go over the budget with her. And I remember thinking, "Yeah, the fruit of me being a bad spiritual leader is that my wife yells at me and makes me feel like dirt. It's the fruit of my poor leadership."

We'd go to counseling with pastors, and they'd take her side on some of it. They would tell me I should be a better spiritual leader. They didn't catch on to the truth until our entire situation fell apart. To be fair, later on, the pastor I was closest to said he was sorry for saying those things. He felt bad.

The problem with high-risk start-ups is this: not all startups succeed, and a lot of them fail. So at one point I wasn't making much money, and I started feeling like a failure, coming home and then getting criticized at home. I became extremely depressed. All the time I asked myself, why am I even doing this? Am I even worth this? And at the time, Melissa would say, "You've got to stop this. You've just got to stop this, why are you doing this?"

Melissa wanted a nicer home. She said, "I can't find good friendships here, and I always want to grow a garden, and you can't afford to buy me a house here, so let's move out to the country."

So we moved further from my work. Now I commuted an hour and a half to work so that she could live in the house that she wanted. I'd wake up at 5:30 AM to do my twelve-hour work day, starting with a long commute. And it just wore on me. She said, "If you weren't so selfish, you'd get an easier job." It wore away at my heart and my soul until the point where I really was suicidal at that time.

In time, the trust and emotional closeness eroded. There wasn't a sense of two-way companionship or support. David wanted a partner, but his hope for that kind of marriage was almost gone. By this point, David and Melissa's only positive connection was sexual.

Our intimacy was completely based on sex, because we couldn't have emotional intimacy. So [I told myself] if we were having sex, things were okay because we had that intimacy.

The problem is [that sex covers the problems and] works for a little bit. It's a distraction. But you feel the emotional connection eroding. Towards the end of our relationship, it all culminated in one huge argument where she said, "I just don't think you care about me; I just don't think you love me."

And I remember thinking, I don't want to have sex with a person who doesn't think that I love her. That doesn't seem right. Because if she thinks that I don't love her, then what's the point of sex and intimacy in that context?

I was at my lowest point, and I remember thinking, "Okay, how do I get away with a suicide? How do I do it in a way that my kids don't know?" You read the stories about the kids who have parents who commit suicide, and they too learn to see suicide as a good option. I don't want to do that to them. But I was thinking that the only way I can get out of my vows is if I die. How can I do it? How do I do it without burdening my children? Even Melissa was saying she would be better off without me.

Where could I go? My church told me secular psychology and therapy were really bad. I had no options. I had no concept that secular therapy could be something useful.

Melissa said to me, "I can't deal with you. You need to go see somebody." I just felt like going to see somebody was just the nail in the coffin of failure, so why should I go do that? I'm already a failure.

Looking back, I can see Melissa was right about getting counseling, but at the same time, she didn't really care about my wellbeing. None of her old tricks were working, and she saw me as a burden. It reinforced the whole thing of me being a failure.

One evening we were having an argument about something, and she said, "I don't think you love me, but let's have sex." And I said, "No, I don't want to have sex with somebody who doesn't think I love them." She said, "No, having sex will make it go away, and we should just make it go away."

I said no and made the comment that maybe she should get a vibrator, which made her really angry. She said, "I don't need a vibrator; I can get volunteers to have sex with me."

That was the crushing blow for me. That was it. It was very typical for us to have sex in the morning. The next day, I told myself, "This is what we're supposed to do, and I'm going away on this business trip," so we started having sex, and I remembered in the middle what she had said about getting volunteers, over and over again, and I just got angry about what she said. And we stopped. I couldn't have sex with her.

So I went away on my trip, and I decided I would give counseling one last chance. I called this counselor that we normally had and scheduled a meeting with him. But unbeknownst to me, Melissa went to see the pastor at the church and told him I had abused her.

She told the pastor, "I just want David to have help, I don't want him to die, I don't want him to kill himself, but this is what happened." And the pastor called the police.

[When I returned home, the police contacted me and started an investigation.] I was trying to figure out what I had done. At the time I was thinking, I'm the worst person: I feel bad, I got angry, maybe this is what spousal abuse is. And that's how I ended up going to [an inpatient treatment program in another state]. The staff there deal with two things: Sex addictions and love addictions.

So everybody thought I was going there for sex addiction because I was angry while we were having sex… And to be honest, at that time, I didn't know. It didn't feel right [to say I had abused

> *her], but I had been so brainwashed at that time, the only way for me to get back with my wife was to agree to whatever she said and to agree to the whole process.*
>
> *Now, the silver lining is that going to this place was the greatest thing for me. I spent more than a month in that inpatient care facility. It was the first time [during the marriage] I ever felt safe, that I could remember.*

After meeting with David many times, the staff at the inpatient facility started understanding the story. To them, it was obvious David wasn't a sex addict. In fact, just the opposite.

> *[And the counselor said something to the effect of,] "You're more in the love addiction [category]. You're willing to harm yourself for a relationship and drag yourself through the mud and admit to things that you didn't do and take responsibility for things. That's not really the pattern that we see for sex addictions."*
>
> *Going to the treatment program was the greatest thing because… [they do a lot of testing. They told me,] "Look, unless your wife is willing to do the work to make herself healthy, you guys aren't going to stay together." And I remember thinking, "This program was actually very good, because they have a week for the family to come down and they do work with the family to kind of create a good environment."*
>
> *Melissa went down there for a week. And they told her the same thing: that she needed help too, and she had to do the work to make herself healthy.*

So David and Melissa went back home. Melissa found a therapist and told her David was a terrible monster, but when the counselor asked what she planned to do, her story didn't make sense. Rather than being afraid of "the monster," Melissa wanted to go back to the way things were and continue to live together in the home.

> *The therapist turned to her and said, "You can't do that if he's the monster person that you're describing." And Melissa explained, "No, you don't understand, I've got total control over the situation. I need him to help me with the kids and stuff like that."*

So we ended up getting this house that had two different levels. I was in the basement, and she was out there in the main area.

David and Melissa continued their counseling, but the therapists realized David was putting in effort to make the home safe, and Melissa was not.

Slowly during this time, the therapists started asking her more questions, and she started getting angry. Her claws came out in the middle of the therapy session. Unlike the pastoral counselors we had known, where it was all the husband's fault, these therapists weren't buying it. They basically said, "Melissa, you need to start working on your stuff."

Melissa decided she wasn't going to keep going to this therapist because the therapist would not say that Melissa had PTSD from the abuse. To the therapist, Melissa wasn't acting like a person with PTSD, and she wasn't working on things in her life.

I started going to the group therapy, and the therapist I worked with said, "Your wife is not okay, and she is not getting help, and she's not doing the work."

Over time, the therapists were seeing David's work to improve the marriage, but they weren't seeing Melissa put in effort to get healthy.

And then Melissa changed her story. [The new version was that] I'd pulled the wool over the eyes of all the therapists. That I have this great, magical power to convince people that I'm the innocent spouse in the whole situation. So she started switching therapists. And she had a criteria: Unless they said that she [was a victim], she wouldn't keep going to them.

We went to probably four or five different therapists at that time. And all along, I'd been working on myself, I had my own personal therapist, I had group therapy. I was going to 12-step meetings and stuff like that. It was really good for me. And I realized I could not go back to our old relationship, where she [makes accusations and threats].

David was finding more clarity. Sometimes the person trying to improve gets stronger, and they believe they can protect themselves from the abusive spouse's behavior. David thought there was hope because

Melissa was still going to counseling. He told himself she would get better over time. He wanted to try to get the marriage back together. He had made his marriage vows to her before God and took them seriously.

> *[After a year,] we got back together. [Shortly thereafter we had a] wedding anniversary, and on the anniversary she said, "I don't think I can be married to you."*
>
> *And I said, "Okay, but I still want to be married to you. I feel like I made my vows, and those aren't something that anybody can take away from me."*
>
> *[By that time] I'd almost lost my job because of [her accusation]; I almost lost my freedom because of what she did. And the court ended up dismissing the whole case because there was nothing there. [Editor's note: David provided legal documents to verify his story.]*
>
> *And at some point, I gave balance to that. We were going to couples therapy at that time. And [I wanted to keep trying]. I thought: How do I give her time to get help? I still had a lot of hope.*
>
> *Looking at it now, I know that sometimes abused women just cannot see the truth. They still feel hope and think it is going to turn out. Switch the genders, and that's where I was. I was telling myself, I just have to endure. If I hope hard enough, if I care hard enough, and [protect myself better], I can make it through this. [I still believed] my love and patience and ability to endure the worst would be the saving grace for her.*
>
> *Later on, when we [started changing therapists over and over], I finally said, "Look, this has got to stop." And I started suggesting that she possibly go do an inpatient care program like I did, because it was so good for me. [I thought perhaps she would be open,] because she had been saying, "You're a completely different person, you're doing so great, I'm so proud of all the work that you've done." And then she would flop over to, "You're the same person, you're horrible, you're just really good at hiding things."*
>
> *Finally she told me, "I'm not going to do this, I don't want to do this anymore." And I said, "Okay, how do you want to do this?" She wanted to stay in our home with the children.*

> *I ended up moving in with a friend for a while because it was the only place I could live for free. I gave nearly one hundred percent of my money to my wife. I ate one meal a day because that was all I could afford. I hoped she would see that it's difficult to be on your own, that she would want to be her own adult, and that we could make it through this, but she decided she wanted to divorce.*
>
> *We got divorced, but every issue went before the judge because we couldn't agree in mediation. She wanted the kids and continued to accuse me of all kinds of things. But the court-approved forensic psychologist said, "The dad is a wonderful dad. He relates to the kids well; they love him."*
>
> *Melissa got caught in lie after lie after lie. And the problem is, when you lie to normal people, you can get away with it for a while because there's no authority. When you start lying to a judge, it does not go well with you.*

The divorce finalized after several years. It was very contentious, and his wife got into serious legal trouble for refusing to comply with the court. Since then David is happily remarried and has joint custody.

Let's review David's story—

- While dating, his wife-to-be demanded he do things he felt were wrong. She routinely ignored his sense of morality and integrity. She coerced him into having sex. He hadn't expected a Christian woman to do this and was confused about how to handle it.
- Messages he had gotten from books and his homeschool community gave him the impression that if he married a woman who wanted to be a stay-at-home mother, he could expect a good marriage.
- Additional messages implied that if David and Melissa were dating and had kissed and grown emotionally close, the only honorable step was to marry, or else David was guilty of defrauding her. This message is unsafe. People need to be able to exit unsafe relationships, at any point, without fear of criticism.
- When David spoke up and objected to her demands for sex, Melissa berated him for not loving her or comforting her when she was upset. David had been taught that a wife's happiness was top priority, so he went along with her demands. He felt uncomfortable with this, but he had been taught that saying "no" was unloving.

- Melissa would manufacture conflict situations, demanding that David rescue her. David was confused. He sensed this wasn't right, but he had not been prepared to deal with this type of behavior. The message he had gotten from his pastor was that godly spiritual husbands are to protect their wives no matter what. He couldn't refuse. This led him to support his wife's destructive and sinful behavior.
- Knowing that his career would have financial ups and downs, David included Melissa in budget discussions. He was up front about his income not being predictable and laid out a plan. She did not engage in the budgeting process in good faith, then blamed him when she bought furniture and a vehicle they could not afford.
- David gave into her demands at great expense to himself. She called him selfish for choosing this career. She criticized him when their income was low. She considered him a failure she had to "put up with."
- David felt like a failure and became suicidal. He wanted to plot a way to kill himself without affecting his children.
- Being forced to go into an inpatient treatment center saved his life. Trained, licensed counselors realized he was debasing himself to keep the marriage.
- David made progress in counseling and got better at establishing boundaries. He wanted the marriage and hoped he could improve the situation. Melissa understood that David wasn't going to give in to all her wants anymore, and she decided to divorce.

Several weeks after the interview, I asked David about his spiritual life. He said, "I would say my relationship to God has never been better. When everything has been taken from you and you are left with nothing, you have to turn to God. It is a sweet thing, because you aren't turning to God because of what he has given you or can give you. You are turning to the Lord because it's the only thing that can't be taken from you. That is a powerful bonding that I have with my Lord. It is more real and more close than it has ever been. I have the scars to prove it and the peace that seals it."

David told me he wanted to share his story so people would be warned about the false messages that his church promoted. He also wanted people to know he no longer believes the complementarian (hierarchical or "patriarchal") view of marriage. He is concerned that messages that put the burden for the marriage on just one spouse, without teaching boundaries, pave the way for abusive marriages.

Will I Be Safe in a Particular Denomination?

Many people wonder if doctrinal beliefs about men and women matter in their marriage. Does church denomination matter? A husband and wife who care about each other's wellbeing—no matter what doctrine they hold or denomination they attend—can love each other well.

But a spouse who feels entitled to use control and dominance can destroy a marriage—even if they claim to be progressive, conservative, egalitarian, complementarian, or have no viewpoint at all.

The truth is that abusers can be found in all parts of society and all types of churches.

Abuse occurs regardless of the doctrine you hold. People want to believe that *their* group is less abuse-prone than others, but researchers say abuse happens across all major denominations.[195] It's the specific religious messages the vulnerable spouse receives that cause much of the problem.

Married to a Cheater—Gary's Story

Wives who are adulterers—like unfaithful husbands—aren't interested in being vulnerable, loving, and emotionally close, unless it helps them get what they want. Cheaters display a pattern of treacherous behavior. It is deliberate and planned.

They plan to cheat, often lying and gaslighting, explaining away their absences, the strange phone calls, and the condoms in their purse. They launch a smear campaign on their spouse to justify their behavior and to punish the faithful spouse, but they may not actually want to divorce.

Often, they want to have their cake and eat it, too. They want the stable, reliable home life—and the affairs. The attraction and sexual connection are part of the emotional high.

---

195 Westenberg, "When She Calls," 4.

It may take years for the husband to finally believe his own eyes and set boundaries to hold a spouse like this responsible for their behavior. Like women who are married to unfaithful husbands, these betrayed men may not face the truth about their wives for decades.

> *I met my first wife in college. I knew her for probably about 18 months when we got married.*
>
> *Her family background was different, very conservative, Southern. I don't think I misrepresented who I was or anything, but I didn't have any kind of a faith life. My parents were really involved in their conservative Baptist church, but I had just seen too much growing up in that church, and I didn't want anything to do with it. She had expectations that I was going to get involved in church life and things, and I wasn't the least bit interested in doing that.*
>
> *We had a lot of ups and downs in our relationship and our marriage, but I considered that normal, although she was way more emotionally volatile than I was used to or had ever experienced in the past. I'd never known anybody who was that volatile.*
>
> *We eventually had a couple of kids, and she went back to school to become a schoolteacher. When she started her student teaching and got into her teaching career, looking back, I see a lot of change in her and our relationship. She became way more intolerant of who I was and how I acted, and she had more specific expectations of how I was supposed to act and dress and wear my hair.*
>
> *I couldn't quite figure out what was going on with all of this stuff. Looking back on it, I realize that she was having an affair, or actually multiple affairs. The picking on my appearance just got worse and worse until at one point, my oldest son, who I think was about 14 at the time, wrote her a letter telling her, "Stop picking on Dad. Why are you doing this? He doesn't deserve this, and you're just really mean."*
>
> *He handed the letter to her, and she gave it to me and told me to punish him for it, and I said, "No. Everything he said is true. This is what's going on." I really didn't understand what was happening.*
>
> *And then she started developing more male friendships at school, at her work, and other places, which I was not enthusiastic*

about at all. But I was raised in the '60s and the '70s and not inclined towards controlling people in relationships. It's just like, Okay, you make your own choices, but the fallout is yours. That is how I felt about it and talked to her about it. It just got worse and worse.

Anytime I tell my story, I don't want to come across as like I was a perfect husband, which I certainly was not. I was always faithful, I supported the family, and I was good with the kids and not abusive towards her in any way.

But emotionally, I did not have a very high emotional IQ at that time in my life. I didn't have a lot of relationships with women before we got married, so I think a lot of what I had to learn about a relationship was with her.

Anyway, I discovered in a very painful way that she was having an affair. I found the leftovers of her motel night stay in one of her bags at home, and a checklist of all the things that she had planned to bring for this one-night stand.

Well, what are you going to do? Another time, she left some stuff behind, papers and things which made it very clear that this wasn't the only guy at work. Then that caused me to realize that the strange phone calls I had received from people from her school were legitimate.

[I had brushed them off] as harassment from her coworkers, because she told me that some of her coworkers were out to get her and they were giving her a hard time. Well, yeah, they were giving her a hard time because she was probably having sex with the janitor in her classroom or the closet or somewhere. They saw it happening.

I got a phone call one time saying, "They're doing it right now!" And I just assumed because I loved and trusted my wife, that the [school staff] were just out to get her.

This was a year or two before the big blow-up happened. I finally realized this had been going on for a lot longer than I had any idea, and this was why she was criticizing me all the time. Nothing I could do was right.

Now, when I look back at it, she had launched a campaign to make me into a terrible person, and it went on for years. She would assign [negative, racist, or hateful] motivations to me that had nothing to do with anything I was thinking. She would paint me as this horrible person, but she was out screwing around. Yet somehow I'm the terrible one.

She wanted a divorce, but I wanted a legal separation. We were trying to rotate weeks at home with the kids [where the kids stay in the house and the parents take turns living there]. She [wanted a schedule so that] I was there on the weekends all the time. That way she could go out and screw around. So after this happened once or twice, I said I'm not doing this anymore.

At this time I was resisting the divorce. I didn't want it. You know how it is. It's something that you don't want to have happen, and so you don't see it. You don't want to do the math and see what's happening. You think that somehow things are going to turn around.

At the same time, I have to tell you that I was having a lot of spiritual revelations and things that were happening in my life that were encouraging me to think that God was going to provide some sort of a solution to this. I had started going to church, and I had this Christian counselor. So I was hoping, I was expecting, I was being led to expect that God was going to change her heart.

She just wasn't dealing with reality at the time at all. She was in this lost world where you're just living for the weekend and screwing around with guys, and none of this was really sinking in. But finally it hit her hard.

[At one point we] had what they call a reconciliation, spelled like WRECK-conciliation. If you know the author Tracy Schorn, that's a "Chump Lady" term. You try to make a reconciliation, but it turns out to be a wreck. It didn't work out. [We were headed for divorce.]

My wife was extremely bitter, and I tried to buy her out of the house, pay her off for her equity. I could qualify for the loan, but she refused to do it out of spite. One day, she accidentally left papers behind which revealed to me that she and a woman friend, who was a mortgage broker, were plotting ways to get my name off the title.

So that gives you an idea of the level of intrigue going on behind the scenes. Anyway, she forced the sale of the house. We put the house up for sale, and it wasn't a good market at the time. This was 2001. We had to drop the price and finally got an offer. We [accepted] it and opened escrow.

Then September 11 happened, the terrorist attacks. The buyers got cold feet, and they backed out. The real estate market just turned to cement. Nobody was buying or selling anything. So nothing happened. I was in the house and paying her rent on her half of the house.

We went on for quite a while until finally, at one point, she called me up all tearful and thought that God was telling her to reconcile. Despite it all, I was excited, and I got a good marriage and family therapist who had been recommended and actually was very good. So we started this 12-week commitment, and she was not supposed to see the other guy.

The therapist gave us a lot of homework to do, and it was going well from my perspective. But this therapist wouldn't put up with any of her excuses. My wife would say, "Well, I did this because Gary did this," and the therapist would say to her, "Wait. You didn't have any other choice? Gary put a gun to your head and he made you screw around with other guys? Couldn't you have said, 'This relationship isn't working. We need to see a therapist'? Wasn't there any other option?"

She didn't like that, and eventually she admitted that she was still seeing this guy. Then she met with the therapist privately for three sessions, and then we met back together again one last time, at which point my wife said she didn't want to reconcile; she wanted a divorce.

I said, "Great, just go. Go out the door." I sat down with the therapist, and she said, "You dodged a bullet. This woman has a lot of problems, and you can't fix them. You need to let go of this. You need to look at what God has for you in this. There's a lot here."

She was very encouraging to me and very validating about the experience that I had, and what I had gone through. It was great. It was a tremendous experience. It was as painful as could be, but looking back on it, she was really, really good.

It was just done pretty much at that point, and I didn't really have to see her very much after that. When the divorce was final, we had one child in college, and the other had just finished the last year in high school, so they weren't little kids. That was another issue; I really felt that they needed to know what happened.

So I just straight-up told them that their mom was having an affair, and that is what broke up the marriage. I didn't go into any great detail.

I was encouraged by the therapist and some other people that I respected. They said, "Your kids need to know what it was that caused the divorce. It wasn't just two people growing apart or difference of opinion or something like that, but there's real consequences to behavior."

I wanted them to know the truth. It wasn't a fuzzy thing where no one knew what happened and Mom and Dad just got a divorce. For me to tell the truth may not have been appropriate for a six-year-old, but for a sixteen-year-old, it was. Of course, my wife blew up about that, but I was learning not to care anymore. The concept of having boundaries was a revelation for me, and I learned that one pretty well.

My brother is a therapist in another state, and he taught me about establishing boundaries and learning not to let other people's craziness affect you. That's theirs; it doesn't belong to you. They can be as crazy as they want, but that's not yours to be concerned about.

In the past, I would get wrapped up in her craziness, but I learned to set it aside and just go on with my life. I applied it practically... I applied my new insights on boundaries to a lot of other areas. I discovered that my professional life was a lot better if I was more intentional about boundaries. The other boundary I had to set was with my boss that during this time period. I think he learned something from it, too. Years later, I taught Henry Cloud's Boundaries *classes at my church; it was a very popular course, and I've done it many times since.*

As a result of establishing better boundaries, I dealt with my ex-wife better. I learned to communicate by email; no more face-to-face or phone calls. She expected me to just hand over things to her on her promise that she would give them back. I'd say, "I would have to be crazy to trust you, and I'm not crazy."

That would just set her off, and I didn't care. I didn't say it to upset her, but it was just truth-telling. If somebody stabs you in the back and enjoys twisting the knife, why would you believe them if they said they're not going to do that again? It doesn't make any sense. But that didn't stop her from trying to get information and documents that were not legally hers from me, our kids, and my elderly parents.

Anyway, for the most part, I was able to put her off to the side, and when I didn't have to deal with her on a regular basis, it was just great. I feel really bad for people who have to co-parent with exes who are hard to live with. I have a lot of empathy, even though I didn't experience it. I had my moments, but not on a regular basis.

Our kids did okay through it all. They both have done well in their careers. We are close. And they are close to their mom. I encouraged that.

A couple years later, I remarried. I met somebody on one of these Christian dating services. We emailed online for a month or two and then started talking on the phone. We got to know each other. We dated for a year and then were engaged for a year and got married.

We had similar experiences in our divorces, having been married to unfaithful spouses. We both did a lot of work during the divorce and afterwards to heal and repair and try to discover where we went wrong or how we could've done things differently. It's a good marriage.

Some things I learned:

1. Don't buy the propaganda of the "Recovery Industrial Complex,"[196] *the therapists and authors and "marriage intensive programs" that keep promising you they can fix your troubled marriage. [They use scare tactics, saying your kids are going to have lifelong damage if you divorce. But "We can save your marriage at our conference!"] Tracy Shorn [author of* Leave a

---

196 Tracy Schorn coined the phrase and defines the Recovery Industrial Complex as the "vague conspiracy sense that religious and for-profit institutions want you to try to reconcile indefinitely," including the "save your marriage" books that blame the victim.

Cheater, Gain a Life] *says it's self-serving, and it manufactures millions of billable hours for therapists. I think she would say that adultery is generally so devastating that marriages don't really ever recover. You're generally better off just to cut bait and run, because you're going to be living with the lies and the betrayal.*

2. The people being abused don't think the way abusers think. Normal people think others are fair and equitable and want the best for each other. They don't understand that abusers want *to take advantage of others.*

3. It's important to be angry about the infidelity. Many of the counselors I met with were not very good at allowing me to be angry and be hurt and validating that. It was too much emphasis on attempting a reconciliation and then smoothing it over when it didn't happen. If you don't express the anger and have that validated, it's like having a big abscessed wound that heals over the top, but that infection is still down there [and it's going to ooze out.]

4. Dealing with anger at God and at overly optimistic therapists [is an important part of the process]. I was done with the anger-at-God thing a while ago. That was very real. That took a long time. Most of my Christian therapists were telling me, "Oh yeah, your marriage will come back together again." It didn't happen, of course, so who are you going to blame?

Through it all, I developed a different understanding of who God is and what God's relationship with me is. I used to think that God would protect me, and if I said the right words, I would be safe, and everything would be good.

I tried that; it didn't work out well. Now I've learned that working with God and knowing that God is working with you is much more satisfying and realistic than thinking that I can control God if I do all the right things and say the right things and believe the right things.

These men offered many good insights:

1. They grew in their relationship to the Lord through their divorce. They are closer to God today.
2. They each projected their own goodness, reasonableness, and sense of fair play onto their wives, believing that surely the wife

would eventually come to her senses, know when to stop, feel genuine remorse, and change. But as they learned the hard way, the most blatant abusers/betrayers don't. They feel entitled to injure the marriage, trash your reputation, and take your share of the family resources.

3. Typical Christian wedding vows have included four promises: care, nurture, love, and faithfulness. Who would willingly bind themselves to a person who refused to care about them? Choosing to marry is completely voluntary. No one forces spouses to make these promises in front of the world (at least, not directly; social and religious pressure to marry can be pretty forceful, though we don't always realize it). So when their wives did not love, care, nurture, or stay faithful to them, these husbands had difficulty believing it. It took them years to grasp it. How is this a God-honoring marriage? How is this not a mockery of the "oneness" God intended?
4. Some counselors and marriage book authors are helpful, and others are not. Good ones help you understand that abusers are responsible for their own actions, not you. Good counselors say that you can speak up when faced with controlling, mean, and sinful behavior, and that you can be angry at the betrayals, set boundaries, and expect change.
5. Often people who have a deep sense of commitment to values and integrity are harder on themselves than any pastor would be.
6. God meant marriage to be safe and loving (or at least respectful), where both spouses are appreciative of each other's capabilities. If a person chooses to cheat and smears your good name, why are they still choosing to be married to you?
7. These men are happy they got out. They have no regrets, other than having stayed so long. But even in staying and then divorcing, they felt they gained a deeper relationship with the Lord, and they realized that what their churches had told them is not what they now believe. They no longer buy the easy answers about finding a spouse or the shallow claims about marriage.

The road to safety, recovery, healing, and freedom is often long and hard, whatever your gender, and male victims of abuse deserve support and help along the way. If you resonate with these struggles and want to learn more, turn to the back of this book for recommendations of other books you might find helpful: books on boundary-setting, on abuse recovery, and on the unique experiences of male victims of abuse.

A Favorite Bible Verse for You

I want to share one of my favorite Bible verses, and I'd like to also explain its back story. Jeremiah 29:11-13 is a much-beloved Bible passage. And many people have never read it in context. It promises that God has a good plan for his people.

It's a lovely statement. You might expect that God said this because he was pleased with them, and that everything was going well.

In reality, the reverse was true.

God was displeased with them. Their idolatry and evil were so extreme, the Lord allowed the mighty Babylonians to destroy Jerusalem and the temple and carry people off to exile in another land eight hundred miles away.

This was the worst thing they could imagine. Yet God told them he was watching over them and cared about them. Notice the last phrase, "I will be found by you, and will bring you back from captivity."

God is in the business of setting the captives free and in restoring lives.

Even if you feel you have lost everything, and your life has been destroyed by a bad relationship, it's not the end of the story. God cares.

"For I know the plans I have for you," declares the Lord, "plans to prosper you and not to harm you, plans to give you hope and a future.
Then you will call on me and come and pray to me, and I will listen to you. You will seek me and find me when you seek me with all your heart. I will be found by you," declares the Lord, "and will bring you back from captivity."
—Jeremiah 29:11-14a (NIV)

MOVING ON: FINDING HAPPINESS AGAIN

So do not fear, for I am with you;
do not be dismayed, for I am your God.
I will strengthen you and help you;
I will uphold you with my righteous right hand.
—Isaiah 41:10 (NIV)

Almost every person of faith who experiences a life-saving divorce is worried about their future, and feels the some of these things at first:

- I've got a black cloud over my head.
- I've got a red D for "divorced" on my forehead.
- I will never be happy again.
- No one good will ever love me again.

And they wonder if they've messed up their lives forever, thinking:

- I have missed God's Plan A and Plan B, and now I'm down to Plan ZZ.
- I'm disqualified now. God can never use me again.
- I've let God down.

The truth is: These are lies coming from our own sense of shame.

Most of these natural, normal fears will go away in time,
especially if we take them to the Lord.

When people walk through the door of a divorce recovery group for the first time, they are either numb and silent, or scared or crying. They don't believe me when I say that the first twelve months of the divorce process are really tough and miserable, but someday they will smile again.

By the end of the first year, most can laugh aloud again and feel hope. By the end of the second year, most people feel as though they will survive. By the end of the third year, most feel optimistic about the future.

Not everyone who comes to my groups is religious, but there is still something comforting to them about God's promises of love and care:

The Lord is close to the brokenhearted and saves those who are crushed in spirit.
—Psalm 34:18 (NIV)

For I am the LORD your God who takes hold of your right hand and says to you, Do not fear; I will help you.
—Isaiah 41:13 (NIV)

God doesn't see you as a failure. He knows you are merely human, full of flaws and frailties. He sees you the way any loving and trustworthy parent does: He is kind and patient and has a twinkle of joy in his eye when you come to him.

He sees you with the affection of a good father. He's not judging you for everything you've done wrong. He's not itching for an opportunity to punish you. He sees you as his beloved creation. You were made in his image, and no amount of abuse, betrayal, or trauma will take that away.

Of course, I know that many childhood abuse victims don't view "father" as a good image, so if you had a father who used you for his self-gratification, or took out his egotistical rage on you, perhaps the father-image of God isn't safe.

I think sometimes that God must have known this, and that's why Scripture is full of many different names and images for God:

- a mother hen or mother eagle (Matthew 23:37; Luke 13:34; Deuteronomy 32:11-12)
- a tender shepherd (Psalm 95:7; Psalm 100:3; Isaiah 40:11; Psalm 23; Matthew 18:12-14)
- a mother bear (Hosea 13:8)
- a healer (Exodus 15:26; Jeremiah 30:17)
- a potter (Isaiah 64:8; Jeremiah 18:1-9)
- a woman (Luke 15:8-10; Psalm 123:2-3)

- a mother with her baby (Psalm 131:2; Isaiah 49:15; Isaiah 66:13; Hosea 11:3-4)
- a woman in labor (Isaiah 42:14; Deuteronomy 32:18)

If "father" hurts more than it helps, leave that one by the wayside and choose another of the Bible's beautiful images, to help you feel and connect to God's love for you.

My hope is that the stories I share and the thoughts I give you in this chapter will simply serve as a stepping-stone on your road to safety—and a hand of encouragement along the way, to help you know that—

You're not crazy, and you're not alone.

Getting to Safety

The first all-important goal in moving on is *getting safe*: putting some distance between you and your ex, and even between you and all those who have conflicted, unhelpful feelings about your divorce. That might include your ex-spouse's family, your friends, and perhaps even certain people at your church.

For those who went through a life-saving divorce, most godly spouses gave it their all to hold their marriage together. They turned over every stone, followed every bit of advice, forgave and sacrificed over and over. They were harder on themselves than anyone could be.

Yet they *still* get some well-meaning pastors and biblical counselors saying something to the effect of, "Your marriage isn't over until *we* say it's over." Usually the message isn't that direct. But it's clear nevertheless.

People like this withhold their approval and support until they feel convinced that you've tried hard enough—according to *their* standard. And that standard, that goal post, often keeps shifting further and further away, always out of reach. In these situations, they try to cast doubts in your mind about your God-given desire to get yourself and your children to safety. They try to make you doubt your own judgment and wisdom.

That's called spiritual abuse.

To them, you can say, "Sorry, it's not your call. You don't know what goes on behind closed doors. You don't speak for God; and you aren't the mediator between God and man. You have no right to keep me from protecting myself and my children."

Getting to safety is the first step.

Dealing with the Trauma Inflicted During the Marriage

Most divorcees who've been through a life-saving divorce have experienced a lot of stress, confusion, and trauma, and so have their children. They need some peace and calm and stability.

You may think I'm exaggerating when I say *trauma*, but many of the people I interviewed for this book were married for more than twenty years, and they had suffered a great deal, including physical abuse, marital rape, threats, and fear. Many said they'd been diagnosed with a variety of health problems, including post-traumatic stress disorder (PTSD). In fact, rape victims have reported symptoms resembling those of combat veterans: "insomnia, nausea, startle responses, and nightmares, as well as dissociative or numbing symptoms." The "fear of death during the assault" is a common theme.[197]

Many, but not all, told me they had benefited from therapy and treatments such as "prolonged exposure" or EMDR to reduce their symptoms of anxiety disorders, depression, addiction disorders, and chronic pain.[198] (Ask a trained therapist if these are advised for your situation.)

It is not surprising that a family that looks great from the outside is suffering within. People in families with abuse become great actors, excellent at pretending in public that everything is okay. Yet it does affect them physically and emotionally.[199]

PTSD: Post-Traumatic Stress Disorder

Dr. Judith Herman, a professor at Harvard Medical School and an expert on PTSD and trauma, wrote about two World War II military psychiatrists who worked with soldiers with stress-induced combat reactions after the war. They concluded that "200-240 days in combat would suffice to break even the strongest soldier; 'There's no such thing as getting used to combat'..."[200]

---

197 Judith Lewis Herman, ***Trauma and Recovery*** (New York: Basic Books, 1992), 31.
198 A. Valiente-Gómez, A. Moreno-Alcázar, D. Treen, et al., "EMDR beyond PTSD: A Systematic Literature Review," ***Frontiers in Psychology*** 8 (2017): 1668.
199 The landmark book on the ways that trauma affects physical health is Bessel van der Kolk's work, ***The Body Keeps the Score***.
200 Herman, ***Trauma***, 25.

If 240 days in dangerous conditions is enough to give even the strongest soldier PTSD, imagine the family members in a 20-year marriage (7,300 days) who are always walking on eggshells, always nervous that they might set the abuser off, always worried about danger. They are hyper-vigilant, constantly gauging the mood of the abuser.

They live in a state of constant vigilance
for signs of an emotional landmine
that might go off from the slightest vibration.

Those who studied these returning World War II soldiers concluded that "the strongest protection against overwhelming terror"[201] was the relationships between the soldiers and their leader in their small fighting unit. Knowing the power of camaraderie and loyalty to your team, the military tried to keep the soldiers together as much as possible, returning them to their unit after being wounded and going through recovery.

Together, the soldiers were able to talk for hours through their "terror, rage, and grief,"[202] and this made a big difference. Simply retelling their stories to one another, and giving the details of the trauma, helped them find relief from the emotional injuries. After the war, many of these "rap groups" became opportunities to advocate for others and end the stigma of PTSD. They wanted respect and wanted to be treated with dignity,[203] just like life-saving divorce survivors do.

Whether you find a friend who really understands and has walked in your shoes, or whether you connect with kindred spirits in a divorce recovery group, or whether you find a good therapist, this comradeship is important. If you can find one person who understands what you've been through and will stand by you, you're very fortunate. And like the World War II soldiers who found comfort in their leader, many of us find comfort in the Lord:

Even though I walk through the darkest valley,
I will fear no evil,
for you are with me;
your rod and your staff, they comfort me.
—Psalm 23:4 (NIV)

---

201 Ibid.
202 Ibid.
203 Ibid., 27.

Kids Need Help, Too

The same goes for your children. They need a safe place to talk through their hurts, pains, and feelings, too. Many children need therapy or a group designed for children of divorced parents. They need to talk over their grief, anger, fear, and confusion with someone safe: someone who is sensitive to the fact that they had nothing to do with this situation.

In the case of a high-conflict home, they were helpless victims of the terror, unable to stop it, unable to fix their parents, and unable to get away. In some homes, there was a code of silence that protected the badly behaving parent; nothing got talked about. Everything was covered up, dismissed, or lied about. So kids did not get the information they needed to process what they saw.

As we've discussed, children are likely to need some counseling. Researchers say that the vast majority, about 8 in 10 of kids, will end up doing fine in life, having no serious longterm emotional or social problems,[204] but it's good to get them some counseling early. About one in ten kids in *married* families have serious emotional or social problems; and about two in ten kids in *divorced* families do.

Depending on their age and emotional stability when their parents divorced, some children don't have the tools or maturity to interpret the situation. Sometimes they get it wrong. They need a therapist they can talk to, someone who can help them sort through the issues, and who can help children maintain stability as their parents go through their own processing of anger, grief, and despair.

Some parents spiral down into depression; others develop alcohol or drug problems. Some children become their parent's caretaker, feeling they must encourage and prop up their depressed or out-of-control mother or father, which is not good for anyone. (If you see a role reversal happen, where your child is now acting as your parent, get some help for both you and your child; everyone who is hurting deserves support.)

But the bottom line is that most kids are unbelievably resilient after

---

204 Virginia Rutter, "Divorce in Media vs. Divorce in Research," ***Sociology Compass*** 3, no. 4 (2009): 707-720. Note the percentage of children who have serious emotional problems. When taking all research findings into consideration, the estimate is that 20-25% of kids from divorced homes have serious emotional, social, or psychological problems, compared to 10% of kids from married homes, which makes sense, because many have experienced or witnessed long periods of abuse before the divorce.

divorce, as study after study has shown. Getting them counseling is a big help in many cases.

The God who is in his holy dwelling place
is the father of the fatherless and the defender of widows.
God places lonely people in families.
He leads prisoners out of prison into productive lives...
—Psalm 68:5-6a (GW)

Emotions During a Life-Saving Divorce

Alicia's story, below, is a story about accepting reality: "It's over. I gave it my best, but it didn't turn out the way I wanted." Alicia put up with more than 25 years of cheating, abuse, and disrespect from her husband, Estefan. Each time she caught him, she swept it under the carpet and blamed herself—or the other women—but never him.

Why?

Because she had been taught to be a survivor and to deflect and bury painful moments.

Alicia's Story

Growing up, I loved church. At age eight, I begged my parents to take me to kids' Bible and Scripture memory programs. Jesus loved me, and he was my Savior!

I'll never forget when I met my husband, Estefan.

I thought Estefan was different, very smooth-talking. He wasn't from my area. He was from the Midwest. He was older than most of my previous boyfriends. He knew exactly what to say and how to say it. He called me "Beautiful," something I hadn't heard often. He was different, not like the other guys.

I was happy we had law enforcement jobs in common. I was just ending my police work and starting a new career. We had so much in common in other ways, too. And he was handsome. I couldn't figure out why he was divorced. I decided it was his ex-wife. She accused him of being abusive, but I brushed it off. Yes, it must have been her fault, because he was so nice. And besides, I had taken martial arts on the police force as well as domestic violence training. I was trained to deal with abusers. There was no way he would ever consider abusing me.

My friends were getting married, and I felt old. It was time to marry. Estefan said he would be there for me. So we planned to marry a year later. At first, Estefan was happy. Then my dad got ill, and we moved the date up several months because we weren't sure Dad would live long. Looking back, I realize Estefan felt rushed and was blaming me. Nothing verbal, just a sense of emotional disconnection.

Despite this, the wedding was special. My father had been in the hospital up until the day before, yet he walked me down the aisle. Everyone went crazy cheering for my dad.

After the wedding, I wrapped my life around Estefan. I felt he was searching for someone to take care of him. And I just wanted someone who would be nice to me and not too demanding. He was easy-going like that. He got unemployment payments, and all my pay went into providing for us. He won an occasional bodybuilding contest and earned a little money. He allowed me to spend it, no questions asked. In my mind, that was great. I wanted to be there for him because he didn't have family who cared.

Eight months later, we got pregnant. The moment I told Estefan, everything changed.

We needed more income, and I got three more part-time jobs to make sure we could survive as a family of three. I had been an apartment manager, but I was replaced just before our daughter was born. I had my day job, but it was exhausting. I just couldn't take on any more. We had to downsize to a smaller apartment. Estefan got a part-time job at a local gym.

I was happy about his new job until he started hooking up with women he met at the gym. He would bring them to the apartment when I wasn't home. He claimed they were his workout partners. He would ride his bike to the gym because we had only one car, and he wouldn't come home all day.

At one point he suggested having a "girlfriend" move in. "No way," I thought, and I confronted her. How could she cheat with a married man who had a baby on the way? I threatened her, and she went away.

(Let me stop here in the story. You wonder why I was angry at her and not him. All I can say is that I excused him. I thought he was swept off his feet by a seductive woman and the blame was all hers. I didn't hold him responsible. I minimized his bad behavior.)

He was unfaithful with another woman six months later. He left us and moved in with her.

I should have walked away, but I didn't. I got mixed messages. He would come back to our apartment and say, "I miss you." He kept reaching out to me. His new girlfriend would ask why I was calling him, not realizing he was calling me first. At the time, I didn't realize he was playing both of us.

One day, I went to their apartment and confronted her. I grabbed her by the hair and threw her over the hood of her car. She looked at me and said, "Why are you so mad at me when your husband is the one who made the commitment to you?"

That was a turning point for me. I stopped going after the women, and I went after him in anger over the betrayals. Now he turned physically mean. I was pregnant again, but he pushed me, slamming me up against the wall. He got violent when I spoke out about the cheating. The more I accused him, the more violent he got.

This went on for 25 years—cheating and abuse—probably twenty affairs, eight women I knew by name. He would hit me in the face and push me into the wall. He raped me in front of our children.

I stayed because I thought that's what good Christian wives did. I thought I could help him. I loved him, and I thought if I prayed enough, God would turn him around.

Estefan stopped bringing home a paycheck. He was working, but I never saw another dime. He put it in his own account. I had to support the entire family. I would demand that he pay for certain things, such as a car, but I had no say about anything, not even the type of car.

The financial strain was too much on me. I moved our family into my parents' home. Estefan continued cheating, and he continued his greed—keeping his paycheck for himself. I was afraid to talk back. Speaking up got me slammed against the wall.

My dad was too ill to protect me or himself. My mother pretended not to see. Estefan demanded my elderly parents put him on the title to their home, take out a $40,000 home equity loan, and give him the cash, or he would get revenge. They did what he wanted.

I was almost ready to end the relationship, but as a last-ditch effort, I had a third child. I thought it would make him more committed to me. Instead, he accused me of cheating on him. He turned everything on me, even though I had always been a faithful wife.

Now he had to work full-time and stop bodybuilding. He was resentful. After the baby came, I went back to work again. Estefan had used up the $40,000. I never saw any of it. We found a babysitter for the kids, one of my coworkers from years before. Estefan would drop off the kids, and soon he started cheating with the babysitter. To my horror, my oldest child informed me about the affair. Another blow-up.

That was the last straw.

I realized my love had not changed him. He was a serial cheater, a financial abuser, and a wife batterer. There was no reason to expect his attitude and actions to change.

At a high school reunion, an old classmate said, "I think you're wonderful. You still love to have fun, and you love to laugh." He didn't see me as old or ugly or worn out. He saw me as God saw me. Those two sentences were like streams of water in a desert.

I called out to God: "If you get me out of this alive, I will reach out to other women in the same situation."

I joined a church support group for single mothers. I had to sneak out at night to attend the group.

After a lot of prayer and support from the women, I got the courage to file for divorce. I braced myself for Estefan's violent response. All my friends in church support group were praying for me. I told the police officer couple who lived next door what I was about to do. I had my emergency backpack and plan ready to go. I knew that leaving violent men was dangerous. My police background taught me that many men kill their estranged wives. I was terrified. Fortunately, it went okay.

My ex-husband continued to try to manipulate me, but in time I

> *got better at avoiding his traps. It's been several years now. It's still tough financially, but the freedom from constant fear and anxiety are worth it—to me and my children. We're so much happier. The kids are glad I left. I'm grateful to God for giving me the strength and courage.*
>
> *I had finally come to the realization that God won't force Estefan to follow him. He gives people a choice. Estefan chose to follow his own way. I didn't fail God. Estefan did.*

In Alicia's story, she's married, but her husband is not—at least, he's not *acting* married. She tenaciously hangs onto her marriage, turning herself inside out to make a difference, but Estefan doesn't invest much into the marriage. He doesn't care how destructive his behavior is to her and the children.

Adulterers and abusers like Estefan rarely reform. He used Alicia. He didn't want the responsibilities of a loving marriage, but he wanted a warm bed and a personal maid and cook—someone who kept the home clean and the kids fed while he ran around. Experienced counselors don't offer much hope that someone who has cheated multiple times and who turns to abuse in this way will ever change.

Acceptance: Knowing When It's Over

Each person comes to accept reality at their own time and place. Sometimes you don't have a choice. You were left in the dust, and your ex-spouse is off with a new love, having a good time. The classic prayer (attributed to Reinhold Niebuhr) is a help in times like this:

"God, grant me the serenity to accept the things I cannot change,
Courage to change the things I can,
And wisdom to know the difference."[205]

We cannot change the other person. We can only change ourselves and our attitudes. Some people figure out the difference right away, and others take years to figure this out.

---

205 There are many versions of this prayer. It is attributed to Niebuhr in ***2012 Bartlett's Quotations: 18th Edition*** (New York: Little Brown and Company, 2012), iv-v.

Mixed Feelings: What if I Still Love Him/Her?

While some divorcees never look back when they recognize a final betrayal, many have mixed feelings: "I still love this person."

I see this all the time. People almost feel guilty about feeling love toward their ex. But it's true, you can love and care about that person. A lot of people do. It's perfectly okay to feel that way. It's also okay to remember the good times.

It's not necessary to hate a person in order to divorce them.

You're just saying that their betrayal, abuse, sexual immorality, or neglect has broken the marriage.

But when your feelings of love draw you back into a hurtful relationship over and over, despite their destructive behavior, you may have a "trauma bond" or "betrayal bond" to your ex-spouse, rather than love.

This strong but misplaced loyalty makes it difficult—sometimes impossible—to leave, even when you know your spouse is using you and will hurt you again. Some experts say it is caused by going through the Abuse Cycle (Chapter 4, abuse—honeymoon—tension) repeatedly until a powerful emotional bond is formed.

Are You the Leaver, or Were You Left Behind?

Spouses who get left by their partners suffer a big blow. They may have thought their marriage was okay, and then out of the blue their spouse leaves or is discovered to be living a secret life. Or they may have watched the infidelity over time.

The rejected spouse not only feels betrayed, they also have the sense of being a failure. They may feel angry, vengeful, and unworthy of being loved. But they, too, bounce back within two or three years, on average.

One of the leading researchers on divorce, Mavis Hetherington, writes,

"In the early period, the 'left' spouses were the most unhappy and resentful, but by the end of the second year, there were few differences between those left and the 'leavers'... [In] the second year there was an upsurge in emotional wellbeing as people began to adapt to their new life situation."[206]

---

206 Hetherington and Kelly, ***For Better***, 50-51.

If you filed for divorce, you had already concluded the betrayals were a feature, not a bug—you had given up trying to change your spouse or the dynamic between you two. In other words, this is who your spouse is. Their behavior has been consistent: a pattern of chronic abuse, unfaithfulness, or neglect, alternating with apologies and attentiveness.

Many spouses have lost any reasonable hope that their partner will change on their own, short of a personality transplant. They are ready to call it what it is: a one-sided marriage that is, in reality, no marriage at all.

The spouse who sees the truth and initiates the divorce heals faster.

But that is easier said than done. Most of my interviews were with people who were betrayed for decades, yet stayed.

Sandra's story gives us a bit of insight on the difficulties of accepting reality. As a devout Christian, she refused to give up hope, believing she had to wait and pray for her husband to return.

Sandra's Story

I met him right after high school. We were friends for about six months. He was an active Christian, and he brought me to church. I became a Christian, too. We worked in church ministry together. He was the man of my dreams. I didn't see any red flags until after the wedding. We were married almost ten years, and he took off with another woman. His father had left his mother, and it was heartbreaking to him as a child. Now he was doing it to me and his own kids.

He cut me out of his life. There was no communication. It was awful. I gained a lot of weight. I struggled with depression. Then he filed for divorce. I felt like a failure. I couldn't accept he was gone for good. I waited and prayed for three years, hoping he would come back.

It hit me when I saw him with another woman. Then it really clicked. It took me visually seeing them together to realize he was never coming back. I just knew: God made it clear.

As a Christian, I prayed for a miracle. I know God can change people. But seeing my ex-husband being mean to me and hearing him admit that his disdain for me was the "true him" was eye-opening. Did I really want that in my life?

In that single moment, when Sandra saw her ex-husband with another woman, she finally faced the betrayal that made her accept reality. When he said his contempt was genuine, the blindfold fell off.

Sandra had seen the red flags but was powerless to stop her spouse's exit.

Alicia saw the red flags but minimized and ignored them.

At one point, both women blamed themselves for not holding their marriage together. But in the end, their husbands had made their own choices, and they had to figure it out.

Seeing the truth is a vital step to healing. Truth is very tough to accept. It hurts so much. It cuts deep in the soul, especially if you got the message that God *always* answers your righteous prayers the way you want. It's not that easy.

As the Bible says, "The truth will set you free." But it sure hurts first. When you can admit the truth, you can start to deal with it. Or as another wise person said—

"Betrayal leads to revelation."[207]
—Michael Alvarez, MFT

Betrayal is a gift to us. It wakes us up! In other words, we can learn a vital lesson from the betrayals. Betrayal reveals character. When you are betrayed, you can learn to say, "Ah, now I see who this person really is. The mask is off, and now I see the real person, rather than what I wanted them to be." Now you know.

The next step is yours, not theirs.

Three Ways We Deal with Betrayal: Denial, Self-Blame, or Revelation

Most people who are committed to a relationship more than their partner is experience denial, anger, bargaining, hopefulness, and despair. Many cling to hope that something will change miraculously. Somehow their spouse will finally appreciate their love and generosity.

And of course, some people do set boundaries, speak up for what they want, hold their position, and demand good behavior. And some

---

207 Personal conversation.

self-centered spouses do have a pang of conscience and start to invest more into the marriage when they see what they might lose. I've seen this happen in my groups as women get stronger.

But if you're reading this chapter, you probably didn't get that happy ending.

This section is for those who've hoped and prayed, and who finally need to accept the truth.

Here are three ways we deal with betrayal.

1. ***Denial and excuses.*** (We don't want to see it. We gaslight ourselves.)
    - "He says the affair is over, and it will never happen again. This time he's truly repentant."
    - "He was nice to me. I know he would care about me all the time if I pleased him."
    - "I will single-handedly save my marriage by praying more, even if she continually acts like she's not married."
    - "It's not him. It's that *other woman*."
    - "She wouldn't cheat on me. We're in love, and I trust her."

    [He] started cheating, pretty much right out of the gate. I say I had no idea, but I did sort of suspect it. [The] minute it would enter my mind I thought, oh, no, he would not do that to me. You know, because we project ourselves and our values and things like that onto other people sometimes... I ended up getting an STD... I still didn't believe he cheated on me. A few years later, when I got another STD, he accused me and asked, "Are you cheating on me?"

2. ***Self-blame.*** (We see the betrayal, but we think we can fix it.)
    - "If we just have more sex, he won't molest children or watch porn."
    - "My love will fill the empty place in his heart. He just needs someone who believes in him."
    - "I can win her back."
    - "I can save my marriage if I dress better, lose weight, and never mention his affairs or abuse."

3. ***Revelation.*** (We see the betrayal, and we understand we cannot change another person.)
    - "He has cheated many times. I can't fix him."

- "Whenever I catch him lying and get angry, he brings me flowers. But I don't see any long-term change in him."
- "Her bad behavior is not a one-time mistake. It is a feature, not a bug."
- "He apologizes because he got caught, not because he betrayed me."
- "He has an alcohol problem. I didn't start him drinking. I can't stop his drinking. Only he can make changes, which so far he refuses to invest enough time and effort to do."
- "No reasonable person would trust her again. I see no evidence of change."
- "He blames me (and others) for his bad behavior. He takes no responsibility. I don't think he can earn my trust again."
- "Despite her promises, her actions don't match her words."

The New Normal: Questions for Journaling or Discussion

The first six months after a divorce are the worst. It's tough to accept reality. Many spouses swing from numbness to anger to despair. Some people can hardly function; getting out of bed and off to work is tough. They wonder if they will ever be happy again. Caring for children feels robotic and mechanical. Many parents don't have anything to give emotionally to those little faces looking up at them.

It's tough to survive each day.
If you struggle with major depression, it is even tougher.

But there is a bit of good news: About 4 in 10 people who have a history of major depressive disorder do not have a subsequent depressive episode after the divorce.[208] In a study of marriages that already had been "very unhappy" for twelve years or more, researchers said, "Our results show that… remaining unhappily married rather than divorcing is never beneficial on average to the psychological wellbeing or overall

208 David Sbarra, "Divorce and Health: Current Trends and Future Directions," ***Psychosomatic Medicine*** 77, no. 3 (March 2015): 227-236.

health of the individuals."[209]

You likely did the smart thing to get out.

With God's help, the shattered pieces will come back together in time, and you will start feeling emotionally like you used to. One year later, most people feel a bit better. You slowly adjust to the new normal. You can smile. You take over the tasks your ex used to do: bill paying, taking out the trash, making basic repairs, cooking meals, working, planning, caring for the kids.

In most cases it takes about two to three years for a divorced person to feel they've put it behind them and moved on in life. Some people take longer. That's okay, too. Your mileage may vary based on the length of your marriage and the amount of damage.

[God] gives strength to the weary and increases the power of the weak.
—Isaiah 40:29 (NIV)

In a journal, write some of your thoughts:

1. Why is it so tough accepting that my marriage is over?
2. What was the turning point for me that forced me to acknowledge the truth?
3. What has been the most painful adjustment so far? Did I see it coming?
4. What has God been teaching me during this time? Or has he seemed silent to me? (Explain.)
5. What are my next steps toward healing?

Anger, Grief, Telling Your Story, and Forgiveness

Remember Sandra's story? The man who had introduced her to Christ, brought her to church, and had done ministry with her side by side, had left her and the children for another woman. Sandra prayed and

---

209 Daniel Hawkins and Alan Booth, "Unhappily Ever After: Effects of Long-Term, Low-Quality Marriages on Wellbeing," ***Social Forces*** 84, no. 1 (September 2005): 464. The authors of this study mention an earlier study (Waite et al., 2002) that got a lot of attention from religious organizations. That study used only one item to determine marital quality, and it said that two thirds of unhappily married couples who stayed married for 5 more years were happier. The Hawkins and Booth study was different. In addition to being much more thorough, it specifically focused on people who had been married (very unhappily) for more than 12 years; it used several items to measure marital quality, and it determined that those who divorced from these chronically long-term at-risk marriages were significantly happier after divorce than they had been before.

waited three years for him to come back, but he never showed any sign of wanting to reconcile. Let's continue with her story.

> *I felt like a failure. I was a horrible mom. My depression was bad; I nearly committed suicide. I had no job, so I lost my children to my husband in court. I was couch-surfing at friends' houses. It took me a long time to get stable…*
>
> *I beat myself up. I told myself: "You should have tried harder. The kids don't need you. You should have been nicer to the kids. You're ugly; you're fat. You're not supportive. You'll never get out of this."*
>
> *The enemy (Satan) wants to tell you how horrible you are. That you are no good.*

But God seemed to have another message for Sandra: Find community and loving, safe people. She was able to share her story and get support.

> *"You need to get well," God seemed to say. "How can you be there for your kids if you can't be there for yourself?"*
>
> *I needed my church family. That's where my husband and I had served together. The church was such a big support… They bought groceries for me. I moved in with one woman and lived in her back house and rented from her. I lived there two years.*
>
> *She mentored me, counseled me, and prayed with me. The enemy tells you it's all your fault. I would tell myself I wasn't pretty enough. My landlady told me to read the psalms and put my own name in. For example, "Sandra is perfectly and wonderfully made," from Psalm 139:14.*

At one point, Sandra was in despair and planned to die by suicide:

> *My ex tried to tear apart my relationship with my kids. It seemed as though he had succeeded. My kids were disgusted with me.*
>
> *I was at friend's house, feeling suicidal. "I'm done. The kids don't want me or need me."*
>
> *I decided to drive off a cliff. It was after midnight. As I got close, at about 1:00 AM, I pulled over to the side of the road. My mobile phone rang. My pastor was calling. "Hey Sandra, what's going on? It's as if I can hear your voice in a dream. Your ex-husband is not your savior. Jesus is your Savior. Your divorce story will be used for God's glory someday."*

I didn't get it at the time, but I do now.

I turned around and drove back to the house. When I got home, I got on my knees and said to God, "Here I am. Use me."

Sandra had friends who listened to her and cared about her. In her own time, she determined that she was in bondage to rage, and it wasn't healthy. She forgave her ex-husband, ended her own vicious self-condemnation, and used her story to bring comfort to others.

> *I forgave my husband, and I was free. I stopped holding onto that stuff inside myself—the stuff that brought up more rage and that wasn't healthy. Knowing true forgiveness and forgiving those who hurt you is the most freeing thing to do! You automatically feel a release of the ugliness of the sin, the sin that kept you in bondage! God's peace and grace just comes over you like a flood. And for myself, I can say that I was reminded that I'm a sinner, too. Forgiving him allowed me to forgive myself.*
>
> *God has used me and my story. Now I serve in children's ministry and women's ministry at my church.*
>
> *Today I have a good job, and my kids turned out great. It's unbelievable. Today they are both adults and have good jobs. I'm proud of them, and we are emotionally close even though their dad had primary custody.*

One of the steps to recover from trauma is telling your story and mourning the losses. Grief over the trauma is very important and should not be shortchanged. Many Christians want victims to forgive right away, and that is usually not helpful.

Forgiveness is a process, and it cannot be rushed or forced.

It also is about more than just the perpetrator. Notice how Sandra not only forgave her ex-husband for his betrayals, but she also forgave herself for her faults. She chose not to take revenge on her ex-husband. She decided not to waste her time, energy, or money looking for ways to pay him back for the pain he caused. Instead, today, she is putting her efforts into friendships, finding healing, giving back through service and church ministries, and maintaining good relationships with her children.

"How Did I Get into This Relationship?" (Forgiving Yourself)

Part of the process is forgiving yourself. And one of the things we ask ourselves is: How did I get into this relationship? Why didn't I see the red flags? How could I have fallen for the lies?

To be honest, sometimes there's no way we could have identified a problem in advance. Some people don't reveal their dangerous behaviors at first, and there's no way we could have foreseen it.

But there's still a big question in our mind: If I ever want to remarry, how can I make sure I never get into a bad marriage again?

Let's look at some traits that make us more vulnerable. In any normal circumstance, around people who reciprocate, these traits are lovely. (You definitely want loving friends who see you in a positive light.) But abusers take advantage of these same kind, hopeful, and generous traits.

- *Naïveté* — Our own belief that all Christians (or everyone at our college or town or ethnic group or denomination) are good people. We may not notice red flags, or we downplay them. Sometimes this assumption comes from being raised in a loving family where everyone was giving and reliable and supportive, and there was no reason to set boundaries, so the children never learned to say no to someone's bad behavior. They rarely saw it in their home.

  Sweetness is a lovely trait, and it is not something we need to abandon, but it does make people vulnerable. The Bible's advice for us is to be as "wise as serpents and innocent as doves" (Matthew 10:16), which means that we are to discern: Is this person's behavior trustworthy, or not?

  We can keep our sweetness and good assumptions, using them in trusted relationships, and at the same time intentionally hold back that trust from someone who doesn't show integrity, reliability, or support.

- *Lies/manipulation by abuser* — We are deceived by the cleverness of the abuser. There might be red flags, but the abuser explains them away. Or there may be no warning at all.
- *Projection* — We might be mature and trustworthy, and we project our own traits (our "reasonableness" and "reliability") onto our spouse. We assume they will feel a pang of conscience when they do wrong and will stop. We expect them to sincerely say they

want to change, and that they will then be successful at making their actions fit their words. We think they'll improve once we're married. When they don't, sometimes we don't face reality. We just double down and act more giving and loving, believing that they will eventually reciprocate. Most of the time, once it is a pattern, they don't.

- *Delusions when dating* — We may believe our partner is (or will become) faithful, loving, and mature, despite signs of the opposite. We fall in love with an idea, not the real person. For example, sometimes we identify lies, but we tell ourselves our partner is "honest, except for these slips." Or they are "faithful, except he had a woman sit on his lap last month," or "She's faithful, but I worry she'll hook up with someone if I don't go places with her."
- *Delusions about God* — We might believe that God will miraculously fix all troubled marriages if we are godly enough.
- *Over-confidence* — We might be so optimistic and hopeful we are sure we can overcome any challenge, even serious marriage-threatening problems that are highly resistant to change.
- *Lack of information* — About one in ten people in the U.S. have serious psychological problems or other issues that make it difficult, perhaps impossible, for them to contribute to a good, safe, loving, respectful marriage. This is not to say they are unworthy of love, because all human beings have value. But having value is not the same as being a good candidate for a marriage partner.
- *Neediness* — We might be at a low spot in our life, so needy, down, and desperate that we will take anyone who will put a roof over our head. There's nothing wrong with having needs (in fact, we should be honest about putting our needs for love, affection, sex, closeness, financial support, etc., on the table when we start dating again).

But being desperate makes us too vulnerable to predators. If you find yourself thinking things like, "I'll never find someone else," "Beggars can't be choosers," "I can't make it on my own," or "I've got to take what I can get," you may be driven by desperation, and it's a good time to slow down and think: If I wasn't desperate, would I be getting involved with this person?

Many of us who have come out of dangerous marriages beat ourselves up for being "too trusting." Maybe we call ourselves names, saying *I'm so stupid* or *I'm such an idiot.*

These names don't apply to a beloved child of God, like you are.

And the truth is, being trusting is a *good, God-given* trait—a very important and necessary quality for building a loving relationship.

The problem wasn't that you trusted—
it was that your spouse took advantage of that trust.

You can grow in discernment and courage (learning to recognize untrustworthy behavior, and learning to stand up for yourself, take a stand, and distance yourself from untrustworthy people) while still holding on to your trusting nature. You'll need it!

It's time to forgive yourself for being human, for being trusting and kind, and for being hopeful and optimistic. It's okay. In fact, it's very good that you have those God-given qualities. When you bring those qualities into a relationship with a person who is safe and trustworthy, they will help your relationship to flourish!

Married to a Child Molester—Brittany's Story

I fell in love with Joshua, a guy I met at in the singles group in my church, and we dated for nearly two years. Just before we got married, he told me he used to be attracted to children sexually, but that was all in the past. He admitted to fondling kids when he was a volunteer in the junior high ministry in the church, but he claimed that was long ago.

The pastor who was doing our pre-marital counseling was a trained counselor and very skilled at getting us to communicate better. The pastor believed Josh's claim and was in favor of us marrying. He felt my love and stability would be good for Josh. He even performed the wedding. I was just so naïve and optimistic, I trusted them both. (Since then I learned that pedophilia never goes away, and every professional counselor knows that. I was betrayed by my counselor, too.)

A few years went by, and Josh told me he needed to talk with me. He confessed he had been molesting kids. He was sorry and was seeking help with a new counselor. I was shocked and horrified, and embarrassed. We had just started trying to get pregnant. We were very active in our Sunday school class, on the hospitality committee, and now my husband admits he's a child molester. I wanted to believe God could heal anyone, and I wanted to be a loving and supportive wife. I figured if he had admitted it to me, he was willing to get help and could be "cured."

I prayed and wrote in my journal daily and constantly looked for ways to be a better wife. I agonized every time I raised my voice or criticized my husband. I decided to be the best Christian wife in the world. I tried to be a loving, supportive spouse. I felt incredibly guilty for mentioning even the slightest hint of frustration with his lies or selfish behavior. I begged God's forgiveness every time I criticized my husband. I determined to be nicer, sweeter, and more understanding. I felt if I were the perfect wife, I could keep him from being attracted to children.

Josh went into therapy with a Christian counselor, and he started attending Sexaholics Anonymous every week. For several years I hoped and believed that my husband was okay. And I was watchful, on high alert all the time. I was thinking I could protect my kids, my neighborhood kids, and the kids at church. And besides, I was pregnant again. It was hard to imagine being a single mother raising small children alone. I prayed and fasted and clung to the hope that God would save my marriage. I was so stressed out trying to be a good wife, I maximized my faults and minimized his. I took all the blame without thinking about why I should.

Years passed. I trusted Josh, even though he stopped seeing his therapist. I wanted to believe it was all okay. In all those years, I never caught him in the act. I discovered the truth by accident. I'll never forget the day I found out Josh had fondled our thirteen-year-old babysitter. I was shocked and numb, and I told Josh to leave. Josh quickly found another counselor, and thankfully, that new counselor insisted he report himself to law enforcement using the phone in his office. He had no choice.

I filed for divorce even though I didn't think I had the strength to go through with it. I didn't think I could make it on my own.

Even though my parents were in favor of the divorce, my confidence was low. I had tried to walk away before, but I always went back to him. I asked my mother to help me find a Christian counselor who would help me leave. She found one. He listened to my story and told me I had tried everything. I was free to go.

Six months later, I was so lonely and exhausted trying to handle the children alone, I started to have second thoughts. I asked my pastor if I should invite my husband back. He asked if it was due to my loneliness or due to a complete character change in my husband. I admitted I had not seen any real change in my husband. My pastor counseled me not to reconcile.

From that point on, and almost every year for the next eight years, Josh tried to get joint custody of our children through the courts. Josh's mother was wealthy, and she paid for his lawyers. He didn't pay a dime. I hated Josh, and I secretly hoped he would die in a car crash. I imagined the brakes going out on a winding mountain road at night.

I was terrified he would get custody. He looked so dignified and professional when he went to court. He lied so smoothly, I was sure he would convince the judge. I was scared he would succeed.

The judge required Josh to attend a sex offender treatment program, but that did not stop Josh's constant barrage of legal attacks. Nearly every year, Josh dragged me into court to get joint custody. He already had monitored visitation every week, but he wanted to spend time with our children alone overnight. Every time we went to court, it cost me thousands of dollars to fight back.

To make matters worse, Josh was spiteful and skipped a lot of child support payments. My total legal expenses were already $30,000, and Josh owed me nearly $40,000 in back support. The children and I had so little money, I often had to decide between buying a gallon of gas and a gallon of milk.

I hid my fury from the children. I didn't want the kids to know their father was a child molester, so I didn't badmouth him to the kids. And I didn't tell the kids he wasn't paying child support. I felt those issues were too heavy to be dumped on children. But I was angry and bitter at Josh. I wanted him out of our lives forever.

But no, Josh kept attacking and lying.

Josh found yet another therapist, one who testified that Josh was fine and no longer a threat. Josh demanded that the court allow him a forensic evaluation so he could prove himself a fit parent.

I was terrified. I was praying constantly that the Lord (and the judge) would protect my children. Worry and anxiety filled my mind. I couldn't sleep. I could barely focus on my job. My parents, Bible study group, my divorce recovery group, a coworker, and friends prayed for us. But I felt helpless and frightened. My nerves were shattered.

The forensic psychologist interviewed many people, including Josh, myself, the kids, his new therapist, past counselors and pastors, our family members and friends, and the sex offender program staff. The report was dozens of pages long, and it said no, Josh should not have joint custody of the children. It also said Josh had admitted to having fifty victims. And it revealed that Josh's mother had been making up outlandish lies about me for years.

I felt vindicated, but believe it or not, Josh dragged me into court again. All his legal fees were paid by his mother, so he didn't care. She never came to court. Didn't she realize her son lost every time? I hated her, and I hated Josh. In my mind, they were an all-powerful, evil empire.

Finally, in the tenth year, the judge put an end to it. "I don't want to see you back here, Josh. And you will pay your back child support from the sale of the house."

For the first time in years, I could breathe. I had survived the storm.

Once we felt safe from the barrage of legal and financial attacks, I was in a place to forgive.

The kids were now over 18, and they finally had been told the story and were able to ask questions. They said they were glad I had protected them and had divorced their father. They said they couldn't imagine being brought up in the same home with their dad. They loved their dad and cared about him, but they knew how selfish he was.

To me, forgiveness means I let go of my hatred, but I never let go of my commitment to protect my children and myself. I don't wish ill on my ex-husband. He has never confessed to his behavior to his

> *pastor. He has never admitted it to his own children. But I decided I didn't want to destroy him. I no longer hoped he and his mother would die. I don't hate him anymore. I forgive him, but I will never trust him. No one should.*

Brittany had a lot of support: parents who lived nearby, a good Bible study, a divorce recovery group, and a couple of friends who had survived divorce and had rebuilt their live many years before. She was able to tell her story and give weekly updates in her divorce recovery group. She benefitted from hearing other people's stories, working through the anger and tears, and grieving and mourning with one another.

As they went around the room and shared their experiences of new betrayals, failures, and triumphs, she found support and understanding. They prayed for each other and supported each other practically. They gave hope and faith and comfort to each other. They cheered the victories, and they cried together about the setbacks.

It took years before Brittany found other ex-wives of child molesters online and started talking with them through a secret online forum. She benefitted from their stories and insights. They shed light on aspects of her own experience that she'd never recognized.

What Forgiveness Is Not

In Brittany's healthy community, forgiveness really meant something. That word was not blithely thrown around. It didn't come from being pressured by others to forgive.

Forgiveness was a decision that she made when *she* felt it was right.

It didn't mean:

- forgetting what Josh had done
- trusting Josh again
- pretending it never happened
- staying silent and not telling her story (it *was* her story, after all, and she could tell it)
- being friends or reconciling with Josh
- lying for him to Child Protective Services

In Brittany's case, it meant releasing the bitterness and desire for revenge, even though her ex-husband never apologized and shows no signs of having changed.

Jesus calls his followers to forgive. And that teaching is explosive. So it's important to understand what it really means—and what it doesn't mean.

Just like any source of power, the concept of forgiveness can be used in wrong ways, to do damage instead of to bring life and freedom. Secular authors, people of other faith traditions, and Christians alike sometimes push back on this teaching of Jesus, expressing concern that forgiveness lets abusers off the hook, and that it's easy to cow a devout person into granting forgiveness prematurely.

They're right.

Forced forgiveness isn't true forgiveness, and it hurts people.

Forgiveness for Trauma Is on Your Timetable, No-One Else's

Forgiving an abuser isn't easy. It is not on par with forgiving someone who accidentally rear-ended your car or shattered your grandmother's antique wedding crystal. In the case of long-term, systematic abuse during a marriage, regardless of the abuser's intentions, it takes a long time to process all the pain.

That's because it is *not* a series of "accidents." There is a complex pattern of manipulation and betrayal—from someone who ought to have loved you—that goes with the injury and makes the injury exponentially worse.

In many interviews, I heard stories of Christian friends applying coercion to make the abuse victim forgive on the spot—often in the form of threats or messages saying God won't forgive you if you don't forgive (implying that your forgiveness must be on their timetable).

But let's look at the Bible. It's interesting to notice that we have no evidence that Jesus forgave those who plotted to kill him, attempted to trap and trick him, told lies about him, and smeared his character, in real time.

There are no stories of Jesus forgiving his attackers until the very end of his life.
During his life and ministry, he called his enemies vipers, whitewashed tombs, and hypocrites.

These "forgive and forget" messages keep the vulnerable spouse confused and isolated. The victim is told to stay silent, not to tell their story. If they do tell it, they are accused of not "letting it go." So the healing process is shortchanged.

They need to talk, to be believed, to identify the abuse and the abuser, and to get support in the form of empathy and outrage, as well as comfort and care. When a person is forced to "forgive and forget," they get the message that the damage done to them is minor, that they are over-reacting and whiney, or that they don't have the right to speak up or ask for restitution or get to safety.

The victim of abuse who isn't believed or taken seriously may give up trying. They resign themselves to being trapped with the abuser. If it is not a safe and loving marriage, the abuse is swept under the carpet. The victim is voiceless and may feel they have no choice but to obey the abuser. No wonder depression and suicidal thoughts are pervasive in these situations.

You can forgive and still tell your story.

Many people who have endured significant neglect, abuse, or betrayal are silenced and accused of gossip or slander. They wonder, "Am I sinning against my ex-spouse by telling my story (which makes my ex look bad)?"

The answer is no. Your story doesn't make them look bad: *Their own sinful behavior* is what makes them look bad. It is not a sin to tell your story, to identify the abuse and the abuser, to ask for empathy, to want support, and to put responsibility where it belongs. If you are telling the truth, you are not slandering.

Slander is a legal term:
Oral defamation,
in which someone tells one or more persons an ***untruth***—
which they know is ***untrue***—*about another,*
which will harm the reputation of the person defamed.[210]

210 Definition for slander based on "Slander," ***www.USLegal.com***, accessed 11/3/19, https://definitions.uslegal.com/s/slander/.

"Remember, truth is an absolute defense to libel and slander."[211]

To slander someone, you have to meet three criteria. You have to be (1) telling an untruth, (2) which you know is not true (or should have known wasn't true), and (3) passing it off as truth with the intent of harming the other person. In other words, if your story is true, it is not slander.

Truth is the best defense against slander.

Forgiveness Is Complex because Abuse, Betrayal, and Neglect Are Complex

For example: Let's say your spouse slaps you. If you were confident it was accidental—perhaps he was swatting a fly and missed—that would be easy to handle. But in the case of abuse, there is a tangle of actions, behaviors, words, and attitudes. A slap is more than a slap.

There's a build-up of tension: a threatening glance, word, or gesture; a demand; unspoken expectations of certain conduct; a promise of punishment. The atmosphere is dangerous. You feel anxiety building.

After the slap, the blame is put on you. You are told it was just an accident, or it wasn't as bad as you said, or you deserved it. It didn't leave a mark. You're over-reacting and being hysterical. Later your spouse apologizes and promises better behavior, but within days, the actions don't match the words.

Maybe it's not a slap this time, but the pattern of built-up tension repeats.

That's why forgiveness requires untangling your story and unwinding all the injuries that accompanied the slap.

It may have been one slap, but there were ten other injuries that went with it.

Forgiveness doesn't necessarily mean dropping charges against the batterer, or ending divorce proceedings, or foregoing a restraining order. You can forgive *and* keep your boundaries up: even removing this person from your life by going "no contact," meaning you have no interaction with the other person, unless required by the court on certain topics.

---

211 "Libel vs. Slander: Different Types of Defamation," ***Nolo Press***, retrieved 11/3/19, https://www.nolo.com/legal-encyclopedia/libel-vs-slander-different-types-defamation.html.

No one should tell that you must forgive on their timeline. That's an indication they don't really understand their God-given duty to protect the vulnerable. Often survivors are given the impression their church doesn't think they were seriously injured or have a legitimate grievance. And even if they do, it they should be able to "get over it" or "snap out of it."

My interviews include many stories of people who were pressured by their pastor or biblical counselors to forgive. But how is that really forgiveness? Can you really forgive long before you've identified the extent of the offense? It needs to come from the heart when *you* decide to do it.

Those who encourage you to smooth things over too quickly, before an inventory of the damage, hurt, and pain has been done, are dishonoring the suffering you experienced. They are sweeping the sin under the carpet and not addressing it. Long-term abuse and betrayal must be fully explored, the anger expressed, and the losses mourned by you and the community.

Forgiveness as Part of Trauma Recovery

Forgiveness starts by retelling your story, recounting the offenses and/or wounds, and acknowledging the damage that the person caused: the broken trust, the physical, emotional, sexual, and financial injuries. Many times, the victim needs to identify each part of the trauma and speak to other survivors about the horror of what was done to them. It requires righteous indignation, rage, and contempt for the evil.

And if we're honest, forgiveness is not a one-time event. As time passes, new memories of betrayals come up in different forms. Those injuries too must be acknowledged, grieved, and denounced as evil.

In some cases, the perpetrator can be required to make restitution. Sometimes not. God knows your heart. He knows your motives. But if that anger is eating you up and sucking life out of you, affecting all your good relationships, it may be best to release it. Forgiveness is for *us*, not for the offender. Forgiveness sets us free.

Forgiveness is not...	Forgiveness is...
Forgiveness is **not** letting the offender off scot-free.	Forgiveness is holding the offender responsible, including requiring reparations and accepting the legal consequences of their actions. Forgiveness wants repentance and compensation, if possible, not revenge.
Forgiveness is **not** saying the abuse, cheating, sexual immorality, and addictions are okay.	Forgiveness is saying that the abuse, cheating, and betrayals are wrong and destructive, and there are consequences for the offender, such as the loss of trust and often the loss of the marriage.
Forgiveness is **not** acting as if it never happened.	Forgiveness is saying it happened, and it shouldn't happen again.
Forgiveness is **not** refusing to look at the offense. It is **not** sweeping the injury under the carpet or refusing to see the damage done.[212]	Forgiveness is looking at the full damage and expressing the horror and rage. It is to name the injuries and express your anger/sadness/grief aloud. It is speaking about the unspeakable.
Forgiveness is **not** saying "forgive and forget."	Forgiveness does not require forgetting. Forgiveness doesn't erase the offender's guilt or wipe out the consequences for the offender. Even if you have forgiven a person, you can still divorce them. Forgiveness doesn't give them a clean slate or a fresh start to hurt you all over again.

---

212 Top author on trauma and recovery, Dr. Judith Herman of Harvard, says, "The ordinary response to atrocities is to banish them from consciousness. Certain violations of the social compact are too terrible to utter aloud: this is the meaning of the word 'unspeakable.'" She goes on to write, "Remembering and telling the truth about terrible events are prerequisites both for the restoration of the social order and for the healing of individual victims." Herman, ***Trauma***, 1.

Forgiveness is **not** a one-time event.	Forgiveness is a long process. As you tell your story and think about the past, you will uncover some pain or hurt you hadn't seen before. You may have to forgive various parts of the abuse/betrayal.
Forgiveness is **not** becoming friends again, trusting again, or reconciling again. It does not require you to trust this person again, or to befriend them, or even speak to them ever again. It doesn't mean answering their letters, emails, voicemails, or messages.	Forgiveness is permission to protect and distance yourself.
Forgiveness is **not** saying, "We'll go back to the same warm feelings we had before the betrayal."	Forgiveness is facing the truth about the pain and injury. It means staying away from a dangerous person if possible. In some cases, it might include cooperating with law enforcement to keep this person from injuring others.

Radio counselor June Hunt says,

> "Forgiveness isn't letting someone off the hook for the bad they've done. It is moving them from your hook onto God's hook."[213]

In some sense, in the spiritual realm, they are now God's problem, not ours. "Vengeance is mine," says the Lord (Deuteronomy 32:35, NKJV). And God knows how to deal with each person. He knows how to right the wrongs.

A Biblical Example of Caring, but Keeping Your Distance—1 Samuel 15

The prophet Samuel had anointed Saul and made him the first king of Israel. But when King Saul repeatedly sinned against God, then lied,

---

213 June Hunt, ***Self-Worth: Discover Your God-Given Worth*** (Peabody, MA: Rose Publishing, 2013), 65.

made excuses, and played mind-games when caught red-handed, Samuel rebuked him.

After that, Samuel never went to see Saul again.

Samuel mourned for him, but he kept his distance.

Anger at an Ex's Family

Sometimes the pressure to "forgive and forget" comes from family. Sometimes the ex-spouse's family tries everything in their power to keep you married. They may try all kinds of manipulation—

- telling you you're over-reacting
- telling others *you* are the real problem
- pressuring you to reconcile when you don't feel safe
- minimizing the bad behavior of their loved one
- claiming you are trying to ruin your ex-spouse's life
- threatening to damage your reputation
- saying you are ungrateful when you don't accept your ex-spouse's tokens of affection or expressions of love
- lying about your behavior

Our first task is to get some distance from them. Their loyalty to your ex-spouse is frustrating, but sadly, it's also very common. The old saying is often true: "Blood is thicker than water," meaning they will side with your ex because they are related, even if they know the truth down deep inside.

Sometimes they wake up to the truth, but not always. Regardless of what they decide to do, though, being connected to them can come at a huge cost to you, at a time when you can't afford any extra "costs."

For now, set good boundaries around these people. Limit your contact with them to an amount that you can handle—even if that is *none*.

Anger at God

But what do you do if you're angry at God? What happens when you do everything right and your marriage fails? Many Christians were taught if they did everything right, they would have a great marriage.

There's a myth in Christianity that we can't be angry at God—that it's a sin.

This myth is not true. The Bible contains many examples of people getting angry at God and expressing it in the Psalms. God is big enough to handle our anger. He understands. He knows that anger is a natural response to being hurt, and he knows we are human—he made us this way.

Our God is a God who holds out his arms to his children, even when they are angry, and says to them, *I will never leave you. You can never do anything to make me stop loving you.*

Your anger is not too much for me.
I've got you.
I've got this.

Everyone I interviewed for this book said they prayed and prayed that God would fix their marriage. It wasn't a one-time prayer; it was a constant prayer.

When their marriage continued to get worse rather than better, they doubled down and tried harder. They genuinely tried to live a righteous Christian life: They prayed, attended church, volunteered, donated, and read their Bible daily, but God didn't make things better. The abuse got worse; their health declined; in some cases, their children were molested; several people I interviewed contracted an incurable sexually transmitted disease from their unfaithful spouse. They searched their soul for some hidden sin. They tried to find that one sin that opened the door to this betrayal.

One woman who had been beaten hundreds of times, and who stayed because she thought her children would be damaged if she divorced, lost everything after her 25-year marriage. She cried out to God:

> *"I've done everything for you, God. I wanted to honor you by staying in my marriage. You allowed me to be beaten and left for dead. You allowed my kids to be raped repeatedly. You didn't protect them or me. I witnessed a child being molested at my church and reported it to the pastors. They believed me but kicked me out. You didn't protect me. I find it hard to believe you care about me. I had complete faith in you, but you don't even stop my ex-husband from making our life a living hell."*
>
> *My mom told me I was going to hell if I yelled at or questioned God. But I looked at God's deeds in the Bible and thought, "God,*

you did miracles for people in the Bible, but you didn't do it for me." I was so angry, I literally screamed and tore out pages of my Bible, the HOLY Bible. There was nothing left for me to stand on. No idols left on my shelf once I shredded my Bible. It was gone. I had no good deeds. There was nothing. I was a failure. I felt that I had lost everyone, including God and my kids. I lost every court battle. My close friend wasn't talking to me. I didn't think I could get lower, but I did.

I would not have said this at the time, but now I can see it. God began to speak to me in my gut. I could hear God say, "I love you. You're going to be okay."

So How Do I Tell God I'm Angry?

You may need to express your anger toward God that your life didn't turn out the way you planned. It's okay. God is a big God. He can handle your rage, disappointment, and anger. He already knows exactly how you feel.

You can't hurt God's feelings. He's not fragile. He can take it. When you tell God the truth about your emotions, it means you actually believe he exists. It means you believe him when he says he is a loving God.

May I recommend something like this sample lament prayer? "Laments" are a common type of prayer in the Bible, especially the Books of Psalms and Lamentations. There are dozens of them.

Laments always have one thing in common. They include a complaint. Here are the *complaint* lines from Psalm 44:

But you have rejected and humiliated us;
you do not march out with our armies.
You make us retreat from the foe,
and those who hate us
have taken plunder for themselves.
You hand us over to be eaten like sheep
and scatter us among the nations.
You sell your people for nothing;
you make no profit from selling them.
You make us an object of reproach to our neighbors,
a source of mockery and ridicule to those around us.

You make us a joke among the nations,
a laughingstock among the peoples.
My disgrace is before me all day long,
and shame has covered my face,
because of the taunts of the scorner and reviler,
because of the enemy and avenger.
—Psalm 44:9-16 (CSB)

Many laments express frustration. And that's okay. They often (but not always) also include:

- an acknowledgement of God's protection in the past
- a confession of sin OR a claim of innocence
- a desire to trust and praise God when he does respond
- a cry to God to rescue them

If you like, you can write your own. Feel free to adapt this one, or come up with one in all your own words.

O God,

I wanted our marriage to be a shining example of a good Christian couple. I was not perfect, but I tried to do everything to please you. Despite all my prayers and tears, the marriage failed anyway.

Why, O Lord? Why me? Other people have good marriages, even people who don't care about you. Why didn't you answer my cries for help and fix my marriage?

Instead of having respect and a good reputation in my church, I am seen as a failure.

I am humiliated. And to be honest, I sometimes feel so angry at you, I could scream!

Yet I have believed in you for a long time. You have come through for me in the past in many ways.

Please help me as I walk this unexpected path. Please bring me comfort. Help me deal with the emotional, financial, and legal challenges. Please protect me [and my kids, pets, business, etc.].

You promise never to leave us or forsake us. We trust in you and will praise you.

In Jesus' name, Amen.

Anger and Forgiveness: Questions for Journaling or Discussion

1. Why does it take a long time for people who are traumatized to forgive?
2. Give an example of the difference between forgiveness and trust. Can a person forgive without being willing to have a friendship with the person who injured them?
3. How have you learned to forgive yourself during this season? Why is God's grace and forgiveness so important for us?
4. How can a person forgive someone and set boundaries so they are unable (or less likely) to hurt them again?
5. If we obsess about revenge on those who hurt us, how does that affect us (and our children)?
6. Optional: If you are one of those people who tried so hard to have the perfect marriage, how can you express your anger and frustration to God using the idea of a "Lament"? Look at the full text of Psalm 44 in the Bible for ideas.

Dealing with Overwhelming Loneliness

What does loneliness feel like?

- It's those nights when you're alone, the kids are in bed, and it's quiet.
- Or it's the feeling inside when you're going to a party alone.
- Or it's going to the company Christmas dinner and realizing you have no one beside you for the first time in years.

The feelings of loneliness come in like a giant wave on the shore and crash down on you. You tumble in the surf, struggling and gasping for breath.

And the loneliness whispers lies in our ear:

- No one will ever want me. I've got baggage.
- There is no one to protect me.
- I am unlovable.

Most of the day, we can ignore these feelings because we are busy at work or running errands. But at night, when no one is around—perhaps the kids are with their other parent—loneliness sweeps in and crushes you. You sit there alone in misery, while other people continue their happy lives.

Loneliness sucks us dry. It empties us and takes away our ability to cope. We struggle to get out of bed and to get the kids dressed. Our children sense it, and they need comfort: "We are going through a tough time right now, but the Lord will help us."

These fears are natural and normal to feel after a deep betrayal. And many people who are going through a life-saving divorce feel this loneliness intensely.

I hear these stories all the time, and I've felt these feelings myself. Here's my story—

> *Loneliness hit me like a tsunami—a giant tidal wave.*
>
> *It was like standing out on a beach and seeing a wave coming toward me, rising above my head, then crashing down on me. I couldn't outrun it. I couldn't stand against it. It was going to hit me—and it was going to hit hard. I would be tumbled in the waves gasping for breath, clawing to get to the surface.*
>
> *Every wave of loneliness was overwhelming. The first year was absolutely miserable. I wondered if I would survive. I was raised in a Christian home, and I knew the Bible contained a lot of comfort for difficult times. So I reread the promises given by God.*
>
> *As I memorized these promises and desperately held onto Jesus, I observed something: The waves of loneliness would roll in, but eventually they would also roll out. And that taught me something: Loneliness comes, but it also goes.*
>
> *At times, it felt like it would kill me.*
>
> *Eventually the loneliness tsunamis would last only a few hours. And I realized loneliness would not physically kill me.*
>
> *I realized that as long as I had Jesus walking with me, that wave wasn't going to stay forever. It would eventually wash back out to sea.*
>
> *The loneliness tsunami continued to overwhelm me from time to time. Eventually I accepted it as part of the normal grieving process.*
>
> *It's not as though loneliness ever ends completely, but you learn to accept it and learn how to deal with it. The waves get smaller, and they roll back out faster.*

Four Truths about Loneliness

1. Healing takes time. The first year is the worst. You will feel as though the earth is swallowing you up; you will feel you've got more than you can possibly handle. But God is there.
2. Loneliness will reduce as you spend time with people who are safe and caring.
3. Loneliness makes you insecure and wanting affirmation; it makes you lower your romantic standards. Make sure you've learned to set boundaries. Don't let desperation force you to get involved with someone unsafe.
4. Loneliness wants to isolate you. Instead, find others who understand the pain of divorce. Many have walked in your shoes.

Five Ways to Cope with Loneliness

Don't be passive. Do something to find new friends, new creative activities, and a place to share your story with others. This requires you to take initiative and get going. No one will do it for you, though there are people out there who will help along the way. But the first steps are yours. You've got to look online, pick up the phone, or ask around. You had the courage to get a life-saving divorce, and you do have the courage to rebuild your life. Take one small step this week.

Find friendships. Find safe and understanding people among your family, friends, coworkers, church, or neighborhood.

I was in a women's group at my church, and one of the women had been through a divorce many years before. She often gave me encouragement, saying (with a wink and a smile): "Divorce isn't the worst thing in the world." She was a happy, successful woman who had raised three kids herself. Her kids had turned out great. I clung to her friendship!

Find hobbies. Look for groups that gather around shared interests, like art, music, crafts, hiking, book clubs, sports, working out.

I took up photography. It was an inexpensive hobby that was easy and creative. It took my mind off the pain and gave me an artistic outlet. I took classes and read articles. I developed friendships with other passionate photographers.

Find support groups. Join a divorce recovery group, a single parent group, or try group therapy.

Another divorced woman and I started the Single Mothers Support Group at our church. We met Sunday mornings when there was Sunday school for our kids, and we shared our stories and prayed for one another. It was a great group of women who wanted to get stable, be good mothers, and find hope. We were at different points in our journey and gave each other a lot of care and encouragement. We all became very close friends, and many of us are friends to this day—more than twenty years later.

Make connections through serving others. Mowing a lawn, bringing a meal, tutoring a child, assisting in a classroom, sorting books for the library: all of these things connect you to community.

Whenever I got down and negative, I went into a spiral of self-pity. I learned to break the spiral by finding someone I could help. For example, serving in soup kitchens with my kids. I also found a woman who had four children under the age of 6, who was pregnant with her fifth. I babysat her children one night per week free of charge for a few weeks. It felt good to help someone else. And seeing the challenge of raising four little ones helped me put my pain in perspective.

Note: Another way to make connections through service is by *accepting* the service of others. When people from your community offer to help, take them up on it! Receive with gratitude the gifts of time, energy, attention, and support that others want to extend to you.

Receiving and giving ***both*** *forge bonds between people.*

For those of us who grew up in the church, we're often much more comfortable in the role of giver than we are in that of receiver—but *both* roles are important. If you've been a giver your whole life, maybe ask for God's help in learning how to gladly receive in this season.

It was great to have people who knew me well stand beside me and encourage me. They didn't abandon me. They made sure I was included in the church. They prayed with me and spent time with me. Three families paid for me and my children to go to family camp. When I had healed a bit, church staff encouraged me to reach out to others and start a prayer-and-share group.

Dealing with the Loneliness Tidal Wave: Questions for Journaling or Discussion

1. When do your "loneliness tidal waves" come crashing in most often?
2. When loneliness strikes you, what mistakes are you quickest to make? What do you expect to get out of those behaviors? Then notice: What actually comes out of them instead?
3. When you are lonely, what verses or promises from God's Word give you the most comfort? Do you ever sense God with you in your loneliness?
4. How simple or complicated is it for you to accept loneliness as simply a normal part of the grieving process?
5. Can you identify a few safe, loving people in your life that you can talk to about what's really going on inside?

Fear and Worry—My Kids, My Finances, My Future

For I am persuaded that neither death, nor life, nor angels nor principalities nor powers, nor things present nor things to come, nor height nor depth, nor any other created thing, shall be able to separate us from the love of God which is in Christ Jesus our Lord.
—Romans 8:38–39 (NKJV)

In the stillness of our bedroom at night, there are fears that wake us up or make it hard to fall asleep. We worry that things will only get worse… that our lives will fall apart. We are afraid that God either doesn't care or doesn't have the power to help us. Our worries tell us we are completely alone, and that things will never get better.

As we look to the future, all we see is looming disaster. Fear about the future grips us. But there is a God who loves us and knows how to bring us hope and comfort.

The Perfect Storm

Why is divorce so painful? A Rutgers University professor[214] said one of the reasons divorce is so hard is the combination of changes that happen *all at the same time*. To put his findings in simple terms, it's a perfect storm—which means the convergence of multiple problems at the same time.

No wonder we are frightened and overwhelmed.

In divorce, all these factors happen at once—

- conflict, turmoil
- view of self: "I feel like a failure"
- change in social status and loss of friendships
- economic stress, uncertainty about the future
- change in living situation: Moving, changing schools/neighborhood
- children's fears and stress

If we faced these issues one at a time over ten years, we might be okay. But all of them at once, compressed into one or two years? It's overwhelming!

One of the problems about fear and worry is that we project them into the future—and nothing else. We don't factor God's provision into our vision of the future. We don't factor in the support of others. We don't factor in our own growing strength.

Jesus knows we have the tendency to obsess about the future.

During these seasons, it helps to remember these two Bible promises about God's care for you:

Cast all your anxiety on him because he cares for you.
—1 Peter 5:7 (NIV)

Be anxious for nothing, but in everything by prayer and supplication, with thanksgiving, let your requests be made known to God; and the peace of God, which surpasses all understanding, will guard your hearts and minds through Christ Jesus.
—Philippians 4:6-7 (NKJV)

---

214 Allan Horwitz, "Marital Status and Mental Health," PowerPoint presentation (3/18/00), slide 17.

I like the second part of that verse, because it says that God will give us peace that surpasses our understanding or "transcends" our understanding. That means God's peace defies logic. It doesn't make sense. How can we be in such turmoil and still believe that we will come out okay? Somehow God's peace will guard and protect our hearts and minds.

Will I Ever Be Happy Again?

Yes, on average most people do go back to their normal level of happiness within two or three years of divorce, but that first year is tough. Trusting God, calling out to the Lord, and prayer help many people, but everyone is different.

Fears & Lies We Tell Ourselves	Affirmation & Bible Promise
I've got a black cloud over my head.	***I will not fear, for God is with me.*** God promises: "So do not fear, for I am with you; do not be dismayed, for I am your God. I will strengthen you and help you; I will uphold you with my righteous right hand." —Isaiah 41:10 (NIV)
I've got a red L for "loser" on my forehead.	***God turns ashes into joy.*** "Though the mountains be shaken and the hills be removed, yet my unfailing love for you will not be shaken, nor my covenant of peace be removed," says the LORD, who has compassion on you. —Isaiah 54:10`(NIV)
I will never be happy again.	***It's always hard at first. But in time, I will smile again.*** Weeping`may stay for the night, but rejoicing comes in the morning. —Psalm 30:5 (NIV)
No one will ever love me again.	***I am deeply loved by God, and he will help me find love and companionship.*** "For I know the plans I have for you," declares the LORD, "plans to prosper you and not to harm you, plans to give you hope and a future." —Jeremiah 29:11 (NIV)

Going After Life with Both Hands

One woman, who had a been married more than 25 years to a cheater who had lived a double life as a marriage mentor and elder at their church, gave this advice about rebuilding your life. She says it doesn't happen automatically. You need to work at it.

One is: trust your gut. It's the Holy Spirit guiding you.

Two is: you can flourish after divorce. Never give up. On your darkest days when you feel like life will never be good again, that's a lie. It's a lie. I used to think life will never be good again.

And people told me it would be, and I didn't believe it. It's true. It's true. You have to go after it with intentionality, though. It doesn't happen by osmosis. You have to go after it. Even if you don't feel like it. You have to go after it.

What does it look like to go after life with both hands? It means taking small steps to make one improvement in your life, health, education, job, child-raising, skills, and abilities. It isn't passive.

Developing a Positive Mindset

I like journaling, and it's been helpful to me to look back at those entries from long ago, to see how I viewed my ex-husband's bad behavior before we married. My optimism and trust that God would fix anything were remarkable. I should win some award!

But during tough times, I started to ruminate on my frustrations and unhappiness, writing the same thoughts and phrases over and over. Reading those journal entries thirty years later made me realize I can get stuck. And that's not helpful. Maybe you can relate.

One day I came across a lecture on happiness and decided to try its simple tips. The speaker suggested people do these five things for 21 days.[215] I found it helpful, and I hope you do, too.

At first, finding things to be grateful for was easy: a roof over my

---

215 Shawn Achor, "The Happy Secret to Better Work," ***Ted Talks***, accessed 12/1/17, http://www.ted.com/talks/shawn_achor_the_happy_secret_to_better_work?language=en.

head, food on the table, my best friend, my job. But after the first week or two, I ran out of new things to be grateful for, and I found myself watching for glimpses of goodness all day so I had something to write down. It was a very clever way to get out of a pattern of negativity.

A 21-Day Gratitude Journal

1. List three new things you're grateful for today (not something you've already listed).
2. Write about one positive experience that's happened in the past 24 hours.
3. Exercise for 10 minutes.
4. Pray or meditate.
5. Describe a random act of kindness you did for someone (it can be secret).

Give it a try. It helped me.

You might want to add one more thing: one small step you plan to do tomorrow to "go after life with both hands." (It might be to sign up for a class, polish your resume, do something creative, read about boundaries, apply for a job, or read a website on how to negotiate.)

The Next Step? Using Your Experience to Bring Comfort to Others

When a new person comes to a divorce recovery group, they are often devastated. But by the second or third meeting, after they've shared their story and found understanding and compassion, they start realizing that they can extend that care and compassion onto others.

This is how we turn our pain into hope for others.
This is how we become "healed helpers."

In our group, the women eventually developed a domestic-violence radar. Soon, they were reaching out to strangers with compassion and love, telling them that the Lord cared about them and didn't want anyone used as a punching bag.

One of my favorite Bible verses about divorce recovery is:

Praise be to the God and Father of our Lord Jesus Christ, the Father of compassion and the God of all comfort, who comforts us in all our troubles, so that we can comfort those in any trouble with the comfort we ourselves receive from God.
—2 Corinthians 1:3-4 (NIV)

To me, this says that God comforts us so we can comfort others. We just keep paying it forward. We are reaching out and bringing comfort to people who think they will be miserable forever.

The #1 Evangelist in the Gospels Was Divorced

Did you know that the person in the Bible with the worst luck in marriage was also the greatest evangelist in the four Gospels?

In John 4:1-42, Jesus talks with a woman at a well who has had five husbands. She probably wasn't a five-time widow. It's more likely one or more of her husbands divorced her and sent her away.

Yet this "loser" brought more people to believe in Jesus than any other person in the Gospels.

It's remarkable. Her failures and humiliations in life made people pay attention. When she claimed she had met the Messiah—a man who knew everything about her—her testimony drew people to leave their homes and meet Jesus.

From Despair to Hope—From the Pit to the Place of Honor

Where is God taking you next?

As a new divorcee struggling with the humiliation of a failed marriage, all I could do was call out to God for help. My nose had been dragged in the dirt. I had gone from being a Gold Standard Christian from an honorable family to being a second-class citizen.

During this time, I decided to read and meditate on one psalm from the Bible every week. I would read it aloud and then look at each verse. I started with the famous psalms, like Psalm 23, and moved on to others. I'll never forget reading Psalm 71 for the first time. Near the end were these two verses.

You have allowed me to suffer much hardship,
but you will restore me to life again
and lift me up from the depths of the earth.
You will restore me to even greater honor
and comfort me once again.
—Psalm 71:20-21 (NLT)

These verses seemed like a mockery. They made me angry. How could God lift me from the depths of the earth and bring me to greater honor? I had lost my good name, my reputation, and my future as a respected person in my community. It was ridiculous to believe God could do that. How could he? My life was over.

But in time… he did.

At my job, I worked hard and started getting acknowledgements. It took me five years to get back on my feet financially after the divorce, but I did. At church, I led a single mothers divorce recovery group, and my church saw my ministry as an important service to the community. People from the surrounding neighborhood, even from other churches, came to our group.

Over the next twenty years, I saw God open doors
to ways of serving I never thought possible.

Back then, I thought that divorce was the worst thing that could happen to me, but in reality, it stripped away my dependency on outward appearances and forced me to rely on God. And yes, God did restore me to honor and comforted me. I believe he can for you, too.

To Remarry or to Stay Single: Finding Love Again and Learning to Respect Yourself

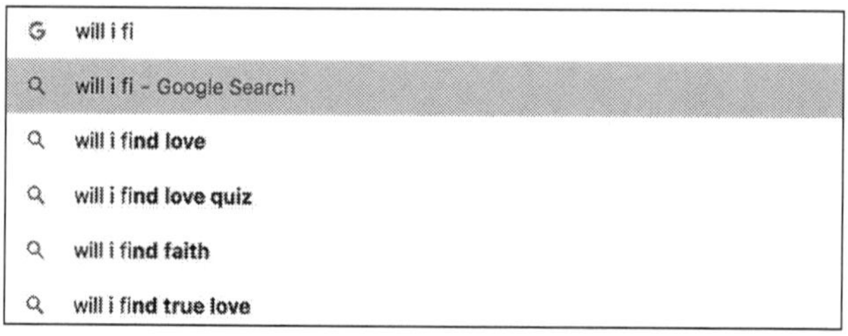

will i fi
will i fi - Google Search
will i **find love**
will i **find love quiz**
will i **find faith**
will i **find true love**

If you do an Internet search and enter the phrase "will I find," the autocomplete fills in "love" as the first option. A lot of people are asking that question. People ask Google "will I ever find love" far more often than they ask, "will I ever feel better," or "will I ever get married."

Wanting to find love and belonging is deep in the human heart. But getting married again? Not as much. Some people want to remarry; some do not.

Let's look at some of the myths about remarriage. (Some of them will be very surprising.)

Myth 1: Everyone wants to remarry.

Some people want to remarry; others do not. Usually younger people wish to remarry, and three in four women who divorced (at ages 15-44) do remarry within ten years.[216] The remarriage rate is very high for those under twenty-five.[217]

Of women who divorce at age forty or older, however, more than two in five (43%) say they do not want to remarry. And for men who divorce over age forty, one in three (33%) say they don't want to try again. Another 26% of women weren't sure (and 24% of men), and the vast majority say they don't want to run the risk of having another bad marriage. Many say they don't want the trouble of finding another partner. Some say they like the freedom to make their own plans and decisions.[218]

For people who divorced when they were age forty or over, many prefer to stay single:

Nearly half of women in this age group do not want to remarry. Men are much more motivated to find a new spouse than women are: 27% were sure they wanted to remarry (compared to only 17% of women who said the same). As a group, women are very wary ("once burned, twice shy"), and so it's not surprising that we find that the men's remarriage rate is twice as high as women's.[219]

---

216 M. D. Bramlett and W. D. Mosher, "Cohabitation, Marriage, Divorce, and Remarriage in the United States," ***Vital and Health Statistics*** 23, no. 22 (2002): 78.

217 Valerie Schweizer, "The Retreat from Remarriage, 1950-2017," ***Family Profile*** 17 (2019), accessed 12/12/19, https://www.bgsu.edu/ncfmr/resources/data/family-profiles/schweizer-retreat-remarriage-fp-19-17.html.

218 Xenia P. Montenegro, "Divorce Experience: A Study of Divorce at Mid-Life and Beyond," ***AARP The Magazine*** (2004), A-23, accessed 12/18/19, https://assets.aarp.org/rgcenter/general/divorce.pdf.

219 Schweizer, "The Retreat from Remarriage."

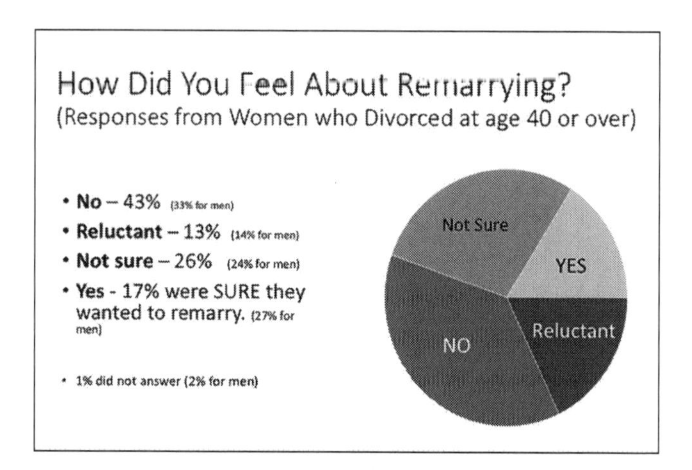

How Did You Feel About Remarrying?
(Responses from Women who Divorced at age 40 or over)
• No – 43% (33% for men)
• Reluctant – 13% (14% for men)
• Not sure – 26% (24% for men)
• Yes - 17% were SURE they wanted to remarry. (27% for men)
• 1% did not answer (2% for men)
Not Sure
YES
Reluctant
NO

Myth 2: Your second marriage is likely to end in divorce and won't be any happier because you bring your problems with you.

The first part of this myth is only partially true. The divorce rate for second marriages nationwide is indeed higher than first marriages: 60%.

But that likelihood is for *all* remarriages, not remarriages after a life-saving divorce.

Research shows that people whose marriages had been very unhappy for a long time—people who needed a life-saving divorce—are likely to have a happier second marriage.

Researchers Hawkins and Booth studied people who were in long-term unhappy marriages (a minimum of twelve years of being unhappily married). They followed these couples for many years beyond the twelve-year point. They compared those who stayed married and those who divorced, and they tracked their wellbeing in several different ways.

They concluded that both those who divorced and remarried, and those who divorced and stayed single, were *much better off* on average than they would have been if they had stayed in the bad marriage:

> "**Divorced individuals who remarry** have greater overall happiness, and those who **divorce and remain unmarried** have greater levels of life satisfaction, self-esteem and overall health than unhappily married people."[220]

---

220 Hawkins and Booth, 468. Dr. Linda Waite (2002) also found that 81% of those deeply unhappy spouses in her study who divorced and remarried were happy.

Myth 3: You will never remarry, and you'll live a miserable, lonely life.

As I mentioned, I was single for more than twenty years after my divorce. Yet I was very happy once I got past those first two years.

I never dreamed I would be single for twenty years,
and I definitely never dreamed that those years would be
so rewarding, purposeful, and meaningful.

Dr. Ryan Burge, using Baylor University's 2014 Religion Survey data, found that 7 in 10 Christians who divorced reported that they were "somewhat happy" or "very happy" after divorce. But researchers could have predicted that. They had already found that people were happier once they got out of a destructive long-term marriage. Based on their findings, it doesn't matter whether you remarry or not. You likely will be happier, on average, than if you had stayed.

If you choose to stay single, your life is likely to be healthier and more satisfying, and you'll have more self-respect.

Researchers Hawkins and Booth concluded this about these long-term unhappy unions:

> "Remaining unhappily married rather than divorcing is never beneficial to the psychological wellbeing or overall health of the individuals in this study."[221]

Happiness and Long-Term Singleness after Divorce

In Chapter 8 (Safe Churches and Friends), I tell the story of how my best friend and I started a divorce recovery group at our church and how it provided a lot of great friendship and support. Those women are some of the strongest and most courageous people I know. They are amazing survivors. I was honored to hear their stories and get a front-row seat to watch how the Lord healed them and gave them a new passion for growth.

In addition to that group, I also joined groups made up of men and women who were interested in the same things I was: friends who loved photography, business, travel, and books. My circle of friendships grew. Between my children and my close friends, I found the love and belonging I craved.

---

221 Ibid., 464.

Here are some reasons to stay single (adapted from my article originally published by Psych Central):

1. *Being single can force you to be a better person.* As a single person, you are more likely to have built-in motivation to be a good employee, friend, relative and neighbor. You have no automatic safety net, in the form of a spouse, and because of this, many single people create and nurture their own circles of people who are important to them. They are reliable and responsible, whereas some married people stop growing and just coast.
2. *Being single gives you time to contemplate life and become deeper.* You get to know yourself when you are alone. You find out what really matters: integrity, self-awareness, and your core values. You don't have to conform to peer pressure. You can be authentic.
3. *Being single allows you to be available for interesting adventures.* Married people spend a lot of time with each other. In fact, they feel *obligated* to spend a majority of time together. But single people have the freedom to explore new ideas, new places, and new people.
4. *Singles have rich friendships.* Most married people spend time with their spouse and kids, and maybe a handful of friends. Singles develop deep relationships with all kinds of people,[222] including their extended family members.

Moving Forward after a Life-Saving Divorce

Whether you remarry or not… whether you wait one week or twenty years to tie the knot… the choice is yours.

My goal in this chapter is to give you reasonable expectations for the future after divorce. Expect big adjustments and a lot of stress the first two years. You can expect it to take a while to get stable financially. Tell God how you feel. Get therapy, if you can afford it.

But if you can't (or even if you can), find a divorce recovery group or single parents' group. Find one or two people who've walked in your shoes and have coffee once a month. Many people find that closed or

---

222 Bella DePaulo, "Put a Ring on It—A Singleness Ring," ***Psych Central*** (2017), accessed 12/12/19, https://blogs.psychcentral.com/single-at-heart/2017/09/put-a-ring-on-it-a-singleness-ring-guest-post-by-gretchen-baskerville/.

secret Facebook groups are a good place for telling their story. You may be able to set up anonymous social media accounts to protect your privacy.

Don't be passive about moving on in life; figure out who you are apart from your ex-spouse. It will take a year or more to get their "voice" and their preferences out of your head. Many life-saving divorce survivors lived years in turmoil, and when they finally got out, they realized they didn't know their own favorite movie, book, TV show, restaurant, color, or decorating style. Their entire life was focused around pleasing or placating their spouse.

If this is you, please know that that's okay. It's normal. Building a new separate identity takes time. Get out there and connect with others who share your interests.

Many of your old friends, especially the married ones, have no idea what to say to someone going through divorce. They may distance themselves from you. That's okay. You may have to distance yourself from some of them too, especially the critics.

This is not the time to educate your friends or pastors about abuse and divorce and why you believe your children will be better off if you leave. You've got enough challenges in life. Spend your time and energy on traveling your own path (and if you really want to educate them, just give them this book).

Moving forward also means taking on household tasks you never did before. Many of my interviewees were stay-at-home wives who never touched the finances, never paid a bill, and never looked at the taxes.

It's time to get up to speed. There are basic budgeting and financial life-skills classes and videos you can use. And for home maintenance, you can find YouTube videos to learn about common repairs and the names of various tools and parts. They'll help you sound more knowledgeable when you call the plumber or talk with a mechanic.

Once you've gotten past the anger and grief of your divorce, it's good to learn to protect yourself and identify your vulnerabilities. Many people have to learn how to have better boundaries, know what to say to those who try to control them, and learn to negotiate. In the back of this book, you will find recommendations for further reading that can help you develop these skills.

A Blessing for You

So many of the people I interviewed were thankful someone wanted to hear their story from start to finish. Most of my interviews were one to two hours, but there were several that took five to fifteen hours. One battered wife who had finally gotten free said this: "You are an answer to prayer. I wanted to tell my story."

Many of them expressed to me how their view of God changed because of the suffering they went through. But most of the people I interviewed said their lives are better and their walk with the Lord was closer than ever. Here are a few quotes:

I would not have said this at the time, but now I can see it. God began to speak to me in my gut. I could hear God say, "I love you. You're going to be okay." I could not accept or acknowledge it at that time.

God has shown me so much this year. It's not about reading the Bible. it really is about abiding with each other. Just living life… I'm so thankful for all of the losses, as hard as they are… [And I'm] thankful for the peace and lack of trauma for the first time in our lives.

I think God calls us to peace and to not be punching bags for abusive spouses.

I'm really amazed at where my life is right now and to think where I was six years ago. It's absolutely crazy, and I thank God for it every day.

I have more of my heart available to love the Lord with. I feel so much better physically, emotionally, and spiritually [now that I've left]. I truly felt I was dying internally. I had no idea how to survive the marriage I was committed to for the rest of my life.

Over and over, [God] has been so faithful. I wrestle with him in prayer, and he answers me in his time. Financially he has provided in some big ways, outside of my job.

While I was still in my abusive marriage, I thought God was like my husband. My view of God was that he had an ego, there was a narcissistic part of him. Because if God wasn't like that, then God wouldn't be okay with my husband treating me like that. When I was able to talk about the abuse, then I realized the picture in my head was wrong. I know who God is now.

I would say the divorce didn't change my view of God. I just finally decided to get healthy for myself, and that act of getting healthy was the part that changed my view of God. God stopped being this far-off entity who was judging and proscribing challenges in my marriage, work, and family life. When everything fell apart… I had to decide whether God was wrong and screwed up, or whether my perception of what God wanted and asked for was wrong. So I let go of everything and gave my old perception over to God and laid my belief in God on the altar to be sacrificed…

I would say my relationship to God has never been better. When everything has been taken from you and you are left with nothing, you still have to turn to God. It is a sweet thing because you aren't turning to God because of what he has given you or can give you. You are turning to [the Lord] because it's the only thing that can't be taken from you. That is a powerful bonding that I have with my Lord. It is more real and more close than it has ever been.

May the Lord,
who loves you and your children more than you can imagine,
bless you,
heal you,
and strengthen you
as you continue your journey.

FURTHER READING

Helpful books come and go. For more recommendations than those included in this list, and for the most up-to-date recommendations, see my blog www.LifeSavingDivorce.com and look under "Links" for videos and updated book, article, and blog recommendations. Note: Not all of these resources are from a Christian standpoint. You are intelligent, and I trust you to use your best wisdom and judgment as you choose which resources will be the best for you in your situation.

Book on High-Conflict Divorces or Parental Alienation

Co-Parenting with a Toxic Ex, by Amy J. L. Baker.
    This book is practical and easy to read. It gives tips on what to watch for, as well as actual phrases to use when responding to your kids. It has a workbook-format section at the end of each chapter.

Divorce Poison, by Richard Warshak.
    The book is basic and practical. It covers more of the legal aspects of child custody, including situations such as kidnapping.

Toxic Divorce: A Workbook for Alienated Parents, by Kathleen M. Reay, Ph.D.
    Toxic Divorce is an excellent workbook to help parents with their feelings, providing strategies and tips to de-escalate parental alienation so it doesn't progress from moderate to severe.

Welcome Back, Pluto, by Richard Warshak [video].
    This video is for parents, containing tips for parents who wish to reconnect and reunite with their alienated children. [Note: It is not meant to be watched *with* your children.]

Splitting: Protecting Yourself While Divorcing Someone with Borderline or Narcissistic Personality Disorder, by Bill Eddy.
    Authored by an attorney, mediator, and clinical social worker. The book covers the court/legal process of divorcing, including hiring a divorce lawyer, gathering evidence, and what to expect from your ex and their attorney. Also his book, BIFF, on responding to conflict.

The Narc Decoder, by Tina Swithin.
    When your ex-spouse turns hostile during the divorce process, and attacks you with insinuations, false accusations, and threats, this book will help you

decide how to respond. Using real-life correspondence and a touch of humor, the author helps you see past the words and look at the underlying message, then decide how to respond in a way that will help you in divorce court.

Books on Making Close Friendships and Improving Relationships

The Friendship Factor, by Alan Loy McGinnis.

Many people who find themselves needing a life-saving divorce want to build new, healthier friendships that are supportive and nurturing, especially if they feel alone as a single again. This old classic is still an excellent book on making and keeping friends.

Nine Thoughts That Can Change Your Marriage: Because a Great Relationship Doesn't Happen by Accident, by Sheila Wray Gregoire.

In this book, the author explains how the solution to a happier relationship is not found in being a more patient, more perfect wife, but in taking responsibility for what you can do—and especially for how you think about your marriage. She challenges you to replace pat Christian answers with nine biblical truths that will radically shift your perspective on your husband, your relationship, and your role in God's design for marriage.

Books on Developing Boundaries and Learning to Deal with Manipulators

There are some basic tasks we each need to learn in life. As Christians, we are taught to be people-pleasers: We have trouble saying no to people. We take the blame when others behave badly. We feel we must say yes to every request, even if it jeopardizes our health and our wellbeing. These books can help with this issue.

Boundaries: When to Say Yes, How to Say No to Take Control of Your Life, by Dr. Henry Cloud and Dr. John Townsend.

This acclaimed Christian book on godly boundary-setting will help you learn how to set boundaries so you aren't run over by others and taken advantage of by them. (While this book is very helpful for people who are rebuilding their lives after divorce, trauma survivors have criticized the authors for being too optimistic about the effects of setting boundaries, and for appearing reluctant to condone divorce as a healthy consequence for abusive spouses who don't respect boundaries.)

Who's Pulling Your Strings?: How to Break the Cycle of Manipulation and Regain Control of Your Life, by Harriet B. Braiker.

A guide on how to navigate boundaries in your workplace, including a substantial section (the second half of the book) that includes phrases to use when faced by a boss or coworker who tries to manipulate you.

Emotional Blackmail: When the People in Your Life Use Fear, Obligation, and Guilt to Manipulate You, by Susan Forward.

This book specifically addresses setting boundaries with family members and loved ones.

Christian Books on Abuse

The Emotionally Destructive Marriage, by Leslie Vernick.

This book is written from a Christian perspective and speaks to women specifically, to help them identify and get free from emotional abuse in a marriage.

Is It Me?: Making Sense of Your Confusing Marriage, by Natalie Hoffman.

This book is also written from a Christian perspective for women struggling to make sense of a damaging marriage. It is a particularly gentle book that would work well to give as a gift to someone you know and love who seems to be in an abusive marriage, but hasn't admitted it yet. Watch for the new small group curriculum that goes with this book.

Redemption from Biblical Battering: Your Path to Faith-Based Freedom, by Shirley Fessel.

This is a workbook-style book for Christian women in physically abusive relationships who are looking for a faith-based path to freedom. It is appropriate for a small group curriculum.

Out of Control: Couples, Conflict and the Capacity for Change, by Natalie Collins.

This book, written for the Church, gives an in-depth look at domestic abuse, using case studies and knowledge about abusive behavior traits gleaned from the author's years of work leading workshops and helping the Church recognize and deal with signs of abuse in its midst.

Books on Abuse (General)

Healing from Hidden Abuse: A Journey Through the Stages of Recovery from Psychological Abuse, by Shannon Thomas.

Written by a licensed, practicing therapist, this book covers the effects of psychological abuse and recovery for victims in easy-to-read language. This book can be useful for male victims of abuse as well. If a person isn't sure if they are being abused, this is a good starter book.

Steps to Freedom: Escaping Intimate Control, by Don Hennessy.

This best-selling book, written in an easily understandable manner, addresses controlling and abusive behavior from an intimate partner, especially of men towards women. It offers a path out of this control and into freedom.

Why Does He Do That? Inside the Minds of Angry and Controlling Men, by Lundy Bancroft.

Lundy Bancroft is a counselor who specializes in working with abusive men, and he has written this book from that perspective, helping enable women to recognize when they are being abused and devalued and find ways to get free of abusive relationships.

Healing Well and Living Free from an Abusive Relationship, by Dr. Ramona Probasco.

Dr. Probasco's own emergence from an abusive relationship and over twenty years of experience as a licensed marriage and family therapist enable her to offer this compassionate guide for victims of abuse to make the transition from victim to survivor to overcomer.

The Verbally Abusive Relationship, by Patricia Evans.

This book offers real-life stories of abuse victims, along with strategies, sample scripts, and action plans to help those in dangerous relationships deal with the abuse and get free.

The Betrayal Bond: Breaking Free of Exploitive Relationships, by Patrick Carnes.

This book explains how trauma bonds work—emotional and relational ties that bind a victim to someone who is dangerous. It is a book that also works well for male victims, as the author himself was in a chronic abuse cycle.

Books on Sexual Addictions and Adultery

Treating Trauma from Sexual Betrayal: The Essential Tools for Healing, by Dr. Kevin Skinner.

In this work, Dr. Skinner uses his insight from over ten years of research to explain why and how victims of sexual betrayal often experience symptoms that match those of post-traumatic stress disorder (PTSD). He also provides practical guidance in recovering from this unique form of trauma.

Intimate Deception: Healing the Wounds of Sexual Betrayal, by Dr. Sheri Keffer.

This book is written for women, and it has special applicability for those who live (or lived) with a sex addict or a partner who sexually betrayed them in any number of ways.

Leave a Cheater, Gain a Life, by Tracy Schorn (a.k.a. The Chump Lady).

This is a funny, wry, irreverent look at being dumped by an unfaithful spouse. Tracy Schorn is the daughter of a Methodist minister and has a blog at www.chumplady.com. [Note: She sometimes uses profanity.]

Books on Spiritual Abuse

The Subtle Power of Spiritual Abuse, by David Johnson.

Written for both those who have been spiritually abused as well as those who may be (inadvertently or not) *causing* spiritual abuse, this book helps explain how people get hooked into spiritually abusive systems, the impact of controlling leadership on a congregation, and how the abused believer can find rest and recovery. (This is a good book for a person who is addicted to pleasing religious leaders, as many of us raised in the church are!)

Untwisting Scripture, by Rebecca Davis.

This book takes scriptures that have often been used to harm people, or take away their rights, their voice, their boundaries, and their safety, and teaches us how to "untwist" those verses so that we can understand them as God intended us to, presenting the beautiful truth of God's Word. It is a book about shaking free from spiritual abuse.

Books on Helping a Friend Stuck in an Abusive Marriage

Helping Her Get Free: A Guide for Families and Friends of Abused Women, by Susan Brewster.

Simply telling a person to leave their abusive marriage often backfires. In fact, it tends to drive them back to the abuser. If you want to speak in a way people will listen, this book is written as a practical guide for family and friends of someone in a dangerous marriage.

Books on the Bible and Divorce

Divorce and Remarriage in the Bible, by David Instone-Brewer.

This is a long, scholarly book for people who really want to dig into ancient languages and biblical customs. Instone-Brewer's findings support divorce for infidelity, sexual immorality, abandonment, neglect, physical abuse, and chronic emotional abuse.

Divorce and Remarriage in the Church, by David Instone-Brewer.

This is Dr. Instone-Brewer's shorter version of his work in *Divorce and Remarriage in the Bible*. It was written for pastors.

And Marries Another: Divorce and Remarriage in the Teaching of the New Testament, by Craig S. Keener.

Keener deeply considers the biblical text and cultural context of the Bible in order to help us understand the true meaning of the words of Jesus and Paul on divorce and remarriage and develop a soundly scriptural view of the "forgiven" status of all believers: married, divorced, or not.

Not Under Bondage: Biblical Divorce for Abuse, Adultery and Desertion, by Barbara Roberts.

This book addresses interpretations of biblical texts about divorce from the perspective of a survivor of domestic violence and concludes that the Bible permits divorce when a marriage has turned dangerous.

Unholy Charade: Unmasking the Domestic Abuser in the Church, by Jeff Crippen and Rebecca Davis.

Together with co-author Rebecca Davis, pastor and author Jeff Crippen presents Christ's body with a work steeped in Scripture that lays before us a map of the abusive mind, the tactics of abuse, the effects abuse has on its victims, and the tragic way our churches have failed the victims of this sin. He issues a clarion call for those who love Christ to answer the call to love the oppressed and speak for the victims, as Proverbs 31:9 says: "Open your mouth, judge righteously, defend the rights of the poor and needy."

Divorce: A Gift of God's Love, by Walter Callison.

Using Scriptural support, the author addresses the question, "What does God really think about divorce?" He urges readers to view divorce as a gift that, like grace, is often misused, but is a blessing from God. He advocates a movement from a judgmental attitude to a redemptive one.

So You are a Believer... Who has been through Divorce, by Joseph Pote

For MEN OR WOMEN. When the life of a Christian believer is struck by the tragedy of a failed marriage, what is a godly response? What is God's heart toward His children who have experienced divorce? This book cuts through biblically unsubstantiated myths we hear.

First-Person Stories of Men Who Are Victims of Abuse or Infidelity

It Does Happen to Men: A diary of abuse by a male survivor, by James Mackie.

This book is a very informally written diary from the author's personal experience in an abusive marriage, and how he finally came to grips with the fact that this was a toxic marriage that needed to end.

Cheated On: The Divorce Minister Guide for Surviving Infidelity and Keeping Your Faith, by Rev. David Derksen.

This book is valuable for those who've had an unfaithful spouse. The author is a minister with an MDiv, who had to defend his ministerial credentials following the divorce and was successful.

First-Person Stories of Women Who Are Victims of Abuse

Black and White Bible, Black and Blue Wife: My Story of Finding Hope after Domestic Abuse, by Ruth A. Tucker.

This is the author's harrowing story of abuse at the hands of her husband—a well-educated, charming preacher no less—offered in hopes that her story would help other women caught in a cycle of domestic violence and would also give a balanced, biblical approach to counter such abuse (for pastors and counselors).

Give Her Wings: Help and Healing After Abuse, by Megan Cox.

This book is the author's personal story of abuse. She gives excellent advice on knowing what to do, why abuse is wrong, and why and when to leave—all with a solid basis of powerful Scriptures.

Trauma, Recovery, PTSD, Medical Effects of Abuse

Trauma and Recovery, by Judith Herman

Classic book on the history of trauma and PTSD by leading Harvard Ph.D. researcher. Explains the treatment and stages of recovery for trauma victims, whether from military combat or from sexual, physical, or emotional abuse or assault. It starts with getting to safety. This book will help you understand people who've experienced horrific life events.

The Body Keeps the Score, by Bessel van der Kolk

Trauma from abuse or combat or being exposed to it can change both your body and brain. It's no wonder that some people who were in long abusive marriages have health issues, often a "whole range of physical symptoms, including fibromyalgia, chronic fatigue, and other autoimmune diseases..."

ABOUT THE AUTHOR

Gretchen Baskerville

Gretchen Baskerville is a divorce recovery leader and researcher. For more than 20 years, she has worked with Christian women and men going through difficult, life-saving divorces, listening with compassion to those who have suffered from domestic violence, betrayal, infidelity, and emotional abuse. She helps heartbroken people find strength and courage and healing.

Herself the survivor of a toxic marriage, she walked through her own life-saving divorce and was a single mother for many years. Today she is happily remarried and writes about divorce recovery. She is a graduate of Wheaton College with a degree in Bible and Christian Education, and she regularly gives interviews on podcasts, blogs, and radio programs on the topic of Christianity and divorce.

For more information, view her blog at`www.LifeSavingDivorce.com. Follow her on Twitter at` http://twitter.com/GGBaskerville` and on Facebook at http://www.facebook.com/gretchen.baskerville/ and on Instagram at https://www.instagram.com/gretchenbaskerville/ and on You Tube under Gretchen Baskerville.

INDEX

A

B

C

I

K

L

M

N

P

R

S

T

U

V

HELPFUL LINKS

If you want to teach a group using *The Life-Saving Divorce*

- *FREE study guides for each chapter*
  http://lifesavingdivorce.com/bookstudy/
- *FREE videos for each chapter*
  http://lifesavingdivorce.com/bookstudy/

Teaching Aids for Church Leaders

- *Jesus' Greatest Sermon, with graphics*
  www.lifesavingdivorce.com/luke13
- *Intro to Domestic Violence Awareness training*
  www.lifesavingdivorce.com/dvoctober
- *Divorce and the Good Samaritan Story*
  www.lifesavingdivorce.com/samaritan
- *Sermon ideas Domestic Violence Awareness Month*
  www.lifesavingdivorce.com/dvoctober

Pastors who Condone Physical and Emotional Abuse as Grounds for Divorce

- *List of pastors and their sermons, videos, or blog posts*
  www.lifesavingdivorce.com/pastors

First-Person Stories on Video

- *See 5 testimonies of God's release from abusive marriages*
  www.lifesavingdivorce.com/thriving

Questions and Answers

- *Jesus Said, "Love My Enemy"—Can I Still Divorce Them?*
  www.lifesavingdivorce.com/enemy

- *But I Thought it Was God's Will for Me to Marry this Person!* www.lifesavingdivorce.com/godswill
- *Should I stand for my marriage?* www.lifesavingdivorce.com/one-womans-story-adultery-and-the-bible
- *Is Marriage an Unconditional Covenant?* www.lifesavingdivorce.com/unconditional-2

How to Find a Good Supportive Church

- *7 Ways to Know if a Church is Safe* www.lifesavingdivorce.com/online
- *Church Denominations and Divorce Policies Comparison Chart* www.lifesavingdivorce.com/comparison
- *Do My Pastors Have a Say about Me Getting a Divorce?* www.lifesavingdivorce.com/excommunication
- *Good vs. Bad Pastoral Counselors* www.lifesavingdivorce.com/good-vs-bad

More on the misinterpretations of Malachi 2:16, the so-called "God hates divorce" verse

- *How Malachi 2:16 has been translated in Bible over the centuries* www.lifesavingdivorce.com/malachi
- *Timeline from Malachi to present* www.lifesavingdivorce.com/malachitimeline

Life-Saving Divorce on You Tube

- Search You Tube for Gretchen Baskerville

Interviews with Gretchen Baskerville

- *To hear podcast interviews featuring Gretchen* www.lifesavingdivorce.com/interviews

Made in the USA
Columbia, SC
17 March 2023

13937992R00241